African Slavery in Latin America and the Caribbean

African Slavery
in Latin America
and the Caribbean

Second Edition

HERBERT S. KLEIN AND BEN VINSON III

OXFORD
UNIVERSITY PRESS
2007

OXFORD

UNIVERSITY PRESS

Oxford University Press, Inc., publishes works that further
Oxford University's objective of excellence
in research, scholarship, and education.

Oxford New York
Auckland   Cape Town   Dar es Salaam   Hong Kong   Karachi
Kuala Lumpur   Madrid   Melbourne   Mexico City   Nairobi
New Delhi   Shanghai   Taipei   Toronto

With offices in
Argentina   Austria   Brazil   Chile   Czech Republic   France   Greece
Guatemala   Hungary   Italy   Japan   Poland   Portugal   Singapore
South Korea   Switzerland   Thailand   Turkey   Ukraine   Vietnam

Published by Oxford University Press, Inc.
198 Madison Avenue, New York, New York 10016

www.oup.com

Oxford is a registered trademark of Oxford University Press

Klein, Herbert S.
African slavery in Latin America and the Caribbean / by Herbert S.
Klein & Ben Vinson III.—2nd ed.
    p.   cm.
Includes bibliographical references and index.
ISBN 978-0-19-518941-4;   978-0-19-518942-1 (pbk.)
1. Slavery—Latin America—History.   2. Slavery—Caribbean Area—History.
3. Slave-trade—Latin America—History.   4. Slave-trade—Caribbean Area—History.
5. Plantation life—Latin America—History.   6. Plantation life—Caribbean Area—History.
I. Vinson, Ben, III.   II. Title.
HT1052.5.K54 2007
306.3'62098—dc22   2007021258

Printed in the United States of America
on acid-free paper

To Yolanda
and the memory of
Louis and Rose Friedman
and
Charles and Anna Klein

Preface to the Second Edition

Since the publication of the first edition of this book some twenty years ago, there has been an impressive output of new and significant research on African slavery in Latin American and the Caribbean. The recent work on Brazil has been especially impressive. The centenary celebration of the abolition of slavery in 1988 led to a revival of studies on slavery in Brazil. At the same time, several schools of research have emerged that have developed often unique interpretations of slavery in the Americas. These have included the São Paulo school of economic historians, the demographic historians of Minas Gerais, the social historians of Rio de Janeiro, and the continued output of a new generation of scholars from the Bahian historical school. These have created a major new and original historical interpretation on the functioning of slavery and the role of free coloreds in Brazilian society. At the same time, African slavery in the societies of mainland Spanish America has finally become a serious area of research by both native and foreign scholars. An outpouring of studies has occurred on the role of blacks in colonial and early national society in Mexico, and similar types of research have begun to appear for places like Colombia, Peru, Nicaragua, Venezuela, and Costa Rica, to name just a few. Parallel to these national studies has been the increasing influence of the African diaspora as an international and comparative research theme. In this new edition we have tried to bring this survey up to date with the latest materials. The addition of a coauthor has enabled us to provide more extensive coverage than a single author could accomplish. Ben Vinson brings to the volume his intimate knowledge of blacks in Mesoamerican society, the economy of African slavery, and the world of free coloreds, themes on which he has published extensively in the past ten years. During this same period, Herbert Klein has actively continued his research and publications on the Atlantic slave trade and slave society of Brazil. For their assistance with this second edition the authors would like to thank Anthony Kaye, Matthew Restall, Robert Schwaller, Pier Larson, Lolita Brockington, Rachel O'Toole, Karl Offen, Russell Lohse, Sherwin Bryant, Paul Lokken, Charles Beatty Medina, Herman Bennett, Paul Zeleza, and Toyin Falola. We would also like to thank both the National Humanities Center in Research Triangle Park and the Hoover Institution of Stanford University for their support during the writing of this manuscript.

Preface to the First Edition

In recent years there has been an outpouring of studies on the institution of slavery and the role of Africans and their descendants in America. To the impressive body of literature produced in the 19th and the early 20th century has now been added a new genre of modern social and economic studies, both on individual periods and societies, but also in a comparative framework. The earlier work was much influenced by anthropologists, and the more recent studies have seen an impressive participation of economists and sociologists. Given the commonality and the differences of the African experience in America, recent cross-national awareness has also led to better insights into individual national experiences. Scholars in the United States were much influenced by the work of Brazilians in the 1950s and 1960s, just as, for example, today Brazilian scholars are very aware of the new research done in the United States in the past two decades.

Despite this new research, however, there still exist few modern comprehensive comparative studies, and none which systematically include the regions with which I am concerned in this volume. This history of African slavery in Latin America and the Caribbean is a survey of the experience of African slaves in the Portuguese-, Spanish-, and French-speaking regions of America. To understand these Latin countries, it has been necessary to study in depth the Dutch and, to a lesser extent, the English Caribbean colonies. Although I offer some comparative materials from the Afro-American experience in North America, I have excluded more detailed treatment of the United States because of the abundant literature which already exists on this country. Knowledgeable readers, however, will be aware that I have consciously framed my questions and analysis around many of the same historical issues and debates that have informed recent historical analyses of the North American experience.

In this study I have tried to incorporate the latest research on the economics of slavery and the demographic evolution of African slaves, my own particular areas of investigation in my earlier work on Cuba, Brazil, and the Atlantic slave trade. I have also sought to summarize for the general reader much of the older research on Afro-American culture and the evolution of the plantation regimes in America, as well as the newer debates within African history related to African slavery in the Americas.

The organization of the book is somewhat unusual for surveys of this type, as I have tried to provide both a chronological framework and structural analysis at the same time. I felt it necessary in the first chapter to distinguish slavery from all other servile labor institutions and also to examine the origins of both the slave system and the plantation economy as they emerged in the context of Western European history. In the next five chapters I deal with the slave economy and slavery as they developed in Latin America and the Caribbean from the 16th until the 19th century. The stress here is on understanding the timing and causality of these developments and examining the differing patterns of urban and rural slave labor that emerged. The second half of the book is more synchronic in nature, emphasizing the social and political aspects of slave and free colored life and culture. Even here, however, I am concerned with relating underlying economic patterns with these structural changes and delineating regional and temporal variations. The last chapter returns to a more strictly chronological approach but tries to provide as broad a model as possible to incorporate the multiple experiences that made up the long process of transition from slave to free labor.

Since this is a general survey of a broad field, I have not attempted to footnote the text, but have provided students and scholars interested in supporting documentation or in further investigation with detailed bibliographical notes for each chapter. Because of varying terminology applied in the several languages to Afro-Americans, readers should be aware of my definitions. When using the term "blacks," I am referring to a person defined by the society as having only African ancestry. In contrast the term "mulatto-" refers to a person of mixed African and European or even African and Amerindian or Asian background. This is the current usage in most American societies, except for the United States. "Afro-American" is the term used to designate persons born in America who are defined as blacks and mulattoes in their respective societies. I use the term "colored," as in "free colored," as inclusive of both blacks and mulattoes regardless of their place of birth.

In the writing of this work I have had the support of many friends. I would particularly like to thank Stanley Elkins, Stanley Engerman, Harriet E. Manelis Klein, Nicolás Sánchez-Albornoz, and Stuart Schwartz for their careful readings of the manuscript and their helpful suggestions. The production of this book was greatly facilitated by the invaluable technical assistance provided by my colleague Jonathan Brezin.

New York
January 1986

Contents

MAP 1. Mexico in the Eighteenth Century

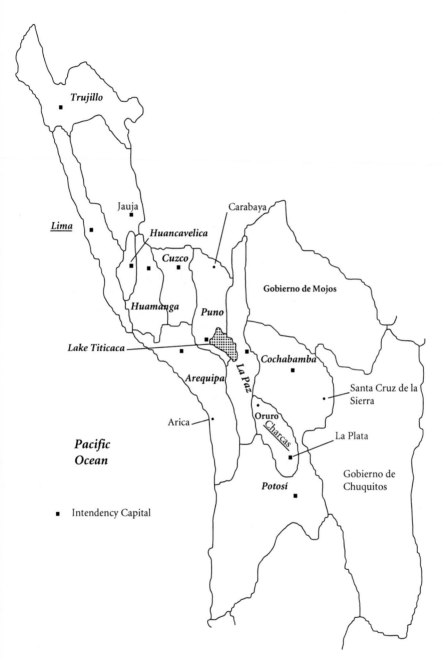

Trujillo

Jauja

Lima

Carabaya

Huancavelica

Cuzco

Gobierno de Mojos

Huamanga

Puno

Lake Titicaca

Cochabamba

Arequipa

La Paz

Santa Cruz de la
Sierra

Arica

Oruro

Charcas

La Plata

Pacific
Ocean

Gobierno de
Chuquitos

Potosí

■ Intendency Capital

MAP 2. Peru in the Late Eighteenth Century

C.Verde I.

Senegal R.

Gambia R.

Senegambia

Niger R.

Sierra Leone

Volta R.

Winward Coast   Gold Coast

Bt. Benin

Bt. Biafra

Gulf of Guinea

São Tomé I.

SOUTH ATLANTIC

Congo R.

Loango/Congo

Angola

Map 3. West Africa

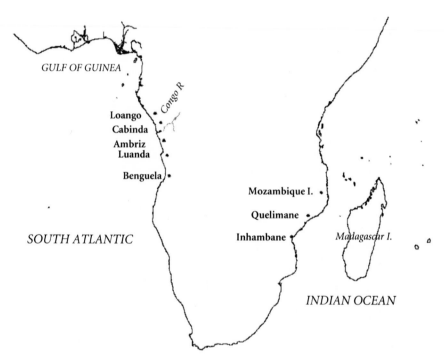

GULF OF GUINEA

Loango
Cabinda
Ambriz
Luanda

Congo R.

Benguela

Mozambique I.

Quelimane

SOUTH ATLANTIC

Inhambane

Madagascar I.

INDIAN OCEAN

MAP 4. Southwest and Western Africa

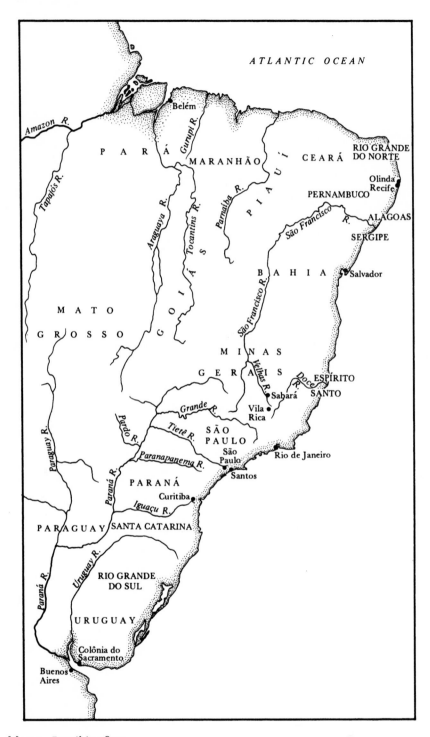

MAP 5. Brazil in 1800

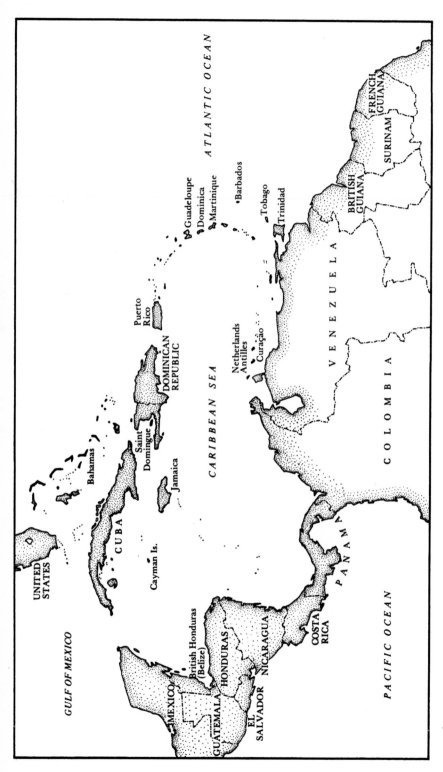

MAP 6. The Caribbean in the Late Eighteenth Century

African Slavery in Latin America and the Caribbean

I

Origins of the American Slave System

African slavery in Latin America and the Caribbean is a late development in the evolution of slavery in human society. Since the origins of complex societies, slavery was known to most cultures and regions of the world. Typically, slavery has meant domestic slavery, in which the labor power of the household was extended through the use of non-kin workers. But slaves have performed all known tasks and in some societies even formed separate classes and groups beyond the household level. Few peoples have escaped slavery themselves, and almost all societies have treated their slaves as outsiders, rootless and ahistorical individuals ultimately held against their will by the threat of force. In all societies in which they existed, they were also the most mobile labor force available.

Slaves, of course, were not unique in either the work they performed or in their lack of control over their own lives. Peasants, serfs, even clansmen and kinsmen, were often in temporary conditions of servitude. With peasants tied to the land, obligated to the nonagricultural elites for corvée, and often severely restricted in terms of age gradations and rules within their own kin groups, there was often little to distinguish slaves from other workers in terms of the labor they performed or the rights immediately available to them. But where slavery came to be a recognized and important institution, it was the lack of ties to the family, to kin, and to the community that finally distinguished slaves from all other workers. It was, in fact, their lack of kin, community, and land that made slaves so desirable in the preindustrial world. True slaves were persons without the bindings and linkages common to even the lowest free persons, and were thus completely dependent on the will of their masters.

3

Masters could use their slaves at far less cost in reciprocal obligations than any other labor group in their societies.

Although many pre-15th-century societies held slaves, in most cases such slaves were only a minor part of the labor force and were not crucial producers of goods and services for others. Most complex societies rested upon the labor of settled village agriculturalists and of part-time artisans, who equally shared the peasant status. These two groups were the primary producers, and slaves were relegated to very specialized work for the elite—domestic service in the better households—and sometimes very hazardous state enterprises, such as mining, to which even obligated peasants could not be assigned to work. Sometimes conquered warriors were enslaved and used in special public works activities, but in most societies it was the peasants who performed most of this labor.

Thus, while slavery was an institution known to many complex societies, slavery as a system of industrial or market production was a much more restricted phenomenon. Most scholars now date its origins for Western society in the centuries immediately prior to the Christian era in the Greek city-states and the emerging Roman Empire of the period. It is now argued that for slavery to become a dominant factor in society it was essential that an important market economy at the local and international level be developed, that a significant share of the agricultural production for that market come from nonpeasant producers, and that slave labor become the major factor in that production. All these conditions, it is now assumed, were met only within our historical memory, in the two centuries before the Christian era under the Romans.

With large artisan shops using slave labor and producing goods for an international market, the classical Greek economy of the 6th and 5th centuries B.C. was distinguished by the utilization of slave labor, which historians would later define as an original development of the institution. But the concentration of slaves in urban areas, their limited use in rural production, and other constraints on slave production meant that Greek slavery would not be as fully elaborated an economic institution as that which developed in the Roman Empire.

It was the Roman conquest of a greater proportion of the Eurasian land mass than any other previously known empire that created a major market economy. Market economies obviously existed before, just as previous conquest states created large numbers of slaves as booty for the conquering armies, but the Romans carried all these factors to another level of intensity. Their enormous armies absorbed as much as 10 percent of the male peasant workforce in Italy at the same time as their nobility began to purchase large tracts of land with their earnings from conquest and subsequent taxation of the conquered. In a time of economic expansion and limited supplies of free labor, and an initially cheap supply of conquered slaves, it was natural to turn to slave labor. Although slaves became more expensive as conquests slowed, they were always a less costly alternative than paying wages high enough to attract peasants away from subsistence agriculture. It is this traditional problem of expanding markets and limited labor supplies that creates a condition ideal for slave or other servile labor arrangements.

The Roman case is unusual among documented preindustrial historical societies in the size and importance of both its major urban centers and its long-distance markets. It has been estimated that up to 30 percent of the peninsula's population was urban at the height of the empire, with another 10 percent being urbanized within the empire beyond. To feed these nonagriculturalists required supplies more abundant than could be produced by traditional peasant agricultural arrangements. Thus the growth of large landed estates manned by slaves and supervised by overseers for absentee landlords became a major force in the supply of foodstuffs for market consumption. The high degree of specialization of labor and the demands of the market for mass-produced goods to satisfy international as well as interregional consumption also provided an incentive for slave artisanal labor.

Finally, the sheer size of the slave labor force was unusual in premodern times. While all such figures are extremely speculative, it has been estimated that at the height of the Roman Empire the population of Italy contained some 2 to 3 million slaves, who represented between 35 and 40 percent of the total population. Peasant agriculture was still the predominant form of rural labor, but the size of the slave population meant that it played a vital role in most of the productive enterprises. Slave gangs were a common feature of rural agriculture, and slaves could be found in all parts of the empire and were owned by most classes in the society. It was also evident that slaves were often a large element in many local populations, and well-developed slave communities appear to have been common. This is especially evident at times of major slave rebellions, when there existed a community of interests expressed among the slaves despite their diverse origins.

All this does not mean that Romans did not have household servants and domestic slaves, or that elites did not use slaves for highly specialized tasks, roles common to all societies in which slaves were held. But in terms of the production of goods and services for the market, the Romans can be said to have created a modern slave system similar to those established in the Western Hemisphere from the 16th century to the end of the 19th century. It is for this reason, as much as its historic role in the origins of modern western European institutions, that Roman law and custom in regard to slave labor would prove so important to post-1500 slave regimes.

In their definition of the legal status of slaves, the Romans also profoundly influenced such legal precepts for American slave societies. It was the primary aim of Roman law to guarantee the total rights of property for the master. All slaves were absolutely denied the legal right to personal liberty. But beyond this, the society for its own purposes could put restraints upon masters and their power over their slaves. Other fundamental aspects of legal personality, such as the rights to personal property and security, were not totally denied slaves. So long as these rights did not deter the mobility of the slave labor force, they could be partially or fully accepted. This more "humane" attitude often sprang from the self-interest of the master class, whose desire was for a stable labor force. This stability might result in the qualification of the master's absolute rights in the name of greater efficiency and social peace.

An example of these qualifications can be seen in the Roman practice of emancipating slaves. As in most slave systems, emancipation was fundamentally a right of masters to dispose of their property as they saw fit, even if it meant reducing their patrimony. Unlike all other property, humans could be freed and often made equal to the master who owned them. Thus manumission recognized the humanity of the slave, just as it accepted the absolute property rights of the master. But manumission could also occur at the will of the slave or the state, and this could be done in the name of state interest or even of economic efficiency. It was, for example, highly profitable for masters to manumit slaves through the system of self-purchase arrangements. To obtain the funds to buy their freedom, slaves had to be allowed their peculium, or personal property, reasonably secure from the master's control. The state, for its own reasons, could free deserving slaves even against the will of the master.

The right to personal security also need not be totally denied to get the most out of one's slave labor force. The Romans were not squeamish about allowing masters to use physical force to obtain obedience from their slaves. In most daily situations the master's will was law and could be enforced to the fullest. But killing slaves was not permitted by the state because it could lead to a serious threat to social stability. All this is not to deny that pain, whippings, degradation, and marginality were the daily lot of the slave. But it does suggest that in an otherwise harsh regime it was not essential for the efficiency of the system to go to the absolute limit by depriving the slave of all legal rights. Leaving some legal personality was in fact considered essential for the smooth and profitable functioning of the system. Given that many ex-slaves would eventually become Roman citizens, the divisive forces of ethnicity and racism, which were present in most slave systems, were held in check and not allowed to destroy many of the secondary residual rights of the slaves, such as those to religion, education, family, and even extended kin ties. The potential for full postemancipation equality for some slaves marked the Roman system as more "open" than many that would appear in the Americas after the 15th century.

Roman slavery was a thriving institution so long as the Roman Empire survived. Although slaves did not disappear from Europe until well into the modern period, slavery as a major economic institution collapsed with the barbarian invasions from the 5th to the 8th century A.D. The same causes that gave rise to the importance of the slave regime earlier also explain its collapse at the end of the imperial era. The decline of urban markets, the breakdown of long-distance trade, and the increasing self-sufficiency of agriculture all created a situation in which slave labor was no longer viable, and peasant agricultural labor again predominated. More and more, slavery was reduced to the level of household and domestic tasks. In the early Middle Ages the retrenchment of the international market and the stress on defense and security led to the rise of a new semiservile labor force with the creation of the serfs, peasants who sacrificed part of their freedom in return for protection from the local elite. Serfs soon became the predominant labor force easily displacing the last vestiges of slave labor in agricultural production in Europe.

At no time during this period of retrenchment and enserfment did slavery itself disappear from Europe. Among the Germanic peoples on the northern frontiers, it remained important as warfare continued to create a supply of slaves. In the non-Christian world of the Mediterranean, slavery actually experienced a renaissance between the 8th and the 13th century. The Muslim invasions of the Mediterranean islands and especially of Spain brought the increasing use of slaves in agriculture and industry. Moreover, the existence of Islamic slave markets encouraged a lively trade in Christians.

It was the revival of international markets as a result of the first of the Crusades that again brought Christian Europeans more actively into the slave trade and into slave production. From the 10th to the 13th century the expansion of the Genoese and Venetians into Palestine, Syria, the Black Sea, and the Balkans, with possessions in the eastern Mediterranean islands of Crete and Cyprus, all created a new impetus for slavery. A lively market in Slavic peoples developed in this period, which gave rise to the use of the term "slave" to define this status. Slavs, of course, were not the only peoples to be enslaved. On the islands of the eastern Mediterranean, for example, black slaves could be found in the early 14th century, along with all types of Muslims from North Africa and Asia Minor, Christians from Greece and the Balkans, and northern Europeans.

Along with slavery, plantation agriculture and sugar production were also common to parts of the Mediterranean world after the 8th century. Sugar was introduced from Asia to Europe during the Islamic invasions, but it was the First Crusade at the end of the 11th century that gave the Christians a chance to become sugar producers in their own right. In the 12th and 13th centuries, Christian estates in Palestine began to produce sugar with a mixed labor force made up of slaves, villeins, and free workers. After the fall of these lands to the Turks at the end of the 13th century, the center of sugar production moved to Cyprus. Here Italian merchants and local rulers used slave and free labor to produce sugar. Cyprus in turn was soon replaced by the Venetian colony of Crete and then by Sicily, which had been producing sugar for the European market since the late 11th century. With the fall of Palestine and Syrian centers to the Turks, Sicilian production became preeminent. The Mediterranean coast of Islamic Spain in the late 13th and early 14th century became another important production center for northern and western Europe. The western-most advance of European sugar production reached the southern Portuguese Atlantic province of the Algarve at the beginning of the 15th century. In not all these cases was sugar produced by slaves, nor were they the exclusive labor force in any particular area. But the identification of slavery with sugar was well established long before the conquest of America. The techniques of sugar production and slave plantation agriculture that developed on the Atlantic islands and later in the New World had their origins in the eastern Mediterranean in the early Middle Ages.

After the 8th century, slavery in mainland Christian Europe was reduced to a minor labor arrangement almost exclusively confined to domestic activities. Without major market economies to sustain them, slaves no longer played the vital role within European agriculture that they had under the Romans. The slow revival of commerce and activities after the 10th century led to increases in land utilization and colonization and a subsequent growth of the peasant population, which proved more than sufficient to maintain the slowly developing market economies. In such a situation slave labor was too costly.

Only in the more advanced Islamic Mediterranean world could slaves be purchased in large quantities and the institution of slavery be revived as a major factor in production. The sole European state in this period to provide an important market for slaves was therefore Islamic Spain, which was a significant importer of Christian slaves from the 8th to the 10th century. But the decline of the Iberian Islamic states led to the closure of this market. The subsequent conquest of these states by the northern Iberian Christians resulted more in enserfment than slavery for the captured Muslim peasants and artisans. The experience of the Egyptian rulers, who imported 10,000 Christian male slaves per annum in the late 13th and early 14th century, was not typical of Christian Europe at this time.

By the end of the Middle Ages several varieties of slave regimes existed in Europe, the most important of which were found in the Mediterranean region. No European state was without a few slaves, but the use of slave labor in agriculture and manufacturing on a large scale had long disappeared. The emerging power of the European economy was now fed by an expanding peasant labor force. While the legal structures originating in Roman law were still intact in Christian Europe, the institution of slavery was not a major force by the time the first Portuguese caravels sighted the Guinean coastline at the beginning of the 15th century.

Slavery also existed in the African continent from recorded times. But as in medieval Christian Europe, it was a relatively minor institution in the period before the opening up of the Atlantic slave trade. Slavery could be found as a domestic institution in most of the region's more complex societies, and a few exceptional states influenced by Islam may have developed more industrial forms of slave production. But African slaves were to be found outside the region as well. With no all-embracing religious or political unity, the numerous states of Africa were free to buy and sell slaves and even to export them to non-African areas. Caravan routes across the Sahara predated the opening up of the African Atlantic coast, and slaves formed a part of Africa's export trade to the Mediterranean from pre-Roman to modern times. But a new dimension to that trade occurred with the expansion of Islam in the 8th century. As the Islamic world spread into Asia and the eastern Mediterranean, Islamic merchants came to play an ever more important part in the African slave trade. The frontier zones of the sub-Saharan savannas, the Red Sea region, and the east coast ports on the Indian Ocean in turn became major centers for the expansion of Muslim influence. From the 9th to the 15th century a rather steady international slave trade existed, with the majority of forced migrants being women and children. Some six major and often interlocking caravan routes and another two major coastal regions may have accounted for as many as 5,000 to 10,000 slaves per annum in the period from A.D. 800 to 1600. The primary route remained North Africa, followed in order of importance by the Red Sea and the East African trades.

While the African borderlands became heavily influenced by Islam, and even began to adopt systems of slavery modeled along Islamic lines, the majority of Africa continued to experience slavery as a minor institution within largely kin- and lineage-based social systems. In these societies slaves performed largely domestic and even religious functions, serving as everything from concubines to sacrificial victims, and performed all types of service from those of warrior to administrator to agricultural laborer. But as in most societies in which slaves were to be found, they were not crucial to the production process, which remained largely in the hands of other classes. In these societies, moreover, the status of slaves was not as precisely fixed as in regimes in which slaves played a more vital role in production. Children of free fathers and slave mothers would often become free members of the kin group; second-generation acculturated slaves would become less subject to sale and to totally arbitrary control and assumed far more rights and privileges.

There were, however, a few exceptional societies where slavery was clearly a fundamental institution, playing a dominant role in either the economic, social, or political life of the local state. In many of the sub-Saharan Islamicized borderland regimes, slaves were used extensively as soldiers and also in agricultural labor on a major scale. Several of the Wolof states had agricultural slaves who produced for local consumption as well as for export. The most famous of these agriculturally based slave systems was that developed in the Niger River valley in the empire of Songhay in the 15th century. Irrigated plantations with up to several thousand slaves produced wheat, rice, and other commercial food crops that not only supported the army of the local empire but were also sold to the caravans crossing the Sahara. Slaves were also used in western Sudanese gold mines and in the Sahara saltworks of Teghaza. In East Africa among the commercial towns of the coast, some plantation slaves could also be found near Malindi and Mombasa in the north and on the island of Madagascar.

But these commercial uses of slaves were more the exception than the rule, and the shifting nature of trade, warfare, and ecology on the Saharan border meant that most of the West African Islamic savanna states were relatively unstable. They were subject to attack by non-African border states, which was the fate of the Songhay empire, destroyed by Moroccan invaders in the 1590s. They were also often located in unstable ecological zones, and severe periods of drought usually led to the destruction of local economies and states. Major slave regimes in Africa, especially in the west, were thus relatively few and of limited longevity in the period prior to the arrival of the Christian Europeans.

Although large-scale commercial use of slaves was limited, the use of slaves within most African societies was widespread. The existence of this large number of slaves meant that a lively internal slave market and intracontinental slave trade existed. Thus a dual slave trade came into existence well before the opening of the West African–Atlantic routes. Through the north and to the east slaves were being shipped outside Africa in steady numbers for at least some six centuries prior to the arrival of the Portuguese. In this period anywhere from 3.5 to 10 million Africans left their homelands. These streams of forced migrants tended to contain far more women and children than would the migrants later participating in the Atlantic slave trade, and they also came from regions that would be only moderately affected by the Atlantic movements. Along with this international slave trade there was also a thriving internal slave trade that satisfied the needs of local African states. Given the overwhelming use of slaves for domestic and social purposes, this trade was even more biased toward women. For both these long-term trades, the whole complex of enslavement practices from full-scale warfare and raiding of enemies to judicial enslavement and taxation of dependent peoples had come into use and would easily be adjusted to the needs of the Atlantic slave trade when this came into existence in the early 15th century.

These pre-Atlantic trades, however, did differ in important respects from the European trade. Aside from the far greater participation of women and children, and their concentration on northern and eastern African peoples, they were less intense and had a slighter impact on local conditions. Although the number of persons who were forcibly transported was impressive, these pre-1500 northern and eastern African slave trades still fit in with a level of production and social and political organization in which slave trading remained an incidental part of statecraft and economic organization. There is even some question as to whether the internal slave trade was more important than the external trade in this pre-Atlantic period.

The arrival of the Portuguese explorers and traders on the sub-Saharan African coast in the early 1400s would ultimately represent a major new development in the history of the slave trade in Africa in terms of the intensity of its development, the sources of its slaves, and the uses to which its slaves would be put. But initially there was little to distinguish the Portuguese traders from the Muslim traders of North Africa and the sub-Saharan regions. The Portuguese mostly were interested in controlling the North African Saharan routes by opening up a route from the sea. Their prime interest was gold, with slaves, pepper, ivory, and other products as only secondary concerns. Even when they began shipping slaves in 1444, they were mainly sent to Europe to serve as domestic servants. Africans had already arrived at these destinations via the overland Muslim-controlled caravan routes, and thus the new trade was primarily an extension of the older patterns. The Portuguese even carried out extensive slave trading along the African coast primarily to supply the internal African slave market in exchange for gold, which they then exported to Europe. Their concentration on gold as opposed to slaves was based on the growing scarcity of precious metals in Europe. An expanding European economy was running an increasingly negative balance of trade with Asia, and the direct European access to the sub-Saharan gold fields helped pay for that trade. It was only with the introduction of sugar production to the Atlantic islands and the opening up of the Western Hemisphere to European conquest at the end of the 15th century that a new and important use was found for slaves. As once again slaves became a major factor in agricultural production within the European context, Portuguese interest in its African trade slowly shifted from a concern with gold and ivory to one primarily stressing slaves.

As long as the Portuguese concentrated their efforts on the regions of Senegambia and the Gold Coast, they essentially integrated themselves into the existing network of Muslim traders. The Muslims had brought these coasts into their own trade networks, and the Portuguese tapped into them through navigable rivers that went into the interior, especially the Senegal and Gambia rivers. Even their establishment of São Jorge da Mina (Elmina) on the Gold Coast fit into these developments. Until 1500, in fact, only some 500 to 1,000 slaves were shipped annually by the Portuguese, and a good proportion of these slaves were sold in Africa rather than in Christian Europe. But the settlement of the island depot and plantation center of São Tome in the Gulf of Guinea and the beginning of trade relations with the kingdom of the Kongo after 1500 substantially changed the nature of the European slave trade.

The Kongolese were located by the Zaire River and were unconnected to the Muslim trade before the arrival of the Portuguese. The kingdom also sought close relations with the Portuguese and tried to work out government control of the trade. The Portuguese sent priests and advisers to the court of the Kongolese king, and his representatives were placed on São Tome. These changes occurred just as the Spanish conquest of the Caribbean islands and the Portuguese settlement of the Brazilian subcontinent was getting under way and thus opened the American market for African slaves. The decimation of the native Arawak and Carib peoples in the Caribbean islands, the first major zone of European settlement, especially encouraged the early experimentation with African slave labor.

All these changes resulted in the tremendous growth of the Portuguese slave trade. After 1500 the volume of the trade passed 2,000 slaves per annum, and after the 1530s many of these slaves came from the southwestern coast and were shipped directly to America from the entrepôt island of São Tome just off the African coast. This latter development marked a major introduction of new sources of African slaves for America. Not only were new African regions being brought into the trade, but this also shifted the nature of the 16th-century and early 17th-century transatlantic trade. Acculturated and Christianized blacks from the Iberian Peninsula had been the first Africans forced to cross the Atlantic. Now it was non-Christian and non-Romance-language speakers taken directly from Africa, the so-called *bozales*, who made up the overwhelming majority of slaves coming to America. There even began to appear some African Muslim slaves as well.

Another significant change came about in the 1560s as a result of internal African developments. Hostile African invasions of the kingdom of the Kongo led to direct Portuguese military support for the regime and finally in 1576 to their establishment of a full-time settlement at the southern edge of the kingdom at the port of Luanda. With the development of Luanda came a decline in São Tomé as an entrepôt, for now slaves were shipped directly to America from the mainland coast and from a region that was to provide America with the most slaves of any area of Africa over the next three centuries. By 1600 the Atlantic slave trade was finally to exceed the north and east African export trades in total volume, though it was not until after 1700 that slaves finally surpassed in value all other exports from Africa.

Just as the beginnings of the Portuguese slave trade had complemented a traditional trading system, the first use of Atlantic slave trade Africans by Europeans was in traditional activities. For the first half century, the European slave ships that cruised the Atlantic shoreline of Africa carried their slaves to the Iberian Peninsula. The ports of Lisbon and Seville were the centers for a thriving trade in African slaves, and from these centers slaves were distributed rather widely through the western Mediterranean. Though Africans quickly became a significant group within the polyglot slave communities in the major cities of the region, they never became the dominant labor force in the local economies. Even in the southern coastal cities of Portugal where they were most numerous, they never represented more than 15 percent of the population, while in other Portuguese and Castilian port cities they usually numbered less than 10 percent. Coming into communities where slavery was an already functioning institution and where free peasants were numerous, Africans were used no differently than the Moorish slaves who preceded and coexisted with them. African slaves and freedmen were to be found primarily in urban centers and worked mostly in domestic service. Though not in significant numbers, African slaves could also be found in most major skilled and unskilled trades. There were even some new and unusual occupations for African slaves, such as being sailors aboard both slave and nonslave ships trading with Africa, an occupation that persisted down into the 19th century. But these activities were not of fundamental importance to the local European economies.

Even the wealthiest European masters owned only a few slaves, and an owner who held fifteen African slaves in 16th-century Portugal was considered very unusual. Although slave owners were wealthy aristocrats, professionals, and institutions, and many of these persons and institutions were also major landowners, they infrequently used their slaves in agriculture. Slaves were sometimes to be found in rural occupations but never as a significant element in the local agricultural labor force. Given their high costs, and the availability of cheap peasant labor, African slaves in continental Europe would not play a significant role in the production of basic staples, and a slave system, as defined by the classical Roman model, did not develop in continental Europe in the 15th and 16th centuries.

The African slavery that evolved in early modern Europe blended into an already existing slave system and even adopted traditional Christian institutions to the non-Christian and non-Islamic Africans. As Moors and other groups died out and Africans became the predominant slaves, local institutions such as religious brotherhoods began to stress a more African orientation to the slave community. Special festive days were given over to African Catholic lay organizations in the city of Seville, and they could be found in all European towns where blacks were a significant group. There even developed by the end of the 16th century a free colored population. By the 1630s Lisbon had an estimated 15,000 slaves and an established community of some 2,000 free colored, most of whom lived in a well-defined neighborhood of the city.

Because of their relatively easy integration into an already functioning system, and because they were held in small groups and were never a majority of the local population, African slaves readily adopted the culture, language, and religion of their masters. So rapidly did they integrate into the dominant society that they came to be called *ladinos*, or "Europeanized" African slaves, to distinguish them from the *bozales*, or non-Europeanized Africans. It was these *ladino* slaves who accompanied their masters on voyages of discovery and conquest to the Atlantic islands and the New World and who were the first black inhabitants of America.

But despite their early migration and the important role they played in establishing the legal, social, and cultural norms for the Africans who followed them, the Europeanized African slaves were not the basis for the new full-scale European slave labor system being established in the Americas. Nor were they tied to the evolving plantation system being developed by the Europeans in the 15th and 16th centuries. It was the Africans brought directly to the previously unpopulated eastern Atlantic islands beginning in the first half of the 15th century who were to define the new plantation model of Afro-American slave labor. The use by Europeans of African slaves in plantations evolved not in continental Europe with its *ladino* slaves but in these Atlantic islands.

Just as Portugal was opening up the African coast to European penetration, its explorers and sailors were competing with the Spaniards in colonizing the eastern Atlantic islands. By the 1450s the Portuguese were developing the unpopulated Azores, Madeira, the Cape Verde Islands, and São Tome, while the Spaniards were conquering the previously inhabited Canary Islands by the last decade of the century. Some of these islands proved ideal for sugar cultivation, so Italian merchants were not slow to introduce the latest in Mediterranean sugar production techniques. After much experimentation, the most important sugar-producing islands turned out to be Madeira, the Canaries, and São Tome. Sugar became the prime output on Madeira by the middle of the century, and by the end of the 15th century Madeira had become Europe's largest producer. The Portuguese imported Guanches, the native Canarians, as slaves along with Africans, and by the end of the 1450s Madeira sugar was being sold on the London market. By 1493 there were eighty sugar mills (or *engenhos*) on the island refining on average eighteen tons of sugar per annum. Given the terraced nature of the sugar estates, production units were relatively small, however, and the largest plantation held only some eighty slaves, a size that would be considered moderate by Brazilian standards in the next century.

Madeira had a particularly sharp rise and fall in its sugar evolution, for by the 1530s it was well outdistanced by competition from the other islands. The Canary Islands were the next big entrant into the sugar production race, and by the first decades of the 16th century the local coastal estates were milling on average fifty tons per annum. Here, as in Madeira, Guanche natives were first used as slaves, along with Moors imported from Spain, but very quickly Africans became the dominant slave labor force on the estates. As on Madeira, there were more masters and sugar producers than mill owners, and an intermediate group of small-scale slave-owning planters evolved, employed by larger and richer mill owners who could afford the extremely high costs for establishing sugar refineries.

The final Atlantic island to develop a major sugar plantation slave system was the African coastal island of São Tome, which, like the Azores, Cape Verde Islands, and Madeira, had been uninhabited prior to European penetration. By the 1550s there were some sixty mills in operation on the island and some 2,000 plantation slaves, all of whom were Africans. There were also on average at any one time some 5,000 to 6,000 slaves in slave pens on this entrepôt island being held for transport to Europe and America. Eventually American competition and the island's increasingly important role as a transfer and slave trade provisioning entrepôt led to the decline of the São Tome sugar industry.

Thus all the sugar islands went through a rather intense cycle of boom and bust that rarely lasted more than a century. But all the major sugar-producing islands established functioning plantation slave regimes that became the models for such institutions transported to the New World. Non-Christian and non-Europeanized Africans directly imported from the African coast were brought to work the rural estates on these islands. Urban slavery and domestic slavery were minor occupations, and slaves were held in extremely large lots by the standards of European slave holdings of the period. All the trappings of the New World plantation system were well established, with the small number of wealthy mill owners at the top of the hierarchy holding the most lands and the most slaves, followed by an intermediate layer of European planters who owned slaves and sugar fields but were too poor to actually be mill owners in their own right. A poor European peasant population hardly existed, with only skilled administrative and mill operations opened to non-slave-owning whites. The lowest layer consisted of the mass of black slaves who made up the majority of the labor force, as well as of the population as a whole. Thus, well before the massive transplantation of Africans across the Atlantic, the American slave plantation system had been born.

2

The Establishment of African Slavery in Latin America in the 16th Century

The European conquest of the American hemisphere did not automatically guarantee the expansion of African slave labor to the New World. Africans within Europe and the Atlantic islands were still a relatively minor part of the European labor force, and even sugar production was not totally in the hands of black slaves. At the same time, the existence of some 20 to 25 million American Indians seemed to mean that Europeans would have an abundant supply of labor available for the exploitation of their new colonies. Finally, Europe itself was experiencing major population growth in the 16th century and could probably rely on migrations of its poorer peasants and urban dwellers for its American labor needs. Yet despite these alternative labor supplies, America became the great market for an estimated 10 million African slaves in the course of the next five centuries, and it was in the New World that African slavery most flourished under European rule. Until the 1830s more Africans than Europeans crossed the Atlantic annually and as late as 1750 some 4.5 million of the estimated 6.6 million people who had come to the Americas since 1492 were African slaves.

Before examining the history of the forced African migration to the Americas, it is essential to understand why Europeans turned to Africans to populate their mines, factories, and farms in such numbers. Much has been written of the relative "otherness" of Africans to Europeans and the alienness of African culture to Western norms. But the long-term contact of the Mediterranean with sub-Saharan Africans from at least the time of the Pharaohs onward makes one doubt the importance of this "exotic" phenomenon. Also, the extensive history of Europeans enslaving each other would suggest that there was nothing special about the Africans and slavery in the European mind at the end of the 15th century. Finally, it was not any special need for such Africans within the European economy that was the driving force behind the purchase of enslaved Africans on the Atlantic African coast. It was without question American labor market conditions that most influenced the growth of the Atlantic slave trade. At the same time, the choice of Africans had much to do with their availability and price as opposed to the nonavailability of traditional European slave sources, which were drying up by the time of the European expansion into the Western Hemisphere.

Initially, it appeared as if the few thousand Iberian conquistadores would turn toward Indian slavery as the major form of labor in America. Already using the enslaved labor of Africans, Muslims, and Guanches in Europe and the Atlantic islands, the first Spaniards and Portuguese imme- diately went about enslaving all the American Indians they could find and keep. But, for a series of political, cultural, and religious reasons, the govern- ments of both Spain and Portugal decided against permanently enslaving the American Indians. Both governments had just finished with enserfment and other forms of semifree labor arrangements and were committed to the principle of free wage labor. The Spaniards also faced in Mesoamerica and the Andes powerful peasant-based empires that could be exploited effectively without destroying their political and social systems. Using traditional In- dian nobility and accepting preconquest tax and government structures proved a far more efficient way of exploiting available labor. Finally, the commitment to an evangelical mission and doubts about the legitimacy of enslaving Christians pushed the Spanish Crown toward acceptance of American Indian autonomy.

Not all Indians were treated as free persons, of course. In certain fringe areas of the Spanish kingdom natives were sometimes enslaved. In modern- day New Mexico, for instance, which remained a semiconquered region for much of the colonial period, Spaniards enslaved Indians into the 18th century, well after the law had formally eliminated native slavery. A number of these slaves were the prisoners of Spanish expeditionary and military forces; others were purchased directly from Indians who had taken prisoners in intertribal conflicts. Frontier slavery, in this context, was justified as a means of "civili- zing" these otherwise lost Indians, but rarely did their captivity seamlessly and intimately integrate them into Hispanic life. Although important to the do- mestic sphere, native slaves did not comprise a primary workforce even in this frontier economy, and in New Mexico at least, native slavery was not seen as a permanent condition. By the 18th century their captivity resembled indentured servitude, since slaves retained their status for just ten years. Native slavery probably persisted as long as it did along the Spanish frontier because of the weakness of governing institutions in the kingdom's outer areas, and because constant warfare produced a steady source of captives. Closer to the core of the kingdom, there was more internal stability, and the laws of Spain were more strongly felt. Consequently, in these areas Indian slaves had largely disappeared by the late 16th century.

In the case of the Portuguese there was less constraint exercised by the metropolitan government over the issue of enslaving Indians than in the Spanish colonies. Also, the weakness of the political systems of the Tupi-Guarani Indian groups they conquered on the Brazilian coastline, and the inexperience of these Indians with systematic peasant labor, made them less easy to exploit through noncoercive labor arrangements. Although the Portuguese initially had a large pool of Indians to exploit and wholeheartedly adopted Indian slave labor, such labor would eventually prove too unreliable and costly to guarantee the necessary agricultural labor force needed to maintain the economic viability of their American colony.

Thus, for a multiplicity of economic, political, and even religious reasons, the Iberians eventually abandoned the possibility of Indian slavery. But what was to prevent them from exploiting their own peasantry and urban poor? After all, Spain had a population of more than 7 million persons in the 1540s, and it added another million persons to that number by 1600. But this population grew in a period of major economic and political expansion. Spain's control over a vast European and American empire saw a tremendous growth of its cities, with Seville doubling its population to over 110,000 and such new urban centers as Madrid coming into full growth. Agriculture also flourished in this imperial century, all maintained by a free wage labor force. Finally, the establishment of full-time professional Spanish armies in other European states guaranteed another major area of employment for the Spanish masses. All this created a large demand for Spanish labor within Spain and its extensive European possessions. Thus wages for Spanish workers in Europe were high enough to make mass migration to America too costly an operation.

The situation for the Portuguese was even more constrained. With fewer than 1 million in population, Portugal was straining its resources to staff the vast African and Asian trading empire it had just established. Demand for labor was so high and wages so remunerative that there was no pool of cheap Iberian labor that could be tapped for the initially quite poor lands of Brazil. With dyewoods as the only important export, compared with the gold, slaves, ivory, and spices from Africa and Asia, Portuguese America was a very uninteresting proposition in the European labor markets.

This left the Europeans with only the free Indian peasant masses of America as a potential labor force. In Mesoamerica (the region that is today Mexico and Guatemala) and the southern Andes of the Pacific coast, the existence of centuries-old established peasant societies initially gave the Spaniards the ability to exploit local labor for all its needs. In the former area there existed the Aztec empire, which was a densely populated region of fairly autonomous and only recently conquered states. Here the Spaniards under Cortés were able to quickly ally themselves with key rebellious groups and conquer the rest with relative ease. In the Andean region was an equally recent creation, the Inca empire, which, though less densely populated than Mesoamerica, also had a well-established peasant base. The pattern of conquest and settlement set by Cortés in Mexico was adopted a decade later in the 1530s by Pizarro in his overthrow of the Cuzco-based empire. In both cases, the Spaniards relied on indirect rule, perpetuating the preconquest Indian nobility and re-creating much of the traditional Indian governmental structure at the community level. All this aided in the efficient extraction of labor. Given this organization, it was relatively easy for the Spaniards to exact tribute not only in goods but in labor as well. Thus, when they began to expand mining far beyond the production levels obtained under the preconquest Indian empires, the Spaniards had a ready labor pool from which to extract their labor needs. Through wage-labor incentives and through discriminatory taxation, large numbers of Indian laborers were attracted to the rich silver mines in Mexico and Peru. To supply food for the mines and for the developing Spanish cities, the Spaniards were also able to use a blend of corvée labor, along with market incentives and discriminatory taxes, to force through a major reorganization of Amerindian agriculture. Many of the American foods they incorporated into their own diet, but they also succeeded in having the Indians produce wheat and other traditional European crops for their needs.

In the regions south of Guatemala and north of Ecuador, and within the Amazonian and southern Río de la Plata interior and eastern coastal plains, there existed few settled peasant Indian groups and limited mineral resources. Here the Spaniards encountered largely hunting-and-gathering tribes or only semisedentary Indian communities of relatively low population density. Given the lack of easily exploitable labor or readily available exportable precious metals, and the abundance of both in Mexico and Peru, these regions produced less demand for either Spanish capital or black labor. In the central Mexican and Peruvian provinces of the Spanish empire, there was also initially limited interest in African slaves. Even in this best of all possible situations for the Europeans, there was a slow realization that alternative labor was needed. European diseases were especially virulent among the Indians of the coastal zones, which were soon depopulated. Also, regions outside of the main peasant areas of Mexico and Peru were soon depopulated of their hunting-and-gathering Indians, and it was found that even the creation of church missions in these areas did not acculturate a sufficient labor force for developing major exportable crops. With an excellent supply of precious metals, and a positive trade balance with Europe, the Spaniards of America could afford to experiment with the importation of African slaves to fill in the regions abandoned by Amerindian laborers. They could also use the African slaves to make up for the lack of an urban-poor labor force among the Spaniards in the new imperial cities of America. They found African slaves useful for the very reasons that they were kinless and totally mobile laborers. Indians could be exploited systematically, but they could seldom be moved from their lands on a permanent basis. Being the dominant cultural group, they were also less amenable to Spanish and European norms of behavior. The Africans, by contrast, bereft of their homelands and more closely subjected to the immediate power of European masters, found themselves more compelled to adapt to European norms. African slaves, in lieu of a cheap pool of European laborers, thus added important strength to the small European urban society that dominated the American Indian peasant masses.

The Portuguese experience with their American Indian workers was less successful than the Spanish experience. The thousands of Indians conquered by the Portuguese in coastal Brazil were nowhere near the millions of Indians controlled by the Spaniards. They were less adaptable to systematic agricultural labor and were even more highly susceptible to European diseases. Moreover, just as the demand for their labor increased with the expansion of exports to Europe, their numbers declined and, with it, their relative efficiency. Since the Portuguese already had extensive experience with African slaves in their Atlantic islands and had ready access to African labor markets, once the decision was made to exploit fully their American colony, then the turn toward African workers was conditioned only by availability of capital for importations.

The northern Europeans who followed the Iberians to America within a few decades of the discovery had even fewer Indians to exploit than the Portuguese and were unable to develop an extensive Indian slave labor force, let alone the complex free Indian labor arrangements developed by the Spaniards. Nor did they have access to precious metals to pay for imported slave labor. But, unlike the Iberians of the 16th century, they did have a cheaper and more willing pool of European laborers to exploit, especially in the crisis period of the 17th century. But even with this labor available, peasants and the urban poor could not afford the passage to America, and subsidizing that passage through selling of one's labor to American employers in indentured contracts became the main form of colonization in the first half century of northern European settlement in America. The English and the French were the primary users of indentured labor, and they exploited a significant pool of workers faced with low wages and poor opportunities within the European economy. But the end of the 17th-century crisis in Europe, and especially the rapid growth of the English economy in the last quarter of the century, brought a thriving labor market in Europe and a consequent increase in the costs of indentured laborers. With their European indentured laborers becoming too costly, and with no access to American Indian workers or Indian slaves, it was inevitable that the English and the French would also turn to African slaves, especially after discovering that sugar and other plantation-produced crops could profitably be exported to the European market on a mass scale.

Thus, despite their initially higher cost, African slaves finally became the most desired labor force for the Europeans to use to develop American export industries. That Africans were the cheapest available slaves at this time was due to the opening up of the West African coast by the Portuguese. Given the steady export of West African gold and ivories, and the development of Portugal's enormous Asiatic trading empire, the commercial relations between western Africa and Europe became common and cheap. Western Africans brought by sea had already replaced all other ethnic and religious groups in the European slave markets by the 16th century. Although Iberians initially enslaved Canary Islanders, these were later freed, as were the few Indians who were brought from America. The Muslims who had been enslaved for centuries were no longer significant as they disappeared from the Iberian Peninsula itself and became powerfully united under Moroccan and later Turkish control of North Africa. The dominance of the Turks in the eastern Mediterranean also closed off traditional Slavic and Balkan sources for slaves. Given the growing efficiency of the Atlantic slave traders, the dependability of African slave supply, and the stability of prices, it would be Africans who would come to be defined almost exclusively as the available slave labor of the 16th century.

With their rapid conquest of the American heartland and the enormous wealth that it generated, it was the Spaniards who were the first Europeans to have the capital necessary to import slaves. African slaves were in the armies of conquest and the households of many of the conquistadores, but the formal Spanish slave trade took decades to develop. King Ferdinand and Queen Isabella originally authorized the importation of slaves on September 16, 1501, when they issued a decree describing the type of populations that would be allowed entry into Spain's new colonial holdings. Neither "Moors, nor Jews, nor heretics, nor reconcilables, nor persons newly converted to our faith" would be permitted, "except if they are negro slaves or other slaves born in the power of Christians, our subjects and natives." Although primarily targeted at preserving religious orthodoxy in the New World, this early legislation became the core legal precedent that opened the doors of the African slave trade. In 1502, the governor of Hispaniola, Nicolás Obando, introduced sixteen slaves to the colonies; he was soon followed by a score of individuals who were granted independent licenses to bring their own and other slaves across the Atlantic. The decline on the native population in the island of Hispaniola led the king to authorize the importation of 250 slaves to work in Hispaniola's mining camps in 1510. Shortly thereafter, the Crown implemented a tax of two ducats for each slave brought to the Indies. The combined acts of taxing slavery and placing it under the purview of the empire's House of Trade meant that the slave trade was becoming institutionalized. The first *asiento*—or contract for importing slaves on a commercial basis—was issued in 1518. Don Jorge de Portugal and Lorenzo de Gouvenot o Gavorrod were granted contracts for importing 400 and 4,000 slaves, respectively. Prior to 1518, all Africans brought to the Spanish colonies were required to first pass through Europe, where they were supposed to be instructed in the Christian faith and integrated into European lifestyles. After 1518, this intermediary stop was eliminated, and African slaves could be shipped directly across the Atlantic.

Early Spanish experiences with African slavery in the Caribbean set the stage for what was to come on the mainland. Supplied by *asientos* and individual licenses, in its earliest years the Atlantic slave trade drew Africans primarily toward Mexico and Peru. Although the relative importance of African slaves was reduced within Spanish America in the 16th and 17th centuries, African migrations to these regions were not insignificant and began with the first conquests. Cortés and his various armies held several hundred slaves when they conquered Mexico in the 1520s, while close to 2,000 slaves appeared in the armies of Pizarro and Almargo in their conquest of Peru in the 1530s and in their subsequent civil wars in the 1540s. African slaves and military auxiliaries were present in other mainland conquests and expeditions that extended into Guatemala, Baja California, Florida, and even the Carolinas. Although Indians dominated rural life everywhere, Spaniards found their need for slaves constantly increasing. This was especially true in Peru, which while initially richer, lost a progressively higher proportion of its coastal populations to European diseases in areas ideal for such European crops as sugar and grapes. By the mid-1550s there were some 3,000 slaves in the Peruvian viceroyalty, with half of them in the city of Lima. This same balance between urban and rural residence, in fact, marked slaves, along with Spaniards, as the most urbanized group in Spanish American society.

The need for slaves within Peru increased dramatically in the second half of the 16th century as Potosí silver production came into full development, making Peru and its premier city of Lima the wealthiest zone of the New World. To meet this demand for Africans a major slave trade developed, especially after the unification of the Portuguese and Spanish crowns from 1580 to 1640 permitted the Portuguese to supply Spanish American markets. Initially most of the Africans came from the Senegambia region between the Senegal and Niger rivers, but after the development of Portuguese Luanda in the 1570s important contingents of slaves began arriving from the Kongo and Angola.

The slave trade to Peru was probably the longest and most unusual of any of the American slave trades for it involved two distinct stages. Africans shipped across the Atlantic were first landed at the port of Cartagena on the Caribbean coast of South America. They were then transshipped a short distance to Portobello on the Caribbean side of the Isthmus of Panama, taken by land across to the Pacific, and then shipped to Callao, which was the entry port for Lima. This second phase on average took some four to five months, which more than doubled the usual length of the trip from Africa to America. Also, mortality may have reached 10 percent on this second part of the trip, in addition to the mortality suffered on the Atlantic route, which was probably in the range of 15 percent in this century.

Another slave route into the kingdom of Peru came through the southern port of Buenos Aires. While ships from Africa could reach the port in seventy days, another long overland trip through difficult terrain could extend the journey significantly, depending on the final point of destination. Although the number of slaves legally entering Buenos Aires paled in comparison to the thousands that arrived in Cartagena, a thriving illegal trade added impressively to the numbers. Between 1606 and 1625, a total of 11,262 slaves were recorded as entering the city, of which only 288 had done so by royal permit.

Slaves were sold throughout the viceroyalty, from Upper Peru (Bolivia), Paraguay, and Chile in the south to Quito in the north. Slave prices could be quite high in some of the more remote regions, given the additional distance and geographic barriers that had to be overcome during transit. Initially African slaves tended to be heavily grouped in urban areas, but new economic roles opened up for them at the margins of Indian rural society. Although Indian free labor and conscripted labor were used to mine silver and mercury throughout Peru, gold was a different matter. Most gold was found in alluvial deposits in tropical lowlands far from Indian populations. Thus as early as the 1540s, Africans in gangs of ten to fifteen slaves were working gold deposits in the tropical eastern cordillera region of Carabaya in the southern Andes. These local gold fields were quickly depleted, but the precedent was set, and gold mining in both Portuguese and Spanish America tended to be an industry using African slaves.

But Africans were also used in some commercial agriculture. To serve such new cities as Lima, Spaniards developed major truck farming (the so-called *chácaras*) in the outskirts of the city, which was worked by small families of slaves. These vegetable gardens, orchards, and even small grain-producing farms usually relied on seasonal Indian labor for harvesting. Even more ambitious agricultural activity occurred up and down the coast in specialized sugar estates, vineyards, and more mixed agricultural enterprises. In contrast to the West Indian and Brazilian experience, the slave plantations of Peru were much more mixed-crop producers. On average the plantations of the irrigated coastal valleys, especially those to the south of Lima, had around 40 slaves per unit. But sometimes the larger estates could reach 100 slaves. The major wine- and sugar-producing zones of the 17th century, such as Pisco, and the Condor and Ica valleys, had together some 20,000 slaves. Along with the private owners, Jesuits also got into slave plantation production in a major way after 1600, and their estates were to be found throughout Peru. In the interior there were also several tropical valleys in the north, and even in the southern highlands slave estates specializing in sugar could be found. These interior plantations, like those of the coast, were relatively small, and, given that production was for the Peruvian and relatively limited Pacific coast trade, the dominant characteristic of commercial plantation agriculture was its mix of products. The diversity of goods also included the cultivation of coca, an important highland stimulant used especially by native silver miners in Potosí. In the Mizque region of Upper Peru, southeast of Cochabamba, 16th- and 17th-century slaves were found producing coca along with wheat, sugar, wine, and honey. Some Africans were also used in the coca plantations in the Yungas region near the city of La Paz. Finally, ranching of European animals was also a specialty of the African slave population, except for sheepherding, which was quickly adopted by the Indian population along with their herds of llamas.

Slaves also played a vital role in parts of the viceroyalty's communications infrastructure, being especially prominent as muleteers on the interior routes and as seamen in both private and royal vessels. The royal navy at the beginning of the 17th century employed as many as 900 black slaves, who were rented from their masters. These were used in all tasks except as galley rowers, which was an exclusively criminal occupation.

Slaves were a vital economic element in all the cities of the Spanish empire. In the skilled trades they predominated in metalworking, clothing, and construction and building supplies, and they were well represented in all the crafts except the most exclusive such as silversmithing and printing. In semiskilled labor they were heavily involved in coastal fishing, as porters and vendors, in food handling and processing, and even as armed watchmen in the local Lima police force. Every major construction site found skilled and unskilled slaves working alongside white masters and free blacks of all categories, as well as Indian laborers. In some trades by the middle decades of the 17th century, free and slave Africans and Afro-Americans were dominant and could exercise master status without opposition. Thus of the 150 master tailors in the city, 100 were blacks, mulattoes, or mestizos. Of the 70 master shoemakers of Lima in the same period, 40 were blacks and mulattoes. This was not the norm in all crafts, of course, but it well reflected their weight in the lower status of apprenticeship and journeymen in these occupations. Sometimes opposition in areas where they were fewer in number was quite bitter, but the lack of a powerful American guild organization permitted blacks, free and slave, to practice most crafts even at the master level.

In Peru there even developed major factory labor in the clothing industry. In all the major cities, *obrajes*, or factories for dying, spinning, and finishing textiles, where lower quality cloth was produced, were common and even reached quite impressive sizes. These were exclusively worked by Indian labor, though sometimes free colored persons—often convicted criminals— could be found in these occupations. In Lima there also grew a whole set of hat factories that were all worked with slave labor. In 1630 there were eighteen such factories employing between 40 and 100 slaves per company. Numerous slaves were also employed in tanning works and slaughterhouses and in kilns and quarries producing bricks and finished stone for the major construction works going on in the wealthy city of Lima. Finally, all government and religious institutions, charities, hospitals, and monasteries had their contingent of half a dozen or more slaves who were the basic maintenance workers for these large establishments.

As the city of Lima grew, so did its slave population. From 4,000 slaves in 1586 the number of Africans and Afro-Peruvians grew to some 7,000 in the 1590s, to 11,000 in 1614, and to some 20,000 by 1640. This growth was initially faster than the white and Indian participation in the city, so Lima was half black by the last decade of the 16th century and would stay that way for most of the 17th century. Equally, all the northern and central Andean coastal and interior cities had black populations that by 1600 accounted for half of the total populations. As one moved farther south into the more densely populated Indian areas, their relative percentage dropped, though black slaves could be found in the thousands in Cuzco and even Potosí, which in 1611 was supposed to have had some 6,000 blacks and mulattoes both slave and free.

Slave ownership in Peru would be a model for all of Spanish and most of Portuguese America as well. In the urban and sometimes even in the rural areas, slave rentals were as common as direct ownership. Most skilled artisans were rented out by their owners, who could be anything from institutions to widows who lived off their rent to free artisans to whom they brought extra income. Often the skilled and semiskilled slaves maintained themselves and rented or sold their services, supplying their owners with fixed monthly incomes, and absorbing their own expenses for housing and food. For most unskilled slaves, it was common to be rented to Spaniards or other free persons who paid both wages and maintenance costs. Thus a complex web of direct ownership, rentals, and self-employment made the slaves an extremely mobile and adjustable labor force. This is most clearly reflected in the activities of the Crown, which often had emergency recourse in its fortifications, shipyards, and fleets to hundreds of unskilled and skilled workers, almost all of whom they rented from private owners.

Another characteristic of the Peruvian labor scene was the existence in every region and every craft of free black and mulatto workers, employed alongside slaves. Again, in a pattern common to the rest of Spanish and Portuguese America, free blacks and mulattoes appeared from the very beginning of the conquest and colonization period, some of them even coming from Spain itself. Often discriminated against on racial grounds by whites competing for the better jobs, they nevertheless were to be found at all levels of society from unskilled to master positions. In some cases they were paid wages equal to those of white workers; in others they were paid even less than the rental wages of the slaves. In some occupations they could not break into the elite classes, but in construction and shipping, where blacks were well represented, they became shipmasters, architects, and master carpenters and builders. In all cases their numbers grew. By 1600 in most cities they had reached 10 percent to 15 percent of the local black population, and those numbers rose steadily as the century progressed. Neither favoring manumission nor opposing it in any systematic way, Peruvian society allowed the normal operations of the market to lead to manumission and put no social constraints on free fathers manumitting their children or even recognizing them.

With self-purchase arrangements allowing skilled slaves to buy themselves and their families out of slavery, and with a steady stream of children and women freed by masters conditionally and often totally, a very large population of free colored arose and actively participated in the free labor market. The growth of urban centers, the expansion of the hacienda system and Spanish agricultural production, and the decline of the Amerindian population due to massive epidemics throughout the last quarter of the 16th century and most of the 17th century created a tremendous demand for labor in all Peru. The more mobile the freedman, the more discrimination he or she faced, and the more unsettled the times, the more he was singled out by whites as a threatening element. Free blacks and mulattoes were disproportionally found as convicts in Peru's jails, galleys, and factories. But the society was too desperate for their labor to prohibit them from actively competing for jobs and from attempting to rise out of the lower classes. In Peru, as in the rest of Spanish and Portuguese America, the dynamics of capitalism would not be constrained to any significant extent by the inherent racial prejudices of the white elite. As the 17th century progressed, greater and greater would be the percentage of free among the blacks and mulattoes, especially as the post-1650 mining crisis led to a slowing of African arrivals into Peru.

The second major zone of slave importation into Spanish America in this early period was the viceroyalty of Mexico, which from the first moments had *ladino* and *bozal* slaves in the armies, farms, and houses of the Spanish conquerors. As in Peru, the first generation of slaves probably numbered close to the total number of whites. They were also drawn heavily into the sugar and European commercial crop production in the warmer lowland and coastal regions, which were widely scattered in the central zone of the viceroyalty. These sugar estates were usually quite small, with the average size approaching the forty-slaves-per-farm arrangement in Peru. Several hundred slaves were to be found in the largest sugar estate of the Cortés family in the 1550s, but this was the exception.

In a significant departure from the Peruvian experience, African slaves were initially extremely important in the silver-mining industry. By the second half of the 16th century, major deposits of silver were discovered in the northern fringes of the viceroyalty, in areas with few settled Indians. Given the immediate need for labor and the relative availability of African slaves, these were quickly brought to these newly developed mining camps to undertake the first work of exploitation. Thus the mines at Zacatecas, Guanajuato, and Pachuco initially used large numbers of slaves to perform all types of mining tasks, both above and below ground. In a mine census of 1570, some 3,700 African slaves were listed in the mining camps, double the number of Spaniards, and just a few hundred less than the Indians. At this point they represented 45 percent of the laboring population. But the increasing availability of free Indian laborers who quickly migrated to these new settlements lessened the need for the more expensive African slave labor. At the same time, the number of African slaves who were available to work in the mining industry fluctuated. The period from 1576 to 1600 saw erratic slave shipments to Mexico, resulting in unreliable levels of slave imports to the colony's mining regions. Very quickly, the numbers, relative importance, and even occupation of the African slave miners changed. By the 1590s the slaves in the mining camps were down to 1,000 workers and represented only one-fifth of the combined African and Indian labor force. They were now confined to less dangerous above-ground tasks. Although slave imports to Mexico picked up pace and increased in volume during the first three decades of the 17th century, Africans declined as a significant element in the mining industry.

Mexican slaves also appear to have worked more heavily in the textile *obrajes* (or workshops) than did their Peruvian counterparts, especially as the government struggled to decide whether to allow or prohibit Indian labor in these factories. In fact, while the African slave trade to Mexico began to wane after 1640, *obraje* labor, along with a renewed sugar industry, helped sustain slavery, supporting several internal slave markets in central Mexico that lasted until the 1750s. Even as the Indian and mestizo population grew throughout the colony in the late 17th century, black slaves remained a key element of the *obraje* labor force well into the 18th century. So important was this use of slave labor that when the textile industry finally moved to free wage labor after 1750, Mexican slavery in central Mexico began to decline quickly.

Elsewhere in Spanish America, African slaves comprised an essential component of royal construction projects, but in Mexico black slaves played a lesser role in this arena, compared with convict, corvée, and free Indian wage labor. The fact that most of Mexico's major urban centers were built either over preexisting Indian towns or inside zones of dense Indian population also meant that urban slave labor competed with native labor. Though slaves performed many of the same urban tasks in Mexico City as they did in Lima, the former was more of an Indian town, so slaves did not achieve the same proportional importance in the labor force. Obviously, this did not mean that urban slaves were invisible. Indeed, they were highly visible, and scholars believe that most of Mexico's slaves may have lived in cities, with Mexico City being their point of greatest concentration. Slave numbers grew so high that the Mexican viceroy Luís de Velasco wrote an urgent letter to the king in 1553 requesting restraints on African slave imports, since he believed that the colony was being inundated with blacks, inspiring great confusion and chaos. While his was an alarmist view, it signaled a growing perception among colonists that blacks were transcending their assigned place at the bottom of the colonial order. Some of this, ironically, was the result of the colonists' own habits and behavior. Urban black slaves, for instance, were highly valued for their symbolic worth, and owning slaves typically improved one's rank and honor. Some owners provided their slaves with fine clothes, shoes, stockings, jewelry, and even weapons, particularly in certain public settings, so as to display their positions as patrons and masters. As late as the 17th century, it was not uncommon to see a royal official strolling along the streets of Mexico City in the company of immaculately groomed black body-guards with roses on their feet and swords at their sides. The symbolic value of urban slaves was complemented by their value as domestics, which was one of the professions dominated by slaves and blacks prior to the 1640s. Important Mexican cities representing geographically diverse areas of the colony, such as Valladolid in the central interior, Saltillo and Colima in the north, and Merida in the southeast, had large contingents of black slave servants and domestics into the 17th century. Even in the mining town of Guanajuato, the majority of slaves may have been domestics in the 17th century.

White and mestizo colonists who could not afford to own large numbers of slaves aspired to own at least one. But for members of the middle and lower classes, Mexico's urban slaves were drawn into a more diverse labor arena. Slave women, largely unskilled, hawked their wares as street vendors or in small shops (*tiendas*). They were employed in nunneries and convents, walked the streets as prostitutes, served as wet nurses, or were entertainers. Male slaves were skilled and semiskilled craftsmen, served as apprentices, and became carpenters, candle makers, blacksmiths, hatters, and silversmiths. Blacksmithing was especially important in Mexican urban slavery but was outpaced by tailors, cobblers, and hatters. In the early 17th century, as slave participation in mining declined, a transition took place in Mexican slavery whereby urban slaves became more important to the personal economies of the middle class. The wages brought by slaves could mean a fundamental difference in lifestyle for a widow, small merchant, or artisan. Increasingly these colonists took advantage of the economic support that slaves provided. Meanwhile, for the ranks of the urban poor, gaining access to the services of just a single slave could mean salvation from a life of poverty. Colonial court cases bear record of poor families refusing to release their slaves or allowing self-purchase, given the dire hardship that the sale would inflict upon their lives.

The relative importance of Mexican slavery was well reflected in the growth of the slave population. In 1570 there were an estimated 20,000 slaves in all of Mexico. At their peak in the first decades of the 17th century the total slave labor force reached a maximum of 45,000, although less reliable ac-counts from contemporary observers have placed the total at 80,000 in 1645. By and large Mexican slaves represented around 2 percent of the viceregal population in the 1640s. In contrast, the number of slaves in Peru during the 1640s reached close to 100,000, representing between 10 and 15 percent of the population. Though the Peruvian slave population would stagnate in the next century, it would not go into the decline shown by the Mexican slave population in the 18th century. Indeed, between the 1680s and 1730s, intermittent sugar booms kept slaves coming, being sold in places like Trujillo from Panama. But only 20,000 slaves entered Mexico in the 1700s, playing specialized skilled roles in the sugar industry and key roles in the textile industry. Mexican slave numbers generally leveled off in the second half of the 17th century, before declining steeply in the 18th century. By the last decade of the 1700s, Peru had close to 90,000 slaves, while Mexico had only 6,000 left. The Mexican experience clearly demonstrated the importance of the relative weight of the much larger Mesoamerican Indian population on the labor market. Because of complex regional variations among the local ethnic groups, Mexico also had an Indian population much more mobile and responsive to the demands for free wage laborers than the Andean Indians of Peru. Finally, it was an economy with a large population, but with a much slower rate of growth. Thus the mining and agricultural sectors of Mexico grew slowly enough to fulfill most of their labor needs from the increasingly large propertyless and mobile Indian labor force, which grew out of the Spanish conquest and subsequent pressures of taxation and exploitation, as well as from the rising mestizo and free colored populations. Exceptions to this pattern came in industries where slaves filled specialty roles, such as in sugar processing and refinement, where the high turnover rates of Mexican free labor militated against their acquiring the skills needed to properly perform tasks. Slaves, meanwhile, being bound to estates for long periods of time, proved more ideal in these circumstances and continued to account for a small but valuable portion of the Mexican labor force at the end of the 18th century. In both Peru and Mexico, however, the 1650s marked the end of their great period of massive slave importations. By 1650 Spanish America, primarily Peru and Mexico, had succeeded in importing from the earliest days of the conquest some 250,000 to 300,000 slaves, a record they would not repeat in the next century of colonial growth.

Outside of the two major mainland colonial economies of Spanish America were smaller areas of settlement that also witnessed an influx of African slaves in the 16th and 17th centuries. Central America was prominent among these, receiving direct slave shipments from the ports of Honduras, Guatemala, and Panama, but also from overland routes that extended from Mexico and Cartagena. Perhaps as many as 20,000 slaves resided throughout Central America by 1650, with the first of the region's slaves arriving in Panama well before blacks were transported to either Mexico or Peru.

Being an initial area of settlement on the mainland (1502–10), Panama was a pioneering slave market that encapsulated features of the earliest Spanish trade in Africans. For example, instead of being shipped in large groups through contracts, most of Panama's earliest slaves arrived as the personal attendants of officials and colonists, entering by means of licenses issued to specific individuals. Slavery's initial scale in Panama was also quite small. Although thirty-six black slaves accompanied the explorer Diego de Nicuesa in his expeditions between 1511 and 1513, and thirty more assisted Balboa in several construction projects launched shortly after he reached the Pacific in 1513, the majority of the region's early slave owners had only a few blacks in their employ, typically between two and eight. African slave numbers would increase markedly over the course of the century, however, thanks to important changes in the colony's demography and economic profile. As was the case in the Caribbean, Panama's indigenous population declined sharply just a few years after the Spaniards' arrival. Those who survived were rapidly absorbed into a thriving market for native slaves, who staffed the emerging transportation and service industries that were associated with the Spanish expeditions of conquest and discovery in South America. When the conquest of Peru uncovered grand riches in mineral wealth, the Isthmus of Panama was transformed from being a platform for exploration into a critical passageway for the transport of goods and treasure back and forth from Spain. Shipments bound for Europe arrived at Panama's Pacific coast from Peru and were taken by land and river routes to the port of Nombre de Dios. Native slaves, many of whom were imported into Panama from places like Honduras and Nicaragua, were called upon to fill the labor market's growing need for cargo bearers. The influx of Indians continued throughout the 1530s and 1540s, but in 1550 the Indian slave trade came to an abrupt halt when a decree was issued granting freedom to all natives. However, the increasingly vigorous growth of the South American export economy meant that the need for transporters did not decline. In place of Indian laborers, locally bred horses and mules, combined with imported African slaves, filled the void.

Africans had established a presence in the Panamanian transportation industry from the mid-1520s. Not only did they haul goods, but they were also entrusted with the care and upkeep of roads. Panama City and Nombre de Dios used municipal funds to purchase teams of slaves to inhabit huts outside of the city limits, from which they monitored the royal roadways while ensuring that these thoroughfares remained paved and clean. By the 1550s, the end of Indian slavery helped to solidify the black presence in other sectors. African slaves worked in rock quarries, hammering and breaking stones for the seemingly endless construction projects in which they toiled, particularly building Panama's fortresses. Black slaves were domestics, artisans, and agricultural laborers. They represented a critical element of the colony's hospital workforce, working in nearly every staff position available in Panama City's hospital apart from being doctors themselves. A snapshot of the capital's slave population in 1575 reveals several arenas in which African labor was employed. That year, nearly 1,600 slaves were domestics, 102 worked in the city's vegetable gardens, 401 served as muleteers along the route from Panama City to Nombre de Dios, 363 dived in search of pearls off neighboring islands, 150 were cattle herders, and another 193 worked as loggers in nearby forests. Slave numbers would increase in many of these industries in the 17th century. By 1600, as many as 1,000 blacks worked in the pearl industry, 576 were muleteers, and 600 appeared as rowers in the cargo boats that sailed the Charges River during the rainy season, bound for the Gulf Coast.

The unique development of Panamanian society, especially when compared with Mexico and Peru, meant that African slavery would occupy a much different role. The other two colonies were highly stratified societies based on free and Indian tributary labor and sustained by rich mining economies. Panama never quite reached such a stage of development. Instead, early colonial Panama was a more socially and economically fluid world. Food supplies could be scarce, hunting for native slaves was commonplace, significant interracial and interclass conflict existed, and, ultimately, blacks came to saturate the overall population. By the late 16th century, blacks and mulattoes accounted for nearly 70 percent of all of Panama's residents. In the mid-1570s, the colony had only 800 whites, but 2,809 black slaves, 2,500 runaways, and 300 free coloreds. By 1610, the number of whites had increased, but the number of slaves also rose proportionately. Approximately 1,267 whites inhabited the colony, with 3,696 slaves and only 27 Indians. It seemed that just as Panama's economic identity was becoming solidified as a broker of trade between Spain and South America, it grew increasingly clear that the population responsible for filling this economic niche would be Africans and their descendants.

Whereas Panama was an important component of the Spanish transatlantic commercial network, it remained an outlier to more politically powerful regions, particularly Peru. By contrast, the colony of Guatemala became home to the seat of an *audiencia* (regional high court) and developed into one of the most politically prominent regions in Central America outside of Mexico. Slaves trickled into this colony, perhaps arriving with the conquistador Pedro de Alvarado in 1524, and then picking up pace with the first shipload of slaves being delivered from Santo Domingo in 1543. Guatemala's capital city of Santiago emerged as a primary slave market but developed slowly. Just 249 slaves were bought and sold in the city from 1544 to 1587, and rather than Santiago being a destination for slave traders, its earliest slaves were purchased elsewhere before being brought to town. By 1570, a public space had finally been created for slaves to be sold in the capital. This development occurred alongside the growth of Santiago as a commercial center, engaged in the exchange of cacao and textiles. In the 1580s, the entry of the Portuguese as a supplier to the Spanish slave market dramatically increased the availability of slaves, and in 1601 an *asiento* was signed authorizing 200 Africans per year to be brought to Guatemala. These numbers could not always meet the colony's rising demand. Despite improvements with the supply of slaves between 1580 and 1640, it appears that no more than 150 slaves entered Guatemala annually for much of the early 17th century, either legally or illegally. When the formal slave trade declined more definitively after 1640, colonists were still requesting new shipments.

African slaves in Guatemala performed multiple urban tasks, along the lines seen in Peru, Panama, and Mexico. What differentiated the Guatemalan experience was that the greater scarcity of Africans made them costlier. The dearth of liquid capital in the colony compounded the problem. An untrained male *ladino* (born in the New World) cost roughly 250 pesos in the early 1580s, and trained male slaves could typically be worth more than 500 pesos. The scarcity and slightly higher prices in Guatemala may have had favorable implications for slave treatment, as well as on the types of labor they performed. For instance, black Guatemalan slaves, unlike Indians, were seldom subjected to the horrors of branding in the 16th century. Moreover, black bondsmen entered the agricultural labor arena only gradually (appearing after the 1550s) and seldom worked in gangs. When black slaves did work in large groups, they tended to do so in the most profitable enterprises. As in Mexico, some Guatemalan slaves were miners and could be found working collectively to extract gold and silver, but the mining industry was only briefly profitable given the colony's minuscule ore deposits. However, slaves also cultivated cacao and indigo, which produced more solid and longer lasting revenues. Much of the indigo was grown in El Salvador, which was part of Guatemala during colonial times. Since indigo production needed significant amounts of labor only during its short harvest season, the slaves used in this industry were concentrated in smaller groups, often of no more than four persons. They were also used principally as skilled laborers, or as the supervisors of Indian work gangs, who did most of the harvesting. In the 17th and 18th centuries, sugar operations in the agricultural region near Lake Amatitlán accounted for the largest Guatemalan estates. Sugar cultivation began to thrive after the 1590s, and in 1680 the Dominican-owned Anís and Rosario *ingenios* (sugar mills) held 225 slaves, while a Dominican *ingenio* called San Gerónimo employed 700 slaves in the 18th century. These church-owned estates were unusual properties in terms of their size and scale of operations, although a few privately held plantations could hold in excess of 100 slaves.

Unlike those in Panama, black slaves in Guatemala constituted a minor segment of the overall colonial population, which was heavily dominated by Indians. But in the hot and unforgiving climate of Guatemala's Pacific coast lowlands, where whites and mestizos were few, black slaves and freedmen comprised the primary nonnative population group. As early as the first decade of the 17th century, their numbers had reached a point where the colonial government authorized the creation of a black township. San Diego de la Gomera, founded by blacks and settled in 1611, was supported by the Crown largely in an attempt to lure blacks away from the surrounding Indian villages they were rumored to have infiltrated. In the confines of their own town, black slaves and freedmen apparently intermingled, with free blacks having access to political office and exerting control over local saltpans and fisheries.

Regardless of whether blacks comprised a significant or small element of certain regional populations in the colony, the lower amount of slave imports to Guatemala definitely affected key personal relationships, such as marriage. When compared with slaves in colonies like Mexico, black slaves in early 17th-century Guatemala tended to marry outside of their race and status with far greater frequency. It seems that the small number of African women reaching Guatemala compelled male slaves to seek other wives. Many took Indian brides, particularly those classified by the colonial government as tribute payers, thereby representing one of the lowest and most accessible categories of native women. Yet, despite their tributary status, these women were free, and their children with African slaves were born into freedom. Evidence from Mexico City, by contrast, shows that from 1595 to 1650, most slaves married other slaves. Given the large numbers of male and female slaves coming into the city, there were greater possibilities for slave intermarriage to occur than in Guatemala. Meanwhile, in the Mexican countryside, particularly in the sugar-growing region of Jalapa, slaves did marry outside of their group with greater frequency than in Mexico City, but seemingly not to the same extent that slaves married Indians in Guatemala during the early 1600s. It would not be until the late 17th century that black Guatemalan slaves would begin marrying other blacks in significant numbers. As might be expected, these marriages were conducted largely by slave men, who toward the 18th century began marrying free *mulata* and black women, both of whom were considered to be of higher status than the socially inferior native tributaries. The attractiveness of slave men as viable marriage partners for free women represents an interesting and unexpected twist in the pattern of colonial social relations. In Guatemala, part of the answer to this apparent paradox rested in the fact that Indian tributary women realized that blacks actually enjoyed a slightly higher status in the social hierarchy. Securing a marriage to a black, even a slave, ensured that their children would benefit from being of mixed-race ancestry (an Indian mulatto, or *zambo*). Meanwhile, for slaves, marrying native women not only guaranteed liberty for their offspring but also ensured them partial access to the world of the free.

As in all other regions, the economic importance and mobility of Guatemalan slaves meant that they were not only a prime source of labor but also that they could be sold and transferred, and were often used as collateral for loans. Skilled slaves generally ranked highest in value and helped secure the most sizable loans. In the case of default, slaves represented commodities that could be easily confiscated and were routinely among the first elements of a borrower's estate to be seized.

Outside of Guatemala, Costa Rica probably represented one of the main areas of Central America where slaves factored into the economy in similar ways. This cash-strapped colony regularly saw slaves exchanged as currency in the 1600s, especially to settle debts. Slaves were also used as payment for indemnities, as dowries, as security deposits, and as partial payments on homes and property, or they were simply sold for cash. Some members of the Costa Rican elite even used slaves to pay for elaborate funerals and for a series of annual masses to commemorate them after death. Importantly, slaves also represented investments that could grow in value. Unskilled slaves could be taught a trade, which dramatically raised their overall worth, while the reproductive capacity of females could be exploited to bring new slaves, and consequently new cash, onto Costa Rican estates.

The weakness of the Costa Rican economy in the 16th and 17th centuries translated into a few important differences in its slavery from places like Guatemala, Mexico, Peru, and even Panama. From 1569 to 1611, the colony largely relied on profits gained from vessels built in its shipyards and from exporting Indian tribute for profit. Since tribute was collected in goods rather than specie, a variety of native products were exported, including corn, cacao, sarsaparilla, wood, limestone, animal fat, birds, and meat. The devastation of the native population, combined with competition from more important shipyards in Guayaquil (Ecuador), forced economic change. Throughout most of the 17th century, Costa Rica concentrated on supplying its internal markets through farming, fishing, and cattle enterprises. As a provider of basic foodstuffs, it remained in the orbit of larger economies such as those of Peru and Panama, but it was only after 1680 that cacao cultivation jolted economic production and profitability, reawakening Costa Rica's export markets.

Thanks partly to the sluggish economy, slaves entered Costa Rica very slowly, serving primarily in the households of the elite and as field hands. By 1700, only 2,415 blacks and mulattoes lived in Costa Rica, which had a total population of 19,293 individuals. Albeit scant, these numbers represented substantial increases over the 275 blacks and mulattoes who lived in the colony in 1611. Evidence from slave sales during the early years of the cacao boom suggests that slave imports probably experienced a nearly sixfold increase between 1670 and 1700. But this simply meant a rise from 20 slave sales per decade to just under 120. Clearly, in light of these demographic figures, the overall scale of 17th-century Costa Rican slavery was small.

The colony also lacked a legally recognized port where it could receive slaves. Combined with economic retardation and low slave demands, this meant that Costa Rica's status as a secondary, or even tertiary, slave market was reflected in the type of slaves that arrived there. The robust *bozales* imported directly from Africa were saved for more vigorous slave centers. Costa Rica's 17th-century slaves were overwhelmingly creoles, born in the New World, and frequently of mixed racial origins. Moreover, the critical role that Costa Rica's slaves played as economic capital, as opposed to elements of production, altered the tenor of slavery. Certainly, slaves were sold on the auction block to work for their masters. But when slaves were exchanged as parts of dowries and inheritances, or to repay debts and serve as down payments, slavery was transformed into a different mode. Such slave transactions constituted a redistribution of preexisting wealth among the Costa Rican elite, rather than serving as the base for the production of new wealth.

The rest of Spanish Central American slavery in the 16th and 17th centuries resembled the basic patterns seen in Guatemala, Mexico, Costa Rica, and Panama. As in Mexico, mining served as an important catalyst to the importation of Africans into Honduras. Arriving in the port of Puerto Cabellos, which would emerge as a key supplier of black slaves for Central America, nearly 1,500 blacks toiled in the gold mines of Olancho and the Guayape River by 1545. Gold deposits would decline substantially within a decade, but slaves remained important. Silver was discovered in the region of Tegucigalpa toward the end of the century, and with it, African slaves quickly came to play an important role here as well. Because the mining industry never reached the magnitude of that in either Mexico or Peru, the long-term use of slaves in the Honduran export economy was limited. Instead, as in Costa Rica and Guatemala, slaves in the 17th century acquired greater importance as elements of the internal economy, serving as agriculturists for local markets, domestic laborers, and even as capital and currency. In neighboring Nicaragua, the slave market was probably one of the smallest in Central America in the 16th century. In 1583 the governor Francisco Casco wrote a letter to the king explaining the dire labor situation in his colony. The depletion of Indians in Nicaragua had been exacerbated by years of widespread hunting for native slaves, who were rapidly sold and exported. Without natives, Casco stressed the pressing need for African slaves to serve as workers, especially in cultivating indigo, but the result was no new slave trade. Instead slaves entered sporadically into the colony as they always had.

The black presence in Nicaragua enjoyed a markedly different history along the Caribbean coast. In a region known as the Mosquito Coast, which extends into Honduras, the native population successfully resisted domination by the Spaniards in the 16th century. In the early 17th century, these Indians began intermingling with African runaway slaves and freedmen. In 1641, fugitive British slaves who were fleeing a shipwreck in nearby Providence Island accounted for hundreds more blacks entering the Mosquito zone. As they settled in the area, many worked themselves deeply into the local culture. The result was a unique African-native population that thrived at the fringes of the major European colonies. The newly categorized "Miskitu Indians" possessed both an Africanized branch (*zambos*) and a native branch (Tawira), which jockeyed for power and influence, and which made strategic alliances with multiple European states. The *zambos* aligned with the British, who began establishing themselves as a power in the Caribbean during the mid–17th century and had started entering Nicaragua by the 1630s. The Tawira, on the other hand, favored the Spanish. By the 1720s, however, they had become a weak voice in the Caribbean coast region, making the *zambo* branch the dominant group.

The Miskitu presence complicated the dynamics of slavery and blackness in Central America. To meet the demands of growing British labor needs in the Caribbean, the Miskitu served as slavers raiding the Spanish colonies of Honduras, Panama, and Costa Rica for their remaining Indians, especially the so-called wild Indians who had not been completely conquered. They also entered into agreements with the British government to serve as bounty hunters in search of black fugitive slaves. In the 1720s, they boarded ships bound for Jamaica to destroy maroon settlements.

In the meantime, a limited number of black runaway slaves from various Spanish and British settlements in Central America found their way into Miskitu-controlled areas. Here, they either became absorbed into the culture or were shielded and protected from their former masters. On a number of occasions, the Miskitu also refused to answer the British call to serve as bounty hunters. In retrospect, the social institution of slavery proved crucial to the development of the Miskitu people and their identity. Not being purely black, the Miskitu conceived of themselves as free from the legacy of African slavery. Not being completely Indian, they further saw themselves as beyond the scope of being captured as slaves for the British market. Yet, at the same time, being both Indian and black also made the Miskitu somewhat ambivalent in their loyalties to the Europeans. They offered Europeans their services and talents only when they felt it convenient and necessary. Consequently, this unique Afro-Indian population came to occupy a fragile space in between multiple colonial identities.

South of Central America and outside of Peru were a number of important slave regimes that exhibited features revealing additional nuances in Spanish American mainland slavery. Prominent among these was the kingdom of Quito, conforming roughly to the territory of modern Ecuador but encompassing areas in southern Colombia and northern Peru. An Andean region with a highland geography, Quito, like Peru, retained a strong native presence that would not be eclipsed by African slaves. Nevertheless, as elsewhere, black slaves settled quickly into the colony's urban areas and performed a range of urban labor tasks. In the countryside, slaves worked as lumberjacks, polemen, and agriculturalists, and also in local gold mining. Unlike in Central America, Quito's gold mines were among the most profitable in the Spanish kingdom, accounting for nearly one-quarter of all the gold registered in the Spanish port of Seville between 1535 and 1660. Gold-mining production surged even higher in the second half of the 18th century. Slaves came early to work in Popayán, a 400-mile region in the northern reaches of Quito. By 1592, Quito's officials were requesting shipments of 1,000 Africans between the ages of seventeen and forty. Far fewer arrived. In the three major Quiteño slaveholding regions, including Guayaquil, Popayán, and Ibarra, slaves rarely amounted to more than 12,000 out of a population of 430,000 during the colonial period.

The relatively low numbers have not discouraged some from describing Quito as a slave society, even though the colony may not fit the classic definition usually associated with slave societies found in larger plantation economies. The observation rests on a few simple principles. First, slavery was vital to Quito's economic vigor. Although the anchor of the colony's economy until the 18th century was textile production, which generally did not utilize slave labor, the institution of slavery still helped underwrite *obraje* profits, since textile items were frequently purchased by masters to be used by their slaves, and slaves also worked on the agro-pastoral estates that serviced many of the colony's textile mills. Moreover, in the 18th century, the decline of the colony's *obraje* industry reinvigorated the role of African slavery, causing what some have called an "Africanization" of the Quiteño economy. Nearly 20 percent of all slaves entering the port of Cartagena during the 18th century would be brought to Quito. Considering every element of slave production and consumption, slavery's share of Quito's total economy during the colonial period was considerable. A second element helping to situate Quito among the New World's slave societies is that the colony was a place where African slavery fundamentally affected social hierarchies and sociopolitical relations. Quite simply, the master-slave relationship constituted an important component of what it meant to be elite, and a large percentage of the elite owned at least one or two slaves. Third, although Andeans served as the primary workers of the textile industry, indigenous labor may not have taken precedence over African slavery in Quito. Native labor has been perceived to have been in competition with African slave labor in many of the mainland Spanish colonies. When native labor was cheaply and readily available, then African slavery has been viewed as being unnecessary and too costly to compete. For much of the 16th century and some of the 17th century, native labor was readily given to Spaniards by means of individual grants known as *encomendias*. The *encomendia's* decline has been portrayed as a catalyst for the rise of African slavery, but in Quito the two systems were not mutually exclusive and were coexistent. Although the *encomendia* enjoyed a longer life cycle in Quito than usual, African slavery complemented *encomendia*, offering both a mobile enslaved labor force and indigenous tribute and workers.

The development of early colonial slavery in Mexico, Peru, Central America, and South America defines a distinct, mainland Spanish American system of slavery that differed from later Caribbean and Brazilian models. One characteristic of the Spanish mainland system was that among its principal tasks was reconciling the African presence with an influential, preexisting indigenous heritage. In cases where the native population was large and integrated into complex social systems, African slavery filled specialty roles in colonial economic development, often supplementing and compensating for the effects of native demographic decline. In zones where the native population was scattered and minimally organized, African slavery enjoyed a more prominent position as a principal economic force. But even in areas with small native populations, the local economies were quite varied and highly subsistence oriented, and this made local slavery quite varied as well. Although at times slaves could dominate certain individual economic sectors, such as mining, they were distributed simultaneously into so many other arenas that attempting to singularly characterize a mainland colony by a dominant type of slave production was nearly impossible.

Because early Spanish populations were so small, and the task of managing conquered territories was so great, one way of thinking about mainland African slaves is as "auxiliaries" to white and mestizo colonists. Auxiliary slavery contrasts with plantation slavery, where the emphasis of slave life was on production for a market economy, and where slave units of production tended to be larger. Most Spanish mainland slavery in the 16th and 17th centuries was small-scale, with households having just a handful of slaves. Also, rather than being centered on rural estates, Spanish mainland slavery was heavily urban, located precisely in the cities and towns where the majority of white and mestizo colonists were concentrated. As auxiliary slaves, blacks augmented the Spanish urban presence in both number and function. Apart from menial labor, slaves were found performing tasks where there simply were not enough whites to do the job. Consequently, they became artisans, apprentices, and vendors. Slave labor sometimes blurred with the jobs of the free to the extent that in a number of societies, free blacks, whites, and mestizos worked in many of the professions that were also staffed by skilled slaves. In the countryside, especially in remote sections of Mexico and Guatemala, the slaves' position as a Spanish auxiliary often meant that they were charged with managing and supervising free-wage Indian labor. Contract Indian labor on the mainland was frequently cheaper than black slaves and, in many cases, more expendable. Valuable African slaves therefore supplemented the Spanish presence by serving as the nucleus and organizers of broader teams of labor.

An intellectual justification existed for situating black slaves in important intermediary and auxiliary positions in colonial society. This identification derived from 15th-century and early 16th-century Iberian debates about purity of blood and the proper legal status of Old and New Christians, Africans were assigned a position in the colonial world as *gente de razón* (people of reason). Others in society who enjoyed this status included Spaniards and mestizos, but not Indians. As *gente de razón*, blacks were subject to the Inquisition and the full range of judicial bodies affecting the Spanish commonwealth (*república de españoles*). Indians, on the other hand, had their own jurisdictional bodies (*república de indios*). Assigning blacks the *de razón* status provided a space within which African slaves and their offspring were deemed to be members of a broadly conceived Spanish society. In practice, this membership was fraught with restrictions, which further worked to relegate slaves, in particular, to an auxiliary social function.

Of course, auxiliary slaves on the Spanish mainland certainly did not enjoy freedom as such, even if they sometimes administered Indian workers. Nevertheless, in serving as supplements to Spanish household economies, they fulfilled a role that resonated with some slave patterns on the African continent. Lineage, or "kinship slavery," as it has been known, was often encountered in Africa and essentially involved households taking in slaves as supplemental kin in order to fortify family networks and household economies and sometimes providing them with independent economic and supervisory roles. In urban areas such as Mexico City and Lima, slaves who lived alone or independently with their families seemingly possessed more of the autonomy exhibited by the African slave model. In the countryside, too, some forms of Spanish American slave life could enable certain liberties. Slaves who cultivated vineyards or tilled fields sometimes resided in huts that were dozens of miles away from their absentee masters, as was the case in the cacao-growing regions of 18th-century Costa Rica. Here they enjoyed distinct opportunities and moments of independence.

The nature of slavery on the Spanish mainland exhibited a unique chronology that differed from the colonies held by other European powers. By and large, the majority of slave imports came in the 16th and 17th centuries, particularly during the era of the Portuguese monopoly from 1580 to 1640. Consequently, slavery on the mainland had a strong impact on the development of Spanish American societies, especially during the early phases of growth where patterns of governance and legal structures were still being molded. Considerably more slaves arrived than Europeans during these years. Just 188,000 Spaniards crossed the Atlantic, as opposed to 289,000 slaves in the period of the Portuguese monopoly. Subsequent decades would bring more parity, as 141,000 slaves and 158,000 Spaniards landed in Spanish New World destinations from 1640 to 1700. But the period 1700–1760 would once again witness a renewal of slave imports, as 271,000 slaves and 193,000 Spaniards arrived. The flow of these slaves would change in the 18th century. Mainland slaves were channeled away from the dominant Spanish colonial economies of Mexico and Peru and into the secondary economies of places such as Quito, Costa Rica, Venezuela, and Colombia. Their proximity to the thriving British, Dutch, and French colonies offered them access to the illegal slave trade as a supplement to the legal imports that supplied their renewed economies.

The flow of slaves away from Peru and Mexico would continue powerfully after 1650 into previously marginal and neglected areas of the Caribbean, and these regions were destined to become the great slave holders of the 18th and 19th centuries. Moreover, for all the original and early usage of African slaves in mainland Spanish America, it was not the Spaniards but the Portuguese who would define the model of slave societies for all other European colonies that would become dominant in the Americas. With no stable Indian peasant populations to exploit, and with little or no alternative exports in the form of precious metals, the Atlantic islands model—with their slave plantation production satisfying Europe's insatiable demand for sugar—led inexorably to the massive introduction of African slave labor to the fertile soils of the tropical lowlands. The first of the European powers to develop this plantation slave system, and the model for all later developments throughout the Americas, was Portugal, which took possession of the eastern coastline of South America in the early 16th century.

The conquest and settlement of Brazil was initially not a primary concern of the expanding Portuguese empire. Claiming the region through expeditions that found Brazil on the road to the East Indies, the Portuguese were little interested in its immediate development. With the riches of Asia being exploited as the Portuguese opened up a water route to the spice islands and then to India, there was little demand for the development of Brazil. The first commercial exports were in fact woods, from which dyes were extracted. These so-called Brazilwood trees were usually cut by local Indian groups and then shipped by the Portuguese to Europe on a seasonal basis, with no permanent Portuguese settlers residing in America. Castaways and other marginal Portuguese began living with local Tupi-Guarani-speaking Indian communities along the coast and became the crucial cultural brokers who kept the contact with the mother country alive. For some twenty years after its exploration and official integration into the Portuguese empire, Brazil remained a backwater.

This situation changed rapidly, however, when Portugal was suddenly confronted by European rivals willing to contest this transitory control over its American territories. French and British merchants began to send their own ships into Brazilian waters to pick up the profitable dyewoods, and they soon used the coast as a base for attacking the Portuguese East Indies fleets that cruised the South Atlantic. The French and British even went so far as to set up more than temporary logging camps both at the Amazonian estuary in the Northeast and in Guanabara Bay in the south. The establishment of this latter settlement—the so-called French Antarctica colony—finally convinced the Portuguese that full-scale exploitation of Brazil was imperative for the safety of their entire overseas empire. Thus, despite their limited population resources, the Portuguese decided to commit themselves to full-scale colonization.

With Portugal's decision to colonize Brazil came the need to find an export product more reliable and profitable than dyewood. In this context its experiences in the Azores, Madeira, and São Tome showed that sugar was the ideal crop to guarantee the existence of a profitable colony. This decision was greatly aided by the fact that the Portuguese still dominated the Atlantic slave trade at this time and could easily and cheaply deliver slaves to America. Equally, the leaders of the colony were mostly men who had generated their initial wealth in the East Indies trade and could provide the crucial capital and credit needed to import the machines and the technicians who would get the sugar plantation regime going on a profitable basis. Thus by the 1550s was born the first plantation system in the New World, a system that very rapidly dominated the sugar markets of Europe and effectively ended the dominance of the eastern Atlantic island producers.

Brazil was not the first American zone to produce sugar, since Columbus had already brought sugar to Santo Domingo as early as 1493. But all the sugar estates on that island, Cuba, and Puerto Rico were soon reduced to small units producing for just local and regional markets. The headlong rush of Spanish colonists to the mainland eliminated the incentives to develop these islands into full-scale production zones despite the quality of their soils. Even in Brazil enterprising colonists had begun to plant sugar as early as the 1510s. But it was not until the formal establishment of the proprietary captaincies into which Brazil was divided that systematic production began. The Portuguese fleet of 1532 carried along sugar experts from the Madeira plantations, and the new governors who took over their regions all brought plantings from Madeira or São Tome. After many trials and problems with Indian raiding, two zones stood out initially as the most profitable centers of colonization and sugar production. These were the two Northeast provinces of Pernambuco and Bahia. By the 1580s Pernambuco already had more than sixty *engenhos* producing sugar for the European market, and by the last decades of the century it was intimately connected to the Antwerp market. Given the initially marginal interest of the Portuguese in this zone, it was Dutch shipping that played a vital role in linking Brazil to the northern European sugar markets, the site of Europe's fastest growing economies. By the 1580s Bahia had emerged as the second-largest producer, with some forty mills in production, and the two zones produced about two-thirds of all the sugar on the continent.

Quickly becoming Europe's prime supplier of sugar, the mills of Brazil's Northeast soon evolved into far larger operations than their Atlantic islands predecessor. By the end of the 16th century, Brazilian mills were producing six times the output per annum of the Atlantic islands *engenhos*. Much of this increase was due to the greater size of American sugar plantings, through the efforts of the mill owners as well as the smaller dependent planters tied to the mills (and known as *lavradores da cana*). This allowed many owners to construct expensive, large water-driven mills with capacities far greater than their own field production. At the end of the century Brazilians also worked out a new type of milling process that effectively increased the percentage of juice extracted from the canes, thereby greatly increasing the productivity of the mills. With excellent soils, the most advanced milling technology, and close contact with the booming Dutch commercial network, Brazil dominated sugar production in the Western world by 1600. What had been settled in a marginal way and with little interest from the Crown now began to take on more and more of a central role in Portugal's vast empire, with sugar the crucial link connecting Portugal, Africa, and Brazil.

Given the insatiable demand of the mills for unskilled agricultural labor, the Brazilians would experiment with many of the forms of labor organization that later colonists would attempt, exempting only indentured European workers. They imported African slaves from the very beginning, but they also sought to enslave the local American Indian populations and turn them into a stable agricultural labor force. The Tupi speakers who occupied the Northeast coastal region were settled in fairly large villages of several hundred persons and engaged in agricultural production. They were thus not the seminomadic and primarily hunting groups encountered farther in the interior, although they were largely subsistence agricultural producers and nothing like the Andean or Mexican peasants with their complex markets and long-distance trade. Also, their constant warfare and putative ritual cannibalistic practices gave the Portuguese an excuse to conquer and enslave them; their agricultural experience promised the possibility of making them into an effective labor force.

The Portuguese tried converting the Indians and paying them wages, but the primary means of extracting their labor was to turn them into chattel slaves. From 1540 to 1570, Indian slaves were the primary producers of sugar in Brazil and accounted for four-fifths or more of the labor force in the Northeast and almost all the labor component in the southern sugar mills developing in the Rio de Janeiro region. Owners obtained these slaves both through purchase from other Indian tribes and through direct raiding on their own. They also encouraged free Indians to work for wages and quickly tied them to the estates, so that thereafter little distinction could be made between enslaved and debt-peon Indian laborers.

Although Portuguese efforts in this area showed that an enslaved and indebted Indian labor force could be created out of the Tupi-Guarani Indians of the coast, despite an open frontier and constant warfare with Indian groups, the institution of Indian slavery, which now claimed tens of thousands of Indians, was doomed to failure. The most important factor undermining its importance was the endemic diseases the Europeans brought with them, which became epidemic when they affected the Indians. In the 1560s, at the height of Indian slavery, a major smallpox epidemic broke out among these previously unexposed populations of Indians. It was estimated that 30,000 Indians under Portuguese control, either on plantations or in Jesuit mission villages, died of the disease. This susceptibility to disease along with their shorter life expectancy resulted in lower prices for Indian slaves than for African slaves. When combined with increasing Crown hostility toward enslavement, especially after the unification of the Portuguese Crown with that of Spain after 1580, Indian slavery was made less secure and more difficult to maintain.

This decline in the utility of Indian slave labor combined with the increasing wealth of the Brazilian planters led to the beginnings of mass importations of African slave labor after 1570. Whereas the Northeast had few Africans before 1570, by the mid-1580s Pernambuco alone reported 2,000 African slaves, comprising one-third of the captaincy's sugar labor force. With each succeeding decade the percentage of Africans in the slave population increased. By 1600 probably just under half of all slaves were now Africans, with some 50,000 having arrived in the colony up to that time. In the next two decades the Indian slaves progressively disappeared from the sugar fields, and by the 1620s most sugar estates were all black.

Interestingly enough, in the transition period from 1570 to 1620, Africans first moved into the most skilled slave positions in the *engenhos*, working more in the sugar-making processes than in field cultivation. Since many West Africans came from advanced agricultural and iron-working cultures, they were far more skilled in many of these activities than were the native American Indians. Also, they came from the same disease environment as the Europeans, and most of the epidemic diseases for the Indians were endemic ones for the Africans. Thus, in terms of skills, health, and involvement in more routinized agricultural labor, the Africans were perceived as far superior to their Indian fellow slaves, and the three-to-one price differential paid by planters reflected this perception. As capital was built up from sugar sales, there was a progressive move toward Africans on the part of all Brazil sugar planters.

The fact that the sugar trade now boomed was of immense importance to this transition from Indian to African slaves. By 1600 Brazil had close to 200 *engenhos* producing a total of between 8,000 and 9,000 metric tons of sugar per annum, and Brazilian output rose to 14,000 tons per annum by the mid-1620s. All this occurred during a period when European sugar prices were constantly rising. With the introduction of new milling techniques (the three-roller vertical mills) in the second decade of the 17th century, the costs of mill construction were reduced considerably, and the amount of juice extracted from the cane greatly increased. While there appears to have been a price drop in the 1620s, prices firmed up in the next two decades as Brazilian sugar dominated European markets. Thus slave importations began to rise dramatically, and by the 1630s and 1640s Africans were arriving in much greater numbers to Brazil than to Spanish America.

The middle decades of the 17th century would prove to be the peak years of Brazil's dominance of the European sugar market. No other sugar-producing area rivaled Brazil at this point, and Brazilian sugar virtually wiped out Atlantic islands production. It was this very sugar production monopoly that excited the envy of other European powers and led to the rise of alternative production centers. Crucial to this new plantation movement would be the Dutch, who had been firm partners of the Brazilian planters from the beginnings of the American sugar trade in the 16th century.

3

Sugar and Slavery
in the Caribbean in the
17th and 18th Centuries

The establishment of an independent Dutch nation in Europe had a major impact on the distribution of slaves and plantations in America. The long Dutch struggle from the 1590s to the 1640s against Spanish domination would profoundly affect Portugal, Africa, and Brazil. From 1580 to 1640 Portugal was integrated into the Spanish Crown. While this incorporation had opened up Spanish America to Portuguese slave traders and resident merchants, it also brought Portugal into direct confrontation with the rebellious Dutch, who were Brazil's most important and powerful trading partner.

While northern European pirates were systematically attacking the Spaniards in America and the Portuguese trade with Asia and Africa, it was the Dutch who emerged in the late 16th century as the most aggressive, competent, and powerful of Iberia's rivals. A part of the Spanish empire since the ascension to the Spanish throne of the Hapsburg Charles V, the seven northern and largely Protestant provinces of the Low Countries had gone into active rebellion against Spain in the 1590s. For the Spaniards, the Dutch wars of independence proved to be a long and disastrous affair and one of their most costly imperial conflicts. By 1609 the Dutch had secured de facto independence and were able to use their advanced commercial system and their dominance of European overseas trade to carry the war deep into the Iberian empire. While the Spanish American possessions were too powerful to attack, the Asian, African, and eventually American empire of Portugal was less well defended.

Because the Dutch had become deeply involved in the Brazilian sugar industry, Portuguese America was initially protected from Dutch imperial pretensions. So long as the Spaniards did not attempt to interfere with this international trading, all was well. But the war with the Dutch proved to be a long and bloody affair, and the Spanish finally attacked Dutch shipping to Brazil in the first decade of the 17th century. This ended the neutrality of Brazil and of Portuguese Africa in the great imperial conflict, and in the last round of fighting, after the end of the so-called twelve-year truce in 1621, the Dutch assaulted both Portugal's African settlements and the Brazilian plantations.

As early as 1602 the Dutch had established their East Indies Company to seize control of Portugal's Asian spice trade. That competition was not peaceful and involved constant attacks by the Dutch on Portuguese shipping and Pacific commercial networks. With the foundation of the West Indies Company in 1621, the Dutch decided to compete directly in Africa and America with the Portuguese. In a systematic campaign to capture both Brazilian and African possessions, the Dutch West Indies Company sent the first of many war fleets into the South Atlantic in 1624. They temporarily captured the town of Salvador and with it Brazil's second-largest sugar-producing province of Bahia. But a year later, a combined Spanish-Portuguese armada succeeded in recapturing the province. In 1627 a second Dutch West Indies Company fleet attempted to take Recife, Brazil's premier sugar port and center of the province of Pernambuco, the colony's richest sugar plantation region. Though repulsed by the Portuguese, the Dutch fleet succeeded in capturing the annual Spanish silver armada on its return to Europe, thus enormously enriching the Company's coffers.

Another major fleet and army was outfitted by the Company in 1630, and after bitter fighting the Dutch captured Recife and most of the province of Pernambuco. With this base in sugar production, the Dutch were now direct competitors of their former Brazilian partners. The next step in this competition was to deny Brazil access to its sources of African slaves. Thus new expeditions were mounted by the Company to seize Portuguese African possessions, which also resulted in the Dutch themselves becoming a dominant power in the Atlantic slave trading system. First the fortress of El Mina on the Gold Coast was captured in 1638, and then came the fall of Luanda and the whole Angolan coastal region in 1641.

The seizure of Pernambuco and the Portuguese African settlements by the Dutch affected sugar production and the slave system in both Brazil and the rest of America. For Brazil, the Dutch occupation resulted in Bahia replacing Pernambuco as the leading slave and sugar province, it led to the reemergence of Indian slavery, and the ensuing interior slave trade opened up the interior regions of Brazil to exploitation and settlement. For the rest of America, Dutch

Brazil would become the source for the tools, techniques, credit, and slaves that would carry the sugar revolution into the West Indies, thereby terminating Brazil's monopoly position in European markets and leading to the creation of wealthy new American colonies for France and England.

For the first fifteen years, Pernambuco proved to be a source of great wealth for the West Indies Company, and the city of Olinda (Recife), under the governorship of the prince of Nassau, became an unusual multiracial and multireligious community of considerable culture. But the long-drawn-out war for the interior *engenhos* of Pernambuco, especially after the planter's revolt in 1645, led to a decline in production and the emergence of Bahia as the premier zone of Brazilian production. At the same time, the Dutch stranglehold over African slave sources reduced supplies and sent prices up. Brazilian planters once more resorted to Indian slave labor, which the Crown temporarily permitted. The source of slaves was now no longer the Tupi speakers of the coast but distant interior tribes of various linguistic families. These tribes were captured in slave-raiding expeditions by the special bands of hunters (or *bandeirantes*) coming from the interior settlement of São Paulo. These *paulista* (persons from São Paulo) *bandeirantes* roamed the whole interior of Brazil and into the upper reaches of the Rio de La Plata basin seeking slaves and shipping them to Bahia and Rio planters. As a result, much of the interior of Brazil was explored for the first time, and São Paulo itself expanded from its very crude beginnings into a thriving settlement. All this would lead by the end of the century to new uses of slave labor being developed in the Brazilian interior.

In terms of the rest of America, the Dutch control in Pernambuco led to their active intervention in the overseas West Indies settlements of the French and English. Though the fighting between the Dutch and Portuguese in the interior reduced Pernambuco's role as the region's leading sugar producer, it still sent a large quantity of sugar into the European market and revived Dutch sugar commercialization networks, which had been badly disrupted by the previous closure of the Dutch trade to Brazil. In need of furnishing their Amsterdam refineries with American sugar, especially after the precipitous post-1645 drop in Pernambuco production, the Dutch began to bring slaves and the latest milling equipment to the British and French settlers in the Caribbean and carried their sugar into the European market. In the 1640s, Dutch planters with Pernambuco experience arrived in Barbados as well as Martinique and Guadeloupe to introduce modern milling and production techniques. Dutch slavers provided the credit to the local planters to buy African slaves, while Dutch West Indian freighters hauled the finished sugar to the refineries in Amsterdam.

Even more dramatically came actual mass migration of Dutch planters and their slaves to these islands in 1654 when Pernambuco and Olinda finally fell to the Portuguese troops. In Guadeloupe some 600 Dutchmen and their 300 slaves arrived in this period, and an equal number landed in Martinique. To Barbados came another thousand or so. While many of these new colonists eventually returned to the Netherlands, enough remained in America so that their arrival gave a major boost to the Caribbean sugar industry in the 1650s. It was these transplanted Dutchmen who proved decisive in effectively implanting the sugar plantation system on the islands.

The opening up of the Lesser Antillean islands and the northeastern coast of South America to northern European colonization represented the first systematic challenge to Iberian control of the New World. French and English settlers began to take over lands never fully settled by the Portuguese or the Spanish, from the Amazonian estuary to the lands north of Florida. The most successful of these new settlements were those planted by the English, French, and Dutch in the abandoned islands of the Lesser Antilles from the 1620s to the 1640s. Using every style of settlement practice from private companies to fiefdoms, the English and French attempted to settle these uninhabited islands with white European laborers, who mostly came as indentured (or engagé) workers. Fighting off attacks of local Carib Indians, the Europeans immediately began to plant tobacco, which was the first successful commercial crop. Indigo for European textile dyes was also produced, and finally, in desperation, came the turn toward sugar, which was the costliest commercial crop to produce.

In this race for settlement the English initially made far more headway than the French. By 1640, for example, the English had 52,000 whites on their islands of Barbados, Nevis, and Saint Kitts (compared with 22,000 in the settlements of New England), whereas Martinique and Guadeloupe still had no more than 2,000 white settlers. But in the next two decades growth was steady, and by the end of the 1650s there were some 15,000 white Frenchmen in these islands. At midcentury, tobacco and indigo were the primary exports in all the islands, and both were produced on small units, primarily with white free or indentured labor. Though slaves were present from the beginning, their numbers were few, so at midcentury they were still outnumbered by the whites. The fortuitous arrival of the Dutch in the 1640s made sugar a far more viable proposition, especially when the opening up of Virginia tobacco production led to a crisis in European tobacco prices. Sugar had been planted on all the islands from the beginning, but few could get commercial milling accomplished until the Dutch came. They brought the needed credit to import the expensive machinery to get the mills into successful operation. They also supplied African slaves on credit from their factories in El Mina and Luanda.

The transformation that sugar created in the West Indies was truly impressive. The first of the big production islands was Barbados, which probably experienced the most dramatic change. But all islands went through a similar process. In 1645, on the eve of the big shift in sugar, more than 60 percent of the 18,300 white males were property owners, and there were only 5,680 slaves. Tobacco was the primary crop, and the average producing unit was less than ten acres. By the 1670s sugar was dominant, the number of farms was down to 2,600 units, or only one-quarter of the number that were in existence fifteen years earlier. Total white population had declined from some 37,000 to some 17,000, and for the first time in the island's history blacks outnumbered whites. By 1680 there were 37,000 slaves on the island (almost all of whom were African-born) and some 350 sugar estates, and production had climbed to 8,000 tons of sugar per annum. Of the indentured whites only 2,000 remained, and their numbers were falling. Already local society was dominated by the new elite of large planters, and the 175 Barbados planters who owned 60 slaves or more controlled over half the land and slaves on the island. The median size of these large plantations consisted of 100 slaves and 220 acres of land. At this time Barbados was both the most populous and the wealthiest of England's American colonies. The slave ships were bringing in over 1,300 slaves per annum, and by the end of the century this tiny island contained more than 50,000 slaves and was probably the most densely populated region in the Americas.

The experience of the French islands was similar to that of Barbados, though the changes occurred at a slower rate. In the major island of Martinique, as well as the smaller center at Guadeloupe, the free white labor force was more deeply entrenched, and small farm units were still important until the end of the century. Nevertheless, the Dutch impact was profound, and sugar relentlessly began to absorb the best lands and the flow of slaves continued unabated. By 1670 Martinique, Guadeloupe, and Saint Christopher islands had some 300 sugar estates and were producing close to 12,000 metric tons of sugar yearly. This was close to two-fifths of the 29,000 tons produced by all Brazilian regions in that year, and occurred only fifteen years after the Dutch had established the first successful French mill. Increasing sugar production brought with it increasing slave arrivals, and by 1683 the major French islands had some 20,000 slaves. These were mostly carried to the islands by French slave traders who had recently penetrated the Senegambia region of Africa.

Growth also continued for the French in terms of adding new lands, and in the late 1660s a definitive French settlement was finally achieved on the abandoned western half of the island of Santo Domingo, which the French called Saint Domingue. With extremely rich virgin soils, this region began a slow and steady growth. By the 1680s it had 2,000 African slaves and double that number of whites. A government census in 1687 found that there were now 27,000 slaves in the French West Indies, along with 19,000 whites, only 1,000 of whom were indentured.

The wealth from the sugar trade not only attracted new capital and new slaves to the West Indies but also gave northern Europeans the incentive to directly attack settled Spanish possessions. The basic indication of the change in policy was the decision of the Cromwell government to seize Santo Domingo from the Spanish in 1655. This use of government troops to attack the settled islands of the Greater Antilles opened the stage for a major advance by the English and French into the larger Caribbean islands. Though the English failed in their attack on well-defended Santo Domingo, they did take the lightly held island of Jamaica. The French followed shortly after with a successful settlement of western Santo Domingo, which had been abandoned by the Spaniards since 1605. Thus Spain was left in the Caribbean with only Cuba, Puerto Rico, and the eastern region of Santo Domingo, all still undeveloped and lightly settled islands.

By the end of the 17th century, then, a whole new sugar and slave complex had emerged in the French and British West Indies. Whereas Brazil had absorbed a migration of some 433,000 slaves from Africa up to 1700, the non-Iberian Caribbean now took second place in the slave trade, receiving over 408,000 Africans in the same period. This left Spanish America as the third major area of importation, with some 270,000 slaves arriving in these two centuries. The struggling English and French colonies of North America were still relatively small importers of slaves, probably accounting for fewer than 20,000 before 1700.

The West Indies plantation regime began on islands like Martinique and Barbados, which, because of soil quality and hilly terrains, had difficulty developing very large units. Though the tendency was to move toward ever larger estates, the industry in the late 17th century looked in terms of acreage and size of workforce much like that in the Brazilian sugar zones. Fifty or so slaves per plantation was the norm. But in the early days of the 18th century a whole new system began to emerge of truly giant estates, as sugar moved into the more open areas of Jamaica and Saint Domingue. By the 1730s and 1740s, when first Jamaica and then Saint Domingue replaced Barbados and Martinique as the largest sugar producers in their respective colonial empires, the average estate began reaching the over-200-acre range, the number of slaves per plantation was approaching 100, and the modern West Indian plantation system was in place. This size, which became typical for major Caribbean sugar plantations in the 18th and 19th centuries, whether French, British, or later Spanish, was unique by the standards of the other slave societies in the Americas.

The experience of both Jamaica and Saint Domingue was quite similar, though their ultimate trajectories and internal composition would differ in subtle but important respects. Both islands got off to a slow start and were overshadowed by their respective original production islands, Barbados and Martinique. In the case of Jamaica, the first twenty years had seen the very slow growth of both the white and black populations, which were about equal among the 17,000 inhabitants by the late 1670s. But in the 1680s the island's sugar industry took off. Slaves began arriving at the rate of close to 3,000 per annum in the 1680s, and although natural disasters, pirate raids, and involvement in international warfare affected the island, much like the equally exposed Saint Domingue in this respect, the economy continued its steady growth. By 1703, while the white population had stabilized at some 8,000 persons, the number of slaves had climbed to 45,000. The pace continued into the 18th century. By 1720, when the slave population of Jamaica had climbed to 74,000 persons, the island had become the most populous slave colony in the British West Indies. Population increased by 12,000 slaves in the next decade, and by 1740 the 100,000 mark had been passed. In 1768 the slave population reached 167,000, while the white population had grown to only 18,000. The ratio of blacks to whites finally reached ten to one by the last quarter of the 18th century.

With the growth in population had come an increase in the number of sugar plantations, a growth in their average size, and also an increase in output per unit. In this decade Jamaica was producing 36,000 tons of sugar per annum, four times the output of Barbados (though 15,000 tons less than annual production in Saint Domingue). This growth was due both to the increasing size of the average estate in terms of laborers and land devoted to cane-growing and to the increasing capacity of the local mills. By the 1740s, when Jamaica replaced Barbados as the premier English sugar producer, an average sugar estate had 99 slaves, and three-quarters of the island's slave population was employed in sugar. By the 1770s an average estate held 204 slaves.

Along with this growth and concentration of the slave population came a change in the acreage of the sugar estate and an increasing concentration of ownership. The average sugar estate was 327 acres in 1670, with half the estates being 99 acres or less; in 1724 the average estate contained 1,147 acres, and half the owners had 499 acres or less. In 1670 there were only two planters out of the 724 enumerated sugar estate owners who owned more than 5,000 acres, and they held only 6 percent of the total lands dedicated to sugar. In 1754, there were 61 out of 1,599 planters in this category, and they held 28 percent of the land. Over three-quarters of the land was now held by planters who owned 1,000 or more acres.

Thus by the middle of the 18th century Jamaica had many of the features of a prototypical Caribbean plantation society. Blacks dominated the population by a ratio of ten to one, some 75 percent of them were involved in sugar, and 95 percent of them were found in the rural areas. Urban slavery of the kind developed in 18th-century Spanish and Portuguese America, with their twenty-one cities of 50,000 to 100,000 persons, was of minor importance in a society where the leading insular towns held fewer than 15,000 persons. Also, diversified commercial foodstuffs production for local consumption, which was a major occupation of Peruvian blacks, hardly existed in societies that were so dependent on foreign imports or slave subsistence production for all their basic food supplies.

Certain features of plantation society, however, were special to either Jamaica or the British West Indies. Jamaica, for example, had few blacks or mulattoes who were free, and these free colored were a distinct minority even of the small free population. In terms of plantation size and structure, Jamaica was an extreme example of monoproduction for export, with sugar accounting for over three-quarters of the value of all exports. The Jamaican sugar estate, while organized like all others in its use of slaves, was larger than elsewhere, with a typical workforce of more than 200 slaves. Jamaica was prototypical, however, in that its leading planters dominated everything from owning the majority of productive lands and slaves to controlling the local and even imperial political scene.

Saint Domingue demonstrated many of the patterns of growth set by Jamaica. It was slow to develop, it was as much exposed as Jamaica to the problems of international wars and interventions, and it had to compete with an already well established dominant sugar center. It took Saint Domingue about eighty years from its definitive settlement to overtake Martinique, in terms of slave population and the quantity of sugar exported. Sustained growth began only after 1680. At that time its total population of 8,000 was exactly half of Martinique's, and only 2,000 of that number were slaves. It took until 1701 for the number of sugar mills in operation and in construction to approach the 122 mill total found at that time in the latter island. Martinique then had 58,000 slaves, and Saint Domingue had only half that number. Growth in Martinique began to slow in the first quarter of the new century, however, just as Saint Domingue experienced an extraordinary expansion of its economy and population. By 1740 the size of its slave labor force had passed that of Martinique by a considerable margin, and Saint Domingue's 117,000 slaves represented close to half of the 250,000 French slaves now found in the French West Indies. Growth of the white population continued, but, as in the case of the English islands, it slowed considerably as the black population started increasing at such impressive rates. Unlike the British West Indies, Saint Domingue also developed a relatively powerful, if small, class of free colored persons who made up almost half of the 26,000 free persons on the island.

By the middle of the 18th century it was clear that Saint Domingue was the dominant island in the Caribbean. It was the greatest sugar-producing colony in America, it now held the largest West Indian slave population, and it was also quickly becoming the world's largest producer of coffee, which had only been introduced into the island in 1723. By the late 1780s Saint Domingue planters were recognized as the most efficient and productive sugar producers in the world. The slave population stood at 460,000 people, which not only was the largest of any island but also represented close to half of the 1 million slaves then being held in all the Caribbean colonies. The exports of the island represented two-thirds of the total value of all French West Indian exports and alone were greater than the combined exports from the British and Spanish Antilles. In any one year well over 600 vessels visited the ports of the island to carry its sugar, coffee, cotton, indigo, and cacao to European consumers.

As is obvious from this trajectory of the history of production and population growth, Saint Domingue began to differ substantially from Jamaica by the middle decades of the 18th century. Its rate of increase in population and production was much more rapid than that of Jamaica, its free colored population was a far more significant element of the free population, and, even more unusual, its economy was far more diversified than that of any island in the British West Indies. While all the islands had experimented with tobacco, indigo, and coffee, only the French, who continued to experiment to the end of the century, succeeded in maintaining important alternative commercial crops even as sugar emerged as a major force.

The rise of the French and British sugar colonies in the 17th and 18th centuries had been made possible by the dynamic intervention of the Dutch in the first half of the 17th century. Until the late 1650s the British and French West Indies had been dependent upon Dutch assistance in all aspects of production, commercialization, and the provisioning of their African slave laborers. But the growing importance of France and England led to their emergence as major imperial powers in Asia and as competitors in the African slave trade as well. By the end of the 17th century, British and French slave traders, acting as free traders without resort to formal factories, as in the case of their Portuguese and Dutch rivals, seized a major share of the West African slave trade.

This growing imperial power of the British and French soon brought them into direct conflict with their former Dutch partners. In 1652 there occurred a war between the two Protestant powers of England and the Netherlands. This was followed by several more English and French wars with the Dutch that effectively destroyed the naval supremacy of the latter on all the world's oceans. In the next two decades France and England set up imperial tariff walls aimed primarily against Dutch trade with their West Indies possessions. Though political ambitions outpaced economic reality, by the last quarter of the 17th century French and English production, shipping, and marketing organization was sufficiently important to break the dependence on the Dutch not only in the European sugar markets but even in the provisioning of slaves from Africa. By the beginning of the 18th century, only the Portuguese traders came close to the English and French levels of participation in the African slave trade.

Thus the rise of the French and British West Indies slave plantation economy ended the importance of the Netherlands as a major American factor in the production and marketing of plantation staples. This growth was also at the expense of Brazilian sugar production and the role of Brazilian sugar in the markets of Europe. Not only were the French and British islands both equaling Brazilian sugar output by the first quarter of the 18th century, but the trade restrictions raised by these two powers to end the Dutch influence over their new colonies had a direct impact on Brazilian sugar markets. By the first half of the 18th century England and France were satisfying their own needs as well as the demands for sugar of practically all of northern and eastern Europe. Whereas 80 percent of the sugar sold in the London market in the 1630s came from Brazil, that figure had dropped to 10 percent by the 1690s. France, which had been a heavy consumer of Brazilian sugars up until 1690, put up tariffs in that decade which completely eliminated Brazilian sugar from the French market. By the 18th century only the top grades of Brazilian clayed sugar could still be found in any of the northern markets, and most Brazilian output was confined to southern Europe and the Mediterranean. So efficient were the French West Indies producers that they soon dominated even these southern markets, as well as eliminating the more expensive British West Indies producers from the European continent.

This severe restriction of Brazil's international markets and its relative stagnation in production, however, did not eliminate Brazil as an important world sugar producer. Its monopoly position was overturned, but the continued growth of European consumption, the excellent quality of its best grades of clayed white sugar, and the continued growth of demand in the home and imperial markets guaranteed that the Brazilian plantations would be a major force in the world market. Now accounting for only about 10 percent of New World sugar output, Brazil's 27,000 tons per annum output by the middle of the 18th century placed it in third place behind Saint Domingue (at 61,000 tons) and Jamaica (at 36,000 tons). It also became an important alternative source for northern European markets in the frequent imperial wars that France and England fought in the 18th century, which temporarily would halt the West Indian trade to Europe. Thus in the 1760s Brazilian sugar captured about 8 percent of Europe's market for sugar, and in the warfare of the 1790s took a 15 percent share of the market. This continued vitality of the Bahian and Rio de Janeiro sugar plantations guaranteed that even with the massive growth of mineral exports in the 18th century, when Brazil became the world's greatest single source for gold, sugar still represented the single most valuable Brazilian export and alone accounted for half the value of its total exports.

Thus by the middle of the 18th century the slave plantation system, based primarily on sugar production, had been firmly implanted in America. It now accounted for something like 1.4 million slaves, both African- and American-born. This was at a minimum some 40 percent of the 3.5 million African and Afro-American slaves to be found in America, and it represented the single largest occupation in which the slaves were employed.

The reason for the dominance of the slave plantation model in America by the late 18th century was due to its being the most efficient means of production of commercial crops developed by Europeans prior to the Industrial Revolution. Though late 18th-century contemporaries sometimes argued that free labor was more efficient and productive than slave labor, it was clear that white labor would not work in regimented gangs on plantations. Whatever reluctance slaves may have felt about working, however destructive they may have been toward tools, equipment, and crops, and however inherently opposed they were to the demands of the masters, the ability to physically force them to work in regimented groups under close supervision more than compensated masters for these disadvantages.

The organization of plantation labor was probably one of the most efficient labor systems then operating in the Western world. The most obvious way this is revealed is the absence of sexual differences in all major labor tasks associated with the planting, cultivation, and harvesting of crops, and the high percentage of persons who were employed at all ages in life. Women did almost all the same physical labor as men. The only time this rule did not apply was in the distribution of skilled occupations, which was the exclusive preserve of males. From small children to aged persons, everyone was assigned a task commensurate with physical abilities. Older men and women cared for or trained infants and children or had simple cattle-tending or guarding duties. All children worked, starting at simple weeding tasks when they reached the age of eight and gradually moving up the hierarchy of field gangs during their youth. The result of this use of slaves was that plantation populations had among the highest levels of economically active individuals relative to total population ever recorded. Something on the order of 80 percent of the slave population were gainfully employed; in agricultural societies of the developing world today the figure is around 55 percent.

Whatever the disincentives for working that existed among slaves, heavy supervision of laborers organized in gangs based on physical abilities and performing common tasks in a common setting helped compensate for lack of enthusiasm. The constant availability of "negative incentives" (the use of whips and other corporal punishments) may have been more important than any positive rewards of leisure, extra food and clothing, or special provisioning ground rights, but both types of incentives were constantly available and used. Thus between force, rewards, high labor participation rates, close supervision, and systematizing and routinizing of the labor tasks, the plantation slaves produced high levels of output.

The distribution of tasks on the plantation shows both consistencies across crop types and some surprising differences from our classic images of the plantation. While there was some variation depending on type of crop, soils, and location, the structure developed with sugar did not differ significantly from that found in coffee, cotton, or cacao production. Sugar, because of the existence of manufacturing facilities on the plantation, had a higher share of skilled and semiskilled labor that was not related to field labor. But in all types of plantations, the ratios that were to be found among the Antillian and Brazilian sugar estates were common.

Only between 50 and 60 percent of the total slaves were engaged in field labor related to production of agricultural crops. On a typical 18th-century sugar plantation in Jamaica only 60 percent of the plantation's slaves worked in the field. Ten percent of the workers were involved in milling and refining the sugar, and fewer than 2 percent were servants in the master's household. The rest of the slaves either were involved in transport of crops to market or were too young or old to work. Even more surprising is the fact that in all work gangs women dominated. Customarily workers were divided into several groups or "gangs" ranked according to their age and physical characteristics. On an 18th-century Jamaican sugar estate field hands were grouped into four gangs based on their relative youth and vigor; women represented approximately 60 percent of every one of these gangs, from the first or "great" gang to the fourth or "weeding" gang.

In the French islands, a three-gang organization of field workers was more typical on the sugar plantations. There was the same first or great gang (grand atelier), made up of prime-age and able-bodied males and females. Then came the second gang (second atelier), which was composed of the less able-bodied (newly arrived Africans, recent mothers, convalescents, etc.). These two were the basic field work gangs and were composed primarily of females, who made up three-quarters of their labor force. These gangs prepared the soils, planted, and cut the cane.

The only work to which males of the grand atelier were assigned exclusively was heavy land clearance tasks such as tree and stone removal. A last gang, the "petit atelier," was made up of children eight to twelve or thirteen years of age who performed simple agricultural work and was much like the weeding gang on the English estate. While three-quarters of the women on the plantation were to be found in the field gangs, less than half of the men were located here. Of the men, one-tenth were assigned to the work of the refineries, and the rest were in skilled trades.

The Saint Domingue coffee estates of the 18th century had a slightly different breakdown than that of the sugar plantations, largely because of the lack of any milling and refining activity. Thus the 10 percent fewer skilled tasks to be assigned on these estates meant that a higher percentage of men would be found in the field labor force. The actual ratio of field hands to total slaves differed little from the sugar estates. On a typical coffee plantation, less than 60 percent of the total slave labor force were to be found in the three field ateliers. The sex balance of the field gangs, however, shifted in favor of men.

The occupational division on Brazilian sugar estates was similar to that on the Saint Domingue plantations. Cane workers formed slightly more than 60 percent of the total slave population, were divided into field gangs, and had roughly the same distribution of skilled (about 35 percent) and domestic servants (just under 4 percent). The primary difference was in the pattern of ownership. In Brazil until late in the 18th century, essentially four plantations were grouped around one sugar mill. Three of these were really small cane farms owned by the so-called *lavradores de cana*, who were small-scale sugar planters tied into the mill of a larger *senhor de engenho*. These *lavrador* plantations had around ten slaves per unit, almost all of whom did field labor, with the main mill using around seventy slaves in its fields. There were thus four separate slave owners per milling unit, but they all acted together, so the end result was a plantation of around 100 slaves. Though half the size of the Jamaican estate, this was the average for the French West Indies. Why the total number of slaves on a Jamaican plantation should be double the norm elsewhere is difficult to explain, but it appears to be related to conditions of soil quality, the terrain, and finally the relative efficiency of the local planters. By all accounts, French planters were the most efficient and seem to have gotten the highest sugar yields per acre. The fact that the milling season in Bahia was three months longer than the five- to six-month cutting season in the Caribbean guaranteed high annual outputs even with a less effectively used labor force.

The absence of sexual discrimination in labor assignment of slaves was apparent not only in the organization of the plantation labor tasks but also in the prices and rents planters were willing to pay for slaves. Slave prices of unskilled and healthy male and female slaves remained equal until early adulthood, when male field hand prices rose about 10 to 20 percent above female prices. This differential then declined as slaves passed the prime years. These changing price differences appear to reflect physical abilities that differed markedly only in the prime-age categories. Rental prices for unskilled field hand slaves also followed these patterns quite closely, though they tended to be more reflective of pure physical output potential, since no additional rent was paid for the potential childbearing ability of the women, a factor that did influence slave prices.

While the percentage of the sugar plantation population listed as skilled artisans was relatively high, there is considerable debate about the level of skills taught to these craftsmen. Unlike urban slaves in Spanish and Portuguese America, rural plantation slaves were not formally apprenticed to master craftsmen in their youth and did not go through the standard journeyman and master stages. Usually they were older adult male slaves who were taken out of the field gangs and given rudimentary and partial training well into their adulthood. Plantation slaves were masons, carpenters, and coopers, but there is a serious question about how their skills compared with those of Lima's slave artisans, for example, let alone those of the white or free colored populations. Only the slaves trained as sugar masters and in other skilled jobs related to the manufacture of sugar itself can be considered to have mastered a craft equal to any white level of competency, since these were exclusively plantation-related occupations.

Although the traditional literature placed much emphasis on the household slaves, these proved to be a surprisingly small part of the total labor force in all plantation zones. No more than 2 to 4 percent of the slaves on any 17th- or 18th-century plantation were recorded as domestics. Slave drivers, craftsmen, muleteers, fishermen, cowboys, and others outside the direct supervision of white overseers or with a degree of power over others were in fact more important numerically and occupied anywhere up to a third or more of the slave-defined jobs on the plantations.

By the 1780s, then, the plantation system was in place in Brazil and the Caribbean, and it dominated slavery in America. Close to a million and a half slaves then resident in America lived on sugar plantations. The plantation zones of dense black and mulatto populations ruled over by a few whites became the norm for the Caribbean islands as well as the Portuguese and British mainland colonies. Although the Jamaican ratio of nine Africans or Afro-Americans for every white was the extreme, it was most common for blacks and mulattoes to be in the majority wherever the plantations were to be found. Also common to the French and British colonies was the lack of a significant class of freedmen among blacks. In the 18th century, free coloreds were less than 10 percent of the 380,000 blacks in the British West Indies, a ratio found as well among the 575,000 blacks in the British continental colonies of North America. In the French islands free coloreds numbered but 36,000 compared with the 660,000 slaves. In contrast, the free colored population in the late 18th century was already an important part of the plantation world and its environs in the Spanish and Portuguese colonies. By 1780 in Brazil, for example, there were 406,000 freed persons of African descent and 1.5 million slaves.

Despite differences in the ratios between whites, free colored, and slaves among the colonial powers, the sugar plantation system itself—its means of production, its organization of tasks, and its distribution of workers by types of occupations—remained fairly constant through time and across national boundaries. Sugar plantations were most commonly run with 100 or so slaves, though they varied in size from the 50-slave model in the Spanish mainland to the over 200-slave size in Jamaica. Despite this range, they all shared such basic labor features as the lack of a sexual division of labor in field work, the use of supervised "gangs" for routinized tasks, and the distribution of slaves between skilled and unskilled occupations. Although sugar was sometimes produced by nonslave labor, almost all milled sugar was the product of slave toil, and no American society seemed capable of exporting sugar unless it used African slave workers. Though labor arrangements would differ for other crops, as the early coffee plantations in Saint Domingue demonstrated, the basic features established by the Brazilian and Caribbean sugar estates proved the standard for the next century of slave plantation labor.

4

Slavery in Portuguese and Spanish America in the 18th Century

The growth of the West Indies plantation system in the 17th century and the early 18th century did not put an end either to the Brazilian sugar industry or to the thriving slave system upon which the Brazilian economy rested. The Dutch occupation and the subsequent growth of the West Indies sugar industry did, however, seriously affect the colonial economy. Not only was a large part of the Pernambuco sugar industry destroyed, taking a long time to recover, but also Brazilian export markets were reduced and production stagnated for most of the late 17th and early 18th century. Bahia did continue to grow, but the golden age of profitability had passed. Competition from the West Indies sent sugar prices into a decline relative to the first half of the century, and West Indian demand for slaves meant rising African slave prices, thus squeezing planter profits. By the last two decades of the century the Brazilian economy was in a depressed state, and an anxious Crown was seeking new markets and products to revive the colonial economy.

Among the many attempts to develop new resources, the Crown began to explore the interior with hopes of finding mineral wealth. The success of the *paulista bandeiras* in supplying Indian slaves at midcentury had led to government subsidization of systematic surveys of the interior. After numerous discoveries of minor deposits of gold and precious stones throughout the second half of the 17th century, a major expedition in 1689–90 discovered substantial alluvial deposits of gold in the region of what is today Minas Gerais, some 200 miles inland from the port of Rio de Janeiro. Thus at the end of the century an entirely new type of slave economy would emerge on Brazilian soil, that of slave mining. Gold and, then, diamonds would be the basis of this

18th-century phenomenon, and Brazil would again be the initiator of a mode of production that would soon be replicated in Spanish America.

The rush to these mines by the coastal whites with their slaves was immediate. Before the 1690s the interior region of Minas Gerais in the heartland of the gold region had been totally unpopulated. As early as 1710 there were 20,000 whites and an equal number of blacks there; by 1717 the slaves had increased to 33,000, outpacing the whites, and by the early 1720s their numbers had passed 50,000. The 100,000 population figure was passed in the first slave census taken in 1735. Both the rapidity of the growth of the slave population and its makeup marked Minas Gerais as an unusual zone of slave labor in Brazil.

First of all, the demand for slaves was so high that it was soon necessary to rely exclusively on slaves imported directly from Africa. Even as late as the 1750s approximately 60 percent of the slaves arriving into the port of Salvador, the central city of Bahia, were being reexported to the gold mines of the interior. The gold fever also did not encourage masters to think about long-term population concerns or family structural arrangements for their slaves. At first the sexual balance in the gold fields and towns of Minas Gerais was heavily male, so much so that initially the only way to maintain the slave population at the over 100,000 population level was through heavy and constant migration of slaves from the coastal ports.

Finally the gold fever was such that the whole control system, which had been developed to force compliance and integrate slaves into the labor system, was allowed to lapse in many places. Slaves were of course worked in gangs and were carefully supervised by white overseers. And in certain clearly delineated gold fields, such as those in the environs of the cities of Vila Rica do Ouro Preto and Vila do Carmo, heavy concentration of slaves—something like 4,000 in the former city and 5,000 in the latter—guaranteed a certain stability on a par with the discipline found in a controlled plantation environment. Here and at other well-defined alluvial gold fields, heavy investment was carried out in so-called lavras, which were elaborate sluice constructions, or dredging operations, which required major hydraulic works that in their more elaborate development led to channeling of rivers, excavation of riverbanks, or alternatively the construction of hillside terraces and the setting up of sluices and other water-diverting projects. But these tightly controlled and well-developed mining camps probably absorbed less than half of the mining slaves in the province. Mining was also carried out by very small groups of unsupervised slaves in hundreds of scattered river sites throughout the province of Minas Gerais, and then farther west into the provinces of Goiás and Mato Grosso. In these cases, slave owners late on the scene, and initially with little capital to develop elaborate works, relied exclusively on itinerant slave miners and prospectors known as *fasqueiros*. These *fasqueiros* usually spent considerable time away from their masters prospecting for gold, eventually returning a fixed amount of gold dust to their owners and otherwise paying for all their own expenses. Though local governments attacked this itinerant-style mining, it was simply too widespread to destroy.

The result of all this seeming chaos was the extraordinarily rapid rise, through local self-purchase, of a free colored population in the mining camps. Probably in no other slave region of America did the population of free colored grow as rapidly or become as important an element so early in the settlement process as in Minas Gerais. By 1786, when there were some 174,000 slaves in the province, the number of free coloreds had already passed the 123,000 level. Their growth now continued even more dramatically than that of the slave population. By the first decade of the 19th century, freedmen finally outnumbered slaves and had become the largest single group in this fast-growing provincial population. That growth would continue into the 19th century despite the continued expansion of the slave population. Though the Portuguese government protested the growth of this class and charged that it was based on theft of gold and other minerals, there was little that it could do to stop its expansion. Free blacks and mulattoes even became goldsmiths, though this extremely important and sensitive craft was specifically prohibited to their class, since goldsmiths were crucial to the illegal smelting of local gold. Unable to control the illegal extraction of gold, the desperate Crown in 1735 gave up attempting to tax smelted gold (the usual Iberian manner of determining output and extracting taxes) and resorted to charging a slave head tax for all masters in the mining zones.

The Brazilian gold-mining economy also gave rise to an important regional urban culture. By the second half of the century Minas Gerais had a dozen cities in the 10,000 to 20,000 range, which supported a highly developed urban lifestyle based heavily on both skilled and unskilled slave labor. Thus the interior mining slavery of central Brazil gave rise to a sophisticated urban civilization. In towns like Vila Rica do Ouro Preto, which reached 20,000 population by the 1740s, and in other urban centers in the region, there developed a surprisingly rich Baroque culture, which was expressed in a rather sumptuous display of the plastic arts and of music, much of which derived from the hands of black craftsmen, artists, and musicians.

While gold was the initial metal exported first from Minas Gerais and then from Goiás in the 1720s and Mato Grosso in the 1730s, it was not the only mineral produced. In 1729, diamonds were discovered in the northern end of Minas Gerais. Like gold, diamonds were found in alluvial deposits, on the beds or banks of rivers, or in wadis left by seasonally active rivers. Slave labor was used to obtain these precious stones in the same manner as for gold, through panning, hydraulic works, and active washing of soils. The impact on the European market of the diamond finds in Minas Gerais and Goiás was immediate, and international prices dropped by two-thirds as a result of the discoveries. The Crown tried to create a royal monopoly on the extraction of these stones, but it was only partially successful. In fact, diamonds would prove harder to control than gold, since the latter required smelting. The 18th-century diamond boom, which started and peaked later than that for gold, tended to use fewer slaves in far more scattered holdings than in the gold-washing operations. Though deposits were eventually found in parts of Bahia and Mato Grosso, as well as in the two original provinces, diamond mining probably absorbed no more than one-third of the 225,000 or so slaves involved in Brazilian mining in the second half of the 18th century.

The rise of mining centers in the central interior zone of Minas Gerais would also have a profound impact on the subsequent growth of slavery and black populations in other parts of Brazil. The gold-mining boom of Minas Gerais powerfully shifted the center of gravity of the Brazilian economy and population from the north to the center and south. The mines had been discovered by paulista bandeiras, which were eventually backed by Rio de Janeiro investors. Though Bahians had a considerable say in the investments made within the mining zone, the logistics of interior transport guaranteed that the balance of trade to and from the interior provinces would shift to the southern cities. Thus the mines of Minas Gerais, Goiás, and Mato Grosso became the crucial hinterland of the more southern port of Rio de Janeiro. Rio de Janeiro soon outpaced Bahia in international shipping and trade and quickly approached the 50,000 population size of the imperial capital. The Crown recognized this new geographic reality by shifting the capital of the colony from Salvador Bahia to Rio de Janeiro in 1763. This only furthered the city's dynamic expansion, and by the end of the century Rio de Janeiro was not only Brazil's leading slave trading port and the main port for Minas trade but it was also Brazil's leading urban center with more than 100,000 persons. That made Rio de Janeiro, along with Mexico City, one of the two largest cities in America.

Other regions also benefited tremendously from the growth of this new interior market. Although the gold rush fever initially disrupted coastal production by attracting large numbers of speculators and coastal planters with their slaves, it soon created dynamic new markets that only the coastal zones were equipped to supply. Until well into the 18th century the gold fever absorbed everyone to such an extent that few interior workers, free or slave, engaged in agriculture or stock breeding. Thus all the food and animal needs for the mines were supplied by the coastal provinces. Initially the central and southern highlands around São Paulo began producing animals and foodstuffs for the *mineiro* (or Minas Gerais) market, but these quickly proved incapable of satisfying demand. To supply beef, hides, and the crucial mules for the great inland shipping caravans, a whole grazing industry was fostered in the open plains of Rio Grande do Sul and as far south as the eastern bank of the Plata River (in modern Uruguay). A major series of interior trails were now opened between these southern zones and São Paulo in the 1730s. But the opening of more direct routes from Rio de Janeiro and the fact that only 18,000 persons occupied the *paulista* plains meant that São Paulo could not respond fast enough to the demands of the mining markets, and so it was replaced by the provincial producers in Rio de Janeiro. This involved Rio de Janeiro producers in everything from supplying foodstuffs and locally produced sugar to Rio becoming the chief port for all of the interior mining provinces' imports (slaves included) and exports.

Bahia also began to benefit from this trade. Its location near the São Francisco River, the only major inland river route to the mines, guaranteed steady contact with the mines. At first the Crown tried to prevent trade with the mines and feared for the loss of crucial slave labor from the plantations. But the rise of sugar prices after 1711 eased the pressure on the Bahian sugar industry, so the Crown lifted its ban on the sale of Bahian slaves to the interior. Trade with the mines also encouraged the expansion of the interior northeastern manioc and foodstuffs frontier and promoted the growth of an important livestock industry, which now supplied both the coastal plantations and the interior mines.

All these backward linkages of the mining sector resulted in a more even distribution of population within Brazil and the spread of slavery to all sectors of the colonial economy. Slaves now reached the frontier working in foodstuffs farms, and they also joined the burgeoning cattle industry both in the central northern coastal region and in the new cattle zones of the southern pasture-lands.

The case of the southern province of Rio Grande do Sul was typical of these developments. The early part of the century brought an active opening up of the southern grasslands of the region, both for political reasons to prevent Spanish expansion northward and as a response to the demands from Minas Gerais. By the end of the century there were some 21,000 slaves and 5,000 free coloreds in a population of 71,000. The slaves were linked into the export sector of the economy. While the cowboys on the cattle ranches were mostly Indians or free peon gauchos, the salting and beef-drying establishments were run with slave labor. Jerked or dried beef (called *charque*) was produced in special factories (*charqueadas*), which usually used from 60 to 90 slaves. By the early 19th century these *charqueadas* of the Rio Grande do Sul region were in full production and were employing some 5,000 slaves. The market for the dried beef was domestic, since Brazilian products did poorly in competition with Spanish output from the Rio de la Plata region. The consumers of Brazilian jerked beef were almost always slaves, the dried beef of Rio Grande do Sul being a major source of protein in the diets of plantation and mining slaves in central and northern Brazil.

While the gauchos of the cattle ranches of the Rio Grande do Sul region were mostly free and Indian laborers, those farther to the north in the so-called Campos Gerais area around the city of Curitiba were primarily slaves. Smaller in size and with no access to the Indian laborers of the south, the typical Curitiba cattle *fazenda* (ranch) used one slave cowboy per 800 or so head of cattle. Thus on an average Curitiba 5,000-head of cattle ranch, there would be six gauchos and one overseer, all slaves. There would be another twenty-five or more slaves employed on such an estate, involved in hide and meat preparations, various crafts needed on the ranch, and transporting products to and from the *fazenda*. On these and on the ranches farther south there were also a large number of free colored dependents who worked on the estates, usually in less export-oriented capacities. Finally, in all the southern towns, some of which were reaching the 10,000 level by late in the century, slaves formed the largest single element in the workforce and were the majority of skilled craftsmen. Slaves were also crucial in supplying the labor for the large internal transport network that brought southern goods into the *mineiro* centers.

The southern grasslands thus provided a new area for slave labor, as well as an example of the impact of the mining economy on the rest of the society. Once settlement got under way to the south, local industries could be developed, which created a new labor market for slaves. After strong settlements were established along the coast of Rio Grande do Sul and Santa Catarina to support the grazing industry, Brazilians began to engage in commercial fishing activities with important slave participation. While offshore coastal whaling had been practiced in Brazil from the beginnings of colonization, the industry only became an important factor when the southern provinces were successfully opened to colonization in the 18th century. From Cabo Frio in the province of Rio de Janeiro south to Laguna in Santa Catarina, whaling became a major industry from the second half of the 18th century until the first decades of the next century. The center of the industry was the island of Santa Catarina in the province of the same name, which had a commercial whale oil–producing factory (or *armação*) as early as 1746. By the 1770s the region of Santa Catarina alone was taking more than 1,000 whales per annum. During the June to September whaling season, free colored, poor white, and slave fisherman in open boats did the harpooning and bringing of the whales inshore. Once beached, the whales were then cut down and boiled for their oil, which was sold both nationally and internationally for use in illumination. These very costly and elaborate cutting and boiling factories were run mostly with slave labor. A typical *armação* was a major operation, on average employing between 50 and 100 slave workers. One of the biggest in the late 18th century was the Armação de Nossa Senhora da Piedade on the island of Santa Catarina, which owned 125 slaves, of whom 107 were working adults. Along with unskilled laborers, the slave workforce included carpenters, blacksmiths, and coopers, and those with the specialized skills relating to the cutting of the whale and the production of the spermaceti. Though the work was highly seasonal, the factories could employ as many as 2,000 to 3,000 slaves in a good season.

The opening up of the Brazilian interior stretched Brazilian settlement both southward and westward and also encouraged the creation of major transportation networks to tie these vast markets together. Slaves were vital in the large canoe fleets and mule trains made up by the coastal and southern merchants to supply the enormous import needs of the interior mining provinces. Given the poor records of these activities, it is difficult to estimate the number of slaves involved. Another major area of transport fostered by the interior and southern markets was coastwise shipping. In this case, there is a basis of estimating the relative role of the African- and American-born slaves. Contemporary reports list high rates of participation of slaves as sailors in all types of coastal shipping. Recent estimates of interregional coastwise shipping at the end of the 18th century place the number of vessels employed at approximately 2,000 ships. Assuming a minimum of five slaves per crew on these ships (or one-third of the average coastal trader's complement of sailors), then something like 10,000 slaves were sailors involved in cabotage or coastal trade in the late 18th century.

Brazil was also rather unusual in its use of slave sailors in international shipping, especially in its Atlantic slave trade routes. Because of its direct trading relations with Africa, in which no triangular linkages existed with Portugal, Brazil early developed a very powerful merchant marine. Hundreds of Brazilian-owned ships plied the South Atlantic, taking Brazilian rum, gunpowder, tobacco, and European and American manufactured goods to Angolan and Mozambican ports and exchanging them for slaves, which were then brought to Brazil. Brazilian-owned vessels also controlled most of the carrying trade to Europe, in sharp contrast to the Spanish American areas.

Given the crucial role slaves played in all aspects of the Brazilian economy, it was no accident that even on slavers there were typically slaves listed as members of the crew. In 147 of the 350 slave ships that arrived in the port of Rio de Janeiro between 1795 and 1811, Brazilian-owned slaves were listed as crew members. These slaves numbered 2,058 out of the 12,250 sailors engaged in the trade. On average there were 14 slave sailors per ship, or just under half the total crew on a typical slaver. Since the registers always justified the need to use slaves because of the lack of free sailors, this would suggest that slaves were even more important in the other international routes. Even in the 19th century slave sailors remained a fundamental part of the shipping industry. In the southern Brazilian port town of Porto Alegre in 1859, over half of the 354 sailors involved in coastal trade were slaves; in 1869, of the 3,638 sailors listed as working from the port involved in coastal trading, fishing, and/or local rowboat transport, 1,168—or almost a third—were slaves.

The growth of mining and the revival of the northeastern sugar industry led to a major expansion of the colonial economy of Brazil in the second half of the 18th century. The emergence of a dynamic administration in Portugal under the Marques de Pombal from 1750 to 1777 also brought about the further development of the Brazilian economy and a new slave-based industry in the north of the country. A typical Enlightenment regime, the Pombal administration used classic mercantilist procedures to encourage the growth of previously neglected regions of Brazil. With the interior and the south booming, it turned its attention to the major northeastern region of Pará and Maranhão, which until the second half of the 18th century were backward and sparsely settled areas. In 1755 and 1759, respectively, Pombal created two major monopoly trading companies, the Grão-Pará e Maranhão Company and the Companhia Geral de Pernambuco e Paraíba. Both were given economic support by being allowed monopoly rights to slave importation into these two regions—the only break in the usual free-trade policy that Portugal allowed. In turn these companies were required to invest in the commercial development of the northeastern regions.

After much experimentation, a major new export crop was developed under Pombaline company initiatives in both Maranhão and Pernambuco. This was cotton, which was produced on plantations using slave labor. At approximately the same time as cotton was developing in the British colonies with the aid of slave labor, it was also becoming a major staple export of Brazil. Beginning in the 1760s, Maranhão cotton plantations began to export to Europe. Production rose steadily in the next decades and quickly spread to the neighboring province of Pernambuco. The typical cotton plantation in these two states contained 50 slaves per unit, not too different from what would be the average size of a cotton plantation in the southern states of the United States in the 19th century. With the steady increase in European prices came a continuous increase in production. So aggressive was the Brazilian response that by the early 1790s it accounted for 30 percent of British raw cotton imports. By the first decade of the 19th century, more than 30,000 slaves were involved in cotton production in the northeastern states. The cotton plantation system continued to expand for two decades more until ginned United States cotton production wiped out its comparative advantage and brought a long-term decline to the industry.

The efforts of the Pombaline companies were also important in finally reviving the sugar plantation economy in Pernambuco in the 1770s and 1780s. Though Pernambuco never regained its dominant position in the industry, it became the second-largest northeastern producer after Bahia. But the main change in sugar in the late 18th century was not so much the revival of the older northeastern region as the growth of new sugar products and new sugar production regions. Rio de Janeiro and São Paulo became the centers of production of both *muscovado*, or brown sugar, and *aguardente*, or sugar-based alcohols. While sugar had been cultivated in the Campos region of Rio de Janeiro for well over a century, there began a major expansion of the sugar estates in the second half of the 18th century. By the end of the period Rio de Janeiro would rank third in Brazilian production and account for two-thirds of *muscovado* sugar output. It was also Brazil's major producer of *cachaça* (or brandy made from sugar), which was exported to Africa as well as supplying the internal market. By the end of the century Rio de Janeiro was employing some 25,000 slaves in all aspects of its sugar industry. Neighboring São Paulo, although only a moderate sugar producer and slave zone at the end of the century, finally began exporting from both its coastal enclaves and highlands to the west of the city of São Paulo into the international market in this late 18th-century period, and this evolution marked the beginning of what would prove to be the most important slave and plantation region of Brazil in the 19th century.

Despite the growth of new sugar production areas and the fact that sugar still accounted for one-third of the value of all Brazilian exports, the industry was relatively depressed through most of the 18th century. Whereas colonial production was still averaging something like 36,000 tons per annum in the 1730s, by the 1770s it was down to 20,000 tons and probably accounted for less than 10 percent of total American sugar output. At this time the number of slaves involved in all forms of sugar production, which involved both the exporting of finished white sugar and the semiprocessed brown sugar, as well as the production of *cachaça* for both national consumption and export to Africa, was probably well under 100,000 persons. By the early 1780s, European tensions and the disruptions of trade were beginning to affect prices and to encourage national production, and in the 1790s the profound impact of the French Revolution and the subsequent Haitian revolution would create a new era of expansion for Brazilian sugar.

The final major development in the colonial economy of Brazil related to slave labor was the surprising diversification that was taking place in the province of Minas Gerais by the end of the 18th century. As first gold output and then diamond finds declined after the middle decades of the century, the *mineiro* economy was faced with a serious economic crisis. By the first decade of the 19th century there were only 10,600 slaves in *lavras* and another 2,000 who operated as itinerant prospectors. Whereas as many as 5,000 slaves may have been employed in the Diamond District of the province in the mid–18th century, by the beginning of the new century there were only some 2,000 slaves still extracting precious stones. Yet the slave population of the province at this time stood at over 150,000 persons. The great mystery remains as to how these remaining 135,000 or so nonmining slaves were employed. Urban decay had set in with the decline in mineral extraction and diminished even further the opportunities for slave use. The free colored population, moreover, was now employed everywhere and was greater in number than the slaves. Yet the slave population continued to grow at a steady pace through the 19th century, and by the time of abolition at the end of the century their number had more than doubled, which meant that at both the beginning and the end of the 19th century Minas Gerais had the largest slave population of any province in Brazil.

The major developments that accounted for Minas retaining and expanding its slave labor force seem to have been a combination of diversification into agricultural production, which supplied the internal market, and then, several decades later, an expansion into coffee for international export. In the southern and eastern regions of the province a diversified agriculture developed in the late 18th and early 19th century based on slave production. Sugar, coffee, staples, and cattle were produced in Minas on slave-run farms. Both the total number of slave owners in the free population was higher, and the number of slaves held per owner was lower in Minas than in the coastal provinces, and under the impact of agricultural diversification, this pattern was accentuated even further. There also have been recent studies that have suggested that despite high manumission rates, the natural growth of the Minas slave population was positive and helped to sustain the growth of the local slave population without recourse to importing Africans or Afro-Brazilian slaves in the international or internal slave trades. Moreover, there seem to have been few sales of Minas slaves outside the province, suggesting a steady use of and demand for slaves within the province. If the slave population was growing naturally in the 19th century, as demographers have suggested, then it would also mean that Minas was one of the few regions in Brazil where slaves did not experience a negative natural growth. Most regions required a constant infusion of Africans to increase or even maintain their slave populations.

Although much of *mineiro* economic history is still poorly understood, the vitality of slavery within its borders in the late 18th century and early 19th century made for a nontraditional and highly unusual slave economy by American standards. Some have even argued that slavery was essentially dedicated to subsistence agriculture from the late 18th-century decline of mining to the mid-19th-century rise of commercial coffee production, but this seems too extreme a position. More likely, it would appear that local output was being successfully exported into a national market and that Minas Gerais had reversed the direction of its relations with the coastal economy, for it now became a major supplier of the foodstuffs needed to run the coastal plantation regimes.

In all of Brazil there were close to 1 million slaves by 1800. Brazil thus held the largest single concentration of African and creole slaves in any one colony in America and also accounted for probably one of the most diverse economic usage of slaves to be found in the Western Hemisphere. Although a detailed breakdown of the slave population by economic activity is always difficult, it is evident that no more than one-quarter of all the slaves were to be found in plantations or mines. The rest were spread widely through the cities and rural areas of the nation engaged in every possible type of economic activity. As many as 10 percent of the total slave population may have had an urban residence, but the rest were involved in rural activities, employed in farming, fishing, transportation, and every conceivable type of occupation. Brazil, with its half a million free coloreds, was also the largest center of the new class of black and mulatto freedmen in America. Although sugar, gold, diamonds, and other export products went through the classic colonial boom-bust cycles, the vitality of the Brazilian economy was such that new products were developed, new regions opened up, and a lively internal market created. All this guaranteed that the flow of slaves would not cease. In the last quarter of the century, some 16,000 African slaves per annum were arriving in the ports of Brazil, above all Rio de Janeiro and Salvador de Bahia. By the first decades of the new century that number would steadily rise, reaching into the 40,000 yearly ranges by the second decade of the 19th century.

The growth of Brazil took place in the context of major economic reforms generated by liberal and dynamic ministries in the mother country. The same occurred within Spanish America under the direction of the enlightened ministries of the reformist Bourbon monarchies of Madrid. Especially in the second half of the 18th century, Spain made every effort to promote colonial exports and to bring new regions into commercial production. One of its prime reforms was to make the slave trade more open to competition and to allow the greater importation of African slaves into its American colonies. At the beginning of the century it had allowed the English to take over the *asiento* (or monopoly contract) for slave trading to Spanish America. The English quickly brought some 75,000 slaves into Spanish American ports over a twenty-five-year period. The newly expanding port of Buenos Aires received some 16,000 Africans, most of whom were shipped to Upper Peru (Bolivia) and the interior, while the traditional ports of the Panamanian isthmus and Cartagena got the rest. As others took over the British *asiento* after 1739, the patterns developed in this first third of the century were accentuated. Slaves flowed steadily into the Caribbean corner of the Isthmus of Panama, the north coast of South America, and the Rio de la Plata region.

In the second half of the 18th century a new route developed into the Greater Antilles, which had received few slaves through the legal trade up to the time. But the increasing European conflict in the Caribbean over the fate of the various sugar islands led the Spanish Crown to reevaluate its policies in relation to its own islands. Especially after the temporary capture of Cuba by the British in the 1760s, the Crown decided to open the islands to full-scale commercial development. This meant the eventual adoption in 1789 of free trade in slaves for all nations to the Spanish American possessions. The result of these various actions was the growth of new slave centers in northern South America, above all in sectors of Nueva Granada and Venezuela, and the islands of Puerto Rico and Cuba. It was Cuba that ultimately proved to be the largest slave colony ever created in Spanish America.

Although the older and more populous viceroyalties of Mexico and Peru continued to grow in the 18th century, they failed to participate in this new stage of Spanish American slavery. Mexico's slave population steadily declined to some 5,000 to 10,000 slaves by the end of the century, and even the large slave population of Peru remained relatively stable at about 90,000 slaves. The reasons for this lack of interest in expanding the use of slave labor had to do with the revival of their own Indian labor force and the growth of the mestizo and free colored populations. By 1700 the Indian populations of these two zones had adjusted to the European disease environment and were in the process of rapid population expansion. Each of these viceregal centers also experienced very rapid rates of natural population increase in the 18th century and were thus able to meet their expanding needs for agricultural, mining, artisanal, and service labor from their free Indian and mestizo populations. The dimensions of growth can be appreciated by looking at the Mexican case. In the middle of the 17th century, there were roughly 177,000 mestizos, 1.2 million Indians, and perhaps as many as 116,000 free coloreds living in the colony. By the end of the 18th century, the mestizo population had risen to nearly 1.1 million, the native population stood at 2.3 million, and the free colored population had tripled to more than 360,000 individuals.

In the more marginal lands and islands controlled by Spain, however, such an abundance of native labor did not exist. To develop these previously neglected lands the Spanish Crown was therefore forced to resort to African slave laborers just as its rivals did. To develop the new gold mines of New Granada, the cacao fields of Venezuela and Costa Rica, and the sugar plantations of its Caribbean islands, the Spaniards were forced to import African slaves on a major scale. This newly revived slave trade, in contrast to the older one, went not so much to the main viceregal centers of Peru and Mexico but to these new regions.

The majority of the slave-based economies that developed in 18th-century Spanish America were not created de novo but were extensions of earlier efforts to tap local resources. Now, however, under the aegis of royal support, local entrepreneurs were able to become international exporters. This was the case with gold in New Granada, with cacao in Venezuela and Costa Rica, and with sugar and coffee in Cuba. Also, the urban slavery so typical of Lima and Mexico City appeared in the newly growing marginal centers. Thus Santafé de Bogotá in the first half of the 18th century was filled with *jornalero*, or day-laboring, slaves who lived on their own or in the houses of persons who rented them, performing all the urban skilled and unskilled and domestic labor tasks. There were even *jornaleros*—usually married couples, who worked the small truck gardens and orchards that surrounded the city and supplied it with fruits and vegetables. Interestingly enough, the decline of Quito meant that most of the slaves working in the region were in plantations, mining or working as domestic servants in Quito. Along the coast, however, slave *jornaleros* were most important in the town of Guayaquil, where they served as a major group of skilled and semiskilled artisans in the local shipyards.

Probably the most lucrative of these slave-based industries was that of gold mining in the Pacific slope region of the viceroyalty of New Granada (in what is today the coastal lowlands of Colombia). Alluvial gold deposits were known to exist in this inaccessible and hostile area at least from the 16th century. Stiff Indian resistance hindered intensive, wide-scale mineral extraction during the 16th and early 17th centuries, but small enterprises were launched, especially in the upper San Juan River watershed and, after 1544, in the Cauca valley.

Black slaves were brought into these areas early where they worked alongside native workers. Both blacks and Indians shared technological knowledge, and some African slaves, particularly those from the Bambuk, Bouré, and Akan fields of the upper Senegal, upper Niger, and middle Volta rivers, brought considerable mining expertise with them across the Atlantic. Between 1670 and 1690 the Chocó region in the northwestern section of Colombia finally succumbed to Spanish control, which initiated a long but increasingly vigorous new phase of mining speculation. The Chocó region would emerge as the primary mining site in the viceroyalty between 1680 and 1810. By the 1720s there were 2,000 African slave miners in the region, and by the 1782 census there were over 7,000, accounting for more than 13 percent of the viceroyalty's total slave population. Africans were brought first by ship to Cartagena and then by long and dangerous overland routes to the Chocó. In both the overland routing and the actual organization of the slave mine labor, the Chocó was similar in development to what had occurred a generation earlier in the gold fields of Brazil. As in Minas Gerais, most gold was obtained in placer mining by using sluices to wash selected areas or by rediverting rivers and exposing riverbeds rich in minerals. The abundance of water in these tropical regions guaranteed a steady source of power for earthmoving and cleaning. The mining gangs (or *cuadrillas*) were fairly large, and in the 1750s, 90 percent of the slaves worked in units of 30 slaves or more. Gold-washing operations of several hundred slaves were not uncommon. Despite these similarities, there were some important differences between gold mining in Brazil and in New Granada. Perhaps the biggest differences were in the sex ratios and the sexual division of slave labor. In the Spanish gold-mining systems of South America and the Caribbean both men and women worked in the industry, helping to generate natural growth in the slave population. Slave owners actively sought gender balance so as to encourage slave satisfaction, prevent rebellions, and increase their slaveholdings. In Brazil, by contrast, slave growth in Minas during the mining boom period was maintained largely by new and steady infusions of black males. Ultimately, gold mining in New Granada would prove to be a very ephemeral industry, and by the end of the century a depression had set in. As output declined, slavery declined, and by 1800 most of the black population had been freed or purchased their freedom as mining died out.

Less transient were the cacao plantations of Venezuela. These had started in operation with Indian labor late in the 16th century, and by the middle of the 17th century Venezuela cacao had established dominance over the Mexican and Spanish markets. This was one of the few areas to use Indian labor in *encomendias* for the production of commercial export goods, and the local planters resisted all efforts to convert their tribute to a money payment. But the entrance of the Portuguese into commercialization of cacao finally provided the capital and resources to import African slaves on credit. By the second half of the 17th century, slave labor had totally replaced Indian labor on the "encomiendas," which had in fact become full-scale plantations. Though the industry was affected by plant epidemics in the last decades of the 17th century, it recovered well in the 18th century and began a major expansion. By the 1750s there were five million trees planted, and by the end of the century there were some 64,000 slaves in the colony, at least 60 percent of whom were engaged in cacao production. More like coffee than sugar in its organization, cacao required careful tree management, but the trees lasted a long time and could be kept in production for several decades. There was no exhaustive rush for harvesting or drying, so the labor needs were reasonably distributed over time. Though gang labor was used, supervision was extremely loose by sugar standards. Given that all tasks, from removing the beans from the pods to drying and bagging them, were done with minimal equipment, there were few skilled jobs on the plantation, and a rather high percentage of workers were field hands. The largest group of skilled slaves was that of the muleteers who brought the crop to market. Most plantations averaged around thirty slaves, and there were also a fair number of small marginal producers who entered the market based on their own free labor efforts.

In Costa Rica, cacao cultivation also brought black slaves into the economy, especially at the end of the 17th century and into the 18th century. However, the cacao industry flourished in unique ways, incorporating some features that were characteristic of the gold-mining regions of Spanish America with aspects of the cacao economy seen in places like Venezuela. To begin with, as in Venezuela, the initial development of the cacao industry came at the hands of native laborers, especially the Urinamas, who were subjugated by the Spaniards in the 1650s. But whereas in Venezuela native workers toiled for nearly a century before major infusions of African slaves arrived, in Costa Rica the use of blacks became routine just decades after native labor was introduced. Indeed, from the 1650s through the 1690s, cacao was cultivated by mixed labor teams, including slaves, free coloreds, mestizos, and Indians. From the 1690s onward, the transition to African slavery grew markedly as mestizos shunned the harsh living conditions of the Matina and Barbilla valleys where most of Costa Rica's cacao was grown, and as laws from the *audiencia* (high court) prohibited the use of Urinama laborers on cacao estates. Moreover, the heavy rains, high humidity, predatory animals (including jaguars, pumas, alligators, and snakes), and troublesome raids from European pirates and Miskitu pillagers made these regions undesirable places of residence for the white and mestizo populations even if they were good areas for cacao production. In the wake of the exodus of whites, the Costa Rican cacao valleys became essentially black zones in the early 18th century.

Similar to the gold-mining regions of New Granada, Costa Rican masters sent their slaves to work under circumstances that offered remarkable liberties. Some of these freedoms were unique in the New World for Africans in bondage. Arguably, the relative poverty of the Costa Rican elite when compared with other Latin American colonies affected how they chose to manage slaves in places like the Matina valley. Lacking cash, it was not uncommon for masters to send slaves independently into the region to start or operate a cacao enterprise. Since land was virtually free, any slave could establish himself, plant cacao trees, and begin working. Often, a master might purchase an already established cacao estate in the Matina valley, in which the slave workforce was factored into the price. Regardless of how a master acquired his slaves and property, he quickly found that maintaining his slave investment involved minimal expenses, which caused many of the Costa Rican elite to diversify their portfolios with cacao speculation. The abundance of fruit, vegetables, sea turtles (for meat), and small game meant that slaves could feed themselves, and cash-strapped masters were not reluctant to allow slaves to live by their own devices. Since cacao was converted into legal currency in the 18th century, slaves had access to a ready source of real income for purchases, including their own freedom. A typical European traveler visiting the Matina valley for the first time might have been shocked at what he found. Slaves lived in huts under their own supervision, or under free black stewards. In addition to managing their master's estate, these slaves cultivated property that they sometimes leased and made regular earnings. They moved freely, wielded weapons, took goods to market, and were responsible for virtually every phase of the cacao industry, including cultivation, packaging, and transport. With their disposable income of cacao seeds, they independently made purchases from long-distance merchants and frequently engaged in contraband trade with friendly pirates. Meanwhile, white masters and mestizo supervisors irregularly visited the Matina valley's estates, coming mainly during the short harvest season (once or twice a year) and then staying for only two to three weeks. The casual visitor would have also noticed, however, that black slavery in the Matina valley was primarily a man's world. Few black female slaves made the trek into the cacao-growing countryside. With many slave women residing in urban areas, the cacao-growing slaves' freedom was often circumscribed by lack of family and an occasionally forbidding solitude. However, as in Guatemala during the 1600s, and even in Mexico during the second half of the 17th century, these slaves were able to attract a small number of free spouses with unusual frequency. Many of their brides were mulatto women, but others were mestizas and even a few Indians. By contrast, many of the men were described as *negros* or "pure" blacks. Unlike in much of Latin America, Costa Rican black men actually enjoyed an advantage over mulatto slaves in attracting free brides. While in various circles marrying a black slave was considered a "disgrace," these women saw real opportunities in their husbands. Their high level of independence, access to a private home (even if owned by a master), and access to ready cash made them attractive, eligible bachelors, especially to women who came from lesser means. In turn, the men preferred free brides because of their ability to give birth to free children (despite vociferous protests and challenges from masters) and the women's access to networks within the world of the legally free. Indeed, black male slaves throughout Costa Rica appear to have preferred wedding free women to tap into such networks. The case of Ramón Poveda seems typical. In 1742 Ramón proposed to María Nicolasa Geralda, a free *mulata* whose father was a well-placed, influential militia captain. Shortly after marriage, he assisted his son-in-law with a cash loan of 200 pesos to help him acquire his freedom.

The last major area of new slave labor development was the island of Cuba, which was to have an explosive growth in the second half of the 18th century. Like Venezuela, its major staple crop had been planted as early as the first settlement. Sugar, tobacco, and coffee were established early on the island, and there was even some significant mining in the first two centuries of settlement. The island had been a fast-growing center of production in its first century of European settlement, with a significant Indian slave labor force and even some African slaves in mining and plantations. But the attractions of mainland conquests drew off men and capital from the island, and the economy was allowed to stagnate. Only imperial defense needs at the end of the 16th century brought royal attention to the island in the form of subsidization of a major defensive port in Havana for the protection of the annual silver armadas.

With a market in provisioning the fleet, Cuban agriculture remained reasonably active but was incapable of generating major income. Tobacco, the principal crop with a potential world market, was produced on small riverbank farms, or *vegas*, which were run by free labor. But royal control over production and export throttled the industry, and until the end of the 18th century the island was incapable of paying for its own defense and government. Instead it received an annual subsidy from the Mexican treasury. But in 1763 this slow pace of growth changed dramatically when the island fell to

English troops in the midst of the Seven Years' War. The Crown was shocked by the fall of this military bastion and even more upset by the dynamic growth of the local economy under several months of British rule. Expecting to remain permanently, the British had opened up the island to international trade, with a resulting stimulation to commercial agriculture that was unprecedented. In five months they imported 10,700 African slaves, some five times more than the Spaniards permitted to be brought in an average year. Upon recovering the island, the Crown realized it could not retreat to the old restrictive regime. It now gave subsidies for importing milling machinery for sugar, granted land liberally to Spanish immigrants, and encouraged the opening up of the virgin interior soils to exploitation. The result was an explosion of production and a swelling of the slave population. From a base of about 10,000 slaves at the beginning of the century, the African labor force had increased to about 40,000 by midcentury and reached the 65,000 figure by the end of the 1780s. By this date the island was producing 14,500 metric tons of sugar per annum and was already employing well over 25,000 slaves in sugar production. Coffee production had also begun, and Cuba was entering the world market as a significant producer. On the eve of the Haitian rebellion of 1791, Cuba was already well on its way to emerging as the primary slave and plantation island in the Caribbean.

Thus by the end of the 18th century the importance of slavery within the various parts of the Spanish and Portuguese American empires had been well established. Brazil was unqualifiedly the primary slave colony by any standard. But slavery was also an important institution in all Spanish American societies. It had flourished more in some regions than in others, but in all places it had left important residues in the form of both slaves and free colored populations. In those states where slavery began to decline in the 18th century, such as Mexico and even New Granada, the result was the growth of a free colored class. Thus in all northern South America and Panama, the free colored population represented half or more of the total national populations. In Panama, 50 percent of the 63,000 population were free colored; in Venezuela, where slavery was still an expanding institution, there were almost 200,000 free coloreds, representing 46 percent of the population, while in New Granada an even greater number of freedmen made up close to half of the 800,000 population. The free colored population numbered well over 100,000 in both Peru and Mexico. But it was in Brazil, with its thriving slave population, that free coloreds were most numerous, at almost 500,000. Thus free coloreds were expanding both where slavery was dying out and also where it continued as a major labor force.

The importance and distribution of both slave and free colored labor had been defined for the Iberian-American world by 1790. The shock of the Haitian revolution on American slave societies would also be felt in Latin America, but it would only move to reinforce trends already well established before this first successful slave rebellion so influenced the evolution of American slave societies.

5

Slavery and the Plantation Economy in the Caribbean in the 19th Century

In 1789 the revolution that swept through France had a profound impact on a bitterly divided elite in Saint Domingue. The world's largest, most dynamic, and most efficient sugar plantation society would tear itself apart. White planters fought each other over colonial self-government, and then they fought mulatto planters over the rights and privileges of the very aggressive free colored population. In 1789 the three French West Indies islands were the first colonials to send elected representatives to a European parliament. But the white masters were seeking self-rule and the rights of man only for themselves and totally rejected any participation by the free coloreds, let alone the African and creole slaves. France itself was in the midst of a major debate about basic freedoms and was not about to ignore the internal conflicts within the island. Metropolitan opinion was also much influenced by the development of an abolitionist movement led by the Amis des Noirs. After much debate the Paris Estates-General in May of 1791 accepted the position of the Amis and granted the free colored of the West Indies the right to vote. Both the planters and the local royalist governor in Saint Domingue rejected this decision, and open conflict ensued.

In the midst of these elite struggles, which included mulatto planters versus white ones, and poor free coloreds versus poor whites, the slaves of the sugar plantations of the Northern Plain the center of the island's sugar industry, rose in revolt in August of 1791. In the first few months of bitter and bloody fighting the entire Plain was cleared of planters, with 2,000 whites killed, more than a thousand plantations destroyed, and 10,000 slaves dead. The fighting continued on in the north well into 1793, when slaves finally captured Cap Français, the last of the northern strongholds, and the local Jacobin army declared provisional emancipation. A four-year invasion by English troops and temporary independence only delayed the final destruction of the plantation regime. In 1800 the dams that provided the irrigation for the Western and Southern Plains collapsed; this was followed by two years of intensive fighting by a Napoleonic army attempting to reinstate slavery. The end result was the declaration of an independent Haitian government by 1804 and the abolition of slavery on the island. In 1804 sugar production fell to one-third of its 1791 levels, and by the next decade Haiti dropped out of the sugar market altogether. Even coffee production, which survived the destruction of the plantations, would be maintained at only half the 1791 output in the first decade of the 19th century.

The result of all this violence was the elimination of the world's largest sugar producer. Saint Domingue produced twice as much as its nearest rival (or 86,000 tons of *muscovado* and clayed sugar) in the late 1780s and accounted for 30 percent of total world production. Its elimination as an active producer caused a rise in world sugar prices. Suddenly sugar planters from Cuba and Jamaica to Bahia and Rio de Janeiro found themselves with an expanded market and rising prices and quickly moved to meet this new demand. At the same time the incipient coffee plantation economies in Jamaica, Rio de Janeiro, Puerto Rico, and Cuba were given a significant boost when the world's largest coffee producer lost half its production in this same decade.

The impact of the Haitian slave rebellion was not just economic, however, for it also brought a considerable tightening of the slave laws and slave-control mechanisms in every slave-dominated society. From Virginia to Rio Grande do Sul, harsher laws, a less tolerant attitude toward free coloreds, and a generalized fear of slave revolts were to be the social and political legacy of the Haitian experience. Though this era of fear eventually passed in most slave regimes by the early decades of the 19th century, the Haitian years left a residue of bitter laws and feelings that was not overcome in many of these societies until final emancipation. The Haitian experience also convinced masters that division in their ranks could lead to eventual destruction of the slave system. Though the lesson was learned, it was not always acted on. In the Spanish American case many slave regimes would be destroyed as masters demanded their political liberties from Spain. Hoping to achieve an outcome equal to that secured by the masters of slaves in the southern colonies of the United States, they often got a Haitian outcome in which slavery was weakened if not destroyed. This would be the case in Venezuela. At the other extreme, the burgeoning planter class of Cuba and Puerto Rico read the Haitian experience carefully and, when their fellow colonials revolted in the other provinces of the Spanish empire, elected to remain loyalist for fear of arousing their slaves.

As for the slaves of America, the Haitian revolution proved a vital example of a movement for freedom that could succeed against all the odds. Despite the invasion of French, English, and Spanish troops, along with those of the white colonial masters, the slaves of Saint Domingue were able to obtain their freedom. To the free coloreds everywhere the privileges obtained by their fellows in the midst of the French Revolution also promised a world of equality and justice that the prejudiced societies had never granted to them. In all American societies, the black and mulatto workers, free and slave, were inspired by the Haitian example, just as whites and masters were to fear it.

In its social and political consequences, the Haitian revolution would be felt throughout America for most of the next century. However, the impact of the revolution was immediately experienced in its economic consequences. The elimination of the world's richest and most heavily populated slave plantation regime provided an incentive to the expansion and growth of new slave and plantation regimes in the other colonial societies of America.

In the period from 1791 to 1805, Jamaica, Brazil, Cuba, and Puerto Rico more than doubled their sugar outputs to meet the new demands of the European market. Both British West Indian and Brazilian sugar now made major inroads in the open sugar markets of the rest of Europe. Until close to the end of the second decade of the new century, in fact, these producers dominated the North Atlantic market. But it was Cuba that was eventually to replace Saint Domingue in the world market by the middle decades of the 19th century, and it was the Cuban sugar industry that was to prove the most efficient and dynamic in 19th-century America.

Sugar had been planted in Cuba from early in the colonial period, and the colony had been both a modest grower and exporter for most of the 18th century. By the 1780s it was a reasonably important producer with a total annual production of some 18,000 tons of brown and white sugars. By the 1810s production had doubled to 37,000 tons and was growing steadily. But Cuban output grew less rapidly than either Jamaica's or Brazil's and attained only a modest 12 percent of the market. By the late 1820s Cuban sugar exports were reaching close to 70,000 tons and finally equaled Jamaican output in the early 1830s, just on the eve of Jamaican slave emancipation. The sugar produced by free labor in Jamaica could not compete with the slave-produced Cuban product, and by 1840 Cuba became the world's largest producer of cane sugar, exporting over 161,000 tons and accounting for 21 percent of world production. Growth in the next few decades was even more spectacular. By 1870 Cuba had reached its maximum 19th-century position of world dominance, accounting for 41 percent of world output and producing more than 702,000 tons. This was its highest output under slavery and was a crop record not seriously surpassed until the 20th century.

The boom in world commodity prices and the migration of French capital and technical knowledge led to the growth of an entirely new Cuban export as well, that of coffee. In Jamaica and Brazil coffee was already a known commodity, but in Cuba it was a new crop. While some coffee may have been produced for local consumption in Cuba prior to 1791, there was none exported from the island. It was escaping French planters and their slaves who first organized coffee production on a plantation basis. From no exports in the 1780s, Cuba was up to 14,000 metric tons by the 1810s and 20,000 tons by the 1820s. At the height of the industry in the late 1830s, the island's coffee plantations numbered just over 2,000 units and employed some 50,000 slaves, a number roughly equal to the number employed in sugar. It was then one of the world's largest producers and in active competition for Caribbean leadership with Jamaica, which it soon displaced. While Brazilian coffee production was also stimulated by the Haitian revolution, its initial growth was more modest, and it did not equal Cuban output until the end of the 1830s.

The steady expansion of sugar and the spectacular growth of coffee had a direct impact on Cuban population growth. As was to be expected, there would be a dramatic increase in both slave immigrants and total slave population. But in contrast to the traditional Caribbean experience up to this time, all other sectors of the population would grow as well. The growth of the slave population did not lead to the decline of the free white population, nor did it lead to the elimination of the important free colored population. From a strong 18th-century base the free white population expanded at almost the same rate as the slave population, and there was also a slower but constant increase of free colored persons. Towns were the stronghold of free labor, and the number of such urban centers, defined as concentrations of over 1,000 persons, contained more than half a million persons by the 1860s. Equally, despite the advance of slave plantations, most of the rural industries and occupations remained in the hands of free labor. Cattle, foodstuff production, and Cuba's famous tobacco industry were all run with predominantly free white and colored workers. Though slaves were found in all these occupations, they numbered only some 70,000, compared with 404,000 whites and 122,000 free coloreds on these *vegas, estancias,* and *sitios.* Thus free laborers not only dominated the towns but also were the most numerous in the rural areas, with slaves accounting for only one-third of the rural workforce.

The growth of traditional rural industries and new urban jobs guaranteed occupational opportunity for free labor. The immigration of whites and their positive natural rate of increase, the steady manumission of slaves, and the positive natural growth among freedmen all guaranteed the continuing increase of the free populations throughout the 18th and 19th centuries. In the late 1770s there were 44,000 slaves, 31,000 free coloreds, and 96,000 whites. As the pace of commercial agricultural exports increased following 1791, so did population, with the slaves initially growing fastest. By the mid-1790s they numbered 84,000, and by 1810 there were 212,000 slaves and 114,000 free coloreds, while the whites numbered 274,000. The slaves increased to 324,000 in the mid-1840s and had peaked at 370,000 by the 1860s. But the other classes of the population had been growing as well. Whites now accounted for well over half of the island's population of 1.4 million persons, and the relative share of freedmen had risen to almost two-fifths of the total black and mulatto population, free and slave.

Although an intense trade in African slaves continued into Cuban ports until 1864, the latest date for any region in America, the dramatic growth of the slave population never led to its demographic dominance over the other groups. By the 1860s, when the total colored population reached its maximum level of more than 600,000 persons, there was still an impressive 233,000 who were freedmen. By the middle of the 1870s, under the impact of the first laws of manumission, the free colored population rose to 272,000 and passed the slave population for the first time. By this date the whites numbered over 1 million. Thus just as Brazil would experience considerable growth of its free colored class in the context of a rising tide of slave imports in the nineteenth century, so too would Cuba. The white population in both societies also would expand by both very high rates of natural increase and immigration of Europeans. All of this was in sharp contrast to the standard histories of the French and English Caribbean islands. Thus, as will be seen in later chapters, the social and cultural life of slaves and free colored in these two Ibero-American societies would show important variations from the patterns that developed elsewhere. In terms of labor, however, both Brazil and Cuba were typical American slave societies in that African slaves were identified with the production of export crops, above all coffee and sugar.

In the question of slave ownership, however, Cuba seems to stand apart from other slave societies that had a major free component during the period of slavery. From limited data available in censuses in the 1850s it was estimated that there were only some 50,000 owners of slaves, about 24,000 of whom resided in urban areas. If one assumes that only whites owned slaves, this meant that only 12 percent of the urban and just 9 percent of the rural whites owned slaves. These figures contrast sharply with those found in both the United States and Brazil, where the number of whites who owned slaves was double to triple that figure. Moreover, even among this small elite of slave owners, there were obviously sharp differences in the distribution of slaves. The average urban slave owner held just three slaves, and among the rural owners the average was only 12 slaves. Given that plantations averaged 127 slaves, with many in the 200 to 400 range, it was obvious that even in this limited group of masters there was a markedly skewed distribution, with a few wealthy elite owning the bulk of the slaves.

The Cuban sugar and coffee plantations initially were built along the lines of those in the French West Indies. The average sugar mill and its estate, known in Cuba as the *ingenio*, usually employed three to four times as many slaves and land as the average coffee plantation (or *cafetal*). By 1804 Cuba had 174 *ingenios* employing 26,000 slaves and was producing 22,000 metric tons of sugar. A typical *cafetal* had 35 slaves, and in 1817 there were 779 *cafetales* using 28,000 slaves. By the early 1820s, the coffee and sugar plantations together used close to 100,000 slaves, with another 46,000 slaves working in other rural agricultural pursuits and another 70,000 or so slaves involved in urban and nonagricultural tasks.

Though initially quicker to dominate the international markets, coffee could not compete for land or slaves with sugar. Production peaked on the 1,000 or so *cafetales* in the 1830s at about 20,000 to 30,000 tons just as Brazilian production began to reach world markets on a major scale. Whereas Brazil was producing less than 10,000 tons as late as 1821, by the early 1830s it had overtaken Cuban output. Then came the Caribbean hurricanes of 1844 and 1846, which devastated the *cafetales* on the plains. Production dropped to half the previous output, and the *cafetales* were forced off the more fertile lowland areas by sugar, which soon absorbed the major part of land and capital in the rural areas.

Sugar estates spread from Havana eastward along the coast to Matanzas and in the interior of the western part of the island. As they spread into virgin lands, the sugar estates progressively destroyed the island's dense forests, and for the first time in its history Cuba became a net importer of timber. The period from the 1790s to the 1820s was Cuba's first sugar boom period. It also was an era of rather spectacular changes. The French had introduced the latest in modern techniques to the then totally backward Cuban sugar industry. This had an immediate impact on productivity. The number of *ingenios* kept increasing, and in these extremely unusual boom conditions some rather exotic experiments in slave organization occurred as well. It was in this first sugar era that many of the newer estates in the Western zone experimented with creating a distorted labor force by buying predominantly younger males. The result was that the largest and newest *ingenios* of the period had less than 15 percent of their labor force made up of female slaves and virtually eliminated all children in the belief that this would lead to greater output per worker. This extremely harsh regime violated all the norms of slave plantation labor up to this time, resulting in a particularly brutish life for the slaves. But such an arrangement was ultimately irrational from an economic point of view, as well as unstable socially and politically. By the 1830s, as the industry moved into a more mature phase, the sex ratios in sugar estates became more balanced, with the resulting age spreads being more normal as well.

In the period from the 1830s to the 1860s the sugar plantation regime entered a new phase due to a technological revolution. Now the world's largest cane sugar producer, Cuba would also be among the first to modernize its industry. In 1838 its first railroads were in operation in the rural areas, making Cuba not only the first in the Caribbean but the first in all of Latin America to adopt the new technology. Railroads performed a dual service for sugar. First, they reduced transport costs dramatically and freed large numbers of slaves from transport occupations; second, they allowed acreage to expand because rails could bring large quantities of cane to the mills quickly and efficiently. Next came a revolution in milling itself with the introduction of steam power to drive the mills. By 1846, some 20 percent of the 1,422 *ingenios* on the island were driven by steam and by 1861, when the number of *ingenios* was down to 1,365 units, 71 percent were steam driven.

The impact of steam was profound at every level of sugar production. Output per steam mill was nine times greater than animal-, wind-, or water-powered mills. In 1860 an average steam-mechanized mill produced 1,176 tons of sugar. The resulting demand for cane increased greatly, which led to increased demand for unskilled agricultural labor. In the more advanced regions undergoing mechanization, plantations of 300 slaves or more were common, though for the island as a whole the norm of 120 to 150 slaves per plantation still held for the first half of the century. The demand for labor became so intense that by the 1840s, well before the end of the Cuban slave trade, planters began experimenting with importing alternative types of laborers. In the late 1840s they brought in hundreds of enslaved rebel Mayan Indians from Yucatán and also attracted the first of the more than 100,000 Chinese coolies who would be carried to Cuba in the next twenty years. These Indian and Chinese laborers were immediately put to work in the cane fields alongside the African and creole black slaves, and by the 1860s there was evolving a mixed slave and indentured labor force on the larger slave estates. Nevertheless, slaves still remained the basic labor power of the sugar industry.

In 1862 when 34,000 Chinese and 700 Yucatán Indians were working on the *ingenios*, there were 173,000 slaves living on these estates, with an average estate holding 126. The heartland of the industry still remained the Havana-Matanzas zones, which together accounted for 70 percent of the 512,000 tons produced in the harvest (or *zafra*) of 1863.

The technical revolution that was slowly reorganizing the Cuban countryside with the introduction of steam power and the consequent modernization of the milling and boiling processes was given powerful impetus by the exogenous crisis of a civil war. Faced by a decreasing peninsular market for its exports and an ever restrictive imperial government, many Cuban planters, merchants, and small farmers agitated for a more autonomous insular government. Hostile Spanish official response led to an ever more radical action on the part of Cubans and finally to open revolt in 1868. The resulting rebellion, known as the Ten Years' War, was a brutal, bloody, and quite destructive affair.

The rebel armies were eventually destroyed, but the war had a profound impact on Cuban slavery. The center of the rebellion was the more backward and smaller plantation regions of the eastern region. Here a desperate elite turned toward manumission to obtain its soldiers, and a hostile Spanish force was not loath to destroy plantations. The net result was the virtual elimination of plantation slavery in the east, as well as the physical liquidation of most of Cuba's traditional animal-powered mills. The victorious Spanish government made no attempt to reenslave the emancipated slaves, so the result was that the region now became a center of a vibrant free colored peasant agriculture that would define the Oriente (Cuba's Eastern region) to the 20th century.

The Western zone, which was the region of the largest and most modern estates, also experienced change at this time due to an administrative revolution followed as a consequence of the technical one. The overwhelming superiority of steam-driven mills soon forced animal-powered ones out of production, and from the 1840s onward Cuba experienced the pattern of increasing output created by an ever-decreasing number of mills. The civil war was a major impetus in furthering this decline by eliminating most of the Eastern producers. By the late 1870s, therefore, almost all of the sugar exported from the island was produced in modern mechanized mills. But the increasing demand of these mills for raw sugar, the ever-higher prices demanded for slaves, especially after the effective close of the Atlantic slave trade in the early 1860s, and the very high costs of building these steam-driven *ingenios* forced a change in the nature of ownership and production on the island. The late 1860s and 1870s saw the beginnings of a new organization of sugar production in rural Cuba known as the *centrales*. These were truly enormous factories in the field, which concentrated primarily on sugar refining and handed over sugar planting to smaller independent planters. By the last quarter of the 19th century this led to a new class of slave-owning planters called *colonos*, who were very similar to the *lavradores de cana* of early Brazilian production arrangements. They had no mills of their own and often rented the land on which they produced cane. While the centrales produced their own cane, they also worked out contracts to mill the cane of a large number of private farmers who used both traditional slave and indentured labor. Thus Cubans well before abolition had already begun to reorganize labor arrangements by mixing slave, indentured, and free workers and to experiment with alternative forms of land and mill ownership.

Throughout this growth in sugar output and in plantation expansion and reorganization, and despite the predominant role that sugar played in exports, Cuban slavery was not exclusively defined by the sugar plantation. According to the famous German naturalist Alexander von Humboldt's estimates in the 1820s, only 25 percent of the 262,000 slaves on the island were in sugar, and only 100,000 were on coffee or sugar plantations. In subsequent decades, the relative importance of sugar plantation slaves climbed but probably peaked at 40 percent in the 1860s, when an estimated 150,000 slaves were to be found in sugar. Another 20 to 30 percent of the slaves on Cuba were to be found in rural areas engaged in a whole range of mixed farming activities and living in relatively small units of a few slaves apiece. This was especially the case in the extensive truck gardening around Havana and in the remaining coffee plantations.

Even more varied than the work and lives of the sugar plantation slaves were the lives of the urban slaves of Cuba. Throughout the entire 19th century, half to two-thirds the number of slaves found in sugar could be found working in cities. Havana, of course, was the main urban center on the island. As early as a census of 1811, it had 28,000 of these bondsmen, and one-third of the island's slaves lived in towns. By 1861, when Havana's total population stood at 180,000, the relative share of urban slaves had declined to slightly over one-fifth of the total slave force, but there were still 76,000 slaves along with 120,000 free coloreds living in the cities of the island. These urban slaves were employed in the same occupations common to slaves in Lima in the preceding centuries. There was widespread ownership of slaves by urban dwellers and a well-developed practice of slave owners allowing their slaves to live and work away from home in return for a fixed rental. Urban slaves mingled with an even greater number of free colored workers, providing unskilled and skilled services to the free population and providing for themselves in terms of housing and social arrangements. Small and large commercial establishments used slaves in their work. Particularly important in this respect were the activities related to shipping and services in the port of Havana. With the need to load millions of boxes of refined sugar aboard the thousands of ships leaving for Europe and the United States, it was inevitable that slaves were a major part of the stevedore labor force. Slaves could also be found in every occupation from prostitution and peddling to being masons and carpenters. Domestic slaves, of course, could be found in houses owned by those of even moderate income. These were the slaves who were obviously the most controlled and dominated in the otherwise quite open atmosphere that characterized urban slavery.

Thus, while the large sugar *ingenio* dominated the economic, social, and political life of the colony, it absorbed neither the majority of slaves nor the free colored population on the island. In total numbers the slaves of Cuba were a moderate-size population compared with the United States and Brazil, or even Saint Domingue. At their maximum they numbered some 370,000 strong in 1861 in a total population of blacks and mulattoes of half a million. Nevertheless, Cuba, along with the United States and Brazil, was to prove one of the most dynamic plantation regimes in the 19th century, and it would in the end dominate world sugar production and be defined as the quintessential sugar plantation regime.

The growth of Spain's second major Caribbean production center, Puerto Rico, was to follow much the same pattern experienced by Cuba. Though a few slaves had been on the island from its conquest in the 16th century, the relative importance of slaves within the population as a whole was quite small. Initially the island developed as a gold-mining center based on Arawakan Indian slave labor. But the exhaustion of the gold deposits led in the 17th century to a predominantly cattle and small peasant agricultural economy alongside the provisioning and defense center of San Juan, which was a walled city. In the 18th century the island began to develop exports of coffee, sugar, and tobacco along with its traditional exports of hides and wood. But these newer commodities were still primarily produced by free peasant labor. The growth of a more active export sector also led to the unusually rapid growth of the island's native-born population. Beginning in the late 18th century, the island's free population was growing at the rate of over 2 percent per annum, without the aid of immigration.

This pattern of peasant domination of commercial exports did not remain for long. The collapse of Saint Domingue after 1791 had a dramatic impact on Puerto Rico as well as Cuba. With excellent soils and a perfect climate for sugar, the island became a new center of sugar production. Thus within twenty years following the Haitian revolution, Puerto Rico had developed a thriving sugar plantation system based on slave labor that followed along the classic lines established in other Caribbean societies. But the growth of sugar, coffee, and tobacco did not eliminate the peasant subsistence sector. This continued to expand inland, and in 1830, when most of the coastal lands had been taken over for export crops by planters using slave labor, the amount of lands devoted to subsistence agriculture in the interior was still double the amount of acreage in commercial crops. It was this parallel growth of both a large subsistence peasant sector and the intervention of peasants in some of the commercial crop production that distinguished Puerto Rico from all the other Caribbean plantation societies. While a free peasantry survived in Cuba, especially in the Oriente, it was progressively isolated within the context of Cuban development in the 19th century. In Puerto Rico, however, the more mountainous nature of the island's central core guaranteed a refuge for peasant producers, which even the expansion of coffee into the highlands in the second half of the 19th century did not destroy. This also helps to explain why slavery, though the dominant form of labor for sugar production on the island, never became the island's dominant form of rural agricultural labor.

Puerto Rico's plantation system also differed in significant ways from standard Caribbean developments, especially in terms of the relative size of the production unit and the slave labor force. Sugar was initially grown in the coastal enclaves of Ponce, Mayaguez, and Guayamo. These were relatively narrow bands of land dependent on access to irrigation and other sources of water. The great plains that dominated both Saint Domingue and Cuban landscapes and thereby permitted rather extensive plantations over large areas of the island did not exist in Puerto Rico. The best coastal sugar areas were located, as in Ponce, in rather narrow strips of land, which put strong ecological constraints on the size of plantations and the relative size of their labor forces.

Despite these limitations, the Puerto Rican sugar industry got off to a rather strong start for an island with a population of less than 300,000 in 1827. Exports of sugar climbed from just 2,000 metric tons in the late 1810s to an impressive 16,000 tons in the mid-1820s. Coffee, in the same period, rose from 3,000 tons to 6,000 tons. Thus by the late 1820s Puerto Rico was a major world producer of both sugar and coffee, as well as a significant producer of tobacco. By the mid-1830s sugar production was up to 19,000 tons, and by the end of the decade production had doubled to an annual average export of 36,000 tons, one-third of Cuba's output. By the late 1840s it was producing almost 48,000 tons per annum, which ranked it among the largest world producers of cane sugar. By this date it was supplying 22 percent of the United States import market for sugar, and 9 percent of the newly opened British sugar market as well. In 1870 the industry peaked when its exports reached the 100,000-ton mark, and it then accounted for 7 percent of the world's total cane sugar output. But the increasing competition of European beet sugar production after the 1850s progressively closed off Puerto Rico's European market, and the competition of Louisiana and Cuba moved to cut off its United States market. Faced with higher tariffs on white sugar imports, Cuba moved to export more brown sugar, directly competing with Puerto Rico, which concentrated almost exclusively on *muscovado* output. By 1880 the Puerto Rican industry was in serious decline, abetted by the crisis of emancipation that would occur as a result of the acts of 1870 and 1873, and the number of sugar-producing haciendas (as local plantations were called) had fallen to half their 1870 level. Thus the history of both slavery and sugar were intimately tied together on the island, and the abolition of one institution coincided with the fall of the other.

Though Puerto Rico had been granted the same right as Cuba to freely import slaves in 1789, the initially slow expansion of sugar did not encourage major growth in the slave population. As of 1815 there were only 19,000 slaves on the island. But in that same year the generalized liberalization of the local economy by the nervous Spanish Crown desperate to retain the island, along with the long-term impact of the Haitian rebellion, gave an added boost to the growth of both sugar output and slave imports. The slave population now began expanding at the rate of 4 percent per annum, which could have only occurred through African imports. By 1828 there were 32,000 slaves; by 1834 the total was 42,000. This was the maximum number reached by the Puerto Rican slave population. In the mid-1840s British pressure effectively closed the Atlantic slave trade to Puerto Rico, fully twenty years before this occurred in Cuba. Though sugar production continued to grow, the actual number of slave workers remained constant until emancipation began in 1870. Given the steady loss of slaves to voluntary and involuntary manumission, this meant that the slave population had achieved a positive rate of natural growth prior to abolition and one sufficient to maintain its numerical strength in the next three decades. Since the free population was growing at a rate of over 2 percent per annum, however, the relative importance of slaves within the total population declined from a high of 12 percent to just 9 percent by the end of slavery.

While a slave population of 42,000 in 1834 ranked Puerto Rico as a relatively small slave society by Caribbean standards, the total dedication of slaves to sugar had a major impact on the productivity of that slave force in relation to exports. This meant that an extraordinarily high ratio of the slaves, or two-thirds to three-quarters, worked in sugar. Despite this concentration of slaves in sugar, it was necessary to supplement slave labor with free wage labor on all Puerto Rican haciendas. The existence of a large free population of

317,000 persons (of whom two-fifths were free colored) in that year meant that many of the tasks performed in Cuba or the French West Indies by slaves were performed by free wage laborers in Puerto Rico.

The Puerto Rican sugar plantation slave economy thus differed in many respects from the Caribbean standard. It was defined not only by the relatively small physical size of the average plantation because of ecological limitations but also by one of the smallest workforces per unit of production. It would use free wage labor alongside the slaves from the first to the last days of the industry, whereas elsewhere in the Caribbean this was associated only with the epoch of emancipation. The physical extension and workforce of an average Puerto Rican sugar hacienda made it probably the smallest sugar plantation ever devoted to commercial export sugar production in the Americas. In 1845, for example, the premier sugar zone of Ponce had on average 40 slaves per unit, which was typical for the rest of the island's sugar estates as well. In turn these slaves were supplemented by an average of nine *jornaleros*, or free daily-wage laborers, per estate. The average size of each unit was also small, being around 60 acres instead of the 200 to 300 average in the rest of the Caribbean. But because productivity was high, these plantations were fully integrated into the world sugar markets. Productivity was also high at the small farm end, as well as the large plantation end of the market, thus guaranteeing the survival of quite small units of sugar production in these areas.

As output and the number of the island's haciendas increased in the middle decades of the 19th century and the number of slaves remained at 42,000, there was an obvious increase in the use of *jornaleros* for production. But despite the increasing importance of *jornaleros*, the slaves remained the core and dominant labor force on all plantations. In the 1840s, as a response to the end of the slave trade and increasing prosperity, the planters succeeded in having the first of the vagrancy laws passed, which tried to force free workers to register for work. This was not too successful, and the end result was a progressive increase of wages offered to the *jornaleros*. It also led to an increasing mechanization in agriculture after the 1850s. Initially the constraints of available watered and arable land made use of mechanized steam-driven mills a rather expensive operation that was not cost-efficient. But in the 1850s and 1860s more and more steam-driven mills appeared on the island. The result of all this effort was to saddle the planter class with a rather costly structure that did not survive the crisis of the 1870s. Thus a combination of a failure to pay the promised compensation for the slaves emancipated after 1870, an over-investment in steam, and overproduction in the world market worked together to destroy the sugar industry in Puerto Rico in the last quarter of the 19th century. Puerto Rican exports after 1880 shifted heavily into coffee, and the whole economy moved once again toward closer integration with Spain and away from its former dependence on the United States.

The progress of slavery and sugar on the remaining French-controlled islands of Martinique and Guadeloupe was not that dissimilar from what occurred in Cuba and Puerto Rico. Initially, however, the shock of the Haitian uprising was a profound one that found echoes of revolutionary activity among the slaves on both islands. While the other West Indies islands responded to the elimination of Saint Domingue with increased sugar output and the development of new commercial crops such as coffee, the opposite occurred on the complex of islands that made up the rest of the French West Indian possessions. On the leading islands of Guadeloupe and Martinique, the plantations (or *habitations*, as they were called on the islands) of sugar, coffee, cotton, and indigo all suffered labor unrest, the withdrawal of planter capital, and a generalized crisis due to the French and Haitian revolutionary movements at the end of the 18th century and the very beginning of the 19th century. This was compounded by the invasion of the islands by the English in the last phases of the Napoleonic Wars.

In 1789 the two islands and their dependencies had a total of almost 170,000 slaves, with Guadeloupe being slightly larger in total slave population (at 89,000). The 1790s were a period of such unrest that slave importations stopped entirely and total production declined dramatically. In 1794 the French Assembly abolished both slavery and the slave trade. But this affected only Guadeloupe as Martinique had already been seized by the English. Even in Guadeloupe it took a slave rebellion in alliance with a French invasion to abolish slavery and remove the English. From 1794 to 1802 there was an active black and mulatto participation in the economy of the society, and there were even attempts at running the sugar estates without slave labor through rental arrangements with ex-slaves. Ex-slaves and free coloreds were also vitally important in the armies, and a provisional government was even established in early 1800 under Magliore Pélage, a mulatto and former slave. But Napoleon could not suffer either a Pélage or a Toussaint, and in 1802 a new French army arrived in Guadeloupe, reestablishing slavery and the slave trade over bitter ex-slave opposition. The Guadeloupe reconquest convinced Toussaint in Haiti to finally break with his French supporters over these hostile actions.

With the end of the colonial wars between Great Britain and France in 1815, both Martinique and Guadeloupe were restored to France and again began to prosper. Under the Bourbon restoration government from 1815 to 1830 the slave trade was reestablished, even the limited numbers of manumissions of earlier years were seriously curtailed, and a major push was given to increase sugar production. The result of these efforts was that the two islands finally surpassed their prerevolutionary output by the early 1820s, averaging 20,000 metric tons of sugar per annum each. At the same time, their labor force once again began to expand, though this occurred only on the more dynamic Guadeloupe, whose slave population by the early 1830s climbed to 100,000. Thus the two islands on the eve of the final abolition of the French slave trade in 1831 contained some 180,000 slaves and were producing 70,000 tons of sugar, which placed them in the ranks of the major world cane producers.

But the two colonies entered fully into renewed production when many changes had occurred in the world market, which were reflected in local changes as well. Cotton, coffee, and indigo, which had been major products in the 1780s, declined dramatically in the 19th century in the face of stiff world competition. This meant that more lands and more slaves were put into sugar. By the 1830s more than half of the arable land was in sugar on Guadeloupe, and some 42 percent of the slaves were working the plantations. But the number of plantations had increased faster than the slave labor force so the average size of the workforce on each plantation had actually declined from the prerevolutionary period. Whereas a typical sugar "habitation" had contained 112 slaves in the earlier period, the average dropped to 79 in the 1830s. Coffee, which had been exported at the level of over 3,000 tons per annum in the 1780s, declined to less than 1,000 in the 1830s and absorbed but 9 percent of the slave labor force and averaged only 18 slaves per unit.

The establishment of the July Monarchy in France brought an abrupt change to the evolution of slavery on the islands. In 1831 the slave trade, which had been revived under Napoleon and ineffectively abolished after 1818, was definitely abolished; in the next year all restraints on manumission were removed, and free colored were given full civil rights. With the slave trade closed, the number of slaves began to decline, especially as there now occurred a dramatic increase in manumission. In the 1780s these colonies contained only 8,000 freedmen. Because of the wars and rebellions their numbers had climbed to 25,000 in the 1830s; by the 1840s there were 72,000 free coloreds, compared with 161,000 slaves.

This slow decline of the slave population and growth of the free colored population meant that the planters, even before the end of slavery in 1848, were beginning to experiment with alternative forms of labor. While slaves were the basis for the sugar estates until the end, planters tried both sharecropping and wage labor arrangements for free coloreds. All this was in anticipation of what would become a major alternative labor force in the 1850s when both East Indian workers and even large numbers of indentured African "engagés" would be imported into the island to produce sugar.

While Guadeloupe and Martinique would again suffer a major crisis in sugar production in the late 1840s due to emancipation, the special protection afforded by French preferential tariffs for the island's sugar guaranteed that local West Indies production would survive all the market crises of the 19th century, including the major dislocation caused by abolition. Thus the French sugar plantation system of the 18th century survived the catastrophes of the Haitian and French revolutions, English invasion, and even emancipation. The French West Indies sugar industry would in fact emerge as innovative and even more powerful in the third quarter of the 19th century, being the first region in the world to adopt the central mill system (or *usines*) of modern sugarcane production.

But while sugar remained dominant on the islands for most of the 19th century, the rise of the free colored class in the post-1794 period did bring a significant change in the interrelationship between colonies and metropolitan government. The free coloreds, much as they had done during this same period in 19th-century Jamaica, quickly established themselves as a powerful group of land owners on small farms producing food crops for local markets. In the French islands, however, the constant attack on their rights and their successive resort to arms made the free blacks and mulattoes initially a far more politically conscious and well-organized group within insular society before the end of slavery. Thus the free colored population played a crucial role in agitation for both the abolition of slavery and the demands for equality of all persons regardless of color or class. The result was the emergence of a highly politicized and articulate class of persons who quickly gained local political control after abolition and dominated both insular politics and representation in the French Assembly in Paris. Thus, despite their relatively small numbers, free coloreds both in Saint Domingue in the 1780s and in the other islands in the 1790s to the 1840s played a vital political role in liberating themselves from white domination and eventually in promoting the establishment of freedom for the local slave populations.

The experience of the French West Indies after 1791 thus differed markedly from the Spanish West Indies experience. Their involvement in many aspects of both the Haitian uprisings and the international conflicts of the Great Powers delayed their response to international market developments. But the end result was in many ways a similar one. These societies, like that of Cuba, entered a new period of expansion in the 19th century, adopted a new type of industrial organization, and also developed new labor inputs from indentured workers. Only Puerto Rico differed from these developments in its greater dependence at an earlier date on free labor in sugar production and the fact that its plantation economy did not long survive the abolition of slavery.

6

Slavery and the Plantation Economy in Brazil and the Guyanas in the 19th Century

The impact of the Haitian revolution was not confined to the nearby Caribbean plantation societies. It was also to have a profound influence on South American developments as well, both in such major slave societies as Brazil and in the smaller European continental colonies on the northeastern coast. In these regions the elimination of the world's leading sugar and coffee producer generated renewed growth in both the plantation regime and slavery after 1791. Only in the Spanish American republics was there little economic response to these changes. For imperial Spain, Cuba and Puerto Rico became the center of sugar production and were encouraged to supply the mainland colonial markets of Spain as well. To these islands came a heavy stream of Africans until the middle decades of the 19th century. But few slaves were carried to the Spanish Main after 1800, and the sugar industries of Peru and Mexico remained primarily local producers that even lost ground to Cuban and Puerto Rican imports. Both cacao and indigo production on the mainland, as well as local mining, either stagnated or passed into the hands of free labor. Mostly in the urban centers and their associated industries did black and mulatto slavery continue to remain strong. But this type of slavery was not responsive to changes in international markets. By and large, it appears that the Haitian revolution's primary effect on the Spanish mainland was not in precipitating fundamental fiscal shifts or demographic change. Rather, from the colonial elite and government's perspective, it was the idea of liberty that circulated amongst Haiti's slaves that was potentially most transformative to Spanish American slavery, looming as a specter over the remaining slave populations in places like Venezuela,

Argentina, Colombia, Peru, and Mexico and threatening to destabilize the local colonial and republican regimes.

Triggered by events in Haiti, it was in the eastern half of the continent of South America that growth on the Caribbean style was to be seen in the post-1791 period. In terms of numbers, there is little question that Brazil was the dominant region in 19th-century developments. Before 1791 it was the largest slave society in America. Although that title would be seized by the United States in the early decades of the 19th century, the Brazilian slave population still continued to grow until 1850, mainly through the importation of large numbers of Africans via the Atlantic slave trade. The Haitian collapse came at a time of a classic export crisis in Brazilian history. By the last decades of the 18th century, there was a major collapse of both the gold- and diamond-mining industries in the central interior, while the sugar industry found itself in serious competition with the booming French and British producers of the West Indies.

Thus the immediate impact of the decline of Saint Domingue was to give new life to old industries such as sugar and cotton. Within a decade, sugar production surpassed its old 15,000 to 20,000 tons per annum limit as world prices and demand began a long and upward secular trend. The Haitian impact thus intensified the plantation system of the old Northeast by increasing the number of plantations and slaves in sugar production and by encouraging the expansion of the sugar fields in Rio de Janeiro and São Paulo. Demand was so intense in Europe and even in North America that Brazil suddenly found itself once again competing on a world market. Confined mainly to Portugal and the Mediterranean for most of the 18th century, Brazilian sugars again began to penetrate central and northern European markets. Production grew so fast that Brazil once again moved into a leading position as a major world producer, accounting for 15 percent of world output by 1805.

The most intensive growth of the sugar industry occurred in the older regions of the Brazilian Northeast, with Bahia and Pernambuco leading all other regions. Although the *otahiti* variety of sugar cane was introduced into Brazil at this time, just as it had been into Cuba, there was no other major technological invention in the industry. Mills were not changed in structure, nor was steam introduced until well into the 19th century. In fact the average output per mill in Bahia, Brazil's leading sugar zone, still remained basically the same as it had been in the colonial period. Expansion of the sugar zone into new lands beyond the famous soils of the Reconcova region and the increase in the number of mills accounted for increased production. The existence of a growing national market successfully cushioned the local industry from severe world price shocks. An expanding and contracting sugar frontier was thus the response of the Northeast to international market conditions.

Initially market conditions were quite good, and total exports steadily increased. By the 1820s national output was up to 40,000 tons and climbed to 70,000 tons by the next decade. A decade later it was up to the 100,000-ton range, where it would remain for the next two decades as world prices were buffeted by the entrance of beet sugar into the European market. But expansion got under way again with favorable world prices, so by the 1870s Brazilian production averaged 168,000 tons, and by the last decade of slavery output had climbed to more than 200,000 tons. Although Cuban sugar had taken the lead early in the century, Brazil became America's second-largest producer, especially after the crisis of emancipation disastrously affected British West Indian production. In the early 1880s, when its production was just half of Cuban output, Brazil accounted for over one-fifth of American production and 13 percent of world cane exports.

The 19th century saw a major shift in northeastern zones of production. Between 1790 and 1820, Bahia doubled its mills, to more than 500, and increased its slave population to nearly 150,000 persons. By this date Bahia alone was exporting some 20,000 tons of sugar, or close to half of the Brazilian output. Thereafter production slowed, and Bahia produced only some 30,000 tons of sugar by the late 1840s. At this point, Pernambucan production surpassed Bahian output. The Bahian sugar industry revived in the last quarter of the century, with major capital inputs finally bringing steam mills to over three-quarters of the province's *engenhos*. But Bahia never caught up to Pernambuco, which remained the leader of Brazil's sugar industry.

The impressive growth of Pernambuco in the 19th century had its origins in the revitalization of the local economy carried out in the late 18th century. The work of the Pombaline monopoly company in Pernambuco had been effective and placed the province in an advantageous position to respond to the post-1791 boom in sugar prices. There was an expansion of mills in both the traditional and frontier areas; at the same time the slave trade became quite intense, and the local slave population increased to almost 100,000 by the second decade of the 19th century. Sugar production expanded with each passing decade, and at midcentury Pernambuco had passed Bahian levels. By the mid-1880s it was producing over 100,000 tons of sugar and accounted for almost half of Brazilian exports. This growth was achieved with a declining slave population. In the 1850s, at the closing of the slave trade, Pernambuco had 145,000 slaves; by the census of 1872 this dropped to 106,000, and the number declined further to 85,000 in the next decade. The growth of the free colored population more than made up for this decline, some of which was due to the post-1850 expansion of the internal slave trade, which resulted in Pernambucan slaves being shipped south into the southeastern coffee plantations. Already by the 1850s the plantations in the richest of Pernambuco's sugar zone were averaging 70 slaves and 49 free wage workers in their labor force. This ratio of free workers increased just as the introduction of steam increased sugar output per worker, so that by the 1870s no more than 40,000 slaves were to be found in the sugar fields of this leading sugar center.

A most impressive growth in the sugar industry in the post-1791 period was also registered in the province of Rio de Janeiro. Around Guanabara Bay and in the interior lowlands of Campos, a major industry developed that accounted for one-fifth of total Brazilian production by 1808. By the early 1820s there were more than 170,000 slaves in the province, some 20,000 of whom were to be found on the 400 or so sugar estates of the region. Sugar *engenhos* in this south-central province used the same technology as in the Northeast but were on average smaller than those of the Northeast. The typical mill in the Campos region owned around 40 slaves in the late 18th century, although there were some exceptional mills owning as many as 200 slaves. Production remained steady and was up to 10,000 tons by the second decade of the 19th century. In the middle decades of the century, however, there was considerable growth in the sugar industry. Not only did the size of the sugar estates finally begin to reach northeastern levels, but by the 1850s there were already 56 steam-driven mills out of some 360 *engenhos* in Campos. While more slaves in the province of Rio de Janeiro would be engaged in other agricultural activities than sugar, Campos was still the largest slave county in the province at the end of slavery, and the *fluminense* (referring to Rio de Janeiro province) sugar plantation employed some 35,000 to 40,000 slaves up to the eve of abolition, with total output ranking it just behind Bahia in importance.

The final region to become a significant producer in this period was the captaincy of São Paulo. Along the coast near the port of Santos and in the previously mixed farming region around the city of São Paulo, sugar now began to be produced for world export. Although São Paulo always ranked a poor fourth in national output and accounted for no more than 5 percent of national production, sugar proved vital to the *paulista* economy. Sugar immediately became São Paulo's most valuable export, and even though output barely climbed into the 1,000-ton figure in this early period, it already accounted for well over half the value of all exports. In the 1820s sugar was the province's primary export and was then in the 5,000- to 10,000-ton range, while some 12,000 of the province's 50,000 slaves labored in the local sugar estates. Sugar exports continued to expand into the late 1840s, when some 20,000 slaves produced just under 9,000 tons of sugar, plus a large quantity of cane alcohol (or *cachaça*) for which both São Paulo and Rio de Janeiro became known, especially in the trade to Africa for slaves.

But all this growth in Brazilian sugar was not without its problems, for Brazil was not the only nation to respond to the post-Haitian boom. Several other major American producers now entered the cane sugar market, including the United States, Cuba, and Puerto Rico. Even Peru and Mexico began exporting sugar in the second half of the 19th century with the use of free Indian and Chinese indentured labor. Cuban competition especially had a profound impact on both prices and shares of European markets attained by the Brazilians. There was also the growth of sugar production in Asia, which began to be a serious competitor to American cane production. African slaves were used by the French and British to produce large quantities of sugar in their Indian Ocean island possessions, but also free labor was used in India, Java, and later in the Philippines for sugar production. Even more important was the growth of the European beet sugar industry, which fully came into its own in the 1850s and cut off much of the European market to Brazilian production. Nor could Brazil find an alternative market in the United States, as Louisiana production also expanded to meet national needs, with the shortfalls in U.S. consumption supplied by Cuba and Puerto Rico.

All these negative trends would most affect the big producers of the Northeast, for the regions of Rio de Janeiro and São Paulo had already dropped out of the sugar race as early as the 1820s and had shifted into a new major export crop. In terms of structural change and growth it was not sugar production but coffee that was most affected by the Haitian experience. Though coffee had been produced in Brazil since the early 18th century and was already a minor but growing export at the end of the century, the halving of Haitian production in the new century and the growing demand for coffee in the North American and European markets created a major demand for new American production. It was coffee, greatly pushed by the collapse of Saint Domingue, that would be the slave crop par excellence in 19th-century Brazil.

The production of coffee in Brazil had initially been widely dispersed over the colony. But it was in the captaincy of Rio de Janeiro that the beans became a major product. What is impressive about this growth of coffee production in Brazil was how late it was in terms of development, how quickly Brazil came to dominate world production, and how concentrated the plantations were within Brazil itself. Thus in a complete reversal from the experience of sugar, it was from the West Indies that Brazil learned to cultivate coffee. First from Saint Domingue and later from Cuba, Rio de Janeiro planters learned the techniques of producing coffee on a commercial scale. It was the combination of the crisis created by the elimination of Saint Domingue and the post-1815 rise in

European and North American demand that sent prices rising, finally shifting the industry into its mature phase.

Before the end of the Napoleonic Wars, production was negligible, and even as late as 1821 the planters of Rio de Janeiro were exporting no more than 7,000 tons. This was a third of Cuban and Puerto Rican output and was nowhere near the 42,000 tons that Saint Domingue had been producing in 1791. Even within the province itself, coffee did not replace sugar as the most valuable export until the 1820s. But in this decade the industry began its dramatic growth. In 1831 coffee exports finally surpassed sugar exports for the first time in Brazil, and they finally surpassed the tonnage record of Saint Domingue set in 1791. By the middle of the decade Brazil was producing double the combined output of Cuba and Puerto Rico and was the world's largest producer. In the 1840s output climbed to more than 100,000 tons per annumand doubled again to over 200,000 by the 1850s.

From the beginning coffee was produced on plantations by slave labor. Thus the growth of coffee in the central provinces of Rio de Janeiro, Minas Gerais, and São Paulo, the top three producers, was closely associated with the growth and expansion of the Atlantic slave trade to Brazil, which reached enormous proportions in the 19th century. The expansion of the coffee frontiers up from the coastal valleys and into the interior highlands was also typical of a slave plantation economy. Virgin lands were the crucial variable in determining productivity, and with no serious fertilization carried out, soil exhaustion made for a continuously expanding frontier. From the 1820s to the late 1860s the central valleys of Rio de Janeiro were the core zones of exploitation, with the Paraíba Valley being the heartland of the new industry. From there it spread westward into the southeastern region of Minas Gerais, whose declining mining economy was revived first by sugar production and then by coffee. By the 1860s local production expanded so rapidly that Minas Gerais replaced São Paulo temporarily as the nation's second-largest producer, with more than one-fifth of total coffee exports. For most of the 1860s and early 1870s it gained ground on Rio de Janeiro and maintained its lead over São Paulo. It was only in the late 1870s and the 1880s, at the very end of the slave era, that the coffee frontier finally moved into the West *paulista* plains area, and former sugar plantation regions like Campinas became the centers of coffee production. Even abolition and a shift to free labor did not stop the moving coffee frontier, which by the end of the 19th century had finally reached south of São Paulo into the province of Paraná.

In its earliest days coffee was produced on relatively small plantations in the coastal region of Rio de Janeiro. A typical early 19th-century coffee *fazenda* contained some 40,000 coffee trees and was worked by thirty slaves. Coffee trees began producing in the third or fourth year of growth and could continue giving beans for a life span of thirty years, though of course with widely varying output. It was estimated at this time that an adult slave could care for 2,000 newly planted and preproduction trees and up to 1,000 mature ones. There was wide variation in soil quality, which made annual production vary from half a ton to a ton of beans per 1,000 trees.

The search for better and virgin soils was constantly drawing the coffee frontier inland. The interior valleys of the province were heavily forested and contained excellent soil. For this reason initial output from the coffee trees was extremely high in the first fifteen or so years. But, denuded of forest and improperly planted, these steep valley lands were subject to soil erosion and rapid decline of productivity of their coffee groves. Thus a boom-bust cycle accompanied coffee in these early centers. Typical of this first stage was the interior *fluminense* valley of Paraíba and its central district of Vassouras. Initially settled in the 1790s, Vassouras did not develop coffee *fazendas* until the 1820s. But the richness of the local soils, the high prices for coffee on European markets, and the availability of large amounts of capital and labor allowed for the development of a new type of coffee plantation regime. It was in Vassouras that these first large coffee plantations appeared, with the biggest estates containing 400,000 to 500,000 trees and a workforce of 300 to 400 slaves. More typical, however, was the plantation of 70 to 100 slaves, which was double or more the size of the average West Indian coffee estate even in the 19th century.

During the course of the 19th century the productivity of slaves increased as more stable virgin lands were opened in the highland plateaus and as more experience in planting was developed. It was estimated that an average adult slave could care for over 3,500 mature trees in the mid–19th century, and rough estimates placed an average output of a slave at between 17 and 20 sacks of coffee per annum (at 60 kilograms per sack). In the prerailroad era—that is, in the period before the 1850s—transport costs were a large part of the final price of coffee, so a large percentage of the slave labor force was engaged in the moving of the coffee sacks to market on the backs of mules. A good one-third of the slave labor force on a coffee estate prior to the introduction of rail connections was off the plantation at any given time transporting goods to and from the distant port markets. The railroads eliminated these mule trains in the second half of the 19th century, which were replaced with ox-driven carts and feeder roads that led to the nearest railroad sidings. This revolution in transport reduced costs considerably but did little to change the actual structure of the labor force on the coffee *fazendas*. In surveys from coffee plantations in all parts of the province, the number of field hands never reached more than

58 percent of the total number of slaves on a given estate. These field hands were divided into gangs and driven under supervision of local slave or white overseers. Just like the sugar estates of the Caribbean and the rest of Brazil, it turned out that the majority of workers on these field gangs were women. In coffee, as in sugar, it was men who were exclusively given all the skilled occupations and it was men who were underrepresented in the unskilled field tasks of planting, weeding, and harvesting. Given the large pool of free black and white labor available even in the most densely settled coffee zones, it was left to hired free laborers to do all the dangerous tasks of clearing virgin forests, a task usually reserved for male slaves in the British and French Caribbean.

Since Rio de Janeiro was the leading coffee-producing province up to the 1870s, it was not surprising that the largest number of rural slaves were to be found in the coffee *fazendas*. In the 1860s an estimated 100,000 of the province's 250,000 slaves were in coffee production, and that figure probably rose to 129,000 in the next decade. The growth of the coffee *fazendas* and of the slave population devoted to them was not confined to the traditional areas but was constantly on the move throughout the Paraíba Valley complex. Older zones with aged trees and a low percentage of virgin forest lands, such as Vassouras, saw declining numbers of slaves in the working-age categories as these younger workers were exported to the newer production zones. Thus while an intense African slave trade kept the *fazendas* supplied with slaves until the 1850s, reaching a high of 50,000 African arrivals per annum in the 1820s, most of the post-1850 plantation growth was accomplished through an intense intercounty, interprovincial, and interregional migration of slaves.

A second zone of coffee production would emerge in the province of São Paulo. A late exporter of any major products, São Paulo initially entered the sugar race as a minor producer but ranked fourth in total output by the early decades of the 19th century. By the late 1830s the province held 79,000 slaves, most of whom were in rural occupations, and it was sugar that was the primary occupation. But in the 1840s coffee finally passed sugar in importance. In that decade the number of slaves in sugar probably numbered 20,000, but those attached to coffee *fazendas* reached 25,000, while the province as a whole accounted for almost one-fourth of national production with its 53,000 tons of coffee. Shipping half of its coffee sacks through the port of Rio de Janeiro and the other half from its own coastal ports, São Paulo's provincial production finally passed *mineiro* levels by the late 1840s, began to approach Rio de Janeiro output by the 1870s, and moved into the lead in the 1880s. By then some 74,000 slaves were engaged in coffee production on what proved to be the newest and most efficient units in Brazil. It was these leading Central-West *paulista* planters who first experimented with free wage workers. Anticipating the ending of slavery, it was these planters who introduced immigrant laborers, and by the 1880s there were already some 10,000 immigrants working in the local coffee *fazendas*. Refusing to work with the slaves, the immigrants were assigned the care of the newly planted trees and to the slaves were reserved the task of weeding, pruning, and harvesting the mature ones. But this was a short-lived experiment that showed that coffee plantation labor would have to be organized in an entirely new manner if immigrants were to replace slaves.

Coffee not only moved north and east in Rio de Janeiro but also developed in southern and eastern area of Minas Gerais known as the Zona de Mata. While mining had declined to the point where only some 8,000 slaves were employed in its activities in the 1810s, the region of Minas Gerais still held the largest number of slaves. In the 1820s the slave population exceeded 180,000 and was growing. At this point Minas was involved in a complex mix of farming and cattle ranching and was exporting everything from cotton and hides to sugar and coffee. Not until the 1850s did coffee finally became the major export in terms of total value, and even then it employed only some 13,000 slaves in its production. Although the quality of *mineiro* coffee was considered quite good, the average size and the total number of workers involved in coffee were slightly smaller than in Rio de Janeiro and São Paulo. Estates of 130,000 trees and 36 slaves were the norm, and planters tended toward more traditional labor relations. Local planters, like those of Rio de Janeiro, were slow to incorporate free workers. But the steady importation of slaves from other regions and the growth of a creole slave population guaranteed that an expanding coffee output could be met exclusively by slave workers. Although total numbers are in dispute, the slave population on the coffee *fazendas* of the region probably reached a maximum of 42,000 by the early 1870s.

Despite its dominant position in the total value of provincial exports, coffee absorbed only a small fraction of even the rural slaves within the province. Minas Gerais was unique in that its mixed farming sector, which produced exclusively for a local market, absorbed the majority of the slaves in this largest slave province in the empire. In the 1870s there were 382,000 slaves in the province, which meant that those involved in coffee represented only one-tenth of all the local slaves, or just 15 percent of the 279,000 listed as rural workers. Nor were the counties with the most slaves those most associated with coffee. Cattle ranching, food processing, and the production of grains and root crops were all slave- as well as free-labor activities. Thus Minas Gerais represents one of the very few cases within America of a massive employment of rural slaves for primarily local, regional, or national production. Minas Gerais was also unusual for a center-south state in its distribution of slave ownership. As in the case of Cuba, the average number of slaves held per slave owner was quite small, but, unlike Cuba, the number of slave owners was quite large, and they represented a much more sizable percentage of the free population. Big *fazendeiros* owning large numbers of slaves were few, and they controlled a relatively small share of the total provincial slave labor force.

As time went on, coffee increasingly absorbed more workers and finally became the largest single employer of Brazilian slaves in the last two decades of the slave era. Despite *paulista* experimentation with immigrants prior to abolition, coffee remained a far more slave-labor-dominated crop than sugar. With the abolition of the Atlantic slave trade, the prices for slaves rose accordingly, but the coffee planters were able to import slaves from other regions of Brazil to expand their labor force. By the late 1870s, a total of 245,000 slaves were working in coffee. While the total number of Brazilian slaves actually declined in the 1872–88 period, through major purchases of slaves by local emancipation funds and through the freeing of aged and newborn in 1872, an ever higher percentage of slaves were to be found in coffee. By 1883, when the total number of the empire's slaves had fallen below 1 million, the number of slaves in coffee had risen to an estimated 284,000.

Despite this ever-increasing concentration of slaves in coffee, the majority of Brazil's slaves still did not work even in the central-south zone. Of the 1.2 million economically active slaves listed in the first national census of 1872, some 808,000 were employed in agriculture. Of this latter group, only one-third were in coffee. The rest were to be found in other plantation crops and in every other type of rural activity from ranching to small family farming. The most important of the other plantation crops was sugar, which was still Brazil's second most valuable export. Although the sugar *engenhos* of the Northeast were beginning to employ more free colored wage workers by the 1870s and 1880s, those of the Southeast were still primarily worked by slaves, and some 100,000 to 125,000 slave workers worked the cane fields of Pernambuco, Bahia, and Rio de Janeiro in 1872. The other major plantation-produced crops included cacao and cotton, which together probably absorbed another 50,000 to 100,000 of the slaves economically active in 1872. Brazilian cotton, which had been a vital colonial product and still supplied the European market with a major share of its raw cotton until the first decade of the 19th century, revived in the 1860–80 period. The U.S. Civil War created a cotton famine for European mills, and the result was a revival both of the Maranhão cotton plantation sector as well as the growth of new cotton regions such as those of Minas Gerais. Though impressive in financial terms, this temporary growth in the value of cotton exports had no long-lasting or significant impact on local labor distribution. Production only doubled in the 1860–80 period, while the value of these exports more than quintupled. The result was a temporary and quite local shift of slaves into cotton, which had little long-term impact on slaves engaged in the other plantation crops.

The other 370,000 or so slaves in rural occupations could be found scattered throughout the empire in activities that went toward feeding the growing market of 9.9 million Brazilians. Slaves still remained the backbone of the jerked beef industry in the southern provinces of Rio Grande do Sul, Paraná, and Santa Catarina and were also to be found in meat and hide production, though these were by now primarily free-labor activities. They were also important in general food production and in the manufacture of dairy and pork products for local markets in Minas Gerais. Finally, every major urban center was surrounded by truck gardens, many of which were run with small numbers of slaves.

The remaining 345,000 of the economically active slaves in 1872 not directly engaged in agriculture were often closely allied with plantation life. The most obvious example was the 95,000 slaves listed as day laborers, some of whom were probably employed in the *fazendas* alongside the resident slave forces. Some of the 7,000 artisans listed as working in wood and metal crafts, especially carpenters and blacksmiths, may also have been employed on planta-tions. But as the example of Minas Gerais reveals, there was also within the slave labor force a significant proportion of slaves who were not directly related to export agriculture yet still played a significant economic role in the economy. Thus slaves made up 10 percent of the 126,000 workers found in the textile factories, which were then coming into prominence as Brazil's first major industrial activity. The 175,000 slaves who were in domestic service accounted for 17 percent of all persons employed in that activity and made up 15 percent of the economically active slaves. Slaves also exceeded their 15 percent share of the laboring population in such activities as construction (4,000 of whom made up 19 percent of all such workers), in masonry, stonework, and allied crafts (18 percent), just as they held more than their share of day laboring (23 percent). Finally, there were some occupations in which, even though slaves represented a small share of all workers, the absolute number of slaves was impressive. This was the case with seamstresses, an occupation in which the 41,000 slave women represented only 8 percent of the total workers.

A great many slaves also lived in cities, in which, like the country at large, they formed a minority of the total colored population. A much higher per-centage of the 4.2 million free coloreds than of the 1.5 million slaves lived in urban centers. Nevertheless, slaves were important in the labor force of every city. Of the 785,000 persons who lived in cities of 20,000 or more in 1872, a minimum of 118,000, or 15 percent, were slaves. This was probably not the highest number of urban slaves ever reached, since such slaves were in decline at this time, just as was the total slave population. Ever since the end of the slave trade at midcentury, the total number of slaves had declined from their peak of 1.7 million. As in all the American slave states, the abolition of an intense Atlantic slave trade initially led to a negative growth rate of the resident slave population. The decline in total numbers also led to a shift in their distribution. The steep rise of slave prices as a result of the ending of the Atlantic slave trade, the increasing impact of manumission, and the continued expansion of coffee meant that ever more slaves would be sold from the city into the countryside. In 1849, for example, the city of Rio de Janeiro had 78,000 slaves, whereas in 1872 there were only 39,000. But slaves in Rio still represented more than one-fifth of the city's 183,000 people. Bahia, the second-largest center in 1872, with a population of 108,000 had 13,000 slaves, and Recife ranked third with 57,000 persons, of whom 10,000 were slaves. Even the still quite small city of São Paulo had 3,000 slaves out of a population of 28,000.

Urban slavery in Brazil had both the standard forms of rural master-slave relationship with direct ownership and resident employment along with direct ownership and rental to a third party. There were also a fairly large number of slaves who were self-employed, or, as the Brazilians called them, *escravos de ganho*. These slaves spanned the occupational spectrum from the least skilled and most dangerous of jobs to the most highly remunerative occupations. Many of the porters, vendors, and semiskilled and skilled artisans were self-employed and took care of their own housing or lived as apprentices in the homes of master craftsmen who were not their owners. This was the case, for example, of 4 out of the 5 slaves owned by Antonio de Souza Ferreira, who died in Rio de Janeiro in 1824; 2 of these slaves were apprentices to a carpenter and another to a shoemaker, and still another was already a journeymen carpenter. In the Rio de Janeiro city of Niteroi in 1855, there were 130 slaves employed in the local factories, of whom 85 were owned by the factory that employed them and 45 were rented. In the neighboring city of Rio de Janeiro, half (527) of the 1,039 workers employed in the local factories were slaves, though there is no corresponding breakdown into rented and owned. Artists and musicians were often self-employed slaves, though some of these resided with their masters. This was the case of the African-born Antonio José Dutra, a barber in Rio who on his death in 1849 owned 13 slaves, mostly Africans, the majority of whom formed a band and brought him far greater income than either his two rental properties or his barbering. These slave musicians also served as barbers in his shop. All this flexibility made for a quite complex pattern of slave activity and for a much more pronounced intervention of the slave in the market economy as a consumer and earner of income. Though municipalities often complained about the relative freedom and lack of financial support for self-employed slaves, they proved so lucrative an investment for their masters that the practice was never abolished. Estimates from both urban and plantation slave rentals suggest that rented-out slaves—after paying for their own upkeep of housing and food (estimated at 20 percent of their gross income)—provided an annual profit of some 10 to 20 percent to their masters on their initial investment. They were, however, only moderately used in the rural area and so were one of the major features that distinguished urban from rural slavery in Brazil. There was even a strike organized in Bahia in 1857 of the porters known as *ganhadores*. These haulers of objects, water, persons in sedan chairs, and innumerable other cargoes were organized into work groups usually along African nationalities. They also included both slave and free Africans, as well as creoles both slave and free, though the dominant element were Nagôs or Yoruba. In that year, an attempt by the municipal government to tax their labor and create other forms of limitations on their freedom of contract led to a weeklong strike of all active workers that effectively caused the urban government to abandon most of its tax and control efforts.

The relative decline in urban slavery, if not of the urban colored population, was part of a larger process of geographic redistribution of slaves that occurred in the post Atlantic slave trade period. Not only were a higher proportion of slaves found in the most productive industries such as coffee but also in those regions in which those industries were concentrated. At midcentury fewer than half of the slaves were to be found in three major coffee provinces, but by 1872 over half were located there. An active post-1850 internal slave trade helped to concentrate slaves in the center-south district, with both the Northeast and the far southern provinces shipping their slaves to Rio de Janeiro, to Minas Gerais, and above all to São Paulo. On the eve of abolition in 1887, almost three-quarters of the remaining 751,000 slaves could be found in these three provinces. Thus slavery, as in Cuba, was most heavily concentrated in the most dynamic regions of their respective societies on the eve of emancipation. With the cost of slaves rising and the growth rates of the slave populations still negative, even more slaves were shifted into the export sectors of the two largest slave states in Latin America.

The three remaining slave colonies on the mainland coast of South America—Cayenne, Surinam, and British Guyana—would all pass through stages of growth and change similar to what had occurred in both the West Indies and Brazil. All three colonies were directly influenced by the Haitian revolution. Of the three colonies that shared the northeastern coastline, the one to experience the most immediate impact was of course French Guiana or Cayenne. This was a colony that had its origins in the brazilwood trade of the 16th century and finally developed into a plantation society in the late 17th century. In the 18th century it became an important producer of cotton and the world's most important source for annatto, a red dye developed from locally cultivated trees. The colony was quite small by American standards, with a slave population of some 10,000 in the late 1780s. It then experienced the shock of the French Revolution and the temporary elimination of slavery under the French Assembly from 1794 to 1802. But the expedition that reimposed slavery in Guadeloupe also returned the slaves to planter control in Cayenne. Since the emancipation had only turned the ex-slaves into apprentices, rather than granting immediate freedom, it was relatively easy to do so. A mass exodus of some 2,000 to 3,000 slaves was stopped by free mulatto troops, so the region never developed a serious Bush Negro or maroon society in the interior.

In the post-1803 crisis of French imperial organization and the massive attack on French colonial possessions by the British, the Portuguese were able to seize Cayenne and hold it from 1809 to the end of the Napoleonic Wars. With an economy much like that of neighboring Pará province, the Portuguese did little to reform the economic and social structure of the colony. French control after 1815 did not bring many changes. The chaos of the revolutionary era had given rise to an important free colored class, and there was some growth in the slave laboring class. By the 1840s there were 19,000 slaves, of whom 3,000 were owned by the free colored population, and there were 4,000 free coloreds and 1,200 whites. There was some development of sugar production in the 19th century. In 1840 there were some 3,500 slaves working twenty-nine sugar plantations, of which twenty-seven had steam-driven mills. But total production was only in the 1,000 tonnage range, and the coming of emancipation in 1848 found the planters ill prepared to cope with a free-labor system. Though sugar, cotton, pimento, and the annatto dye were still exported, the colony tended to decline in the postemancipation period as the ex-slaves moved into cattle production and subsistence farming. An attempt to retain a dynamic export sector with imported indentured laborers from India was largely a failure, and the region went into a long period of decline.

This was not the history of either Dutch or British Guyana. These regions, which had come into full-scale development in the late 18th century, were both thriving sugar production centers that accumulated a large slave population and were able to take full advantage of the sugar boom caused by the collapse of Saint Domingue. Each passed through periods of crisis in the 19th century, but each was able to emerge with more powerful plantation societies that easily survived the process of emancipation.

The Dutch involvement on the South American mainland went back to the earliest colonial period and was especially intense in the 17th century. Though the territory would eventually change hands several times between the Dutch and the British, the Dutch eventually emerged with a solid base in British-founded Surinam after giving up their colonies of Berbice, Demara, and Essequibo to Britain. By the 1670s the colony of Surinam had 30,000 slaves, and the number rose to 75,000 before the crisis of the French Revolution created unrest throughout the Caribbean and mainland regions. Adopting the standard techniques of Caribbean agriculture, the few white Dutchmen carved out large plantations producing sugar, coffee, cacao, and cotton. This thriving colony became the center of the Dutch American empire, with the islands of the Dutch West Indies surviving primarily as commercial entrepôts with no important agricultural exports.

While the Dutch colonization was typical of the Caribbean, with few whites and few free coloreds living in a society made up by more than three-quarters black slaves, it also developed features that marked the colony as unique in several ways. Among the planters in the 17th and 18th centuries was an important minority of Jews. In the 1690s there were more than a hundred Jewish families, who owned 9,000 slaves working on 40 sugar estates. Although Jewish slave owners were to be found in the Dutch West India islands and in Pernambuco in the 17th century, few if any owned plantations or were active primary commodity producers. But in Surinam by the 1760s, Jewish families owned 115 of the colony's 591 estates and formed the largest number of native-born whites. There even developed a small free mulatto Jewish community, which in 1759 formed its own synagogue. But both white and mulatto Jews declined at the end of the 18th century, and by 1791 they were an insignificant element in the society.

Much more important was the rise of a viable group of maroon communities in the interior of Surinam in the 17th and 18th centuries. The nature of the colony's interior allowed for an open frontier that was used extensively by escaping slaves. In the late 17th and early 18th centuries local slave rebellions resulted in the escape of the labor force of entire plantations. This was aided by constant colonial warfare in the region, all of which led to the creation of major self-governing communities known as the maroons or Bush Negroes. Between invasions and slave uprisings, some 6,000 ex-slaves had escaped into the interior of the colony by the early 18th century and proved too stubborn for the Dutch to overcome. Established in dozens of villages along the interior rivers, there were three major groups of maroons in the 18th century, known as the Djukas, Saramaacanes, and Matuaris. In the 1760s the Dutch finally came to terms with these groups and signed formal treaties modeled along the lines of the 1739 maroon treaty of Jamaica. By their terms, peace was guaranteed between the colony and the communities in return for closing off the frontier to escaping slaves.

Whereas the maroon communities of Jamaica and other major plantation societies were eventually destroyed, those in Surinam survived and prospered. By the 1840s, when their numbers had increased to over 8,000, government policy shifted from isolation to incorporation as the labor situation turned increasingly critical. At the time a local census found that the Djukas, who were still the largest group, numbered 5,500 persons and were divided into fifteen villages, of which the largest had more than 600 persons and the smallest some 170. Despite late 19th-century attempts at economic integration, the maroon communities never lost their self-governing status or their distinctive culture.

The French Revolution initially had a negative impact both on Surinam and on the Dutch metropolitan economies. The constant local conflicts led to a general decline in production and the consequent decline in the number of slaves. By 1817 Surinam had lost some 25,000 slaves and was down to 50,000 such workers, along with 3,000 free colored and just 2,000 whites. Because of the ending of the Dutch slave trade in 1814, no new slaves entered the colony, so the slave population continued to decline despite renewed prosperity. In the 1820–45 period there was a spurt in sugar, coffee, cotton, and cacao exports. All these were plantation-produced crops, and these large estates often contained fairly large numbers of working slaves. In the census of 1833, which was taken at the height of Surinam's early 19th-century production boom, there were 344 plantations with 36,000 slaves, for an average of 105 slaves per unit. The majority of estates were in this range, but there were to be found two plantations with over 400 slaves each. At this time Surinam was exporting about 19,000 tons of sugar and significant quantities of coffee and cotton. But this prosperity did not last long. The slave population kept declining, and the increasing free colored class demanded higher wages. The labor shortage, plus falling world prices and local climatic and disease developments, all brought production down and created a serious economic crisis. By the time of emancipation in 1863 there were only some 33,000 slaves. The fact that the metropolitan government paid compensation for emancipation would mean that there would be enough capital to keep the export economy growing even as large numbers of ex-slaves moved off the plantations into small farms and into the city of Paramaribo. By the last quarter of the century the economy revived with government assistance, and a major importation of East Indian and

Indonesian indentured laborers began to replace the emancipated slaves on the plantations.

British Guyana experienced the same pattern of development as Surinam but on a larger scale. In a reversal of roles with that Dutch colony, it started as a Dutch possession (known under the name of its three component subparts as Demerara, Berbice, and Essequibo) and only passed into British hands during and after the wars of the French revolutionary era. It was the Dutch who turned this delta land into one of the world's richest plantation areas. Through a system of dikes and other hydraulic works, the below-sea-level coastal plain was made into a rich plantation zone producing sugar, coffee, cotton, and cacao. Responding quickly to the post-Haitian boom in prices of slave-produced commodities, the colony's plantations expanded dramatically. In the 1790s it became the world's largest producer of cotton and was the leading producer of coffee in the British Empire, while its slave population probably numbered close to 120,000. Even as that labor force declined in the next decades, it still numbered close to 110,000 in the late 1800s and early 1810s, which made it the second-largest slave colony of British America. As slave-produced cotton and coffee from the United States and Cuba entered world markets in the first two decades of the 19th century, the local Guyana planters were unable to compete and switched heavily into sugar. From a 12,000 tons per annum output in 1814, sugar reached a very respectable level of 60,000 tons by 1830. By this time as well the slave population, closed to new migrants since 1808 when both the international and interprovincial slave trade to the British colonies was abolished, had declined to some 83,000 slaves. These slaves were now concentrated in sugar, with some cacao production. The cotton and coffee plantations were abandoned.

It was the rich quality of the soil and the potential for continued expansion that enabled the Guyanese planters to survive the impact of emancipation in 1838 and the crisis of free trade in the British market in the 1840s and 1850s. On a grander scale than Surinam, British Guyana became a major importer after 1860 of indentured plantation laborers, from both Asia and Europe. In the meantime, a dynamic group of ex-slaves also created one of the most original experiments in Afro-American economic history in the period from 1839 to the late 1850s. Although some former slaves acquired vacant lands from the abandoned cotton and coffee plantations and formed villages of peasant proprietors who engaged in both subsistence and commercial farming, a few thousand ex-slaves actually purchased functioning sugar plantations with the purpose of maintaining them as viable economic units. These emancipated blacks organized corporate or communal villages, as they were called, to own and operate these sugar plantations. Although such communal villages producing sugar also appeared in Jamaica, those of Guyana were the most significant.

Although these black sugar plantations eventually failed for lack of capital, the white planters, especially with the assistance of government-subsidized immigration, were able to compete on the international market. Planters imported not only African indentured laborers and free black West Indian workers but also several thousand Portuguese peasants. They then turned to East Indians, as in Surinam and Trinidad, and Chinese coolies, as in Cuba. From 1838 to 1918 the white planters brought in more than 100,000 East Indians, some 28,000 free black workers from Barbados and the other West Indies, 13,000 Chinese, and some 8,000 Portuguese from Madeira. Like Trinidad and Surinam, British Guyana became a great melting pot of working-class cultures, in which village agriculture existed alongside a restructured and expanding sugar plantation system.

7

Life, Death, and the Family
in Afro-American Slave Societies

The history of slavery in Latin America has been very much part of the history
of European colonization and the development of American commodities for
the European market. The distribution of the African slave population and
their labor has been the theme stressed in this book up to this point. But this is
only one part of the Afro-American experience, and in the following chapters
the patterns of social, political, and cultural adjustments that the Africans were
forced to make within this New World environment will be examined.

A fundamental starting place for such a survey is an analysis of the
demographic history of the African and Afro-American slaves in the period
of their Atlantic migration and subsequent enslavement in the New World. No
other mass transatlantic migration was ever organized in the same manner,
and the trade itself was the basis for complex international trade arrangements
from Asia to America. Its impact on Africa was profound, its role in shaping
the size and distribution of Afro-American communities fundamental. At the
same time the patterns of demographic growth and decline of the American
slaves influenced everything from the demand for American slaves to the
nature of postemancipation society.

The massive forced migration of Africans in the Atlantic slave trade is one
of the central phenomena of both modern African and American historical
development. Some 10 to 12 million Africans were forced to cross the Atlantic,
and about 1 to 2 million lost their lives doing so. There is little question that this
forced migration was one of the great crimes against humanity in world
history, which was made no better by the fact that Africans as well as
Europeans participated in its rewards. But to understand the Afro-American

experience it is essential that all aspects of this trade be analyzed, for the trade would influence everything from slave culture to the patterns of living and dying experienced by slaves in America.

The slave trade began at a relatively slow pace, and enslaved humans were just one of the major commodities exported by Africa to Europe and America in the first two and a half centuries of Atlantic contact. Though some 2 million slaves had been shipped before 1700, it was not until the early 18th century that slaves became Africa's largest "export." It was in the 18th century and the first half of the 19th that most slaves were transported from Africa to America; four-fifths of all Afro-Americans date their migration to this period.

Though all major western European nations participated in the slave trade, essentially four nations dominated it. From the beginning to the end were the Portuguese, who eventually moved the most slaves. Second in importance were the British, who were the dominant shippers of the 18th century. Next came the Dutch and the French, the former predominant in the 17th century and the latter in the 18th century. Following these main traders were those of every other nation, from North Americans and Danes to Swedes and Germans, with most being moderate or short-term participants.

But no matter what the nationality of the traders, almost all participants carried slaves in a comparable manner, especially by the 18th century. All Europeans transported approximately the same number of Africans per ship in the same size vessels, and crossed the Atlantic in approximately the same amount of time. They housed and fed their slaves in the same manner, and despite the usual disclaimers and prejudices, they treated their slaves with the same amount of cruelty and care. They experienced roughly the same rates of success and failure in carrying slaves across the Atlantic, and no one nation had a mortality record lower than any other.

This uniformity had to do with the nature of the trade itself. The very ships that the Europeans used were determined by African trading needs and an optimal way of carrying slaves. The tonnage of English, French, Dutch, and Portuguese slave ships was diverse in the period to 1700 as Europeans experimented with the best ways to transport slaves. But in the 18th and 19th centuries they became more uniform and approximated the same size in all European trades. Most ships were in the middle-tonnage (approximately 200-ton) range. These were far from the largest merchant vessels at the time, being surpassed by both East and West Indian general cargo vessels. Nor were there ever more than a few of the smallest trading ships, since a minimal tonnage seemed essential in terms of profitability and sailing possibilities.

The size of the crews working the European slave ships was also not the same as for commercial trade in these centuries. Slavers were invariably manned by unusually large crews for their size of ship because of the need for extra men to control the slaves. While there was moderate variation among the traders, the overall pattern was similar in all routes. This commonality of shipping patterns for all European slavers was also evident in the manner of actually carrying the slaves. All traders used temporary platforms between decks to provide sleeping space for slaves; the actual space allotted to most slaves by the 18th and 19th centuries differed little between the largest and smallest of ships. Even in terms of feeding and caring for the slaves, Europeans combined African food staples with a mix of European preserved foods. Yams, rice, and palm oil were standard to all trades.

Although the British may have introduced surgeons earlier than other nations, this had little measurable impact on African mortality or the incidence of diseases aboard ship. The general improvement in European knowledge about diet and the use of crude vaccination against smallpox pervaded all the slave-trading nations by the second half of the 18th century, a fact that seems to account for the uniform drop in average mortality figures from approximately 20 percent in the pre-1700 period to some 5 percent by the end of the 18th century and beginning of the 19th.

Given the very high variation from voyage to voyage of any ship and captain or even among ships of a given route and nationality, the average rates are not the whole story of the decline in slave mortality. In the earlier period the average rate was a poor reflection of a much greater distribution of mortality rates, including a far larger incidence of astronomic losses. The lower average mortality experienced by slavers in the transportation of their slaves in the 18th century more closely reflected the majority of crossings, with far fewer cases of extreme mortality. This decline of both the average mortality and the spread of mortality rates around the mean figure had a great deal to do with the increasing shipping experience of slave traders from all over Europe. Studies of the supplies of shippers show that they usually provisioned for a voyage double that of their average expected days at sea. Also, trade routes became far more normalized, and turnaround times were reduced, just as intensive trading made for far better communications about supply and demand factors.

Though mortality rates were dropping, they were still extremely high and would have been considered of epidemic proportions had they occurred to a similarly aged population that had not been transported. Equally, these rates were high even in terms of the shipping of other persons in this period. Slaves had, on average, half the amount of room afforded convicts, emigrants, or soldiers transported in the same period, and they obviously had the most rudimentary sanitary facilities. While the mortality suffered by these other lower-class groups was sometimes as high as for the Africans, these rates eventually dropped to below 1 percent in the late 18th century and early 19th century, a rate never achieved by the slavers.

Findings of recent scholarship about the nature of the Atlantic slave trade contradict some long-standing myths about the organization of the trade and the carrying of the slaves. To begin with, it is essential to realize that the purchase of Africans was not a costless item for the Europeans. While markup of prices was high, relative to prices paid in Africa, the African sellers of slaves controlled the supply conditions and demanded high-cost goods for their slaves. The single largest item of European imports that paid for slaves were textiles, and these mostly came from the looms of India. It was no accident that the two most famous slave trade ports in Europe, that of Nantes in France and Liverpool in England, first achieved importance as international traders though their East Asian trades. It was their supplies of East Asian goods that allowed them to become early and effective competitors in the African slave trade. Next in importance as a trade item were iron bars, which were worked into tools by African blacksmiths, and various arms and utensils made of iron. Finally came tobacco and alcohol and other less valuable trade items. But all of these items added up to a considerable cost for the Europeans, and even when they used cowry shells and other African monetary items, these in turn had to be paid for by European goods.

Given the considerable cost of the slave purchases in Africa, there was no economic rationale whatsoever to engage in what later historians would call "tight-packing," that is, slavers deliberately packing in as many slaves as they could onto their ships, accepting with equanimity any losses suffered, since even the few who survived made for profit. This was true of no trade for which there are records in the post-1700 period, nor could any traders have made any profit in engaging in such an activity. Finally, no study yet undertaken has ever been able to show any correlation between the numbers of slaves per ton or per space aboard ship and the mortality of those slaves carried across the Atlantic.

Death in the crossing was due to a variety of causes. The biggest killer was dysentery, which was related to the quality of food and water available on the trip. Bouts of dysentery were common, and the "bloody flux," as it was called, could break out in epidemic proportions. The increasing exposure of the slaves to amebic dysentery increased both the rates of contamination of supplies and the incidence of death. It was dysentery that accounted for the majority of deaths and was the most common cause of death on all voyages. The astronomic rates of mortality reached on occasional voyages were due to outbreaks of smallpox, measles, and other highly communicable diseases that were not related to time at sea or the conditions of food and water supply, hygiene, and sanitation practices.

Although time at sea was not usually correlated with mortality, there were some routes in which time was a factor. Simply because they were a third longer than any other routes, the East African slave trades that developed in the late 18th and 19th centuries were noted for overall higher mortality than the West African routes, even though mortality per day at sea was the same as or lower than on the shorter routes. Also, the simple crowding together of slaves from all types of different epidemiological zones in Africa guaranteed the transmission of a host of local endemic diseases to all those who were carried aboard.

While the findings about tight-packing, or the deliberate policy of causing high mortality, have been rejected and the ideas of high mortality rates for all voyages have been challenged, it should be stressed that even a rate of 5 percent for a two- to three-month period for healthy young adults in the 18th century was very high. Such a rate in a contemporaneous nonmigrating European peasant population would have been considered of epidemic proportions, even more so since all those who were carried in the trade were healthy and in prime physical condition. Although the European traders carried out every possible health and sanitary procedure they knew of, most of these were of little utility, for the typical manner of carrying 300 slaves on a 200-ton vessel guaranteed a disease environment from which few escaped unscathed.

The study of the trade also shows that there is no question that Africans dominated African supply conditions. In most cases it was local governments or given classes of Africans who supplied the slaves to the coast. Less often, it was mulatto or nontribal or non-nationalized African traders and brokers who carried the slaves from inland to the European boats. Only in the case of the Portuguese was there an example of European or Euro-African traders who obtained their own slaves from the interior. Even in the Portuguese experience, however, most slaves still came originally through African sellers and/or middlemen.

Another myth challenged by recent studies is that of the so-called triangular trade, which supposedly involved European ships carrying their slaves from Africa, colonial products to Europe, and European goods to Africa for purchase of American-bound slaves. The largest Atlantic slave trade, that carried on by the Portuguese, never involved Portugal directly. Brazilian-owned ships transported Brazilian, Asian, and European goods to Africa and returned directly to Brazilian ports with the slaves. Even in the British and French trades, the slave-carrying vessels were so specialized that they had a limited impact in carrying the American slave-produced goods back to European markets. While these two powers did outfit slavers in their European ports and these slavers eventually returned home, their last leg of the voyage was often in ballast or with limited cargo. The majority of West Indian and American commodities pro-duced by slaves was carried in the far larger West India trade vessels that were specifically built for this carrying trade.

The actual movement of slaves across the Atlantic was seasonal in nature, owing both to prevailing currents and winds, which influenced the crossing, and to the seasonality of American demand considerations. Though the sail-ings from East Africa around the Cape of Good Hope were totally dependent on local weather conditions, the West African routes also seemed to respond to planters' harvesting needs in America. Although seasonality in the movement of slaves was influenced by American demand factors, the nationality, sex, and age of the slaves entering the transatlantic trade was determined primarily by African conditions.

Though planters often proclaimed their desires for a specific nationality or group of Africans, it is now evident that they took what they could get. All studies from all trades show that Europeans, except for the Portuguese in Angola and Mozambique, had little idea of the nature of the societies they were dealing with. In most cases Africans were simply designated by the ports that they were shipped from rather than any truly generic ethnic or national identity. Most traders had no conception of what went on even a few miles inland from the coast and even those who established forts and fixed settle-ments essentially dealt with only local governments. While Europeans fought among themselves to protect a special section of the western African coastline, interlopers from both other European and other African groups went out of their way to guarantee that no monopolies were created. Although the Portu-guese controlled Benguela and Luanda, for example, the French and English were getting their slaves from the same inland areas by landing farther north along the Congolese coast. Attempts by any one African group to monopolize local trade often led to the opening up by their competitors of new trading routes. Some American planters may have thought the "Congolese" to be hardworking, and others thought them lazy, but what they wanted made little difference. They got whatever group was then entering the market in Africa. On a few occasions, such as the collapse of a large state or the aftermath of a major military defeat, whole nations of well-defined and clearly delineated groups entered the slave trade and were known by their proper names in America. But this was the exception rather than the rule.

Equally, the sexual imbalance in the departing Africans was more deter-mined by African supply conditions than by American demand. Though there was a price differential between males and females in America, this was insufficient to explain the two-to-one ratio of males to females in the slave trade. Women performed almost all the same manual tasks as men on the plantations of America and in fact made up the majority of most field gangs in sugar, coffee, and cotton. African women, both free and slave, were in high demand locally, and it was this counterdemand that explains why fewer women entered the Atlantic slave trade. In some African societies women were highly valued because they were the means of acquiring status, kinship, and family. One of the distinguishing features of western African societies was their emphasis on matrilineal and matrilocal kinship systems. Since even female slaves could be significant links in the kinship networks, their importance in the social system was enhanced. Also, slave women were cheaper to acquire than free local women in polygynous societies and were therefore highly prized in societies that practiced this marriage arrangement. Even more important was the widespread Western African practice of primarily using women in agricultural labor. For all these reasons women had a higher price in local internal African markets than men.

Aside from the high incidence of males, the trade also exhibited a low incidence of children, with no more than 25 percent of all those transported being in this age category. Cuba during the middle of the 19th century presents an exception, with consistently high rates of child imports, but even here the rate was only 20 percent. Although children suffered no higher mortality rates in crossing than any other groups of slaves, their low sale prices combined with their costs of transportation equal to adults discouraged slave captains from purchasing them. Also, it seems that children were more prized than adult males in the internal slave trade and may not have appeared on the coast in great numbers because of local supply considerations.

All these biases in the age and sex of the migrating Africans had a direct impact on the growth and decline of the American slave populations. The low ratio of women on each arriving ship, the fact that most of these slave women were mature adults who had already spent several of their fecund years in Africa, and the fact that relatively few children were carried to America were of fundamental importance in the subsequent history of population growth. It meant that the African slaves who arrived in America could not reproduce themselves. The African women who came to America had lost several potential years of reproduction and were incapable of reproducing even the total numbers of the immigrant cohort, let alone creating a generation greater than the total number who arrived from Africa. Those American regions that experienced a heavy and constant stream of African slaves would thus find it difficult to maintain their slave populations— let alone increase their size—without resorting to more migrants. This happened in 17th-century Maryland, just as it did in 19th-century Cuba and Brazil.

This consistent negative growth of the first generation of African slaves explains the growing intensity of the slave trade to America in the 18th and 19th centuries. As the demand for American products grew in European markets, the need for workers increased and could only be met by bringing in more Africans. Thus the flow of migrants tended to reflect the outbound flow of finished sugar products to the European markets. Given its early growth and importance, it was Brazil that absorbed the most slaves sent to Latin America in the period before 1700. Together, Spanish America and Brazil took in almost two-thirds of the 1.6 million slaves shipped from Africa to America in the 17th century. Brazil was the leading American region in absorbing slaves in this period, receiving some 7,000 slaves per annum into its ports in the first half of the century, a figure that would rise to over 18,000 per annum in the last quarter of the century. In its turn Spanish America absorbed just over a fifth of the slaves going to Brazil, with most of these coming in the first half of the century. By the last quarter of the century, the French and British Caribbean islands were approaching the Brazilian migrations, together bringing in some 10,000 slaves per annum.

The increasing volume of slave-produced exports to Europe in the 18th century guaranteed that the pace of slave migration would quicken. While the volume of slaves to both Brazil and Spanish America would increase, their relative role in the total trade declined to some 38 percent of total transatlantic slave migrants. Adding the French Caribbean migrants, however, brought the Latin American total to just over half of the 5.5 million slaves arriving in America. Brazil was still, unqualifiedly, the leading importer of slaves throughout the century, averaging 17,000 Africans per annum in the first twenty years of the century and this volume rose to over 25,000 slaves per annum by its last twenty years. The Spanish American regions brought in a relatively low volume of slaves per annum until the 1780 period, when volume began to rise to some 2,000 per annum because of the coming into the market of Cuba and Puerto Rico. The French Caribbean began the century at a relatively modest rate of some 3,000 slaves per annum and rose to 24,000 per annum by the 1780s.

The termination of the United States and British slave trades in 1808, the destruction of the French slave fleet during the era of the French Revolution, and the formal abolition of most European trading in the first three decades of the new century left the Portuguese as the major traders for most of the 19th century. Then the abolition of slavery in 1834 in the English colonies and in 1848 in the French ones eliminated these regions entirely as slave importers. Thus, from the second decade of the 19th century, almost all the 2.2 million African slaves were officially registered as going to Spanish and Portuguese

America. Brazil still absorbed the largest number of slaves for any New World area. By the 1820s its volume of annual arrivals was up to 50,000, with Cuba and Puerto Rico absorbing 13,000 slaves per annum in this same decade. By the next decade Cuban and Puerto Rican importations peaked at 15,000 per annum and began to decline, while the Brazilian trade still absorbed some 35,000 slaves per annum in the 1840s period. Brazil was eliminated from the trade finally in 1850 by the decision of the local imperial government to comply with international pressure to end America's oldest, largest, and longest-running slave trade, which in total had brought some 4.9 million slaves to its shores. Under increasing British pressure, the Puerto Rican trade was terminated in the 1840s, but the Cubans had a last decade of massive importations in the late 1850s, in which they brought in some 12,000 slaves per annum. The effective participation of the U.S. Union navy in the 1860s, allied with traditional British efforts, finally brought a halt to the importation of Africans to Cuba by the middle of the decade, thus ending the last African slave trade to America. In its three and a half centuries of existence, the Atlantic slave trade had brought more than 1.1 million slaves to Spanish America and some 1.1 million to the French colonies, which, together with those brought to Brazil, made for a grand total of 7.1 million Africans carried to Latin America, or almost two-thirds of all Africans who were shipped to the New World. To these were added another 3.1 million who went to the British possessions in the Caribbean and the northern European colonies on the South American mainland.

The origins of the Africans who migrated to the New World varied over time. In general the trade moved slowly down the coast of West Africa and eventually to the southern shores of East Africa over the three and a half centuries of its existence. The opening up of the Senegambia region in the 15th and 16th centuries was followed by intensive slaving along the Sierra Leone and Gold Coasts. The Portuguese were the first to develop this major supply, and it was here as well that English, French, and Dutch interlopers took their first slaves. By the 17th century the area of exploitation was expanded eastward along the Gold Coast into the Bight of Benin, which by 1700 became the single most important region for the trade. By the first decade of the 18th century, only 1,000 slaves per annum were leaving the northernmost regions of Senegambia and Sierra Leone. In contrast, the Gold Coast and the shores of the Bight of Benin were averaging annually some 22,000 slaves. The southern regions of Congo and Angola were on the rise as major sources for slaves and were already shipping 8,000 slaves in this first decade of the 18th century.

Trading patterns had by now emerged that found each of the Europeans engaging in different business procedures, with different levels of intensity along the coast. The Spanish were the only major receiving nation that did not directly participate in the trade. They obtained their slaves from other European slave traders and were constantly selling the importation rights to different nationals. Thus the Dutch, French, English, and Portuguese slavers all participated in the Spanish American trade and got their slaves from all along the coast, depending on which nation had the monopoly rights to import in any given year and, in turn, on which regions of Africa were currently being exploited. The other American colonial areas receiving slaves were largely supplied by their own nationals and thus tended to have more clearly defined origins for their slaves. The English and the French were essentially boat traders with few fixed forts on the African coast. This meant that they spread their purchases over a wider area than those nations with more fixed local arrangements. The French were particularly successful in the Senegambia region, but they also actively engaged in the Congo trade; the English tended to trade everywhere from the Congo northward. The Dutch and the Portuguese, however, relied more heavily on resident "factories" to develop their slave sources, and the Portuguese were the only ones to establish urban centers in West Africa, these being Luanda, Benguela, and eventually Cabinda—all along the Congo-Angola coast.

Thus the Portuguese tended to get a more uniform group of slaves than any other of the participating nations, with most of their slaves coming either from the Gold Coast or from the Congo-Angola area. The former region initially had been controlled by them, and their factory and fort at El Mina became a prime source of slaves for the sugar plantation of the Brazilian Northeast. When the Dutch seized this region in the first half of the 17th century, there was a temporary redirection of trade to the other areas. But the growth of an intimate trade between Africa and northeastern Brazil prior to the Dutch takeover meant that this connection could not be severed. African demand for Bahian tobacco was so strong that eventually the Dutch were forced to compromise and allow the old trade to continue. The result was that Bahian, Pernambucan, and Maranhão ports were rather heavily supplied with Gold Coast slaves until the middle of the 19th century, paying for their slaves with Brazilian tobacco as well as with textiles, alcohol, metal goods, and even gold. This special relation between these two regions grew so powerful and existed for such a long time that the Northeast of Brazil was probably the most concentrated area for Gold Coast cultures in America. So close and recent was the relation that many slave rebellions in 19th-century Bahia were directly influenced by inter-African tribal conflicts brought from Africa by the slaves.

Elsewhere in Brazil there was a more varied mix of African peoples. Though Angolan and Congolese sources provided the majority of the slaves, there were significant elements coming from the middle areas of the Biafran and Benin regions and also from the Gold and Senegambia coasts. Nevertheless, the increasing importance of the south-central Brazilian coffee plantations guaranteed that the west-central African coast, as the region of Congo-Angola was called, would become an ever larger element in the African trade to Brazil as well as the rest of America.

By the 1790s the Congo-Angolan region accounted for some 44 percent of all African slaves going to the New World, or around 37,000 persons per annum. This increasing weight of the west-central Africa region was matched by the rise of a new region of export just to the north, that is, the Bight of Biafra area. Previously unexploited, the shores of the Bight of Biafra, which exported only 1,000 slaves at the beginning of the century, now became Africa's second-largest trader, with 15,000 per annum by the last decade of the 18th century. Together Biafra and the Congo-Angola region at this time accounted for just over half of African slaves.

The 19th century saw a major new development of the trade as the ports of Mozambique were finally opened up to Portuguese and some French slave traders. Although trading was intense from this new region, at one point in the late 1830s even shipping 18,000 slaves per annum, on average in the 1820–40 period, it shipped only 10,000 persons per annum. Thus the Biafran and west-central African regions together remained the prime areas of the trade at the end, with only a little over one-tenth of the slaves shipped in the 19th century coming from East African sources.

The volume of slaves carried from Africa in these three and a half centuries of the trade was enough to guarantee the growth of the American slave population. The majority of slave populations in the New World initially experienced negative natural growth rates and it was only in those regions where the slave trade died out before the end of slavery itself that positive natural growth rates among the native-born or creole slaves were achieved. The classic case of such a positive growth rate was the slave population of the United States, which unqualifiedly attained the highest level of reproduction of any slave regime in the Americas. But the United States was not alone. Some of the older colonies of the West Indies, such as Barbados and several of the nonsugar islands, also achieved positive growth rates before the abolition of slavery, as did some of the Spanish American colonies and some provinces in Brazil as well.

This pattern of declining populations under the impact of the slave trade was perceived by contemporaries, most of whom assumed it was related to conditions of treatment of the American slave population. Later commentators took up this theme, and a host of claims were made for the better or worse physical treatment on the part of this or that slave regime, or one or the other type of plantation activity or crop. Claims were made for the economic logic of planters rejecting reproduction as too costly and therefore relying on "cheaper" imported African adult slaves. Recent demographic analyses show, however, that none of these claims hold up. In all the American slave regimes, the standardized birth rate among American slave women was comparable with, if not higher than, that of most of the contemporary European nations. While the U.S. slaves in the 19th century achieved very high rates of fertility by any standards—in the range of 50 births per 1,000 population—the slaves of Cuba, Brazil, and British Guyana had birth rates in the upper 30s and lower 40s.

But these high standardized birth rates of the slave women were insufficient to maintain local populations because of the disproportionate number of men on the arriving African slavers. In American slave regimes with a heavy level of importation, the sex ratio was in favor of men. Even accepting a relatively high rate of women on slave ships—on the order of 45 women out of every 100 migrant slaves—and a birth ratio of 40 female births per 1,000 women aged eighteen to forty-five, the result would be a crude birth rate of only 36 children born per 1,000 total population. The fewer the number of women in the total population, the lower the crude birth rate becomes, no matter how high the birth rate of the fecund slave women. Although a crude birth rate in the range of 30 per 1,000 was high by contemporary European standards and close to that of the free populations in the given American societies, it was insufficient to maintain the slave population.

The reason for this failure was the very high rate of mortality. Given the age of the arriving African migrants, which largely excluded children and youths, it was inevitable that the immigrant population would suffer a higher crude death rate due to the migrants' older age structure than native-born free or slaves. If Africans made up a sufficiently large part of the slave population, then their disproportionately higher death rates would influence total death rates. This in fact is what occurred. Once the first generation of Africans died out, the mortality rates of the first generation of creole slaves more nearly approached those of the local free populations. Slave death rates, even under the best of conditions, however, were invariably higher than those of the free populations in almost areas.

For this reason, it required crude birth rates in the upper 40s and lower 50s per 1,000 population to overcome crude death rates in the mid-40s per 1,000 range. By world standards, these were extremely high birth rates, but they were achieved in most slave regimes of America by the native-born or creole slave women. The decline of the total slave population in all American slave colonies often masked a positive growth rate among the creole slave contingent and once the first generation of Africans died off and was not replaced, it was common for local creole slave populations to grow. This growth usually occurred if there were not too many manumissions of young females, which in fact was the group most often manumitted, and if there was no intra-American or internal slave trade to move younger slaves out of the local population. This latter possibility occurred in the Brazilian Northeast, where a major internal slave trade after 1850 drained off the young males and females from the local populations of Bahia, Pernambuco, and the other northeastern provinces, as well as from the far southern regions of Rio Grande do Sul and Santa Catarina. As a result, these regions continued to suffer declining total slave populations despite the high creole slave birth rates and the dying out of their African-born populations.

If no out-migration occurred, and if manumissions were kept to a low level and favored older postreproductive slaves, then it was the case that the slave regimes of America would begin to grow once again about a generation after the end of the Atlantic slave trade. While this seems to have been the rule for most of the American slave regimes, it is true that none of them approached the levels of growth attained by the slave population of the United States. As commentators have often pointed out, the United States and Brazil both began the 19th century with a slave population of 1 million each. Brazil imported over 1 million slaves in the 19th century and had a resident slave population of only 1.7 million in the late 1850s, whereas the United States imported a few hundred thousand slaves and ended up with a resident population of 4 million slaves on the eve of the Civil War. When one adds in the manumitted slaves and their offspring, the difference declines greatly. There were just 4.4 million free and slave Afro-Americans in the United States at the time of the Civil War, whereas in Brazil at the time of the first census in 1872 these numbered 5.8 million persons. This would suggest that both societies saw their original African populations grow positively well beyond their initial slave trade num-bers, though even so the North American Afro-American population still grew at a more rapid rate.

It has often been suggested that slave treatment in the United States was different from elsewhere in America. This has been supported by comparing vital rates of the U.S. slave population with all other American slave groups. But such an argument has serious difficulties on several grounds. To begin with, the birth and death rates of the slaves everywhere in America reflected those of the free whites and colored population among whom they lived, and these rates differed between the free populations of different countries. The slave rates in Latin America were close to those of the free populations in their respective countries, just as those rates in the United States were close to those of the free population. The comparison, then, is not between slave groups across political boundaries but between the slave and free populations within each country. All the evidence to date suggests that while Brazilian slave mortality rates were higher than U.S. slave mortality rates, so too were the rates for whites in roughly the same proportion. This and similar findings for Spanish America and the Caribbean suggest that if one is to discuss the independent influence of treatment, then the entire society must be examined.

Next, if treatment was that different in any given slave regime, we would expect to see different patterns of fertility among women. Since female fecundity is influenced by diet and treatment, one would expect that in regimes with "good treatment" the ages of menarche and menopause would be lower in the former case and higher in the latter than in "bad treatment" regimes. But comparing the ages of West Indian women at the beginning and end of their reproductive cycles with those for U.S. slave women shows essentially little difference. Thus treatment was not in and of itself sufficiently different in the American slave regimes to account for the differences in birth rates. While this does not necessarily mean that treatment was equal in all areas, or that some work regimes were not more oppressive than others, or that some societies were more pro-natalist than others, it does suggest that the "treatment" question is a difficult one to answer, and that the detailed demographic reconstructions undertaken to date give no comfort to those who would readily identify their slave histories as "better" than others.

If it was not differences in potential fecundity that explain the differences in birth rates of creole slave women between the United States and the other slave regimes, what then can be offered as an explanation? It has been suggested that it was a difference in the spacing between children rather than any differences in potential years of fecundity that distinguished the U.S. slave regime from all others. Recent studies show that slave women in North America had fewer months separating the births of their first and subsequent children than did those in Latin America and the Caribbean. Since no slave regimes practiced birth control, it was suggested that either abstinence or other factors explained these longer delays between children outside the United States. The evidence suggests that a sharply different pattern of breast-feeding accounts for most of the differences in spacing. Outside the United States the norm was for breast-feeding to last on average two years, which was the West African norm of behavior. In the United States the creole slaves adopted the northern European pattern of one year of lactation. Since lactation reduces fertility, the extra year helps explain the difference in the number and spacing of children.

Although contemporaries and later commentators have speculated end-lessly about the life expectancy of slaves, it is apparent that it was not that different from that of the free populations in the societies in which they lived. A favorite theme even in the 19th-century literature is of an average working life of seven years for a slave entering adulthood. Even adding in the relatively high mortality suffered in the first months of a new disease environment by the recently arrived Africans, the so-called seasoning process, such a high mortal-ity did not occur even for Africans, let alone creole or American-born slaves. The average life expectancy of native-born Latin American slaves was in the low 20s This contrasts with a U.S. slave life expectancy rate in the mid-30s. But in both cases the slave rates reflected local free population rates, with free Latin Americans having a lower life expectancy than did free North Americans. The life expectancy of a U.S. white in 1850 was 40 years, whereas the total (slave and free) Brazilian population in 1872 had a life expectancy of 27 years.

Saying that life expectancy for a male slave in Brazil was 23 years in this period (an upper-bound estimate) does not mean that the average slave died at that age. It should be remembered that infant mortality was so high in 19th-century Brazil that one-third of all male children born died before the age of 1, and just under half died before the age of 5. For those male slave children who reached the age of 1, the expectation of life was 33.5 years; for those who survived the first 5 years of life, the average number of years of life remaining was 38.4 years. Thus a male slave who survived the extremely dangerous years of infancy and early childhood stood an excellent chance of reaching his 40s. For women slaves, the life expectancy was better. Only 27 percent died before the age of 1, and 43 percent before the age of 5, which meant that life expectancy for female slaves at birth was 25.5 years, with the corresponding expectations of those who survived to 1 reaching 34 years and those who survived to 5 achieving 39 years.

Slaves who survived dysentery and other childhood diseases obviously had an average working life well over the mythical 7 years. Nevertheless, it should not be forgotten that slaves were almost exclusively a working-class population and suffered more than their share of work-related accidents, as well as all the infectious and dietary diseases from which the poorest elements of the pop-ulation suffered. Though their sanitation and housing in rural areas were probably better than those of the average subsistence free farm family, their food consumption was probably little better than that of the poorest elements of the society. Thus in considering their exclusive concentration in the working classes of the nation, along with their high level of work accidents and high rates of labor participation, it is no wonder that slaves suffered the worst disease and mortality rates in their individual societies. While the general levels of disease and mortality in each individual American society may account for the different rates among the slave regimes, there is little doubt that they were at the worst levels in every society in which they lived.

The history of the migration patterns of the Africans who crossed the Atlantic and the rates at which they died and gave birth in America have been among the most significant subjects studied in recent years. This scholarship has shown just how important the reconstruction of these demographic processes can be in explaining the evolution of the respective Afro-American societies. African concerns helped define the age and sex of transatlantic slave migrants. The sexual and age makeup of the migrants in turn influenced the growth of the American slave populations and, along with local economic conditions, determined the intensity and longevity of the Atlantic slave trade. Disaggregating the birth and death rates of African- and American-born slaves not only has reopened old debates about relative treatment by masters but it has also led to new studies such as that of cultural differences of nursing mothers. Finally, understanding the demographic evolution of the slave population provides an important framework for understanding the evolution of Afro-American culture.

8

Creation of a Slave Community and Afro-American Culture

Although they spoke a multitude of different languages and came from different cultural systems and nationalities, the African slaves arriving in the Americas sometimes shared a number of commonalties that may have helped bind them together in the New World. The opening up of Atlantic trade, for instance, contributed to the development of interregional contacts within Africa by creating ever-larger market areas. Meanwhile, the fairly constant expansion and reorganization of African states and societies over time brought many different groups into contact. While the process of African cultural integration on the continent should not be overemphasized, neither should the diversity of Africa be exaggerated. Not every ethnolinguistic group comprised a distinct culture that was estranged from others. Moreover, many Africans of the slave-trade era were multilingual and at least minimally conversant in the dialects and customs of their neighbors. Significantly, the circumstances of the Atlantic slave trade did not completely disrupt this pattern. Slave ships often extracted slaves from regions where intense multinational contact had occurred, and many of the slaves that traders purchased had also slowly migrated to the coasts where they were sold, having passed through numerous territories and interacted with a variety of populations along the way. All this may help explain why newly arrived Africans, when setting foot in the Americas, were sometimes able to create bonds of friendship and community with slaves from different nations.

Certainly, some New World masters expressed preferences for acquiring one or another group of Africans on their estates, thinking it beneficial to cultivating a productive work environment. Others actively sought to diversify their slave holdings, based on the belief that having too great a concentration of a particular group might foment resistance and rebellion. Yet there was no systematic attempt by slave traders to diversify their sources, and New World demand had no effect on the selection of Africans who arrived in America. Shippers took slaves where they could find them, and this depended exclusively on African supply conditions and the forces of European competition. There may have been some ability for masters to selectively choose the ethnicities of the slaves they wanted within the internal slave trade that occurred in the Americas, as slaves sent directly from Africa to one colony were transshipped to others. For example, it has been alleged that Africans from the Gold Coast and Senegambia's Bambuk and Buré mining regions were apparently preferred by mine owners in Brazil and Colombia, while Africans from Upper Guinea, who were known to be excellent rice cultivators, were favored in places like Georgia. When possible, efforts were made to acquire these populations—but again, if such selection occurred, then it most likely occurred within the context of internal New World slave sales.

Specific events in Africa may have led to the clustering of some ethnic groups in the Americas. For example, a series of wars in the middle of the 16th century brought about the decline of the Wolof empire in Upper Guinea, which in turn increased their availability for the slave markets of this period. Another very special case is the collapse of the Oyo Empire, which brought streams of the Yoruba into captivity in the late 18th century. A closer look at evidence of the distribution of specific ethnic groups within Spanish-speaking Latin America reveals some of the broad groupings of slaves that clustered in the New World. In the 16th century (especially before 1580), roughly 80 percent of Mexican and Peruvian slaves came from Upper Guinea. Among the most important ethnicities recorded in these regions included the Wolof, Biafara (Guinea-Bissau), Bañon (Guinea-Bissau), and Bran (Guinea-Bissau) groups. In the 17th century, Angolans, many of whom were Kimbundu speakers from the Kwanza River area in West Central Africa, began to figure prominently in the slave populations of both colonies. Approximately 84 percent of slave arrivals to the Mexican port of Veracruz were recorded as having come from Angola, as were over 95 percent of slave ships docking in Campeche. Unsurprisingly, close to 70 percent of Mexico's non-creole slave population was described as Angolan in the early 17th century. Among arriving slaves, in cases where their ethnic identity was clearly given and recorded in the historical record, one can begin to explore the possibilities for the construction of culturally coherent slave communities, based on mutually shared ethnicities. Yet such efforts must be carefully made and, to some extent, must remain speculative. Many slaves were simply listed as originating from the ports where they were sold, rather than being assigned a more specific ethnic identity based on clan lineages and birthplace. The use of these generic port designations often makes it difficult to assert that certain groups of slaves may have definitively shared a language and culture and, consequently, could form a coherent ethnic "cluster," as some have argued. Among the numerous "Angolans" arriving in Mexico, for example, there may have been some truly from the region, others who were multilingual West Central Africans who could converse among themselves, but also many who could not directly communicate with each other and were Angolan simply because they had been shipped from ports like Luanda. Despite the multiple problems, complexities, and even some inaccuracies associated with ethnic designations, examining the existing record for African ethnicities is among the best surviving means to begin identifying possible concentrations of Africans in the New World and exploring their potential impact on the construction of cultural identities.

In Peru, the concentration of Angolans was smaller but still significant. Baptismal records, marriage registers, and slave sales and exchanges from 1595 to 1650 demonstrate that around a third of Lima's African-born slaves were described as Angolan. Bran (12 to 15 percent) and Biafara (3 to 8 percent) slaves continued to register importantly, albeit in greatly diminished fashion. Apparently, the lower proportion of Angolan slaves entering Peru (as opposed to Mexico) was directly related to the number of West Central Africans being shipped to the port of Cartagena, the primary supplier of Peruvian slaves. Between 1595 and 1650, less than half of all slaves sailing to South America boarded in Angola, as opposed to more than three-quarters of the slaves arriving to Mexico. Unsurprisingly, the percentage of West Central Africans in Lima's slave registers hovered around 50 percent.

Outside of these two major colonies of early Spanish America, the dominance of African regional groups among the slave population is harder to identify. Of the nearly 250 black slaves purchased in Guatemala's capital from 1544 to 1587, less than half came from unspecified locations, and just under a quarter from Spain, Portugal, and other parts of the New World. The remaining Guatemalan slaves came predominantly from Upper Guinea, but in proportions that were roughly evenly distributed among Biafara, Bran, Berbesí (Senegal), Bañon, and Zape (Sierra Leone) ethnic groups. Wolof and Mandinga (Gambia Valley) slaves were recorded as well. Given the importance of Senegambia to the slave trade in Spain and Portugal during the late 15th and early 16th centuries, it is also likely that Wolofs and Mandingas comprised a portion of those slaves who were recorded as arriving from the Iberian Peninsula. While their time in Europe might have affected their sense of ethnic identity, the presence of these slaves would have still increased the overall proportion of

Mandingas and Wolofs in the Guatemalan trade, perhaps bringing them up to parity with the other African ethnicities. In the 17th century, as the colony's slave market expanded, Angolans began proliferating among the slave population, constituting by some counts well over half of slave ethnicities recorded between 1611 and 1630. Yet, later in the century, the decline in the colony's slave trade meant that the majority of slaves would become creoles.

A similar situation was found in colonial Quito. Like Guatemala, Quito's province of Popayán had a small 16th-century slave trade. Just 53 slaves exchanged hands in the town of Popayán between 1583 and 1605, with no appreciable ethnic groupings predominating. Slavery would pick up markedly in the 17th and 18th centuries, but ethnic distributions remained mixed. Of the nearly 3,000 Africans that the Popayán region absorbed between 1699 and 1757, slaves arrived from the Gold Coast, the Bight of Benin, Senegambia, and West Central Africa in proportions that never clearly saw the predominance of any single area or ethnic group.

The experiences of Guatemala and Quito probably came to typify a number of other areas of the Spanish realm, especially prior to the late 18th century. Costa Rica, for instance, drew many of its slaves from Upper Guinea in the 16th century without a prominent ethnicity among them. In the 17th and 18th centuries, while perceptible concentrations of West Central African "Congos" and Angolans could be detected, as well as periodic infusions of Mina, Popo, and Arará (Slave Coast) slaves, it is evident that the number of African arrivals remained small, thereby reducing their influence on the broader slave population. Creoles, quite clearly, dominated Costa Rica's slave demography. Because of this, ethnic Africans may have existed in relative anonymity. In Cuba at the outset of the 17th century, certain estates, such as at the copper mines of El Cobre, held important concentrations of slaves from Angola. But their numbers dropped over the course of the century, with a notable rise in the number of creoles. In Venezuela, the growing cacao industry of the second half of the 17th century brought forth a rise in the slave population. With new slaves entering the market there were opportunities for certain groups to nucleate. However, records from the coastal hacienda of Chuao during the years 1659 and 1671 reveal that despite the prevalence of West Central African ethnicities during both years, the combined number of Lower and Upper Guinean ethnicities was not negligible. Decades later, in 1729 and 1730, records from the city of Nueva Segovia and the mines of Cocorote would reveal high concentrations of Tari, Luango, and Mina slaves. Yet this transpired within an environment whereby the creole slave population was expanding. In Argentina between 1742 and 1806, more than 13,072 slaves legally entered the port of Buenos Aires. While many slaves were transshipped elsewhere and may not have remained in the colony, the regional diversity of the slaves and the proportions in which they arrived was impressive. Nearly one-third came from West Africa, another third from East Africa, and just under a quarter from West Central Africa. No single region clearly dominated the trade.

Within Spanish America after the mid–17th century, the notable rise in the creole slave population competed directly with new African arrivals, eventually overshadowing them in most areas, including Mexico and Peru. In the early 18th century, some colonies like Quito and Venezuela experienced a re-Africanization of their economies, as new and heavy influxes of slaves entered their markets. But the ethnic diversity of these arrivals was greater than might be expected. The rise of Cuba as a prominent slave importer (1760s–1860s) brought scores of slaves who tended to nucleate into three ethnic groups on sugar and coffee estates, namely, Kongos, Karabalís, and Lucumís (Yoruba). Still, even here, shipping records reveal that the island's 19th-century imports were, on the whole, the most diverse of any of the major slave regions in the Americas.

It is important to point out that the ethnic diversity found in parts of Latin America was not insurmountable for forging African slave identities. A case in point is Costa Rica, where by the early 1700s the colony was largely composed of creole slaves and a minority of ethnic Africans. Constituting an extremely small minority were the Yoruba, a few of whom fortuitously came to constitute the majority of nine slaves inhabiting an estate owned by Captain Don Juan Francisco de Ibarra in 1710. One of the two non-Yoruba slaves, María Popo, grew so close to her coworkers that she was mistakenly identified as an Aná (a Yoruba group) by her master and government officials, although she self-identified as being a Popo from the Slave Coast. Being mistaken for Yoruba was more than just a simple error. She developed such close ties with her fellow slaves that she even described one of the Yoruba women, Micaela, as "her sister." Their relationship had deep roots. Both María and Micaela had shared the journey of the Middle Passage. Through this horrifying experience, their bonding grew. Although María did not deny her Popo heritage during her life in the colony, it was clearly overlaid with a complex identity that included Yoruba associations derived from her intense personal interactions with them. At the same time, María found herself adapting to and navigating within a creole slave environment in Costa Rica. After several months on the Ibarra estate, she was sold to an owner who lived 200 miles away in the North Pacific Valley of Bagaces. Here, she entered a non-Yoruba world and probably took a creole husband. Over the years, she maintained communication with another Aná slave who her master had sold in Bagaces. Through these means she continued cultivating a tenuous Yoruba identity, although her direct connections with these people were largely gone.

María's case was not unusual in Latin America. In Mexico City, for instance, two slaves, Antón and María, petitioned for marriage in 1591. Their circle of friends comprised an intricate universe of overlapping and conjoined ethnic identities. Antón described himself as "from the land of Bran" and maintained a number of acquaintances from the same region. Some of these were people he knew prior to the Middle Passage. Others had interacted independently with each other in Cape Verde before being shipped to the New World. All had successfully located one another after being sold in Mexico City. Fortunately, the flexibility of their urban labor routines enabled a certain mobility that allowed them to reconstitute communities based on ethnic ties. Residing in the Spanish American colonies further aided them, since even in late 16th-century Mexico City, slaveholding was fairly limited, and the whereabouts of slaves could be determined rapidly. Interestingly, one of the summoned marriage witnesses was another man named Antón who reportedly came "from the Congo." He, too, had spent time in Cape Verde prior to the Middle Passage. The experience proved formative to his identity. Upon landing in Veracruz, he interacted deeply with other "Brans" and became a welcomed part of their social network. It appeared that simultaneously he maintained both a Bran and a Congo identity. As Antón "from the Congo" stepped forth to testify in favor of the impending marriage, the circumstances of his friendships revealed how differences of African ethnicity were wholly surmountable, given the way in which these ethnicities were themselves open to being reshaped by the common forces that bound African lives to New World slavery.

These life stories from Costa Rica and Mexico, and others like them in the historical record, suggest that African ethnicities in the New World, and the ethnic labels used to refer to Africans were in many ways not exact replicas of ethnicities found in Africa. From the nomenclature used by European colonists, slave traders, and masters to the terms adopted by African slaves, there were important incongruities with continental African self-referencing systems that made the ethnic labels used in the Americas seem elastic and open to reinterpretation. For some scholars, the very imprecision of terminology justifies a serious overhaul of how we are to understand the distribution of Africans in the Americas. While labels like "Gelofe," "Gilofo," or "Jelofe" appear to have referred to the Wolof people who inhabited the region between the Senegal and Gambia rivers, the Wolof themselves used two separate terminologies—"Jolof" to refer to their territorial empire that encompassed a number of separate states, and "Wolof" to refer to the dominant ethnic group of the kingdom. New World terminologies did not fully take into account such nuances. The "Mandinga" or "Mandega" labels suffered from similar imprecision. The original Mandinka were a Mande-speaking ethnic group who inherited the great Mali empire that stretched over the Sahel-Sudan region of West Africa, extending from Mali to the Atlantic Ocean. It is unclear at times whether the New World invocation of "Mandinga" referred explicitly to the Mandinka ethnic group or to the people they captured and sold to European slave traders. Although the Mali empire declined in the 15th century, it retained extensive trade networks throughout West Africa that supplied slaves to the Portuguese in the 16th century. A "Mandinga" slave, therefore, might refer to any of a number of groups within the orbit of the Mandinka commercial region.

While the ethnic labels used to identify African slaves may be construed as imprecise and problematic, nevertheless, we must remember that they were used by slaves themselves. When slaves named their children, assigned nicknames to family members and friends, were called upon to testify in court, served as marriage witnesses, or were tried before the Inquisition, they frequently self-identified with an African ethnic label. In many instances, the terms they used were the same as the ethnicities assigned to them by slave traders and masters. Other times they were not. In 18th-century French Louisiana, the director of the Company of the Indies observed that white colonists typically used the term "Senegal" to describe Wolof slaves, but among themselves slaves preferred using the term "Djolauf." In Costa Rica in 1706, a certain Jacobo, who was sold from slavery in Martinique, asserted that he was a Mandinga slave. This confession was rather surprising to his master, who had thought that he was creole. In Cuba, in the mines of El Cobre, a slave named Manuel Catungue arrived to the colony prior to 1620. By 1647, he had apparently risen in influence and began asserting himself as a member of the nobility, taking the name Manuel Catungue Rey (king). By 1665, he was listed in the census again, this time with the name Manuel Rey Angola. Choosing to incorporate "Angola" into his name conveyed many things, including a personal decision on his part to broaden his own conception of identity. In switching from his narrowly defined African surname, "Catungue," to embracing a more collective group identity, "Angola," he openly exhibited his affiliation with the broader Angolan "community" in the mining settlement. El Cobre proved to be a laboratory for such name toggling. In the early 17th century, many Africans coming to the colony arrived with regional/ethnic surnames—Juan Angola, María Congo, José Bran, and the like. But over time these appellatives fell in and out of favor among the slaves. In El Cobre, many chose to replace them with more personalized surnames that either reflected distinct ethnic or tribal affiliations within an African kingdom or referenced specific lineages in Africa. Hence, names appeared in the record like Antón Mofongo, Salvador Lunguengue, and Pedro Molumba. In several instances, these surnames were passed on to creole offspring in subsequent generations.

It is difficult to determine the extent to which the ethnicities declared by slaves, and found either in naming patterns or in documents, formed a conscious part of everyday slave identities. Equally, it is difficult to determine the extent to which illiterate slaves actually claimed the ethnic statuses recorded for them by colonial scribes. Furthermore, a number of slaves were either slow to assert an African ethnicity or, if they came to the New World as children, never really grasped the meaning of their African ancestry. A number of slaves in Costa Rica reported that although they were African, they did not know their "nation" because they left the continent "when they were small." In French Louisiana, the longer African-born slaves lived in the New World, the more likely they were to claim an African ethnicity. By contrast, new arrivals were frequently recorded as not knowing their ethnic status. Some of this would suggest that slaves may have actually had to "learn" their ethnicity to some degree while in the Americas. This occurred simultaneously as slaves acquired new language skills and began adapting to the conditions of slave life. With both Africa and the New World serving as cultural reference points, and understanding how claiming a particular ethnicity might affect their ability to navigate successfully in their new surroundings, ultimately, the ethnicities that slaves claimed could transcend notions of ethnicity that existed in Africa. In 1595, a black slave named Luísa testified in Mexico City, supporting her friend Isabel in contracting marriage. Both had spent their childhood on the island of São Tomé before coming to Mexico. However, they both declared "Angola" as their ethnic status, although they may have only lived briefly on mainland West Central Africa. Clearly, they had learned the meaning of being "Angolan" while living in Mexico and interacting with others who claimed this ethnicity. Technically African by birthright, these two women were conceptually "Angolan" by means of their New World affiliations and upbringing, more than from any direct experiences on the African continent.

The cultural relevance of African ethnicities in the Americas was not always related to demographic strength. Within a given colony or estate, some slaves, who may have been few in number, originated from ethnic groups that enjoyed primacy over others—either culturally, politically, or both—or in turn were the first to arrive and define the rules of acculturation. Thus Akan day names assigned to children even appeared among the majority Congolese in Jamaica who arrived after these West African peoples. Equally important was that individual aspects of certain African cultures were simply more transferable across the Atlantic than others or were found to be more popular among the broader slave population. Africans in the Americas had no state apparatus and no political classes, and their clan organizations were severely ruptured, thus African beliefs associated with all these activities had difficulty crossing the Atlantic. On the contrary, those beliefs relating the individual to health and well-being, interpersonal relationships, and relation of the self to the cosmos were most likely to retain their power in the New World.

It is also clear that large elements of the emerging Afro-American cultures were influenced by European beliefs. Variants of European Christianity became the dominant religion among slaves, even if syncretized with large elements of African beliefs and deities, and second-and third-generation slaves were raised speaking the language of the local master class. In their adaptation to peasant agricultural practices, Africans and their descendants, though sometimes using African technologies, were often found adopting European tools, technologies, and ways of life. The structures of social stratification within the emerging Afro-American community may also have represented an amalgam of two different worlds, or even a response to the special conditions that slaves encountered under New World slavery. In some cases, differentiation in African social status successfully made the transition across the Atlantic. In others, differences in slave status derived from struggles against the varying social positions that were assigned to slaves by their masters, which frequently did not correspond to the notions of stratification that emanated from within slave communities themselves. Consequently, although a hierarchy of status in terms of occupation and skin color was imposed upon the slave population, internal slave divisions often did not necessarily replicate white standards.

Despite all the cultural amalgamation, there were norms of behavior and beliefs that were unique to slaves and helped them fortify an alternative version of the dominant culture. Some of these were brought from Africa, others were created to make their lives more meaningful in the context of slavery, and others were deliberately oppositionist to the culture that justified and rationalized their bondage. To unravel all these strands is a difficult task, made more difficult by the limited knowledge available on contemporaneous African cultures, and of free lower-class culture within Latin America during the time of slavery.

Certain features of this slave culture were common to all slave societies in America, while others were more especially developed in the Latin American context. It is now generally accepted that in the slave periods in Cuba, Haiti, and Brazil powerful movements of proscribed religious practices developed that were most heavily influenced by a syncretic arrangement of African religious deities. These movements came fully to light in the postabolition period in these Catholic countries but never arose to any significant extent in the Protestant societies. These essentially non-Christian religions were among the more significant features that distinguished Latin Afro-American cultures from the others. But there were also other aspects of cultural behavior and community development that set these societies off from others in the Americas, just as many features were shared by all.

Though whites viewed all slaves as equal before the law, the differential prices paid for skilled slaves as opposed to field hands clearly suggest that whites recognized important variations in aptitudes, abilities, and other individual traits. As for the slaves themselves, there were obviously some levels of stratification within their own commonality of bondage. The traditional definitions of social status among the contemporary free persons, however, are not totally applicable when examining slave society. Positions with control over resources or over other persons—highly prized in the free community—were not necessarily those that guaranteed higher status within the community of slaves, or even those recognized by the price differentials given by whites. Autonomy and knowledge often played an equally important role. Autonomy was clearly related to independence from the control and supervision of whites, whatever the job, just as knowledge could be both of the African culture of the past or of the white culture of the present.

The lives of the slaves in Latin America were defined primarily by work. With only the exception of the very young and the very old, everyone spent most of his or her time engaged in manual labor. More than any other segment of the society, slaves were both the least sexually divided by labor and the most highly participatory group in the market. For this reason, work dominated the life of the slave more than others in the society, and questions of work autonomy or dependency were of vital concern to slaves. In plantation societies, supervision of the strictest kind was the lot of the majority of slaves, but even here, relative control over one's time was available to a surprising number of them. On an average sugar or coffee plantation, gang labor involved only half of the slaves. Another third or so were craftsmen or had occupations giving them freedom from direct white or overseer supervision. In the half of the rural slave populations who were not on plantations there was equally a distribution of jobs under close supervision on family farms, as well as relatively independent families of slaves tilling lands on their own, or skilled artisans or muleteers who could escape direct white control. In the urban setting, domestics made up a large share of the labor force, came into close contact with whites, and were most tightly controlled. But all who worked on a self-hire basis or as independent craftsmen tended to have the most free time for themselves outside the normally controlled work environment.

Control over their time and labor permitted some slaves to achieve a fuller development of their talents and abilities. Short of total freedom, this was considered a highly desirable situation, and slaves who held these jobs had a higher status within the slave community. It was also no accident that many of the leaders of slave rebellions and other political and social movements came from these more autonomous slaves. Interestingly, some of these jobs were highly regarded by the whites as reflected in price potential, and some were not. Commentators on slave occupations noted that these jobs created an independence not found among the field hands or even the domestic slaves. In the coffee plantations of 18th-century Saint Domingue and those in early 19th-century Brazil, for example, the muleteers who carried crops to market were considered a particularly lively group and were thought to be the "kings" of the slave force, as they were called in the French literature.

Knowledge was also an important granter of status within the slave community. This could be an ability to read and write the local European language, or even Arabic and a reading knowledge of the Koran, just as it could be an understanding of the dynamics of the master class and the socioeconomic realities of the free world. These types of knowledge would often be associated with either skilled occupations, those possessing autonomy, or domestic service in which contact was had on a frequent basis with the master class and other nonslave groups. It was also more commonly found in urban settings and could be discovered even at the lowest level of the occupational skills ladder. But knowledge of African ways and customs, or even, in some rare instances, of prior noble or elite status transferred directly from Africa, gave some slaves a leverage in their community in contrast with their official status. Thus, in one of the more extreme examples, the leader of one of the Bahian slave rebellions of the 1830s was an African nobleman who in Brazil was the lowest type of unskilled worker. The same occurred with many of the male and female Africans who were part-time religious, health, and witchcraft specialists, most of whom had a status inside the community completely unrecognized by the master class.

Sometimes this knowledge provided leadership and status potential, and sometimes it offered a potential for power as a cultural broker. Many domestics, for example, might not be considered elites within the community but could provide the kind of brokerage knowledge or contacts of aid to slaves more isolated from the dominant society. Thus house servants often held a special ability to mediate demands between the slave quarters and the master's house. But this role often left them with few leadership possibilities on either side. Some slave leaders did come out of domestic service, but usually they had occupations outside full-time master control.

Thus it was no accident that urban slaves and artisan or transportation workers were usually to be found at the head of rebellions or were persons who were most likely to purchase their freedom. But such leaders did not, in and of themselves, define the culture of the slave world. Afro-American culture as it emerged tended to develop in the small black villages that made up the world of the large plantations, and in the common social spaces that slaves shared in colonial cities. It was in these "black belts" that an Afro-American culture was most coherently created. At the heart of the new black culture was the family unit. Though Latin American masters experimented with every type of com-munal arrangement for their plantation slaves, most slaves lived in families. These households would define the emerging Afro-American culture and would socialize children to these beliefs and behavior. Black culture involved everything from sexual mores and kinship arrangements to language, religion, and the arts. It was a culture whose prime task was to create a coherent and reproducible community that would provide a social network of resources and support for the individual slave. Without this culture slaves could not have functioned, and even white planters recognized its essential quality of provid-ing social stability in an otherwise chaotic and hostile world.

The key role in the slave family unit was played by "married" couples. Though the sex ratio among the Africans guaranteed that many males would not have access to African women, among the creole slaves the sexual balance was equal, so almost all native-born slaves eventually lived in family units. Even when sexual imbalances did exist, slaves found creative ways to maintain families. In early 17th-century Guatemala, black male slaves were able to secure native women as spouses, while Mexican slaves in the second half of the 17th century occasionally took Indian or free black brides. Within Latin America there existed a wide range of family arrangements. The region was unique by contemporary European standards in its extraordinarily high incidence of free unions and illegitimate births among the whites and free population in general. In no European society prior to the 19th century were births among free persons close to the 40 percent illegitimacy rates found in Latin America, and in none were the levels of free union so high. Even among the white upper classes, where formal marriage played such a crucial economic and political role, the rates of illegitimacy and free unions were higher than found in any correspond-ing European elite, including those of Spain and Portugal. Latin America never developed a northwestern European family model, with its extraordinarily low rates of illegitimate births. Because of the conquest of a large American Indian population and the introduction of numerous African slaves, the Iberian males had sexual access to a large subject population with which they could maintain illicit unions. As a result, in the Americas, the Iberians were not constrained by traditional Catholic morality in relation to the family. Indeed, the highly stratified class and caste society that was created in Latin America reinforced old traditions of European concubinage, which spread among middle- and lower-class white colonists. In such an Americanized European culture it was inevitable that marriage and legitimacy would take on meanings and importance different from what they had in contemporary Europe.

Nevertheless, even slaves were married sometimes in church weddings in the Catholic world, though the importance of such marriages varied from nation to nation, and even from region to region. Within Brazil, for example, a much higher percentage of slaves were legally married on the coffee estates of São Paulo than in any other region of the country, whether plantation area or not. Whereas some 12 percent of the slaves were recorded as "ever married" (that is, currently married or widowed) in Brazil in the first census of 1872, in the coffee counties of São Paulo 30 percent of the slaves were so designated. In estates owned by the Church, usually all slaves were legally married, but even this could vary. In some of the early colonial Bahian sugar plantations owned by the religious orders, little effort was made to legitimate local unions formally. Although legitimacy records are few for slave births, several analyses of such records indicate such variation. Thus in the Minas Gerais towns of Santa Luzia in the early 19th century an impressive 45 percent of the 1,006 slave births whose legitimacy was recorded were listed as legitimate children, and in Juiz de Fora and Muriaé in 1851–88, the rate was 47 percent for slave births. These rates seem exceptionally high given the low rates of formal marriage among slaves even in southern Brazil. In contrast, in two different periods in the Minas mining town of Sabará rates were much lower: just 8 percent of the 1,627 slave children born between 1723 and 1757 were declared legitimate, and 22 percent for the 529 slave births were so considered in the period 1776–82. This later rate is roughly the same as reported for some 1,118 slave children born in the parish of Inhaúma in Rio de Janeiro between 1817 and 1842, only 21 percent of whom were legitimate.

The ramifications of a legal Church marriage could be strong in the Iberian world. Especially in the Spanish colonies, the Church upheld the marital institution, and slaves enjoyed certain matrimonial rights. One of the most important of these was the right to preserve the marital union. If a master attempted to sell a legally recognized spouse and break up a family, slaves could lodge a legal appeal. In places like 16th- and 17th-century Mexico, slaves won a number of these cases, despite the considerable social and economic resources that masters had at their disposal. For these reasons and others, masters were not always willing to support a slave's desire to marry. Equally cases of the Church intervening to prevent the separation of married slaves on the death of their owner are also found in colonial and 19th-century Brazil.

As with the majority of all married couples in Latin America, slaves lived in free unions that in effect were formally sanctioned and recognized family units, albeit without the powerful support of the Church. Importantly, slaves themselves recognized these units, and once such families were established, slave communities went out of their way to ensure their internal stability by using the usual mechanisms of community control. Errant spouses or non-responsible parents were condemned by the community and were made to conform. This conformity could be enforced by normal social pressure, witch-craft, or even violence to guarantee community peace and welfare. This did not mean that the slaves kept up a Victorian-style morality, but it did mean that once a slave family was firmly established, it was given legitimacy and sanction by the community itself.

Only a few studies have been undertaken on the sexual and marriage practices of the slaves of Latin America and the Caribbean. Local plantation studies from other regions suggest several alternative patterns, from those observed in the British West Indies at one extreme to those found on some of the plantations of the United States in the 19th century at the other. In one case, close to half of the adult slave parents did not have residential cohabit-ation and lived on different plantations. In the old British West Indian sugar islands in the late 18th and early 19th centuries, a large number of the slaves lived alone or in households made up only of mothers and their children. There were even a few polygynous households for favored male slaves. In contrast, in the French island plantations and most of the major plantation zones in Latin America in this same period, slave families seem to have conformed more to the pattern of the United States, with the majority of slaves whenever possible living in two-parent households and in relatively stable relationships. This dominance of organized family living can be seen, for example, in detailed studies of the coffee plantation zone of Bananal in São Paulo in the early 19th century, where in 1829 some 83 percent of the 2,282 slaves were found living in family units. Equally, a study of the small north-eastern São Paulo town of Batatais in the period 1850–88 showed that only 15 percent of 461 slaves were found in the households of single mothers. The rest lived in family units. A similar study of some 1,240 slaves in the São Paulo plantation town of Lorena in 1874 showed only 25 percent of slaves associated with single female households; the rest were in family units. But, of course, the high death rates of slaves and the impact of sales and forced separations on free unions sometimes led to serial marriages. These processes also led to the emergence of stepfamilies, as well as families with legitimate and illegiti-mate children. However, even in high-mortality regions, on average most slave marriages, legal or otherwise, lasted for a long time. One of the few studies of marriage longevity that has been conducted for Latin American slaves comes from the sugar and coffee plantation region of Campinas in São Paulo. In 1872, for women slaves between the ages of thirty-five and forty-four, living in units of ten or more slaves, the median length of marriage was an extraordinary sixteen years and eight months. Moreover, it was found that there was surprising stability of residence for these married women, with almost all breakups of families coming as a result of the death of one partner, rather than sales off the plantation. From the same census of Campinas it was estimated that in six of ten marriages of young slave couples (in their mid twenties or mid thirties) in 1872, the average marriage lasted eleven years. The average length of marriage in Batatais was ten years. Equally, a study of several hundred postmortem inventories of slaveholdings in Rio de Janeiro between 1790 and 1835 showed that only 17 percent of the slave families in these lists were broken up by the death of their owners. Although there was a moderate inverse relationship between the size of the holding and the ratio of families separated through sales, overall, the data from Campinas and the study of the Batatais slave families showed that the death of the master had far less of an impact on family breakups than the death of the slaves themselves, even among smaller units of slaveholdings. Of course, these studies are for prosperous plantation zones of major slave concentrations and continued slave in-migration even after the end of the Atlantic slave trade in 1850. Thus they were zones with limited out-migration and consequently low levels of family breakup. It might be expected that studies from the Northeast or of the southern provinces, which were subjected to an important out-migration of slaves into the internal slave trade after 1850, may show more family unit breakups through sales, even prior to the death of the slave owners. But in general all the current research suggests a surprising longevity of slave marriages and a relatively low incidence of separation through the death of slave owners or through sales. The overwhelming form of breakup of slave families was from the death of one of the partners.

Whatever the local household arrangements, in most slave societies, slave women began having children quite early, and it was common for them to engage in premarital intercourse rather freely before the birth of the first child. At this point, women usually settled down into a relationship that might or might not be with the child's father. Usually, except in cases of widowhood, the father of the second child was the father of all later children. Although this behavior was considered scandalous in North America, it was much less challenged in Latin America, where the norm among the lower classes of free society—white, mestizo, or colored—was not that different. This pattern, for example, was found in the coastal sugar region of Angra dos Reis in the province of Rio de Janeiro in the mid–19th century, where it was common for slave women to have their first child registered as illegitimate, and their second and subsequent children as legitimate. From this same data it appears that married slave women tended to space their children closer together than single mothers, which would suggest that slave women living in marital unions tended to have more children than women living alone.

When slaves married each other, there is also no doubt that the majority of marriage partners, legal and otherwise, were obtained from among the slaves in the same slaveholdings. Whether this was forced by masters to prevent long-term slave absences and loss of control is an open question. Clearly, slaves who resided in households with just one other slave, or at most a few others, often had to find their marriage partners outside their master's slaveholdings. Thus urban slaves and slaves residing in small farms or workshops were far more likely to seek partners outside their owner's households. But in larger slave-holdings, the norm was for marriage partners to come from among the slaves owned by a single master. Numerous 18th- and 19th-century studies of slave plantations in Minas Gerais, Rio de Janeiro, and São Paulo show that women on larger plantations were more likely to be living with partners than those on smaller units. To give just a few examples, in the sugar and coffee plantation region of Campinas in São Paulo in both the provincial census of 1829 and the national census of 1872, slave women living on estates with 10 or more slaves were twice as likely to live in family units as were women being held on estates with fewer than 10 slaves. In the well-studied province of São Paulo, an analysis of some 200,000 slaves from provincial censuses stretching from 1775 to 1850 shows that there was a consistent increase of married couples the larger the size of the estate. This was more pronounced for women, where there was a systematic correlation between increases in the ratio of married women and the size of the slaveholding, but also showed for men, though there was a plateau reached for men after holdings exceeded ten slaves per owner. Thus, slaves who were owned by masters who had just one slave were legally married in only 6 percent of the cases for men and 4 percent for women. Meanwhile, in estates holding more than 40 slaves, the ratio of married slaves was 21 percent for men and 39 percent for women. Given these findings, it is not surprising to discover that in Campinas in 1872, only 29 percent of slave children under age 9 were declared legitimate on plantations holding fewer than 9 slaves, com-pared with an 80 percent legitimacy rate for children on estates with more than 10 slaves. This finding is consistent with several other detailed studies of baptismal records in Rio de Janeiro and Minas Gerais.

With parenthood and cohabitation came kinship arrangements. Slave families several generations deep sometimes lived in extended families. These extended families, whether cohabiting or not, in turn developed clear rules about acceptable marriage partners. These rules included such universal human taboos as sibling incest prohibitions, and even discrimination about marriage partners from along collateral cousin lines. In the legal marriages of African-born slaves in Bahia and Rio de Janeiro, there were even rules of endogamy about ethnic origins. Thus, for example, in 253 legal marriages of African slaves registered in Rio de Janeiro in the first half of the 18th century, there was an extraordinarily high rate of men and women marrying within their own ethnic group. Interestingly, the high endogamous rates among African groups were reversed in Bahia and Rio de Janeiro, which suggests that when any regional group was less well represented among the slaves, there was less endogamy. Consequently, the majority of Angolans were highly endogamous in Rio de Janeiro and far less so in Bahia, where they were a distinct minority among the Africans. Similar trends could be noted elsewhere in Latin America. Some of the better evidence comes from 17th-century Mexico, where endogamy rates ran high among the dominant Angolan population. When that population began to decline after 1630s, ethnic endogamy started to wane.

Slave families also observed internal rules regarding naming patterns, property inheritance, and even place of residence, as newlywed couples negotiated whether they would live alone or with the "bride's" or "groom's" parents. As for names, children were sometimes named for certain blood kin on the father's or mother's lineage line and in turn sometimes used special kin-related terms in addressing known relatives. Some of these rules of inheritance and association came from African practices of different regions, others from the white masters, and still others from among pragmatic rules worked out by the slaves themselves over time. A detailed study of naming patterns on several North American plantations in the 18th and 19th centuries has shown that some U.S. slaves had a prohibition on cross-cousin marriage (a taboo not found among local whites) and that the naming of male children often involved the use of male ancestors several generations back. In Brazil a few studies have recently been undertaken that indicate detailed kinship networks and these show a far lower incidence of naming children for relatives or parents than was found in the United States. On the Resgate coffee plantation in Bananal (São Paulo), well-preserved records for 436 slaves in 1872, along with their baptismal records from earlier years, provide detailed evidence of kinship on this long lasting plantation. They show that almost 90 percent of the slaves were kin to other slaves or free persons of color. Those not having kinship ties were primarily males and either older Africans or recently purchased creole slaves born in other provinces. All but two of the mothers were legally married on the plantation. The predominant form of family organization was the nuclear family, with only a quarter being extended families. Of the 116 married couples, only a third involved Africans marrying creoles; the rest were endogamous for either group. Among the mixed unions, African men married creole women. When Africans intermarried (29 couples), the age difference between partners was only four years; for couples where both were creoles (46 in number), the difference was seven years, and in the mixed African-creole couples it was fifteen years. These figures suggest that African women—always in the minority to African men—were able to marry quite quickly with men close to their age, but when African men could not obtain African women, they had to be older and of higher status in order to marry creole women. Based on the baptismal records for 568 children born on this plantation from 1860 to 1872, only 67 were named for living or dead relatives. This same low usage of the names of living or dead relatives was found in a study of some 130 slave families and their children in the baptismal records of several parishes in Rio de Janeiro from 1790 to 1830. In this case less than 5 percent of the children were so named. In both of the Brazilian cases, however, the patrilineal naming practices that were apparently the norm in the United States did not appear. The naming of children in Brazil came from both the paternal and maternal relatives. On the Resgate plantation, as in the region of Campinas, these slave marriages were quite stable and of long duration.

A secondary kinship system that developed among slaves in the Caribbean and Latin America is more easily studied. Known as godparenthood, it was a major fictive kin system used by all classes—including slaves—in Latin American and most Caribbean societies. Although few marriages were legally sanctioned, all births were recorded by the Church. In such Church recorded births, a fictive kinship pattern of compadrazgo (compadrio in Portuguese), or godparenthood, was established. This was a formal relationship between adults that bound them through their children. The godmother (comadre in Spanish and madrinha in Portuguese) or godfather (compadre in Spanish and padrinho in Portuguese) was supposed to be a close friend and one to whom the child could turn as a parent either if the child's own parents died or even if they remained alive. The co-parent was obligated to provide for that child on all special occasions and incorporate the child into his or her household if the other household ceased to exist. Equally, the friendship relationship among the fictive and real parents was further cemented by these ties so that special claims could be made between them for support and services.

Among the elite and for the Indians and black slaves, this institution was heavily based on friendship and respect, with either close personal friends or community-recognized elders and morally sanctioned persons as the most likely candidates for such a role. Thus white planters had fellow white planters as their godparent relations, just as Indians and slaves had fellow Indians, slaves, or freedmen from their own communities. Free coloreds, mestizos, and other middle groups were known to have sought godparents from higher status individuals and thus used *compadrazgo* as a means of establishing more formal patron-client relationships, an important but alternative development of the *compadrazgo* system. Slaves, too, were not beyond using *compadrazgo* as a tactic for solidifying such vertical ties, especially with the world of free coloreds. Thus in the Minas Gerais district of Senhor Bom Jesus do Rio Pardo, some 1,715 slaves were baptized between 1838 and 1887. Of this number, only 31 percent of the *padrinhos* or male godparents were fellow slaves, whereas 69 percent were free persons of color. For another 255 births no godfather was listed. The case of godmothers was similar, with only 38 percent of them being slaves. But there were also 385 births where no godmother was listed. This remarkable figure of having close to 60 to 70 percent of all godparents for slave children being free persons was also seen in the Bahian sugar parishes of Monte e Rio Fundo in the period from 1780 to 1789. However, this pattern was not consistent across all of Brazil's districts. In Rio de Janeiro, for example, in the parish of Inhaúma, between 1816 and 1842, only 33 percent of the 1,557 godfathers were free persons, and 64 percent of these slave godparents came from the same household or slaveholding as the child being baptized. Moreover, in contrast to other regions, the majority of the free persons serving as godfathers (almost three-quarters of them) were ex-slaves who had been freed within their own lifetimes (i.e., they were *forros*). In the case of the godmothers, the ratio of slaves was even higher, with 78 percent of the 656 women being slaves and 72 percent of these slave godmothers belonging to the same master as the baptized child. Whatever the variation from parish to parish, which at this point is difficult to explain, it should be stressed that few owners were godparents to their slaves, and that in the overwhelming majority of cases even the free persons were of color, were poor, and, as the case of Inhaúma suggests, were themselves recently freed persons, who may have known the child's parents when they themselves were slaves. Brazil also shows slaves acting as godparents to children born free. In the aforementioned Minas parish of Senhor Bom Jesus do Rio Pardo, roughly 35 percent of the 979 births of free children had a slave godfather, and among the 904 births of free children who had a godmother, slave women stood up for these children over 43 percent of the time. Clearly there was not a rigid barrier between poor free persons of color and slaves, and that friendship routinely crossed this boundary.

Despite the importance of *compadrazgo* as a structuring element in the extended family networks of Latin America's slaves, clearly the poorest elements in the society from which godparents were drawn could not always fully honor such obligations, and sometimes slaves were baptized with only a *comadre* and no *compadre* present. Although this was against Church practice and custom, it did reflect the weaker ties of the institution of *compadrazgo* at the lowest level of the society. Nevertheless, all accounts seem to indicate that it was an effective support system that became an essential part of Afro-American culture, just as it was of free society. This fictive kinship system went to further the growing bonds of friendship and community among slaves, and given the status with which godparentage was held by the governing elite, it even provided white legitimacy to slave community-building efforts.

The growing sense of slave community was reinforced by the very manner in which slaves were housed, especially on plantations. Field hands and most skilled slaves lived in what were often miniature African villages. The French West Indies were typical of many Latin American plantation regimes in this respect. In the 17th century and throughout most of the 18th century, planters usually made their slaves construct their own homes. These were usually built of mud and straw and were grouped around a communal area. Many of these early constructions were quite typical of African ones, and in one specific Martinique sugar plantation, the houses in the late 17th century were described as round with canonical pointed roofs in the African Mandingo style. On some plantations, parents lived in one house and children lived in another. Diversity was the norm, and such villages were common to all coffee estates in the French islands until the 19th century; slaves here were largely allowed to determine their own living arrangements. The result, as most commentators noted, was the creation of a village-style community.

But this was not typical for all plantations, especially in later periods. The increasingly capitalized sugar plantations of the late 18th and early 19th century began to emphasize planter control over the design and construction of slave housing. Planters' fears of fire as well as desire for better control led, in the larger sugar estates, to brick and mortar constructions of attached houses or barracks, which were usually built for the planters by outside contractors. Here the concern was with uniformity, better hygiene, and stronger control. Usually these houses had windows and were internally divided as well, but there was wide variation in space arrangements, and most estates still managed to maintain a number of older style, slave-built huts for a few families and for older slaves. While planter concepts of space began to predominate on the more advanced 19th-century sugar and coffee estates of Latin America, slaves still found ways to organize themselves within the new apartments or attached houses by providing separate quarters for families and separate living arrangements for single men and women. Nevertheless, the well-laid-out permanent construction of these estates was not common to the more numerous smaller plantations and farms found in Latin America. Here, African styles of housing continued to predominate.

Essentially, the experience of the French West Indies seems to have been the pattern adopted in residential construction for most other areas. The first century or two saw mud and straw huts usually constructed in a circle around a common open area. Then as plantations got bigger and richer, carefully delineated housing made of more permanent materials was built. In Brazil the separate houses were usually attached and laid out in a long rectangle. These so-called *senzalas* were usually subdivided into bachelor quarters and family units. They would often be located at a distance from cane fields and mills in order to prevent fire. They also often had walls to keep out small animals. As in the French islands, these *senzalas* were the norm on the richer estates but were not common to the smaller estates, whether dedicated to the cultivation of coffee or sugar.

The one exception to this pattern was the odd development of the so-called *barracones* on the Cuban sugar estates of the early 19th century. These sprung up during a period of very unbalanced sexual division within the early sugar gangs and were essentially long dormitories that had only one entrance, which was tightly guarded by the planters. Though important in only a few sugar zones, these *barracones* represented one of the most extreme anti–communal living structures ever created by the planter class of any Latin American slave regime. The harsh living conditions of these dwellings ultimately would not last long and were soon replaced by Brazilian-style long houses with their separate apartments and separate entrances.

The stress on families was also pronounced in the distribution of provisioning grounds for slaves. In most of the Caribbean and Latin America, plantation slaves were provided with their own separate gardens for raising food, most of which they consumed themselves. These *conucos*, gardens or provisioning grounds, became the basis for an alternative peasant lifestyle that developed within the rural proletarian model of the plantation. All adults had access to these "private" plots and were often allowed to sell excess production on the local market. Here families worked together to produce crops, and even single young adults of both sexes were given land. This arrangement for lands varied enormously from crop to crop and across national boundaries. In some French West Indian estates there was even a separate field gang of children and old people who worked under supervision on these food-producing fields along with personal slave labor on the smaller household gardens. In the British islands the provisioning grounds were quite extensive, and in Brazil they were traditionally treated as private plots.

Sometimes these fields were close to the slave quarters, and sometimes they were a considerable distance away. In all cases the planters allowed extensive work on these plots only in the free time which the slaves had on Sundays and holidays. That these gardens became a fundamental part of slave life was indicated in every protest movement led by slaves in the 19th century. As slave systems began to disintegrate, one of the first demands of the slaves was for more time on their own plots and the use of more lands for their gardens. The European-style, peasant nucleated village, with its centrally situated houses surrounded by fields, slowly emerged on the great plantations of Brazil and most of the West Indies even before abolition. Thus even under slavery, an economic basis was emerging for the development of a peasant village society, which shared many of the features of both the African and European village structure.

In terms of kinship and family, housing space, and land utility, the plantation provided the fundamentals for a community identity among slaves in Latin America and the Caribbean. This identity was even further reinforced by the development of a distinctive means of communication among the slaves. Within these plantation villages, Africans were forced to learn a lingua franca if there were not enough native speakers of their own particular African language. This lingua franca was usually a pidgin speech taken largely from the dominant European language. Over time, pidgin speech would evolve into a more complex creole language. These so-called creoles often had semantic borrowings from African languages, taken either from current slaves or from earlier migrants who most imprinted their norms on the first of the local dialects. But the syntactic structure remained largely Indo-European, and most of the basic vocabulary was shared by the whites and mestizos. The most prominent examples of these separate Afro-creole dialects were Haitian patois, Dutch colonial Papiamento, and the English-based Sranan of the Bush Negroes in Surinam. Local pidgins and creole languages also developed among small groups of coastal slaves in northern Spanish America. Consequently, even in their spoken language, black slaves quickly began to carve out separate but complementary aspects of the major national and regional cultures.

Equally important for the development of a community was the creation of a coherent belief system that would provide slaves with a sense of self, of community, and of their place in the larger cosmological order. The growth of a belief system would be a hard and slow task. One of the first areas where this evolved beyond the family level was in those practices that bound the community together. As in any peasant village, there were inevitable interpersonal conflicts among the slaves over resources. Sometimes these involved garden lands, personal effects, conflicts over potential spouses, sexual fidelity, or just personality clashes. These, plus the common problems of curing and divination, all led to the emergence of part-time specialists in witchcraft and curing.

Given the importance these crafts had within Africa, it was inevitable that African influences would emerge prominently. It was usually older and single African males and females who provided the white or black magic that was an indispensable part of any community structure. Such individuals prepared herbs for curing and for influencing desired emotional or physical states in given subjects. They also provided recourse to a system of rough justice, which guaranteed a limit to the amount of personal violence that the community could afford in fights over resources. Aggrieved adults who could not directly confront their opponents often had recourse to witchcraft to harm their rivals. This use of witchcraft and the knowledge that it was effective kept conflicts within acceptable limits within communities that had little policing powers of their own or any type of communal self-government.

These beliefs and uses of witchcraft, while African in origin, did not evolve from any single African source or completely elaborated set of known rituals. Rather, they tended to be an ad hoc mixture made up of many strands of different African beliefs. This was to be expected in colonial societies where such knowledge was not available in the highly coherent and structured form that specialists had developed it in Africa. In such an ad hoc development of admixtures of beliefs, it was not accidental that much American influence was also present, especially in areas where there was access to the knowledge of local Amerindian and mestizo populations, as in Brazil, continental Spanish America, and mainland South American colonies.

Indeed, in colonial Spanish America, particularly in Mexico, it has been argued that blacks eventually emerged as brokers of native magic and witchcraft. The influx of slaves to the colony brought scores of blacks into close contact with Indians, from whom they learned and shared ritual knowledge. Sometimes masters specifically sent their slaves to learn magic from natives, who they perceived to be experts in the casting of spells and the use of herbs. But also, the low social status of both blacks and Indians encouraged interracial contact. In time, free blacks and slaves alike were consulted on a regular basis by members of the colonial upper class to perform magic. It is hard to determine from the written record the degree to which the witchcraft that blacks practiced was of Indian or African origin. But whatever the relative influence of the origins of these beliefs, it is important to stress that because of the legitimacy that society had conferred upon Indians as being authorities in the supernatural arts, and because of the interrelationships between blacks and Indians, a sanctioned space was inadvertently created for Africans to enact magical knowledge and to legitimately preserve elements of African spiritual systems through their associations with native ritual culture. Of course, there were limits to what society sanctioned. Given the stereotypes about blacks and

Indians, blacks were deemed to be legitimate performers of harmful and manipulative magic, whereas Indians were seen as expert curers. Therefore, if a master sought to seduce someone or harm an enemy, he might consult his slave. But if he sought cures for an illness or the power to undo a spell, he would seek an Indian. Unfortunately for masters, one of the great problems with witchcraft was that its black practitioners could often utilize spells on the elite class, or even turn in a master to the Inquisition for requesting a slave to use magic. As early as the 1530s, a black slave woman denounced her master both for asking her to perform magic and for Judaizing—a fatal combination before the eyes of the Holy Tribunal. A century later in Mexico City, a Spaniard felt forced to confess an illicit relationship with a mulatto slave woman, Catalina St. Joseph, when she successfully conjured a spell to make him impotent after he had left her for the arms of a Spanish woman.

In Peru, another colony with a strong native presence, the role of witch-craft among slaves initially took a slightly different turn. Using Lima as an example, between the 1580s and 1590s the resident black population probably had closer socioreligious ties to the Spanish community than to natives. Some of this had to do with the fact that a number of slave men and women in the city had been exposed to Christianity and popular Iberian magical beliefs prior to being transported to the colony. Many had lived in Spain, Portugal, or Cape Verde, while others had been born there. Second, native contact with blacks in the urban capital was probably far less than in the rural countryside. Consequently, in the 16th century, the magic-ritual traditions developed by slaves primarily involved adapting Iberian and Catholic traditions to African ones. Between the 1620s and 1630s, blacks began to experiment more confidently with native ritual techniques and started integrating them into their magical practices. For instance, the Andean use of ritual cleansings, involving baths with herbs, maize, and guinea pigs, became a feature in the rites of some black female conjurers. As experimentation with native techniques continued, by the 1650s blacks were involved in processes of reinterpreting native urban witchcraft and infusing it with new meaning. Coca mastication among free and slave diviners and witches was routinely used as a source of divination. For some, such as a black woman from Pisco in 1655, the ritual use of coca also became the means of invoking the spirits of deceased Inca rulers who could provide divine assistance in assuring the success of spells.

While the spiritual content embedded within the practices of these black New World ritual specialists integrated multiple non-African elements, at the same time, in a number of colonies of the French, Portuguese, and Spanish worlds, slave beliefs began to evolve into ever more elaborate cosmologies, and complete African-influenced religions began to develop by the late 18th century and early 19th century. Masters were opposed to such formalized religious belief systems, which they held to be antithetical to their own Christian beliefs. Thus all such formal cults were ruthlessly attacked, just as the less threatening simpler forms of witchcraft were left unmolested. But so powerful did these religious systems become that they were able to survive under the guise of alternative forms of the folk Catholicism developed under slavery and occasionally even influenced the practices of the dominant white society, whose members sometimes turned to the practitioners of these religious systems for guidance and assistance in their affairs. Though it often took several generations after abolition for Christian society to accept their legitimacy, the cults were finally able to establish themselves as independent religions in the 20th century.

These religious cults were unqualifiedly African in origin, but, as could be expected, they retained only selective aspects of that original religion. In Africa, religion often had involved a full-time priesthood and was intimately related to family, lineage, and clan. It was also closely associated with hierarchy, social order, and government. Many of these functions were no longer of significance in the Americas and were thus abandoned. A typical case was the many rites and deities associated with agriculture, most of which were now no longer a significant concern of the Africans on the plantations of the white owners. Equally, those cults related to lineages, clans, and state structures became extremely difficult to maintain in the atmosphere of the slave societies in the New World, where such histories could not be maintained and where the clan and lineage groups were broken in the Atlantic crossing. But other deities and beliefs were supported in the New World. Those related to the individual and the immediate family in terms of life and death were given added impetus, and in the American slave society those beliefs that supported the slaves as a class in their respective positions of opposition to white oppression and self-identity and legitimacy were stressed. Thus the figures of Ogoun, the god of war, of Shango, the god of justice, and of Eshou, the god of vengeance, not only were given new importance in the American context but stripped of their agricultural or more mystical features, they took on more social and political aspects as gods of an oppressed class.

The most important of these cults in the era of slavery were Candomblé, Voudoun (Voodoo), and Santería. Each appeared in various guises throughout Latin America, though only one would predominate in any given area. Which one would predominate often had more to do with the history of local acculturation than with the weight of immigrant numbers. Thus a small initial group often established the basic cults that later massive migrations from entirely different areas in Africa adopted in their new environments. Even where many national candombles existed—as in Bahia, for example—it was the Nagô (Yoruba) Candomblé that provided the basis for the theology, ritual, and festival activity of all other candombles, even those named for Dahomean, Angolan, and Congolese tribes or nations. In Saint Domingue, where many cults (or mysteries) were established by groups from all over Africa, it was the Dahomean religious ritual of the Fon peoples that eventually dominated Voodoo practice and belief. Among the Bush Negroes in Surinam and Cayenne it was the Fanti-Ashanti culture that predominated, even though demographically many Bantu peoples were well represented among these escaped slaves. Thus a process of acculturation went on among the slaves themselves, even in terms of the proscribed African cults and practices.

This process of syncretization and acculturation among the African religions helps to explain in turn why these cults found it relatively easy to accept and integrate parts of Christian religious belief and practice into local cult activity. Initially this integration was purely functional, providing a cover of legitimacy for religions that were severely proscribed by white masters. But after a few generations a real syncretism became part of the duality of belief of the slaves themselves, who soon found it possible to accommodate both religious systems. In the Protestant societies this involved the selective acceptance of parts of orthodox religion. The stress on Moses and the liberation of the Israelites from Egyptian slavery, for example, were beliefs that fit in with the needs and aspirations of blacks, just as evangelical conversion experiences could be adapted to African rites. In the Catholic societies the dogma of the elite church was not affected, but a rich tradition of folk Catholicism with its saints and local cults provided a perfect medium for syncretization of African deities. Also, the elaborate structure of lay religious societies and local community saint days was extended to the slaves and free coloreds by the white authorities in their desire to integrate and control slave beliefs. They also hoped these associations, many of which in the early days were based on African tribal origins, would guarantee internal divisions among the slaves and prevent the development of a coherent racial or class identity. Though moderately successful in this aim, these associations and local festival activity proved of vital importance in both legitimating and spreading African religious practices and giving blacks and mulattoes important communal organizations.

After some hesitation, European governments and churches were committed to a policy of evangelizing slaves. This was a policy initially resisted by the planters, but which was eventually successful in almost all American societies by the end of the 18th century. By the 19th century most of the Protestant societies had special churches devoted to preaching to slaves, and some even allowed blacks and mulattoes to become lay preachers. But Catholic societies went even further and from the beginnings of American settlement provided slaves with their own religious brotherhoods and special cult activity. Aside from the formal Church-sponsored brotherhoods, civil authorities promoted voluntary associations of slaves and free Africans based on their own national identities and encouraged their civil-religious activity of mutual aid, cooperation, and social and religious observance. The aim of this policy was both paternalistic, in the sense that they wanted the Africans to accept their place in society, and political. In Cuba and Brazil, where the slave trade was bringing in large numbers of Africans up until the middle of the 19th century, the fear of African conspiracies was constant. Long experience showed that through encouraging ethnic self-identity among arriving Africans it became difficult for them to coordinate their rebellions. There are numerous examples in Latin America of slave conspiracies and rebellions of one group of Africans that were revealed to the authorities by opposing African groups. In the famous Bahian slave revolts of the 1830s there were even indications of rebel attempts to kill other slaves from the non-Muslim nations.

The institutions and beliefs encouraged by the whites for reasons of control and accommodation, however, also provided the slaves with an ideology and structure from which to create an Afro-American culture and religion. Such institutions and beliefs gave African and creole slaves a self-identity distinct from the white culture and also allowed an alternative religious system to develop. This duality of an African base under a Christian superstructure was not a rigid and compartmentalized system, for there were many who fully adopted the religion and values of the white master class. Urban mulattoes with education and wealth often were indistinguishable in their beliefs from white freedmen, just as many urban free coloreds who were skilled artisans became African cult leaders and were prosecuted for anti-Christian behavior. Leaders may have had a pure vision of their African religions, but their followers often confused their African deities with Catholic saints. Finally, the brotherhoods were effective in giving a sense of community to the slaves and free coloreds who had access to them and a stake in the maintenance of the system, just as they were a means of guaranteeing a distinct sense of community among their members.

The Catholic Church was already well organized for a syncretic approach to religious conquest and conversion even before the full-scale development of American slavery. The Latin American Church had worked out most of the norms of this activity in its evangelizing of the American Indians. Local gods were to be destroyed, but sacred places were to be incorporated into the Christian cosmology through the erection of churches and shrines and the miraculous appearance of the Virgin. A brown-skinned Virgin appeared in all the traditional pre-Columbian religious centers, and her devotion took on many aspects of pre-Columbian rites and beliefs. Though the intellectual and upper-class Catholics fought the reduction of their monotheistic religion into a pantheon of virgins and saints who took on the role of local deities, they never succeeded in cleansing the Church of its folk aspects, either in Europe or in America. Moreover the Church in early colonial Latin America was unusually open to the rise of popular nonclerical religious figures, the so-called *beatas*, or lay religious individuals who developed local followings and even founded religious institutions, many of whom came from the lower classes and castes. One of the most extraordinary of such *beatas* was the mystic slave Rosa Maria Egipcíaca da Vera Cruz. Born in West Africa, she arrived in Brazil from the Gold Coast at six years of age in 1725 and was eventually put to prostitution by her owner in Rio de Janeiro. Literate, a significant writer, and a mystic, she developed such an extraordinarily following and support, including that of the provincial of the Franciscan order in Rio de Janeiro, that she and her final owner and confessor, Padre Lopes, were eventually taken prisoner by the Inquisition in 1762 and shipped to Lisbon after the Church attacked her teachings. While *beatas* had been openly tolerated in the 16th and 17th centuries, the Church became more resistant and hostile to their activities over time, and Rosa like others in the 18th century, were more typically incarcerated and condemned if they developed important followings. In Mexico and Peru there also appeared blacks and mulattoes in the colonial period who declared that they were Christian mystics and received major support from the elite. Such was the case with the free mulata Ana Aramburu, who was sentenced in an auto-da-fé in 1802. In Peru, Ursula de Jesús (1604–66) was the slave of nuns for over twenty-eight years. After suffering an almost fatal accident, she began seeing visions and served as a widely known intermediary for souls seeking release from purgatory.

Into this system of syncretic absorption were implanted African belief systems. Very quickly each of the major African deities took on an alternative saint identification. In Brazil, for instance, local Brazilian saints had a dual identity in the minds of the slaves, if not in those of the whites. Church leaders in the colony encouraged local slaves to stress the cult of Our Lady of the Rosary (Nossa Senhora do Rosario), which was reserved exclusively for the special devotion of blacks. Though all slaves were taught to accept the feasts, holidays, and saints of whites, they were also expected to celebrate their own saint days and holidays on an exclusive basis. In the urban centers this meant that slaves were to be grouped into religious brotherhoods (known as *irmandades* in Brazil and *cofradías* in Spanish America) whose major purpose was to act as a mutual-aid society and prepare an annual celebration of the black-related religious figures. There were also special welfare societies (*Santa Casa*), which sometimes had black and mulatto branches. In Spanish America there were also black and mulatto social clubs (or *cabildos*), which were organized along nationality or occupational lines and stressed formal festival activity. It was these *cabildos* in Cuba that were the centers for the diffusion of the African cult of Santería on the island. There were even well-known dance groups or *batuques* in some of the Northeast cities of Brazil that were grouped along African nationality lines.

Every small town and city in Brazil and Spanish America had such black brotherhoods and associations that at any one time may have incorporated up to one-third of the slaves and a majority of the free colored population. But it was in Minas Gerais in Brazil that they reached their greatest wealth and importance. Given the prohibition of the Crown against the religious orders from establishing themselves in the mining zones, these brotherhoods took on far more activities than were typical in the other urban areas and small towns of Latin America. The black brotherhoods of all the towns of the region incorporated a majority of the slaves and free coloreds, possessed large incomes, and engaged in extravagant Church construction. They also played a primary cultural role and were the patrons for a thriving Baroque culture of music and art.

In most Latin American urban centers these associations were famous for their annual festive activities and, equally, for their constant conflict with white authorities. Slave and free colored demands for brotherhood self-government and control over their own churches and cemeteries were constantly opposed by the fraternal organizations of the whites. Despite white fears of their autonomy, in the majority of cases the black and mulatto brotherhoods were accepting of the dominant culture and were primarily integrative in nature. They did foster self-pride and also legitimated African religious activity. In contrast, the African cults were forced to create independent organizations to survive. In so doing, they became essentially rejective and opposed to the values of the master class. It was these cults that competed with and reinterpreted Christianity for a slave audience and most aided the development of an autonomous aspect to Afro-American culture.

From the plantation villages and the colonial cities came a distinctive Afro-American culture that provided the slaves with a self-identity and community, allowing them to survive the rigors of their forced integration into the white society. This Afro-American culture was not homogeneous. Some of its elements were integrative and merely expressive of a subculture within the Western norms established by the white society. Others, however, were unique to blacks and provided an alternative value system to that of white society. Such a pattern was almost inevitable given the very hostility and ambiguity that the white culture expressed toward them. On the one hand, white society incorporated Africans into Christianity as coequal members of a universalistic church. Among the Latin American legal codes there was also a basic assumption that Africans would eventually become freedmen in these same slave societies. But at the same time, these were inevitably racist societies that rejected black self-identity and self-worth and often created a second-class citizenship for those who achieved their freedom. Social ascension and mobility were possible for enough blacks to give a majority a sense of hope, but the terms frequently involved a rejection of elements of their Afro-American cultural identity and their blackness. In such a situation it was inevitable that the cultures that were established by the slaves in America would serve two often conflicting purposes: that of integrating the slaves into the larger master-dominated societies while also providing them with an identity and meaning that protected them from that society's oppression and hostility.

9

Slave Resistance and Rebellion

The growth of a sense of identity and community among African slaves in Latin America was essential for their survival as a society and group. Families were established, children were educated, and beliefs were developed that gave legitimacy to their lives. But many aspects of their lives were controlled by others. Their labor was defined by others and was not typically organized by households, as in the case of other working-class persons. Even their social behavior was restricted by whites when it clashed with the needs for control or the norms of behavior found acceptable by whites. Physical violence was also inherent in chattel slavery and created a level of fear and uncertainty unmatched by any other form of class or labor relations in America. Finally, even the physical well-being of the slave and his family was largely at the whim of his or her master and could be affected by considerations outside the slave's control.

Thus no matter how adjusted their culture and community might make them feel toward the American society in which they found themselves, slaves always felt a degree of dependency and loss of control, which created basic uncertainty and hostility toward the whole system. For those who were unable to conform, incapable of restraining their individuality, or unlucky enough to find themselves with no autonomy or protection within the system, escape, resistance, and rebellion were the only viable alternatives.

In most slave regimes in Latin America and the Caribbean the governments attempted to provide some protection for the slaves. This essential support for the humanity of the slave evolved out of a set of medieval laws, which were influenced by earlier Roman legal precepts. In these Iberian codes, slavery was recognized as an institution that was "against natural reason," as the 13th-century Siete Partidas codes declared (Partida IV, Titulo XXI, ley I), "because man, who is the most noble and free creature, among all creations that God made, is placed by it in the power of another" (Partida IV, Titulo V). This of course did not mean that the state would not legitimate any contract of sale or ownership of slaves. But it did mean that, while recognizing slavery as a necessary and historic institution, it also held that it was incumbent upon the state and its judicial institutions to guarantee certain minimal rights to the slave.

Of the three basic rights recognized in Roman law as defining a human being, that which related to personal liberty was automatically sacrificed under slavery. But the other primary rights, those involving one's security and property, need not be sacrificed for slavery to exist. A host of secondary rights also could be accepted that did not interfere with the definition of slaves as chattel; some of these held slaves accountable for their voluntary actions as a human beings, while others guaranteed them the rights of the sacraments as Christians.

In terms of protection for personal security, both the 13th-century Partidas of Alfonso X of Castile and the elaborated slave laws of the Ordenações Manuelinas (Manueline Ordinances) of Portugal of the early 16th century provided that killing of slaves by their masters or anyone else was a crime punishable by death. Although few, if any, masters on the Iberian Peninsula were actually executed for this crime, there were a fair number of cases of masters being exiled or paying major fines for such acts. These slave laws also protected slave women and children against violation and abuse by masters. In the case of personal property, the Portuguese and Castilian codes granted to the slave his or her peculium (or personal property), though leaving residual rights to such property in the hands of the masters. In contrast to later colonial acts and practices, the Iberian codes were restrictive of contracts made by slaves and of their property rights. But they were firm in the state's role in supporting the transition from slave to free status and guaranteeing in principle the right to self-purchase.

In terms of secondary rights, the codes provided that slaves could be tried by the state for crimes. In the Manueline Ordinances, in fact, slaves were subject to all the same punishments as lower-class free persons. The only difference from free persons was that masters could offer to pay the fines and commute the sentence through monetary settlement with the state. Like dependent children, slaves could sometimes serve as witnesses or even make some contracts. All of these rights usually were quite limited and always took into consideration the master's property rights in the slaves. But no Iberian code or municipal law assumed that a slave was without some of the basic rights of humans, no matter how supportive the laws were of chattel status and masters' needs.

The Catholic Church, although itself an active owner of slaves, accepted Africans as having immortal souls and granted to them all the rights to the sacraments. Though the Church was slow and limited in intervening between master and slave, it did play a role in every slave society in which it operated. In the first synods of bishops in the Americas, much legislation was dedicated to proselytizing among the slaves, granting them time for worship and even determining the legitimacy of their African practices of marriage and kinship in relation to Christian doctrine, although the reality was that the spiritual conversion of the native population was given greater attention, especially in the 16th century. While the Church emphasized that slave access to the sacraments was to be held above all claims of the master, even to the extent of having the Church purchase slaves to guarantee their Christian rights, the implementation of such policies was limited, especially given the restricted presence of the clergy in rural areas where many slaves worked. Nevertheless, slaves quickly came to understand their Christian rights. Equally, the Crown, in its effort to assert an increasingly absolutist authority in the New World, began to act in tandem with the Church to establish slaves as loyal Christian subjects. By these means, the Church and state created conditions to directly challenge the role of slave masters. Slaves often used their legal and Christian rights to defend themselves against exploitation.

One of the reasons the Church involved itself on behalf of African slaves had to do with the intermediary position that blacks held in relation to the New World and the Old World. Since Africans had been interacting with Europeans for centuries prior to the discovery of the Americas, they enjoyed a different and more established relationship with Europe's institutions of power. In a sense, unlike Indians, the experience of Africans in the colonies was partially shaped before they had ever set foot in the New World. Since medieval times, canon law had attempted to reconcile Africans with theories concerning the *extra ecclesiam*—an ecclesiastical term used for those who did not profess Christianity. The writings of Pope Innocent IV (1243–54) essentially established that all pagans and infidels living beyond the state of grace were legally allowed to enjoy temporal sovereignty and its attenuate rights. While Innocent's ideas were challenged, they also guided Spain and Portugal as they interacted with the Atlantic world during the high Middle Ages. Africans, therefore, were perceived as enjoying distinct rights as *extra ecclesiam* until professing Christianity, upon which they were subject to the full weight of Christian law. Strong challenges were made to Innocent IV's writings in the 15th century, effectively curtailing the independence of members of the *extra ecclesiam* that lived under European control. As a result, certain populations, like Jews and Moors, lost specific privileges they had long enjoyed, such as access to being tried in separate courts. African slaves living in Europe felt the weight of these policies as well, as efforts strengthened to bring them within the full folds of the Christian world. In the process, however, these same efforts to fortify Christianity served to more tightly associate Africans with the Old World, providing them both with many of the legal rights of European Christians, while at the same time subjecting them to the same mechanisms of Christian legal scrutiny.

Aside from forcing masters to allow their slaves time to worship and participate in the sacraments, the Catholic Church in Spanish and Portuguese America also tried to legitimate slave marriages. In all societies where the sacrament of marriage was performed, it was required that both the Church and the state could intervene to guarantee the sexual, moral, and even physical integrity of the slave family. This meant that slave spouses could not be separated by sale. In colonies like Mexico, however, this marriage benefit applied mainly when both marital partners were slaves; when one of the spouses was free, then the Church and state assumed that the free partner could relocate themselves and build a new life wherever the slave spouse was being sold. Of course, the laws protecting the sanctity of marriage also did not apply to illegal unions. Generally speaking, the high levels of illegal unions at all levels of society meant that, ultimately, marriage protections were offered to relatively few slaves. Although there was marked variation from region to region and among slave owners, it is probably correct to assume that no more than one-tenth to one-fifth of all married slaves were living in unions legally sanctioned by the Church in Spanish and Portuguese America by the 19th century, a figure well below all other classes in their respective societies. Although there is no clear preponderance of the sex of the slave or free person marrying someone of a different civil status, in parts of Mesoamerica, slave men contracted marriages in greater proportions than women. Nevertheless, despite the fact that the overall number of legal unions was low in the Iberian colonies, the figures for legal slave marriages for the French West Indies were far lower, and in the British and Dutch colonies formal marriages were practically nonexistent until late in the slave period.

In other areas, however, the pressure of the Church more significantly affected the lives of slaves. By the late 18th century and early 19th century, all slaves were nominally Christians, and most slaves were guaranteed their Sundays and holidays, which could be used by them for both work and religious purposes. Slave friendship and support networks through godparenthood were sanctioned and protected by the Church, which also supported fraternal societies of slaves. These were crucial secondary rights by which the Catholic Church guaranteed some of the bonds that held the slave community together, despite master opposition. Finally, the deliberate policy of providing black objects of worship, while quite paternalistic in intent, was vital in aiding the survival of African religious beliefs.

None of the Iberian legal codes on slavery passed to the New World without modification; in fact, many of them had already been revised in the 15th and 16th centuries to take into consideration the changing composition of the slave labor force and the different religious backgrounds of the slaves coming from Africa. In translating Iberian slavery to America, the laws designed for a largely domestic slavery had to be adjusted to the new-style plantation slave regimes emerging in the Atlantic islands and America. In some cases the medieval codes would be modified to support the rights of the slaves in a more concrete fashion, and at other times basic rights would be modified. Nor did all Roman law regimes provide equal access to the courts or equal sensitivity to slave needs. Finally, many of the legal rights of slaves were suspended in times of crisis and slave rebellion and there was even a serious attempt to close down much of the protective legislation during the generalized American elite reaction to the Haitian rebellion in the period from 1791 to about the 1830s and 1840s.

The single most basic change in the Ibero-American legal codes was the full-scale recognition to the right of self-purchase, or *coartación*. This had been implied in much of the Iberian legislation, but it quickly developed in customary practice in the Americas. Crown recognition of this practice came in the early 18th century in Spanish and Portuguese America, and by the 19th century it was recognized as a legitimate right with customary arrangements in all the courts. Such a system required a full-scale recognition of the slave's right to personal property and to the making of contracts. Highly circumscribed in the European legislation, this activity was fully accepted in the slave systems of Ibero-America. In both Spanish and Portuguese America, and to a lesser extent in the French possessions, slaves were allowed to keep the surplus from their own gardens on the plantations or were permitted to keep their earnings above rental if they were *negros de ganho*, or rented slaves. Work performed on Sundays and holidays was considered income-earning time for the slaves and accepted by the Church as a legitimate activity. To allow personal property for slaves made economic sense. It provided incentives for labor and often permitted owners to reduce their own maintenance costs. But it also gave slaves the cash with which to purchase their freedom independent of the will of the master. It was this legal right that was so effective in the case of both Cuba and Brazil in guaranteeing the growth of a major free colored population well before the period of emancipation.

The Ibero-American courts are filled with cases of the state intervening to guarantee sale prices and installment purchases of freedom for slaves.

Coartación was constantly expanded and reinforced in the Iberian colonies from the early colonial period into the 19th century. It was an important and well-known tool for urban slaves to achieve control over their lives even before the granting of full freedom. Slaves who had made a down payment on their purchase price could not be sold or transferred from their normal residence, and they could also appeal to the authorities to protect their claims and rights against masters at any time.

Some American revisions of European slave legislation moved in the opposite direction. This is most evident in the French legislation, which in the Code Noir issued for the French West Indies colonies in 1685 proved to be one of the more oppressive slave codes in the Americas and one that remained in force until the French Revolution and again for some time in the 19th century. Slaves were declared chattel without any rights to property or personal protection. Severe punishments were given for running away, and masters had the right to chastise slaves at their discretion and to the degree that they wished. Slaves could not make contracts and were excluded from even the minimal rights granted to children and other dependents. Even rights to the sacraments were qualified. Slaves could not marry without the consent of their masters and, though required to be baptized, were not granted any specific time for religious education and worship. In only one aspect was the Code Noir at all positive toward slave rights, and this was in terms of manumission. Although no provisions were initially made for self-purchase, any slave who was freed by a master was given full legal rights to citizenship. This aspect of the code was in fact quite advanced for its time and would cause an endless amount of conflict between whites and free coloreds in 18th-century French America. Bitter racial conflict led to constant attempts by local whites to restrict the freedoms of manumitted slaves, which even led to short-term prohibitions of manumission and denial of legal equality to those already liberated. But in the end the free coloreds in the French possessions became one of the most economically powerful and important classes in American slave society, even though the draconian Code Noir kept their numbers much more reduced than in the Iberian possessions. Also, self-purchase eventually became part of customary local law, though not as much used and developed an institution as in the Ibero-American world.

Although historians have sometimes downplayed the relevance of law to slavery and its daily existence in America, there is little question that the entire edifice of slavery could be constructed only with the indispensable assistance of the state. Property by its very nature is a legally based institution, and contracts are founded on the ability of the state and its courts to enforce them. Without state activity slavery would not have existed. Though the master's rights were emphasized far more than those of the slave, the state had every right to interest itself in the "peculiar institution," as North Americans called it. It was no accident that the enslavement of Indians largely ended in the 17th century when the Portuguese and Spanish crowns refused to recognize legal title to such slaves. It is equally clear that abolition effectively occurred in every slave state when the governments declared such legal contracts null and void. This does not mean that the more protective and paternalistic parts of the slave code were always and everywhere enforced. Practice differed quite dramatically among nations and even by region. In most cases, the more rural and plantation bound the slave, the less access he or she had to legal redress of grievances, especially since courts were more prominent in urban zones. But in many cases the fundamental principles of the law were sufficiently well known and recognized to afford some minimal rights of protection to a significant number of slaves wherever they were found.

Despite these customary and legal rights and protections, many slaves were at the unqualified will of their masters and overseers. For these slaves the only recourse open to arbitrary behavior was resistance, escape, or violence. In terms of resistance, there were several options available to slaves, but one of the more interesting ones in the Spanish colonies proved to be blasphemy. Research on 16th- and 17th-century Mexico reveals that slaves, oftentimes in the midst of being punished or whipped by their masters, resorted to renouncing God or Christianity as a means of trying to put an immediate end to their agony. Typically, slaves had several goals in mind. First, the act of blasphemy theoretically required the master to stop inflicting punishment and to denounce the slave to the Inquisition. At a basic level, slaves understood this principle, although in practice a master's wrath actually increased upon hearing blasphemous utterances, bringing about an even more severe administration of punishment. In resorting to blasphemy, slaves also had a second objective, namely, to send a warning to their owners. Both slaves and masters had implicit understandings of what were considered "acceptable" levels of exploitation and affliction under slavery. Masters who breached these levels broke the implicit contract. With respect to whippings, Mexican slaves appear to have understood that between fifteen and thirty lashes might be expected as a slave punishment. They also understood that slaves would be typically tied to ladders, stairs, or chairs for such whippings. But when masters engaged in more extreme cruelty, such as pouring hot oil over a slave during floggings, substantially increasing the number of blows, do using slaves in baths of urine, or maiming their genitals, slaves retaliated with shouts of blasphemy. Slaves were well aware that through blasphemy they stood a chance of usurping the authority of their patriarch. If they could get an audience before Church officials, even though they were being tried for renouncing Catholicism, slaves had a chance to air their grievances and expose owner abuse. As typical blasphemy cases unfolded, slaves might attempt to justify their sin as unintentional, given that their actions came at the hand of severe mistreatment. Slaves could even reveal long-term patterns of abuse in their arguments, which further incriminated their masters. Indeed, slaves displayed remarkable adeptness in using legal strategies. Many appeared before the tribunal as humble and pious Christians, thereby underscoring their claims that their momentary lapse of blasphemy was out of character and prompted by extenuating circumstances. Others, such as Gertrudis de Escobar, who blasphemed in 1659, deftly spun testimony to implicate their masters in prompting blasphemy. Under the duress of being whipped on the back by her master and being struck in the head by an Indian maid with a ring of keys, Gertrudis pleaded "for the love of God, leave [me] alone." As the abuse continued, she cried twice that she would be compelled to renounce the Lord, despite being a Christian. Curtly, her master replied: "Renounce, mulata if you have to."

Few masters were formally prosecuted for their actions in blasphemy cases. But as a consequence of the trials their slaves might be placed in the custody of another, more benevolent owner. Generally speaking, slaves who were recent arrivals to the New World (bozales) enjoyed a distinct advantage in court, since they could always use the plea that it was their unfamiliarity with Christianity that inadvertently caused them to renounce the faith. Interestingly, however, some slaves voluntarily turned themselves in to the Inquisition for blasphemy. This was a calculated act. In one single stroke, the preemptive move affirmed their true inner piety while at the same time opening up the floor to launch a litany of complaints against their master. Meanwhile, outside of the framework of blasphemy, slaves could resist a master's authority through other efforts of religious deviance. Some consciously sought to befriend and employ the power of the devil. Occasionally, if slaves were afraid of being sold to another master, sought to counter a punishment, or aspired to challenge a master's authority, then employing the services of the devil appeared to be a powerful, if not a desperate, move. The fear that masters, society, and the Church displayed toward the devil encouraged slaves to seek him out. Slaves also realized that the devil represented the very antithesis of the world order that kept them in bondage. In this sense, whereas colonial society may have construed Satan as evil, the enslaved could perceive him as a good ally for their cause.

While blasphemy and the occult proved to be interesting mechanisms for resistance, there were other, less spectacular forms of protesting the conditions of slavery. Backed by colonial law, slaves also mounted litigation against their masters in secular courts from the earliest years of colonial slavery. Some of these cases were *reclamaciones* (freedom lawsuits) that petitioned a slave's right to self-purchase or to freedom. But as with blasphemy cases, slaves also commonly protested mistreatment (*sevicia*), broadly defined. This could include the denial of conjugal rights, physical abuse, verbal abuse, neglect, and so forth. In a secular court of law, as opposed to the ecclesiastical tribunals, slave tactics changed slightly. A heavy burden fell upon slaves to present themselves as "honorable" royal subjects who needed the "mercy" of the Crown to overcome grave episodes of dishonor. Being honorable required a courtroom performance and a familiarity with certain colonial protocols. Slaves bringing cases in 17th-century and early 18th-century Quito, for instance, knew to be quietly humble, to bow and prostate themselves before court scribes, placing their heads in their hands. They expressed fealty to the king and the Christian God, emphasizing that they had been "baptized in the faith." In their hearings they explicitly appealed that the court not be "malicious" in its judgment—a caution that emphasized the vulnerability of slaves and the potential hostilities that circulated against them in broader society. In cases of physical abuse, the most compelling evidence was the slave's "body" itself, which, when unclothed, could reveal brutal lacerations, wounds, and permanent scars. In Quito such cases are found in the record from at least the 1590s, and over the centuries, slaves became more adept at employing legalese. Because honor was such an important aspect of colonial life, slaves learned its codes and when to press the issue in court. Some set out to mar a master's reputation by demonstrating how they, as Catholics, withheld slaves from hearing mass or set them to work on Sundays. In the city of Guayaquil in 1794, María Chiquinquirá Díaz tussled with Presbyter Afonso Cepeda de Arizcum Elizondo, her purported master. Chiquinquirá declared that she and her daughter were free, given that her mother had been able to secure their liberty. But as with many black women who alleged their freedom, masters responded with severe character attacks that jeopardized their honor. Many were assumed to be prostitutes who slept with scribes to get their way in court. In María's case, Presbyter Cepeda responded with stinging accusations—calling her a "filthy bitch...worse than a whore, a prostitute and lascivious." María responded with equally slighting attacks on his honor, claiming Cepeda to be lascivious himself, a man of the cloth who fraternized sexually with his own slaves and fathered their children.

While María was more free than slave, the courtroom performances and deference exhibited by litigants who were clearly classified as chattel actually served to cement the fact that they were not simply royal subjects but subservient slaves. In no uncertain terms, therefore, slaves in court resisted their masters by embodying the very stereotypes that marked their status as chattel. In other words, their acts of resistance were enabled because they were model slaves. What partly allowed slaves to use the courtroom as an effective resistance strategy was that there were other slaves in the colonial world who were more rebellious and provided an alternative example of possible slave behavior. From the perspective of the Crown, small slave victories in a court of law might prevent more damaging shocks to the overall system.

So, ultimately, the tactics of blasphemy, litigation, and even resorting to the occult did not precipitate substantial changes in the dominant social order, even if they brought some relief to individual slave lives. Colonial society absorbed the blows and continued on. However, to increase their freedom, slaves did engage in more threatening activities that were not sanctioned within law. From the very first days in all American slave societies, running away, or *marronage*, became a common occurrence. In the majority of cases this escape from the plantation was temporary, for most slaves hid in nearby woods. This so-called *petit marronage*, or temporary absence, was such a common occurrence that in most Latin American and Caribbean societies an elaborate arrangement of intervention was developed. In Cuba, for example, a slave would seek out a third party, often a priest, local doctor, or trusted slave driver, and try to guarantee protection from retribution. Given the costs of prolonged absences, the planters and overseers were often willing to negotiate with the slaves. In some cases, the demands of the runaways could be quite elaborate. Thus some runaways in Bahia in the 18th century refused to return to the plantation unless they were given more time to work on their own gardens.

Though a common occurrence and associated with informal arrangements for mediation, there was no guarantee that reprisals would not be taken. In such cases slaves were whipped, incarcerated, manacled, and even tortured. But in other instances they were accepted back with little punishment. Since *petit marronage* could turn into what the French called the *grand marronage*, or permanent escape, there were some constraints on the conduct of the masters. If no negotiation were possible, or if the terms of the negotiation were violated, then slaves left the vicinity of the plantation and headed for permanent escape. Their ability to do this successfully depended on a variety of factors that varied regionally and from colony to colony. The existence of dense forests or inaccessible mountains within a short distance from the plantations was one crucial factor. Another was the availability in these inaccessible regions of soils and climates that allowed for local food production. Finally, a relatively benign Indian frontier was essential if the escaped slaves were to be able to establish a permanent settlement.

Even where dense settlements of Indian peasant communities would have suggested a rigid frontier, escaped slaves were common. In the southern Andes (in the region of modern Bolivia), slavery existed within a context of high migratory activity. Natives in the region were seemingly in perpetual motion—they could not be anchored to estates or kept within their native communities. African slaves followed suit. In some cases, the very occupations of slaves in this region facilitated *marronage*. A few worked on pack teams that guided mules and horses throughout the cordillera. Routes of escape could be easy here, or just as likely, some slaves switched masters fluidly, running away from one to join the team of another.

In the northern Andean regions of the Peruvian coast, black slaves and native laborers were equally mobile. Slaves frequently traveled from Spanish estates to trade with indigenous villages. Both populations had products that the other lacked, which piqued an interest in commerce. Runaway slaves made use of these long-standing trade relationships. Despite the fact that many native communities in the region, such as those in the valley of Chicama in 1621, requested the colonial government to enforce laws that removed blacks from indigenous townships, some natives were still willing to embrace fugitive black slaves who arrived to their settlements asking for work. Throughout the Andes, it was customary for slaves to be rented from one master to another. Therefore, fugitive slaves could appear at a township, seeking work under this guise, when in reality they were maroons. Natives, having plenty of land but being short on labor, welcomed the situation as a means to improve their local economies. But they tolerated maroons only up to a point. As large settlements of runaway slaves emerged in the northern Andes, some preyed on native communities. In the 1630s and 1640s, natives complained of these attacks, and in 1641 they participated in an incursion against a runaway settlement in the Santa Catalina valley.

An alternative frontier for the escaped slaves was the city or absorption within free colored society. This was possible only if large urban centers with many self-employed slaves and freedmen existed near the plantations. Alternatively, in Brazil there was also a large free colored population living in rural areas that was especially difficult to police and proved to be an ideal group into which escaping slaves could disappear. Numerous were the advertisements for runaway slaves who were defined as claiming they were free persons. While a relatively open and benign rural frontier existed for many of the American slave regimes, the urban and free colored possibilities were relatively unique to the Ibero-American societies. It was only in Brazil and Spanish America that major urban centers and large free colored populations existed on a scale significant enough to offer a possible haven for escaped slaves.

The aims of most runaway slaves were conservative: to escape from slavery and to lead normal lives as free peasants. But to establish viable communities they needed women, tools, seeds, and other supplies. Until that stability could be achieved, such communities often raided the settled plantation areas and otherwise found themselves in bitter and often bloody conflict with whites and other free persons. To hide and escape was their prime aim, but it could often be achieved only by predatory activities that provoked retaliation. In the case of Brazil these slave communities, known as *quilombos*, became havens for fugitives of all kinds and were thus constantly attacked by the authorities. Finally, in some rare instances in Brazil and the Guyanas, some of these settled communities joined in larger rebellious movements of either slaves or other opponents to the established order. So bitter did the conflict between the runaway communities and the masters become that all slave societies employed local militia groups and even paid mercenaries, both blacks and whites, to destroy these communities and recapture the runaways. So intense were these internal wars, and so difficult the requirements for success, that the establishment of viable runaway communities was a complex and difficult task that often required a series of fortuitous developments.

In the case of the West Indies, the so-called maroon communities usually had their origins in mass escapes of slaves that occurred as a result of social and political conflict within white society. Jamaica's famous maroon communities originated from the mid-17th-century English invasions when slaves on Spanish-owned estates escaped en masse into the island's interior. The maroon communities of the Guyana territories mostly dated their origins to foreign military invasions, which disrupted the whole system of control developed by local planters. Once firmly established and well known to local slaves, these communities could survive and prosper without the intervention of external events such as foreign wars and invasions. Prior to the formal maroon treaties, runaway slaves in small numbers could find their ways to these communities and if they were not a threat to the community on account of being actively pursued, they usually received a warm welcome.

Although all slave societies had runaway communities, Brazil probably had the most numerous, longest lasting, and most widespread distribution of such *quilombos* in the Americas. By a decree of 1741 the Portuguese Crown defined *quilombos* as any community consisting of five or more runaway slaves. Such communities had already been in existence for well over a century, and others would be continually founded until the middle decades of the 19th century. The reasons for the intensity of *quilombo* activity in Brazil have a great deal to do with both the size of the slave labor force introduced into the country and the open nature of the frontier in all regions of plantation activity.

This frontier was already inhabited by fugitives from justice and by a large and essentially antisocial class of mestizo frontiersmen known as *caboclos*. Until the end of slavery in the late 19th century most of Brazil's commercial agriculture production and mining was confined to the coastal region or interior zones that were surrounded by frontiers. Unlike the 19th-century United States, the slave zones of Brazil were neither blocked by a hostile Indian frontier nor surrounded by white agricultural settlements, but rather had access to open frontiers everywhere.

Quilombo activity was correlated with the distribution of slaves throughout Brazil. Though they could be as far south as Santa Catarina, most of the early and largest *quilombos* were found in the sugar region of the Northeast. The best known of these was one of the earliest. This was the community of Palmares in the region of Pernambuco, along the present-day Pernambuco-Alagôas border. The Palmares Republic was an amalgamation of several communities, all of which had passed through their earlier predatory stage and had established thriving autonomous agricultural communities. These fortified villages were organized into a tax-collecting centralized state under a king. Their agriculture and religion were a mixture of African, American, and European elements. Originating in the earliest years of the 17th century, these communities gained large numbers of new adherents because of the intense Dutch-Portuguese conflicts in the first half of the century. By the 1690s, when Palmares had reached the apogee of its power and importance, it counted some 20,000 persons, among whom were many who had lived in their communities for three generations. Both the Dutch and the Portuguese attacked these communities from the 1630s on, but they continued to grow and even succeeded in establishing a state-supported army with weapons stolen or purchased from the enemy. In the 1670s their king, Ganga-Zuma, had tried to sign a capitulation treaty with the Portuguese, but younger leaders killed the king and continued the war until extinction. After some sixty years of intermittent campaigning a royally financed army finally succeeded in destroying the republic in 1695.

In the 18th and 19th centuries there were several important *quilombos* established in distant isolated zones such as the Amazon, as well as close in toward the most thriving slave areas. In the mining district of Minas Gerais there were some 160 known *quilombos* in the 18th century. They ranged in size from a few dozen inhabitants to one *quilombo* with a thousand residents. This later was the kingdom of Ambrósio, or Quilombo Grande, whose 1,000 slaves lived in several palisaded villages (or *palenques*). After much resistance, the *quilombo* was finally destroyed in 1746. Many of these communities had formal structures, and royal documents record the existence of kings, captains, and other leaders of the community. One leader captured in Minas in 1777 claimed that he was the king of the stockaded *quilombo* that had been destroyed, and that he had been a *capataz*—or slave driver/foreman—on his old *fazenda*. In Mato Grosso the *quilombo* of Quariterê was probably founded in 1730 and existed sporadically for well over half a century. When it was destroyed for the first time in 1770, it contained 79 fugitive slaves and 30 Indians living together under a king and queen. After being rebuilt, the *quilombo* was assaulted again in 1795, and some 54 fugitive slaves were taken. Mato Grosso also had one of the largest *quilombos* in the 19th century; Vila Maria, or the *quilombo* of Sepotuba, remained in existence for at least a century, and during the 1860s it was said to contain 200 armed ex-slaves. In the Amazon river town of Trombetas to the northwest of Manaus the *quilombo* of Para was created in 1820 under the leadership of the *cafuzo* (or mixed Indian and black) slave Atanasio. By 1823 it had a population of 2,000 runaway slaves and was unusual in its active contact with white society and intervention in the market economy. It not only traded with local Indians and whites but also was exporting cacao and other commercial crops to Dutch Guyana. Destroyed once in 1823, it was re-created by Atanasio and lasted into the 1830s. A group from these communities even went further upriver and founded Cidade Maravilha, which in the 1850s was sending its children to the white communities to be baptized. In the 19th century there even occurred *quilombo* involvement in rebellions led by free whites against the imperial government. In Maranhão in the late 1830s, under the leadership of the ex-slave Cosme Bento das Chagas, the *quilombo* of Campo Grande fielded an army of 3,000 ex-slaves, which participated in a Liberal revolution led by the local whites. An imperial army soon put down the republican revolution in Maranhão and then turned on the maroons, destroying the Campo Grande *quilombo*. The inherent problems of the *quilombos*, however, was reflected in the experience of the unconquered *quilombo* Manso in Mato Grosso, which reportedly had an estimated population of 293 persons in the late 1860s. There were only 20 adult women and 13 children in the settlement. This distorted sex ratio goes a long way to explaining the inherent instability of many these communities, as the need for women drove many *quilombo* residents to raid the fazendas and thus provoked reactions from the slave owners.

These well-known and mostly destroyed *quilombos* were, of course, the exceptions. The hundreds of *quilombos* that left their names in the topography of all Brazil's provinces were most often communities of a few dozen ex-slaves who sought withdrawal and anonymity as much as possible. Some of these communities blended in so well that they eventually became indistinguishable from the general *caboclo* and other subsistence farming villages. Others were so bold that they even temporarily founded their homes close to the country's biggest cities. What is clear, however, is that they existed in all regions and at all times, and served as a viable option for runaway slaves, especially as the Brazilians rarely negotiated formal treaties with the maroon communities to close them off to fugitive slaves. Their importance was recognized by the fact that there was a separate military organization that existed everywhere in Brazil to capture runaway slaves and destroy *quilombos*. In Minas in the 18th century, for example, there was established a separate Regimento dos Capitães-Do-Mato whose exclusive role was to hunt runaways and destroy *quilombos*. Their pay was based on their capture rates, and some 15 percent of these troops were *forros*, or freedmen who had been born slaves. There were even cases of slave owners getting royal patents to be Capitães-do-Mato who armed their own slaves and put them into combat units, one of the few known cases of slaves being armed in large numbers. One expedition in 1769 had 58 armed slaves and an accompanying slave chamber orchestra playing minuets who were owned by the leader of the expedition.

Such runaway communities existed in all the Spanish American colonies, but few could match those in Brazil, in size and number. These settlements were mostly associated with isolated rural industries such as mining or fishing, or with ranching and farming. The largest and most active of the *cimarron* (maroon) *palenques* were those established in the mountains near the coast in Mexico, Panama, and what is today northern Colombia and Venezuela. One of the earliest such communities was founded in 1549 by escaping pearl divers on the island of Margarita off the coast of Venezuela. This was the home of one of the more brutal slave regimes. In the middle of the 16th century as many as 2,000 to 7,000 maroons may have also been scattered about the island of Hispaniola (Santo Domingo) in numerous *palenques*. As many as 30,000 blacks lived in the colony during these years, along with just 1,200 whites. The time was ripe for maroon activity, and one of the most feared rebel leaders of the 1540s, Lemba, routinely launched raids from the Bahoruco Mountains into the Spanish settlements of the central valley. His tactic of choice was to separate his army of 140 warriors into small packs that punished Spanish enterprises. Meanwhile, from 1553 to 1558 another major group of maroons was established under an African nobleman known as King Bayano in the Isthmus of Panama. But the most active period of local maroon activity here was in the 1570s, when Sir Francis Drake came upon some 3,000 maroons in the province of Panama, many of whom joined his raiding expeditions. Venezuela also had some large *palenques*, the most important of which was established in the 1550s under King Miguel, a creole slave from Puerto Rico who led the local gold mine workers in a revolt. Some 800 slaves were organized in a government that shared many features of Spanish civil and religious organization. This, like many of the *palenques* from Panama, was joined by rebel Indians, and the two groups did extensive raiding in the region. By the 18th century, Venezuela approached Brazil in becoming a haven for *palenques* (also known as *cumbes*)—official reports estimated nearly 20,000 maroons in the colony by 1720, and as many as 30,000 by 1800.

The nearby province of Cartagena on Colombia's Caribbean coast was also an important center of maroon activity, which reached its height in the 1690s. At that time a major campaign found some dozen significant *palenques*, four of which contained more than 200 maroons each. These were organized under kings and religious leaders, but farming was done in family units. As in Venezuela and Mexico, this type of major maroon activity died out by the early 19th century, largely because of a decline in local slavery and a shrinking of frontier areas. Though small groups of fugitives survived to the end of slavery, the most active period of maroon activity was starting to wane by the late 1700s.

No slave regime accepted the existence of the maroon communities with equanimity. As in the case of Palmares, local and even national armies were eventually sent to destroy the settlements and reenslave the fugitives. But despite a great deal of effort, many of these communities were able to defend themselves effectively against all assaults. When such maroon communities became too dangerous and too powerful to destroy, the white societies ended by formally negotiating peace treaties with them. One of the earliest of such treaties was signed with a maroon named Yanga in the region of Veracruz, Mexico, in 1609. The hundred or so ex-slaves who had successfully resisted Spanish authority for some three decades finally received their freedom and legal community recognition in return for stopping all raiding and returning all future runaway slaves. The treaty led to the foundation of the town of San Lorenzo de los Negros in 1618, but it was unclear how effective the township would be in thwarting maroon activity in the region. As a security measure, that same year the Mexican viceroy established another town (Córdoba) with a white and mestizo population whose mandate it was to curb insubordinate fugitive slave activity. When major slave unrest erupted again in Mexico more than a century later (1725 and 1735), it was precisely in the sugar mills near the city of Córdoba where the violence occurred. Maroons formed themselves into new *palenques* that proved impossible to defeat, as colonists quickly discovered during five failed military expeditions between 1748 and 1759. New treaties had to be drafted. But Spain's entry into the Seven Years' War changed the context in which negotiations occurred. Fears of British invasion diverted the colonial government and made them willing to grant amnesty to any maroon who was willing to help fight against the English threat. A peace treaty was drafted, and in 1769, seven years after the maroons helped the Spaniards defend the port of Veracruz, the town of Amapa was founded by these former rebels.

Additional treaties were signed throughout the Spanish kingdom, with varying effects. One of the more interesting cases comes from Esmeraldas (Ecuador). Black slaves first arrived at this forbidding coastal region of the kingdom of Quito in the shipwrecks of 1545 and 1553, en route from Panama to the slave markets of Peru. Most of the few Spaniards on the voyages perished quickly; those who were able to survive and reach a Spanish settlement arrived without their slave cargo. In the years that followed the shipwrecks, the maroons of Esmeraldas began founding their own settlements and intermingled with the local native population, even dominating them in some cases. Indeed, Spanish observers noted that many of the emerging maroon chiefdoms gradually adopted native political organization and dress, such that it became hard to distinguish them from the local Cayapa, Malaba, Lachas, and Barbacoas cultures. Meanwhile, native patterns of matrilineal descent worked to integrate other blacks directly into native society, as maroon fathers had children with native women. As these events unfolded, the Spanish government took note and came to construe the emerging maroon settlements as key potential allies in their efforts to bring the zone under colonial control. There were practical reasons for Spanish interests. Not only was the region fabled to be rich in emeralds, but the nearby city of Quito perceived Esmeraldas to be an excellent staging ground for constructing a port that could receive and export goods. It was known that the Guayllabamba River, flowing northwest from Quito, turned into the great Rio Esmeraldas. A port at the mouth of the Santiago and Cayapas rivers was another option—either way, both locations offered excellent shortcuts to and from Panama, potentially saving vast amounts of money for merchants paying daily freight charges. Other Spaniards viewed the region's native population as an important labor base that, if harnessed, could prove useful to the health of the economy and the designs of the colonial elite. Still others sought to curb the rising pirate activity in the area by establishing a strong Spanish presence. Between 1526 and 1590, however, the Spaniards had unsuccessfully launched over 30 expeditions to conquer the region. Some thought that entry into Esmeraldas might better be facilitated through maroon intermediation. In 1576, the maroon leader Alonso de Illescas fortuitously approached the colonial government requesting a peace settlement in exchange for recognizing the freedom of his followers. The Spanish government seized this opportunity to use Illescas as a tool in its plans for conquest, bestowing upon him the title of governor. All he had to do in return was to compel rival maroon settlements and native chiefdoms to settle at the mouth of the Esmeraldas River. Unfortunately for the Spaniards, the plan backfired, and a deep power struggle ensued that brought warfare to the region. When a firmer peace was signed in 1599, the region remained far from Spanish control, resulting in multiple additional periods of negotiation lasting into the 1610s. Some of the new efforts involved resolute attempts at Christianizing the region and, through proselytizing, subduing the maroon presence. But throughout the early 17th century, maroons, Spaniards, and natives remained embattled with one another, with only limited periods of cooperation. Maroons altered existing patterns of warfare, sacked Indian villages, seized native captives for labor, and took women to build up the population base of their communities. At the same time they served as guides to Spanish expeditions and provided limited aid and cooperation in colonizing projects. They also made a habit of rescuing the shipwrecked passengers of Spanish vessels. However, when Spaniards encroached upon maroon territory, or "liberated" natives from mulatto lands in order to put them to work on Spanish estates, the maroons responded with swift violence.

In retrospect, Spanish treaties, titles, and negotiation efforts proved weak in incorporating the maroons on Spanish terms. This resulted from what appears to have been a conscious maroon strategy. By constantly toggling between being the Spaniards' friends and their enemies—in other words, by performing a juggling act of cooperation and resistance—the maroons of Esmeraldas kept the colonial regime at bay. Effectively, the maroons were able to manage the relationship between themselves and the government by deciding to what degree and in what ways they were willing to cooperate with the Spanish. They were able to wield such power in their relationship with the Crown because of the difficulties that Spaniards had in establishing a presence in Esmeraldas. Ultimately, it became clear that in this corner of the empire, communities of former slaves would operate with relative independence into the 18th century. As negotiations with Esmeraldas started to falter, Spaniards began ignoring maroon areas, effectively isolating them by limiting the construction of roads and keeping the settlements removed from the normal channels of communication. They consciously refrained from conferring too many political concessions to the maroons, lest they inspire subordination among other blacks that were starting to arrive to the colony. As Esmeraldas grew further removed from the main body politic, its black and mulatto residents became even more deeply entwined in native ways of life, although retaining an identity that was distinct from that of local Indians. Quite literally, the maroon zone transformed into being a *zambo* (mixture of Indian and black) realm of the empire.

Treaties with runaway slaves were also signed in Colombia and the Carib-bean. In Colombia, the *palenque* of San Basilio, which had existed for sixty years and had nearly 3,000 residents, was transformed into a township in 1686. In the Caribbean, perhaps the most famous treaty was signed with the maroons of Jamaica in the 1730s. This was followed by formal treaties in the next decades with maroons in all the other major islands where they existed. The longest lasting of these treaties were signed with the Surinam maroons in the 1760s and guaranteed their independence. In many cases, particularly in the Spanish kingdom (as seen in Esmeraldas), the intervention of clerics proved important to infiltrating maroon settlements and helping establish the terms of peace. Usually, treaties were also written at the expense of the future runaway slaves, who were to be returned promptly to their masters. Normally, maroons were obliged to accept a representative of the local white government in their midst, even if they otherwise had black political representation. These individuals helped enforce the clauses in the treaty that called for the return of new fugitive slaves. Even in Brazil, where such formal treaties were not developed, local arrangements usually left *quilombos* unmolested if they returned runaway slaves.

In most Caribbean slave colonies maroon communities were eventually destroyed as plantations expanded into previously inaccessible frontiers, thereby ending their isolation. In the case of Brazil, Cuba, and the colonies of South America, however, the frontier continued to exist to the end of slavery, and thus maroon communities could often survive until then, eventually transforming themselves into peasant subsistence agricultural communities. In the case of the Bush Negroes of Surinam and the Black Caribs of Dominica and Central America, these maroon communities still survive as coherent and differentiated societies that are greatly influenced by African or Afro-Amerindian culture.

The ability to escape the system through running away, either for a short time or for longer periods, and hiding among urban slaves or free colored communities, or in hidden frontier communities, all were essentially safety valves for the plantation societies. So long as the option of escape was available, the internal pressures that normally built up in a slave regime could be handled. But often such escape was impossible, or the provocation was too immediate and too dramatic. In these cases, the slaves turned inward with their violence. The result was full-scale rebellion. These rebellions were of many types, from the most spontaneous to the most planned, from strictly race wars against all whites to complex attacks on selected elements of the master class. Some rebellions were hopeless from the beginning and were recognized as such by their participants and some were successful transitions to *marronage*. Some encouraged governments to move more rapidly toward abolition, and one was totally successful in all its aims.

But in all cases, slave revolts were a last resort for desperate men and women who could no longer suffer the abuses of slavery. From the 16th century onward, there were slave rebellions in every slave society in America. Though generalizations about such a complex social process are difficult to make, certain general features can be discerned. If the slave regime was heavily African, the revolts were usually more numerous and intense than in slave communities in which the creoles formed a majority. Since all slaves knew what the ultimate consequences of rebellion were, those with more of a commitment to the current social order tended to be more conservative. Among recently arrived Africans, where the sexual imbalance created fewer families or local ties, rebellion was less dreaded. Creoles with their family and community ties were the least likely candidates for rebellion, though even these native-born slaves were sometimes provoked beyond their endurance and conservative instincts.

In the vast majority of cases, revolt was spontaneous and involved only a few slaves. An aggrieved slave's killing of their master or overseer was probably the most common form of revolt recorded. When a group of slaves premeditated such an act, they usually tried to involve the whole plantation and also tried to plan an escape. Such revolts usually envisioned *marronage* as a final result of their violence. There were, however, a few well-known cases of full-scale race and class wars in which the conspiring slaves sought to eliminate the master class and retain the lands for themselves. Sometimes these wars were directed at whites only, but sometimes they opposed elements within the servile class as well. There even exist cases, in the more mature slave societies, of freedmen and slaves conspiring together in the hopes of forming a black and mulatto republic. In most instances, the reaction against enslavement was instinctive and based on universal beliefs in justice and humanity. At other times, however, these rebellions evolved out of alternative religious belief systems and developed an elaborate cosmology, sometimes with millenarian overtones.

Isolated mining communities were particularly prone to slave rebellious activity, whereas small family farms probably had the fewest uprisings. Anywhere slaves congregated in large numbers, slave conspiracies and rebellions were possible. In those regions with a viable frontier, and/or a large free colored class, the intensity of such revolts was less, just as it was in those societies that had acceptable procedures for dealing with *petit marronage*. Variation in the intensity and timing of revolts was not only related to these demographic, geographic, and structural factors but it was also sensitive to changes over time. By the late 18th century and early 19th century, many of the revolts began to take on a more class-conscious and ameliorative component. The French and Haitian revolutions sparked a series of conspiracies and revolts throughout America among those who sought slave emancipation and equality for freedmen. These revolts were usually led by free coloreds and poor whites, but they also included slaves. Such was the case of the so-called tailors' conspiracy in Bahia in 1798 and of the uprising in the Coro district of Venezuela in 1795. The former was quickly suppressed with much bloodshed, but the latter eventually saw the rebels field an army of 300 that attacked urban centers. Then, in the 1820s and 1830s, as the metropolitan governments were swept with Liberal reformist demands, abolition became a general topic of debate in the colonies. The result was a maturation of slave conspiracies and plots into full-scale, class-conscious movements. As creolized slaves got access to information about government reforms, strikes and mass protest activities were organized demanding better working conditions, more access to provisioning grounds, or even the abolition of slavery.

The earliest recorded slave rebellions were of the immediate and race-war types. These were especially prominent in 16th- and 17th-century Spanish America. The bloodiest of these revolts was one of the earliest. In 1522, African slaves working on plantations went on a rampage of slaughter, killing masters and destroying crops in the area around the city of Santo Domingo with the aim of creating an African republic in the region. A slave conspiracy and attempt at arson were recorded as early as 1537 in Mexico City, followed by another plot in the capital in 1611, and fishermen rose up in revolt on the island of Margarita in the 1540s. Given that slaves in Mexico and Peru were distributed among a larger Indian population, many of the later revolts in these regions were carried out in conjunction with local natives and fugitives. More often than not, they ended in *marronage*. In the 17th century, silver-mining camps in northern Mexico and copper mines in Peru were struck by slave revolts, just as the gold fields of the Chocó region of New Granada experienced slave and maroon attacks in the 18th century. In Latin America and the Caribbean no urban center escaped either slave revolts or conspiracies, and no plantation region was unaffected by slave uprisings. Although the number and frequency of revolts in Latin America seem to have been especially intense in the earlier period of slavery when whites were few, the more intense and far larger revolts came during the periods of rapid growth of the slave system in the late 18th and the 19th century, especially under the impact of massive African immigration.

The two outstanding revolutionary movements were the successful slave uprising in Haiti in 1791 and the series of Islamic rebellions in Bahia from 1808 to 1835. The Haitian example stands apart in terms of its numbers, the level of its violence and destructiveness, and finally its success. It represented the only slave rebellion in American history that succeeded in destroying the local plantation system. It was also the single most important slave revolt in America in that it had a profound impact on everything from sugar prices to slave laws throughout the Western Hemisphere. That it occurred at a time when the master class was itself divided by a major civil war goes a long way toward explaining its ultimate success. The experience of all previous slave revolts showed that escape was the only ultimate victory for a local slave rebellion, since the planter and master class had little difficulty in maintaining their slave systems even during periods of the greatest slave unrest, so long as they remained unified. It required a serious breakdown of the normal social order, plus international warfare, to enable the Haitian rebel slaves to kill the planters, to seize their land, and to liberate their colony from slavery. Once the slave uprising had time to mature because of these exogenous factors, it was massive, well armed, and finally able to destroy professional armies of several nations that came to oppose this fundamental threat to the social order.

The slave uprising in Saint Domingue was intimately linked both to African Voodoo cult figures and to the national and international political scene. In August 1791, in the midst of government confusion and conflict over supporting the king or the French Assembly, came news of the meeting of slaves in the Bois Caiman under the leadership of a slave named Boukman, who was originally from Jamaica. Boukman, who was apparently a priest in the Voodoo cult, claimed that the French king had granted the slaves three days per week to work in their own garden. He also reported that this amelioration decree was being brought to the island by a French fleet, and that the local planters were opposing this reform. Boukman, who showed the slaves documents purported to be from the metropolitan government, said that the slaves should organize a revolt in support of this change. Given the state of local political chaos and the climate of agitation, the authorities did not believe that there was any threat. They were more concerned with a free mulatto uprising in support of their civil rights than with a slave rebellion. On the evening of August 22, two days after the Boukman conference, the movement began. From the number of slaves involved and the coordination that took place, the August 20 meeting must have been just one of many such gatherings and only the final session of what was a well-planned movement with a close tie to the secret African cults. On the first night a large number of the island's best sugar plantations were put to the torch and in the next several days the island's richest plantation region, the Northern Plain' was destroyed.

Once unleashed and with no effective counterattack, the rebellion became a violent machine that destroyed all before it. Boukman died early in an attack on the city of Le Cap. He was succeeded by two other slaves, Jean François and Biassou, both of whom were Africans. There were also two other leaders who now began to play crucial roles: Jeannot, who took a race-war position and wanted to wipe out the whites and mulattoes, and Toussaint L'Ouverture. Toussaint was a respected literate freedman who had been a skilled worker on a slave plantation at the time of the uprising. Born a slave, he had obtained his freedom in 1776 and had been educated by Capuchin missionaries. Though not an original participant in the revolution, he quickly rose to leadership when he joined. His policy was one of compromise and furthering the supposedly political aims of the movement. Alliances were made with the Spanish forces guarding the Spanish half of the island, support was declared for Louis XVI, and contact was made with the most conservative pro-royalist Frenchmen on the island. Jean François was made a grandee, or nobleman, of Spain in these negotiations, and there was even talk of ending the rebellion. But in the meantime the battle over civil rights to be granted to the mulattoes of Saint Domingue by the French Assembly led to the split of white and mulatto forces and the takeover of the local government by the most extreme of the whites. The end result was that the free mulattoes, many of them planters, rose in rebellion in the western zone of Saint Domingue. Though slavery still survived in the eastern and western zones, the growth of conflict at these several different levels brought on the violent end of the entire system.

Eventually Toussaint would obtain leadership of the rebel slave armies of the north, defeat the efforts of the mulattoes of the west under their chief Rigaud, and finally shift toward a pro-republican and antimonarchist position once the king had been executed. He adopted a system of forced labor on the old plantations and tried to keep local commercial crop production going. For these efforts he was rewarded by the French government with full control over the colony. He then led his combined slave and free armies against both British and Spanish expeditionary forces and otherwise put on hold the more radical aims of the rebel slaves. But the increasingly conservative nature of the metropolitan republican government by the last years of the century would force a final rupture of the coalition and the effective end of slavery in the colony. In 1802 a French Napoleonic army seized Toussaint and sent him to France. Then a full-scale attack was launched against the slaves with the declared aim of reinstating slavery everywhere. This aim of the Napoleonic troops was successful in the politically volatile situation in Guadeloupe, where slavery had been replaced by apprenticeship. But in Saint Domingue the ex-slaves violently resisted , and in two years of harsh fighting the French army was destroyed, and under the leadership of Dessalines, Haiti was declared an independent republic in January 1804. Though Haitian leaders would attempt to reestablish the plantation economy, they were never successful. Haitian peasants were ever ready to revolt against any hint of the reimposition of the plantation. Only in the coffee zones could some production be maintained by peasant farm families. The sugar industry was totally destroyed.

The Haitian slave rebellion was thus an intimate part of the French Revolution and as such had both local and international connections. It involved formal military campaigns and the establishment among slaves of a functioning government virtually from the first months of the 1791 uprising. It was to prove a unique event in Afro-American history. The events of Guadeloupe show that it took more than the collapse of the elite to carry such a revolution to success. The vacillation of the black leadership over the maintenance of the old plantations, in turn, shows that only the absolute rejection by the ex-slave masses of any reimposition of forced plantation labor kept the movement committed to the total abolition of slavery. Finally, the rebellion would show to all the white master classes of the Americas that internal civil war or wars of independence against metropolitan power could lead to the destruction of the very regimes that they sought to protect.

The Haitian slave rebellion thus guaranteed that most of the later slave rebellions would be carried on without the support of such classes and groups as free coloreds and poor whites, but rather in the face of their opposition. Typical of this isolation, and rather special in its religious overtones, were the series of Islamic slave revolts that occurred in urban and rural Bahia between 1808 and 1835. Houssa and Nago slaves in 1808 seized sugar plantations and attempted to march on the city. It took a major battle to defeat them. In 1810 came another such plantation uprising of Muslim slaves, followed by an uprising of coastal fishermen in 1814. Some fifty slave fisherman were killed by troops sent from Salvador, but not before many local white masters were slaughtered. Five other uprisings took place between 1816 and 1835, in both the countryside and the city. In 1830, for example, twenty armed *escravos de ganho* attacked an urban slave market and freed 100 captives. But the most important revolt was that of 1835. Well organized by Muslim slaves both in the city and on the plantations, it was eventually uncovered before it could be fully developed. But enough slaves obtained arms that deaths were numerous and destruction to property was quite extensive. More than a hundred of the Nago slaves who led the rebellion were executed, and the city and government were thrown into a panic. So violent was the repression of both slaves and free coloreds in the city that no other major rebellions were to occur in this region after that date.

Though more famous as a frustrated conspiracy than an actual rebellion, the Escalera or Placido slave revolt of 1844 had the same impact on Cuban society as the Islamic slave rebellions did on the Northeast in Brazil. It occurred during a period of increasing government repression within Cuba and during growing unrest of the free population over issues of self-government and even independence. In 1842 the authorities had replaced the rather liberal slave code of 1789 with a more severe one. At the same time the rapid growth of the free colored class increased social and economic tension between the races, which led to great bitterness on the part of the free coloreds, many of whom had achieved important positions among the professional class. Like the free mulattoes of Saint Domingue, they sought greater political expression and rights. The result was the launching of an independence conspiracy led by free coloreds who also envisioned some type of emancipation for the slaves who joined the revolt. The conspirators were relatively inept and also had close contact with the more fiery of the English representatives on the island. Discovered by the authorities long before they could launch their uprising, some 3,000 conspirators were eventually tried by military courts, of whom 300 to 400 would be exiled and 11 executed. Among those executed was the free colored Cuban poet Gabriel de la Concepción Valdes, known as Placido. Ineffectual as the conspiracy was, its discovery led to a massive attack on the free colored class and an increase of oppression of the slaves on the island for the next several years. In all its aspects the Placido conspiracy had much in common with the Denmark Vesey plot in the United States in 1831, since Vesey, a free colored artisan, was also apprehended before the actual uprising ever took place. At the same time this conspiracy and the real uprising of Nat Turner in 1831 led to a general attack on the free coloreds and a restriction of privileges in the slave codes everywhere in the United States.

Revolts, rebellions, conspiracies, and protest movements were only a small manifestation of the hostility expressed by slaves for their condition. Common to all slave societies in America was a high incidence of crimes of violence and property. Slave thefts, vandalism, arson, and destruction of property were constant in all slave regimes in Latin America and were clearly acts of protest against masters and the very system of slavery. But the poverty and oppression experienced by slaves were sometimes turned against other slaves. Two-thirds of the victims of crimes in the city of Rio de Janeiro between 1810 and 1821 were slaves assaulted by their fellow slaves. Many of these crimes came from normal interpersonal conflicts, but many were part of an uncontrolled hostility toward the system in which they were forced to live. Drunkenness, social disorder, and crime were largely urban phenomena, but no slave community even in the most isolated plantation was free of them. In a world where violence and helplessness were daily occurrences, a corresponding level of protest, coherent and anomic, was bound to be part of the system.

Finally, the various American wars for independence presented another opportunity for slave violence and resistance to manifest themselves. In the more violent phases of these movements, mass destruction in the countryside gave slaves opportunities to escape and take up life as free maroons. In some cases, it was difficult for masters to reestablish order and discipline on their plantations even in the aftermath of these struggles, or during times of relative peace. For instance, in Colombia, when royalists recaptured the city of Cartagena in 1815, they were unable to return maroons to their estates, effectively marking the destruction of the region's plantation economy until the 1850s. In Colombia's Cauca valley, many slaves who had fought against their masters at the urging of the Spanish could not be located or returned to their estates after the royalists were defeated there in 1817. Meanwhile, in Mexico, after agents of José María Morelos had incited slaves in Veracruz to join the insurgency by fleeing their plantations, slaves could not be brought into submission even after the region had been subdued in 1817. In fact, slaves continued hiding in the hills until well after independence had been achieved (1821), laying down their arms only when slavery was completely abolished in 1829.

While a number of slaves found freedom through flight during the independence era, others were offered freedom in exchange for military service. Although both royalist and insurgent forces actively recruited from among the slave population, the Spanish Crown was the first to employ slave soldiers. Building upon a successful venture in 1806, when slaves were enlisted to help the Crown defeat a British invasion of the viceroyalty of Rio de la Plata (Argentina), slaves were enlisted by the thousands in royalist armies stretching from Venezuela to Buenos Aires between 1810 and 1813. Slaves responded to the Crown's call for duty both because it initially seemed that Spain would be victorious against the insurgency, and because they believed the Crown to be their best bet at securing liberty. However, as the insurgency came to realize the tactical advantage that slaves brought to the struggle, they intensified their commitment to recruiting slave armies. Between the years of 1813 and 1818, between 4,000 and 5,000 slaves were fielded in the rebel armies of Argentina. In 1817, at least half of San Martín's insurgent forces were slaves; and between 1819 and 1821, Simón Bolívar stood charge of over 5,000 slave troops in Colombia and commanded an army in Ecuador in which slaves accounted for one-third of the troops. Some of these recruits were drawn reluctantly. After 1813, many slave masters residing in regions under insurgent control were compelled to enlist a portion of their slaveholdings for military duty. Even if promised compensation, a number of slave owners resisted the conscription efforts by hiding their slaves, fearing that the loss of labor would ruin their estates. But a number of slaves themselves also hesitated to enroll for service. While promised liberty for their duties, freedom was not granted unconditionally. In most cases, slaves were required to serve in the army for several years (five in Argentina) before becoming free. If slaves managed to survive the brutalities of war during this tenure, their service contracts could be prolonged further. Enlistments for six or more years were not uncommon.

Regardless, the military proved an attractive route to liberty for some, and even female noncombatants found ways to claim their freedom during the wars of independence. The liberal rhetoric of the insurgency provided a language and atmosphere for articulating slave plight that had not been available to previous generations of slaves. Especially in the Spanish domain, rebel leaders depicted their struggle against Spain as one that sought to break the unjust chains of slavery that kept the colonies bound to the metropolis. The metaphor struck a chord with slaves, who now began pleading for their own liberty within the discursive framework newly opened to them. In 1823, Angela Batallas of Ecuador, with the assistance of her lawyer, demanded liberty in the presence of Simón Bolivar himself, eloquently stating: "I do not believe that meritorious members of a republic that... have given all necessary proofs of liberalism, employing their arms and heroically risking their lives to liberate us from the Spanish yoke, would want to pledge to keep me in servitude." Whereas Angela appealed powerfully to the sensibilities of liberalism for her freedom, other women sought to link their fates with those of slave soldiers, many of whom were their husbands. In 1811, Juliana Garcia, from the Banda Oriental, accompanied her husband with their three children on multiple military expeditions throughout South America. In four years of travel the family had participated in two sieges of Montevideo, the invasion of Upper Peru, and the battle of Sipe-Sipe. When Juliana's master sought to reclaim her, she protested: "I consider myself worthy of being free together with my children, not only as a result of my master having lost all his rights, but also from the *patria* [fatherland] for my fatigues over more than four years." Though her husband was the soldier, she too felt physically invested in bringing into being the newly liberated *patria*, the independent nation-state. Although she ultimately lost her appeal, her point had been clearly made. In the years of the independence struggle and beyond, slaves would forcibly push the meaning of liberty to include them, and they would exploit the inconsistencies of the rhetoric describing national freedom, to underscore the limits of their personal freedom. Yet, as they confronted the institution of slavery in these ways, the challenges they faced remained daunting. Many of the insurgents who had led the wars of independence were estate owners themselves, deriving a livelihood from slavery that they did not want to abandon. To preserve their property and maintain the regime, some masters cruelly denied that slaves who had fought for years in the independence struggle had actually served the required amount of time to secure their freedom. Others falsely declared that their slaves had not served in the army at all. While the courts in these instances tended to favor the claims of former slaves, the legal battles they endured could be demoralizing, and for some, they actually returned them to slavery.

10

Freedmen in a Slave Society

Every slave society in Latin America permitted slaves to be manumitted from the very beginning. All such regimes accepted the legitimacy of manumission, since it was the norm in Roman law and was deeply embedded in Christian piety and practice. A free colored class thus developed in every American slave society virtually from the first days of colonization. All such populations grew slowly in the 16th and 17th centuries, and all faced some type of restriction on their freedom. These restrictions were uniquely applied to them because of their origin and color. From the early 18th century onward, however, certain slave regimes began to distinguish themselves from others on the basis of their changing attitudes toward the manumission process, which in turn caused major changes in the growth, number, and ratio of freedmen in the respective societies.

The differences in the numbers and acceptance of the free colored population in each of the American slave societies were determined by a broad spectrum of considerations, from religious and cultural to economic and social. In all cases, however, the minority of freedmen in slave societies faced hostility from their white neighbors and former masters, and in no society were both freedom and total acceptance a possibility. Racism was a part of every American system that held African slaves and did not disappear when blacks and mulattoes became free citizens and economic and social competitors.

There has been a long debate in the North American scholarly literature about the nature of racism and whether it preceded slavery or was a consequence thereof. In the Latin American context, Iberian experiences with slavery long antedated New World colonization and even the arrival of African slaves in the Americas. Thus race prejudice accompanied New World slavery, since official policies of discrimination based on origin, creed, and, to a lesser extent, color were being applied in the new centralizing Iberian monarchies as early as the 15th century. While race and racism are often described as modern concepts, the word *raza* (race) had actually begun appearing in Iberian documents from at least 1438 and, in its earliest manifestations, developed into a term that described the degree to which a person's lineage was free from Jewish or Muslim heritages. The need to distinguish these elements originated from the Castilian and Portuguese conquests in the Old World. The long conflict between Christians, Jews, and Moors led to a discriminatory policy of "blood purity," or *limpieza de sangre*. From the time leading up to the expulsion of the Jews from Spain and Portugal in the late 15th century, royal legislation carefully distinguished between the so-called Old Christians, or those who were Christians from the Middle Ages, and the so-called New Christians, or those who had recently converted from Judaism or Islam. New Christians were denied the right to practice certain occupations, were banned from many civil and ecclesiastical offices, and in many respects were treated as second-class citizens. As an expression of these practices, *raza*, therefore, became enveloped with ideas about exclusion, privilege, and religion as the emerging nation-states of Spain and Portugal used Christian ideology to forge a national consciousness in the 15th and 16th centuries. It became common to speak of people as being of *buena o mala raza*, meaning good or bad race, given their specific religious orientation. A person of "good" race was interpreted as having the blood of a Christian, while that of a "bad" race was either a Moor or Jew.

In the New World, the complexity of phenotypes that were produced as a result of miscegenation added to the notion of *raza*, stretching it beyond the Old and New Christian framework from which it originated. The term *casta* (caste) gradually emerged to explain human differences in ways that moved away from the concerns over purity that governed the notion of *raza*. *Casta* sought more to understand *naturaleza*, or one's inner nature and disposition. In the process, phenotype was emphasized as an indicator of one's inherent qualities. By these means, blackness could be interpreted as signaling a propensity toward shiftlessness, vice, laziness, or intellectual inferiority. Through the interchange of the concepts of race and caste, elaborate human taxonomies were created in Latin America that categorized individuals into multiple groups—mestizos, *castizos*, mulattoes, coyotes, Indians, and so forth. Eventually, notions of class factored into caste hierarchies as well, and through the concept of *calidad* (quality), human rankings could be evaluated through a calculus that involved social, economic, and phenotypic elements. Unlike British North America and its proverbial black-white binary, the Iberian system of classification became rather complex, so much so that it enabled a certain fluidity, as individuals could move between caste categories. Some even solidified changes in their caste status through highlighting impressive economic accomplishments, or through underscoring other social achievements that were seen positively within the framework of *calidad*. Yet, as fluid and negotiable as the system may have been, at its core was finding ways to distinguish among, and ultimately discriminate against, populations that were not white. The system's primary aim was to preserve a privilege structure that benefited the colonizers. It was in this world that the free colored population was compelled to operate and carve out space for its survival.

Unsurprisingly, from the earliest days, local and metropolitan legislation began to attack the rights of the free coloreds. Sumptuary laws denied free colored women the right to wear the clothes and jewelry worn by free white women; free colored persons were denied the right to a university education and the practice of a liberal profession, and even some of the skilled occupations such as goldsmithing were denied to them. For several generations the priesthood and the various religious orders were closed to them, and they were denied access to all higher government offices.

Thus, Iberian ideas of phenotypic difference and the laws and practices of the Latin American societies attempted to solidify a castelike system, in which free blacks and mulattoes entered into the lower ranks. The enforcement of the system depended on the willingness of the colonial authorities to prevent the market from distributing rewards on the basis of individual skills and abilities. To make such a rigid stratification system function, wealth would have to be denied to free coloreds, occupational mobility severely limited, and even geographic mobility constrained. Though proclaimed as an ideal, actual practice would eventually move away from this rigid plan as the economic importance of the free coloreds began to make itself felt.

Of the Latin American and Caribbean systems, the French pattern was much closer to the British West Indian and North American situation. France did not initially inherit a castelike model, and even the harsh 17th-century Code Noir maintained that free colored persons were coequal in rights to all other free persons. Like the Ibero-American colonies, however, the French possessions soon passed numerous laws restricting the rights of free coloreds. Sumptuary and occupational distinctions were decreed, and even differential punishments were employed for free colored criminals, all in the name of guaranteeing that the free functioning of the labor market would not displace whites from their dominance over local society. This, too, occurred in all the northern European slave colonies. Some of these latter societies took these prohibitions even a step further, proscribing interracial marriage and severely chastising whites for having sexual intercourse with blacks or mulattoes.

Although all American colonies were racist and placed restrictions on the freedom of ex-slaves, the actual societies that developed differed sharply among the various slave regimes. These differences had to do with both the process of manumission itself and the acceptance of the legitimacy of free coloreds within the larger social and economic order. All societies began with a fairly active level of manumission, as masters piously freed their slaves—or fathers their children—or faithful service was rewarded with freedom. In all societies self-purchase arrangements for slaves developed early. The major differences began to appear only after the first several generations, when the Iberians not only continued to accept and support the traditional patterns of manumission but also actively accepted and codified the route of self-purchase. This further encouraged growth in the number of freedmen, who in turn gave material support to others seeking manumission, thereby increasing even further the free colored class.

Other societies began in this manner, but, as the number of free coloreds began to grow, so too did the fear of these freedmen. Though they had the same restrictive legislation as the Iberian societies, whites became less and less trustful that these prohibitions would guard their privileges in areas like the British and Dutch colonies. They therefore began to attack the whole manumission process, making it costlier to both the master and the slave. Just as the Iberian regimes were legitimizing self-purchase the North Americans were restricting it, if not prohibiting it altogether. This fundamental opposition to manumission effectively began to curtail the number of freedmen in these societies, which remained relatively limited until the final years of slavery.

Especially following the Haitian revolution, British, French, Dutch, and North American legislation became ever more hostile toward freedmen. Many colonies or states temporarily prohibited manumission but even more severely restricted both the occupational and even the physical mobility of the free colored class. Work registration and prohibitions against making certain types of contracts further restricted economic opportunities, and attempts were even made to ship freedmen back to Africa.

In Spanish America, the free colored population grew slowly throughout the 16th and 17th centuries in all the continental and insular colonies. By the 18th century, however, growth was quite rapid. Despite the continued arrival of African slaves in both Peru and northern South America, the number of free coloreds surged ahead of the slave population in almost every colony. In Panama, to take one example, there were already 33,000 free coloreds in the colony by 1778, compared with 3,500 slaves. Moreover, these free coloreds represented half of the total population. The viceroyalty of New Granada, which included Colombia and Ecuador, was estimated to have 80,000 slaves and 420,000 free coloreds in 1789. The thriving cacao plantation zone of Venezuela had 198,000 free coloreds and 64,000 slaves. Peru was reduced to 40,000 slaves in 1792 and had 41,000 free persons of color. In Mexico, which had 10,000 slaves in 1810, there were probably another 300,000 free coloreds by the late 1790s. Though Mexican scholars have calculated the so-called Afro-mestizo population at over half a million persons by 1810, this may be an overestimate, although there is little question that the free colored population well exceeded the slave population.

In many of the smaller colonies, it is harder to obtain reliable data. Still, the rapid 18th-century growth in free coloreds, combined with limited slave imports, meant that slaves were probably vastly outnumbered. In Costa Rica, by the 1780s both slaves and free coloreds totaled roughly 9,000 individuals. These same groups in El Salvador numbered at least 2,000 by 1807. In Nicaragua, within the province of Granada alone, there were probably 8,400 free coloreds (including *zambos*) and 100 slaves by 1790. In Chile there were between 13,000 and 15,000 free coloreds in 1778, and as many as 22,000 in Buenos Aires and Córdoba, within the Rio de la Plata viceroyalty. Meanwhile, in Guatemala, the capital city of Santiago possessed a population of 2,750 free coloreds by 1740—the largest nonnative racial group in the city. At a rough estimate, Spain's continental colonies by 1800 probably contained a half million to 650,000 free persons of color.

The experience of the insular colonies of Spanish America was somewhat different. In both Puerto Rico and Santo Domingo the pattern resembled mainland Spanish America, and the free colored population exceeded that of the slaves by the late 18th century. By 1788, Santo Domingo had 80,000 free coloreds compared with only 15,000 slaves, and the proportions did not differ thereafter. By 1775 Puerto Rico had 35,000 freedmen and 7,000 slaves; by 1820 it had 22,000 slaves, but its free colored population had grown to 104,000 persons and even outnumbered the whites. This initially was the experience of Cuba in the pre-1800 period, but the growth of the island's plantation economy and its slave population was so great that a steadily growing free colored population could not overtake the slave population until the second half of the 19th century. In Cuba there were 54,000 free coloreds and 85,000 slaves in 1792. By 1810 its free colored population had grown to 114,000 persons, but slaves were now close to double that figure. In the 1840s, free colored growth slowed and had reached only 149,000, compared with 324,000 slaves. But there was a spurt in growth over the next two decades, and by the census of 1861 the number of free coloreds had reached 232,000. Meanwhile, the number of slaves had grown to only 371,000, thus narrowing the gap between the two groups. Following the bitter independence struggle known as the Ten Years' War (1868–78), the free coloreds finally surpassed the slave population, reaching a total of 272,000 persons. They continued to grow in number until the eve of the abolition of slavery in the 1880s, when they reached half a million persons.

In Brazil the free colored population grew at an even more rapid rate than in most of Spanish America, though the timing followed the same trajectory until the 19th century. In 18th-century estimates the free colored were an important element of the population everywhere, but they did not exceed the slaves. In contrast to Cuba, however, the massive arrival of African slaves in the 19th century did not slow the pace of growth of the free coloreds. Rather, their numbers grew even more rapidly in the first half of the century, so that by 1850, when the slave trade finally ended, the free coloreds had already exceeded the total number of slaves. This dominance of free coloreds in the total colored population increased with every passing year. By the time of the first national census in 1872, there were 4.2 million free persons of color, compared with 1.5 million slaves. Not only were the free coloreds greater in number than the 3.8 million whites, but they alone accounted for 43 percent of the 10 million Brazilians. All this transpired more than a decade before the abolition of slavery.

There was, of course, some variation regionally in the growth of Brazil's free colored population. In the Northeast, free coloreds were already dominant in the first part of the 19th century. Pernambuco in 1839 had 127,000 free coloreds, and half that number of slaves. This ratio appeared to be typical of Bahia and Maranhão as well. In contrast, the province of Rio de Janeiro was unique in that it still had more slaves than free coloreds even in 1872. Meanwhile, both Minas Gerais and São Paulo had more freedmen than slaves by this time. But São Paulo only had attained this balance quite recently, whereas Minas Gerais probably had more freedmen by the 1820s. Though free coloreds were probably most numerous in the Northeast, they were well represented everywhere. The two largest states where they resided in 1872 were Bahia, with 830,000, and Minas Gerais—also the largest slave state—with 806,000 freed-men.

All this rapid growth contrasted sharply with that of the rest of the West Indian and North American slave colonies. From the French to the Dutch and the English, restraints were increasingly placed on manumission to prevent the growth of the free colored class. Although these societies began with the same relative numbers of free coloreds as the Iberian colonies, their growth was increasingly restrained. By the late 18th century, free coloreds had fallen well behind even the white populations of their island and continental colonies, and they comprised only a fraction of the total colored populations. Consequently, by the 1780s, the three major French islands of Saint Domingue, Martinique, and Guadeloupe had only 30,000 free coloreds among them, compared with over 575,000 slaves and 52,000 whites. The British West Indies had only 13,000 free coloreds for all islands, compared with 53,000 whites and 467,000 slaves. In the United States the same limited importance was encountered. In the first federal census of 1790, only 32,000 free coloreds were listed, compared with 658,000 slaves and 1.3 million whites.

By the beginning of the 19th century freedmen had come close to surpassing the number of slaves in most of the Iberian colonies, whereas they still represented but a small fraction of the slaves in the non-Iberian areas. Despite this imbalance, the growth of their numbers in the Spanish and Portuguese colonies was such that freedmen made up approximately two-thirds or more of the total number of slaves in America. A rough estimate of the total population of free coloreds in 1800 for all the Americas was on the order of 2 to 2.5 million persons, most of whom were living in the Latin American colonies, while the total Western Hemisphere slave population numbered over 3 million persons.

The imbalance between the Iberian and non-Iberian societies began to change in the 19th century as the impact of the French Revolution and the campaigns of the abolitionists finally began to force the French and British colonies to loosen up their manumission procedures. In Martinique and Guadeloupe a large number of slaves had been freed during the constant civil wars and conflicts of the Napoleonic period such that the two islands and Cayenne by 1815 had 22,000 freedmen as compared to 196,000 slaves, a far higher ratio than during the pre-1789 period. But the restoration monarchy in France was brutal on the question of free coloreds, attempting both to halt manumissions and to reinstate the Code Noir for slaves. The July Monarchy of 1830 changed this position, and from this date until abolition in 1848, the free colored population in France's three American possessions grew quickly. In 1831, freedmen again attained full civil rights, and by 1847, on the eve of abolition, their numbers had climbed to some 77,000 persons, compared with 174,000 slaves. The British West Indian colonies also began to loosen up their restrictions on manumission in the post-Napoleonic period, though their free coloreds never approached the total number of slaves by the time of abolition. In 1832, freedmen in the islands and British Guyana numbered 127,000, with a slave population of 663,000 persons.

Despite this growth of the free colored class in the last years before total abolition, it is clear that freedmen were more greatly feared and restrained in the non-Iberian colonies and republics. Why this fear was expressed in an attack on manumissions, rather than on increasing the differentiation of rights between free coloreds and the rest of society, seems related to the racism that came to pervade all levels of the social structure. Free whites feared uncontrolled competition from free coloreds in the labor market and seemed to feel that color and status had to be identical. Having large numbers of free blacks and mulattoes in these heavily slave states was believed to challenge the very legitimacy of slavery. This fear of competition, interestingly enough, had a basis in fact only in relation to a very small segment of free coloreds in the French West Indies, who perhaps more than any such group in America challenged the power and wealth of even the master class. Whereas the freedmen in most other slave societies entered at the lower ranks of free society, in the French West Indies they were often permitted to enter the class of plantation owners from the start. Although their relative numbers were no greater than those for the northern European slave colonies, the French *gens de couleur* held a power to challenge even the highest elites. This helps explain the ferocity of the attack on their rights, just as it explains their own ability to destroy the dominance of the master class in the midst of the French Revolution. In the other non-Iberian cases, however, it would appear that the mere concept of a thriving class of freedmen challenged the viability of the whole slave system and led to an attack on this class, even though their numbers and poverty rendered them highly unequal competitors to even the poorer whites in these societies. Despite a few striking exceptions, such as Philadelphia's James Forten, the grandson of slaves who became one of the city's leading sailmakers in the 19th century, color and status had become so deeply ingrained in these societies that the free colored class was considered an abnormality that was only barely tolerated.

    In contrast, in Spanish and Portuguese America, the protective (albeit permeable) class structure, the elaborate caste and color distinctions, and the existence of a legal stratification system may have provided Iberian whites with a relative sense of security against free colored competition, thereby making them more willing to accept the manumission process. This relative acquiescence of elite whites led to both a public and a private commitment to manumission from the beginning to the end of slavery. Recent studies have shown that manumission was a complex process that involved both voluntary and involuntary manumission on the part of the master class, and a complex pattern of passive and active intervention on the part of the slaves themselves.

    Although it was initially thought that the more economically minded Iberians were simply freeing their old and infirm slaves, this was not the case. Most studies done of large samples of manumission records for Brazil and Spanish American societies show that overall, the manumitted were primarily young, creole-born, and in the majority women. Slaves who purchased their own freedom, however, tended to be male and African-born. Of course there were important divergences from the typical trends, particularly in areas where auxiliary slavery prevailed over plantation slavery, and where the external slave trade was continually low, or dropped significantly prior to the 18th century. In Mexico, between 1650 and 1750, there was a notable, steady decrease in the number of female manumissions, such that male and female manumission rates reached near parity. This can be partly credited to the role women played in sustaining the institution of slavery. As slave imports declined, masters turned to women to give birth to new generations of slaves. To reflect their new role, the price of slave women even began exceeding that of men, a virtual anomaly compared to the major plantation societies. In Costa Rica, a somewhat similar trend can be detected. Between 1684 and 1750, women enjoyed only a slight advantage over men in terms of manumission. Only 55 percent of 131 known manumissions were female. Interestingly, these women were manumitted at various moments of their lives. One could not predict by age alone if they were likely to be manumitted, and even fertile women in the prime of their lives (aged sixteen to thirty-five) were routinely found among the freed. However, as with the New World's larger slave societies, even Costa Rican masters freed children in greater numbers. Roughly a third of the colony's slave manumissions were youths under the age of eleven. Comparatively speaking, in Brazil, also thanks to a large number of infant and young adult manumissions, the average age of freed slaves in a sample of almost 7,000 cases in Salvador de Bahia between 1684 and 1745 was just fifteen years. In the same city in the 19th century, some 30 percent of the slaves freed were under fifteen years of age. This pattern was also noted in the mining town of Sabará in Minas Gerias. Of 1,011 manumissions recorded here in the period between 1710 and 1819, one-third involved children thirteen years of age and under, and only 1 percent were to slaves older than forty-six years of age. Even in a small sample of manumitted slaves from Santafé de Bogotá (Colombia) during the years 1700–1750, of the 83 freed slaves whose age was known, 45 percent were fifteen years old and under, with 25 percent being under the age of six.

The sex ratios of manumitted slaves in Brazil, however, clearly emphasized the greater manumission of women, unlike late 17th-century and early 18th-century Costa Rica and Mexico. In the Brazilian city of São Paulo in the periods 1800–50 and 1871–88, the sex ratio for 1,338 manumitted slaves was 71 men for every 100 women freed. The case of São Paulo illustrates a trend found in most major slaveholding regions in the New World's plantation societies. Recent studies suggest that, on the whole, approximately two-thirds of the manumitted population were women (60 to 67 percent), and few were found to be forty-five years or older. Thus it was no accident that in the Minas Gerais parish of São

José d'El Rey in 1795, the sex ratio among the 1,411 *alforrias* (or manumitted slaves) was 84 males per 100 females. A study of 4,609 manumissions in the city of Rio de Janeiro in the 1840s found the overall sex ratio to be 74 men per 100 women, but the sex ratio differed considerably by origin. For Africans (representing 57 percent of the total manumissions) the sex ratio was 84 men per 100 women and for creole slaves it was just 61 males per 100 females. Hence, while creole slave women clearly enjoyed an advantage at acquiring liberty here, African men gained freedom to greater degrees than their creole male counterparts. Nevertheless, African women still joined the ranks of the free in greater proportions than African men. These general patterns help explain why in the census of 1872, for the province of São Paulo, for example, the sex ratio for the 355,745 freed persons of color was 79 men per 100 women. This can be compared to the sex ratio of 125 men per 100 women among slaves, and 99 men per 100 women among whites. In the Brazilian empire as a whole, however, the sex ratio among the 4.2 million free coloreds was more balanced, but even so, free coloreds had the lowest ratio of men of any group in society, with 102 males per 100 females, compared with 109 males per 100 females among whites and 115 males per 100 females among slaves.

In most manumission studies, self-purchased slaves represented from a quarter to half of all manumissions, while between 10 and 20 percent of manumitted slaves were granted conditional freedom, mostly in exchange for promising to continue rendering their services for a fixed amount of time. The rates of self-purchase varied considerably from region to region. The diverse landscape of Brazil offers excellent examples to study the phenomenon. In the two Minas Gerais regions of Rio das Velhas and Rio das Mortes between 1716 and 1789, of 932 manumissions, 36 percent purchased their freedom. In the city of São Paulo, samples from the 19th century show that 31 percent of 1,338 manumissions were self-purchases, of which a minority involved slaves being bought by one of their own relatives (called *pagantes na família*). Meanwhile, in Rio de Janeiro and its hinterland, the ratio of self-purchases for 17,162 slaves manumitted between 1840 and 1871 was just 28 percent (30 percent for Africans and 26 percent for creoles). In the 1840s, 22 percent of the slaves who purchased their own liberty here did so with the help of a third party, and, surprisingly, only 19 percent of all liberated slaves were granted conditional freedom. In the Minas town of Juiz de Fora, between 1844 and 1888 there were 992 manumissions recorded, of which only 12 percent involved self-purchases. Of these, 60 percent involved slaves buying their own freedom, another 10 percent were paid for by family members, and 30 percent by third parties. Finally, in the southern town of Porto Alegre, some 3,429 slaves were manumitted between 1858 and 1878, of whom 41 percent purchased their freedom. Of these, third parties paid for 25 percent of the sales, a figure quite similar to that found in Rio de Janeiro.

The relative importance of recently manumitted slaves within the free colored population is little studied, and the few data available suggest quite wide variations. Thus, in Porto Alegre, recently freed persons represented an unusually high 44 percent of all free persons of color residing in the parish between 1858 and 1878. In the few other available studies providing the ratio of persons born in slavery versus those born free among the free colored class, the *forros* (or those free coloreds born in slavery and freed in their own lifetimes) usually comprised roughly 10 percent of the free colored class.

On the whole, except for places like Mexico and Costa Rica (particularly between 1650 and 1750), the age and sex biases among manumitted slaves meant that the free colored class was receiving a dynamic element into their midst that was more heavily female and relatively young. The reproductive rates among the free colored population were thus consistently higher than among the slaves. Not only were the creole freedmen reproducing themselves at a positive rate of growth, but they were also receiving from the slave class a steady stream of entrants who were apt to be more reproductive, that is, younger and fertile women. However, in late 17th-century and early 18th-century Mexico, the reproductive rates of both slaves and free coloreds were almost parallel. This did not mean that the fertility rates of free coloreds were necessarily lower than elsewhere in the New World, but that those of slaves were higher than what would normally be expected. While more work needs to be done on this topic, preliminary findings suggest that the decline of Mexico's slave trade helped spark natural growth among the colony's slave population far earlier than in other parts of the Americas. Accompanying the decline in imports came a shift toward using creole slaves in the colony, who had higher fertility and lower mortality rates than African *bozales*. Moreover, Mexican creole slaves possessed particularly high life expectancy rates compared to other New World slave populations and enjoyed better health conditions.

It is hard to say if the trends found in Mexico were the norm in other Mesoamerican colonies, or in other regions of the Spanish empire where slavery was less prevalent than in places like Brazil. But even if slave reproductive rates were higher than has been commonly assumed, the clear overall trend for free coloreds in areas like Guatemala, Nicaragua, Panama, and Mexico was toward remarkable growth. At least in Guatemala, the expansion of free coloreds came about through both manumission and marriage strategies. Male slaves in the late 17th century inordinately married free women here, who in turn gave birth to free colored children. Almost 10 percent of all marriages in the colony by 1700 involved a free woman and a black slave.

The process of manumission was not an uneconomic one as far as the masters were concerned. For the manumitted who paid for their own freedom or had someone buy their freedom, the price paid was usually the slave's current market price, not the original price of purchase. This was especially irksome to skilled slaves and others whose original purchase price was considerably less than their current market value. Freedmen and slaves constantly lobbied the courts to have their manumission price set at what was considered a "just price," which for them meant either their original purchase price or, if they had been raised in slavery, the average price for an adult slave. Sometimes the courts ruled in their favor, but in most cases they did not. Thus, upon manumission, masters were frequently reimbursed with the current value of a slave, which meant a gain above the costs of maintenance and security and not counting the steady income generated by the slave during his or her working career. Consequently, masters could reenter the market for new slaves. In one extraordinary and illuminating case, the Maestro de Campo (field marshal) don Francisco de Cisneros of Cuzco, Peru, allowed his mistress, the Mexican-born black slave Teresa, to purchase herself and her mulatto son Francisco (whom Cisneros admitted having fathered) for 1,000 pesos in 1670. This was virtually the same price he had paid for Teresa and her four small children when he bought them at a public auction in Mexico City in 1652. He evidently lost nothing financially in this transaction, and of course had gained enormously from her service of eighteen years.

Self-purchase arrangements were typically done in installments, usually with one-third to one-half down, and a stipulated number of years set to complete payment. During this period of *coartación,* a *coartado* slave could not be sold to another master without his or her permission, and other restrictions applied that protected their rights. The master continued to receive the earnings of the *coartado* slave until such time as the final installment was paid. The master thus not only recouped the slave's full price but also received a considerable benefit in earnings. As payments and earnings were being remitted, *coartado* slaves received an official document, called a *carta de corte* (in Portuguese), which legally allowed them some physical mobility away from their masters and the right to make contracts in order to obtain the funds needed for their self-purchase.

From Mexico City to Buenos Aires, the ratio of blacks and Africans was high among slaves who purchased their own freedom, especially in urban areas. But when gratis manumission was carried out by masters, then creoles and mulattoes could be found in greater proportions. Clearly, the racism of the master class was evident in their choices when freeing slaves. However, other factors were also at play. Several of the mulatto women receiving their freedom were liberated by female owners and mistresses. In Quito, Costa Rica, Mexico, Suriname, and parts of Brazil, many slave women, particularly creoles, developed close ties in the domestic sphere with their mistresses, who occasionally rewarded them with gratis liberty for their dedicated work in the household. But close and intimate ties also developed between male owners and their female slaves. Mulatto women in Costa Rica, given their favored status as consorts, were almost seven times as likely to be manumitted as blacks. Overall, the high number of mulatto manumissions partly explains the very high ratio of mulattoes in the ranks of the free colored class, as compared with their numbers within the community of slaves.

Aside from freeing their slaves in public acts notarized by officials, the master class in Latin America also manumitted slaves at baptism. This was the typical route used by fathers freeing their bastard offspring and required only the declaration of parents and godparents to set the child free. All foundling children were also declared free, no matter what their color. An analysis of the parish registers of Paraty, a sugar- and *cachaça*-producing coastal region of Rio de Janeiro in the early 19th century, revealed that 1 percent of the total local births were slave children being freed. These children were not registered with formal *cartas de alforria* (certificates of manumission), which were the usual records used for all other manumissions. Thus studies on manumission based on the formal certificates overlook an important number of persons who obtained their freedom at birth, and in this case these seemingly few births added 16 percent to the total number of manumitted slaves in the five-year period under consideration. In another recent study of the 271 newborn slaves manumitted at the baptismal font in the Minas town of São João del-Rei between 1770 and 1850, none indicated that the father was freeing their children, even though subsequent wills and testaments showed that several of these children were fathered by their masters. These children were also about two-thirds female, further strengthening the female predominance among freed slaves. If this ratio was typical for the rest of Latin America, it would have the effect of further reducing the age of the new entrants into the free colored class and further encouraging positive rates of growth.

There is little question that manumission occurred more frequently in urban rather than the rural settings, and that skilled slaves more readily purchased their freedom than unskilled ones. Urban slaves had more opportunities to gain income than rural slaves and were seemingly more cognizant of their rights than the more isolated plantation slaves. But even in rural areas, manumission was possible and practiced with some frequency. A number of rural slaves purchased their own freedom using funds they accumulated from selling foodstuffs produced on their individual slave *conucos*, or provisioning grounds. Others saved money from extraordinary work that they managed to perform on Sundays or other "rest" days. One study has tried to calculate the chances that rural slaves throughout Brazil had at being freed in the second half of the 19th century. It estimated that out of a cohort of ten-year-old slave children who survived to the age of forty, some 16 percent would be manumitted by that age, and 26 percent would be manumitted for those who survived to sixty years of age. This was based on a crude manumission rate of 6 per 1,000 per annum, a fairly high death-rate schedule, and an assumption of a constant manumission rate across all age-groups.

Once freed, ex-slaves in all societies except the French West Indies entered at the lowest stratum of the society. Even skilled slaves came into the free population with their savings exhausted through the act of self-purchase. It was usually these same persons who then purchased their spouses and children in order to free them and in turn mortgaged future savings in this manumission process. In only rare cases, and then principally in the French islands, did masters grant their ex-slave offspring any income and support in their life of freedom, and such children of white masters made up a very small percentage of the manumitted slaves. Because of this pervasive poverty, particularly among first-generation freedmen, free coloreds in all American slave societies typically had the highest mortality and disease rates among the free populations.

But at the same time the available evidence suggests that free coloreds had a much higher fertility rate than the native-born whites. In Minas Gerais, which had the second largest of Brazil's free colored population, the crude birth rate of the free coloreds in 1814 was 42 per 1,000, and its death rate was 34 per 1,000. In contrast, the white population had a birth rate of 37 per 1,000 and a death rate of 27 per 1,000. Several other estimates support the idea that the free coloreds had intrinsically higher fertility ratios than any other population group in their respective societies.

Because of their high fertility and the constant flow of more women than men into their ranks through manumission, the free colored had the highest ratio of women and was the youngest of the three population groups that made up most of the slave societies. In terms of marriage, family, and kinship, however, they differed little from the free society around them. In a census of the São Paulo plantation region of Campinas in 1829, there was little difference in the ratio of female-headed households, married couple households, and widows with children between whites and free coloreds. For the entire population of Brazil in the census of 1872, married whites again were 30 percent of their respective population group, 26 percent of all free coloreds were in this category, and only 8 percent of slaves were married.

The size and mobility of the free colored class led to tensions with the dominant white elite. From early on there were cases of elite white males who accepted fines and sometimes exile to stay with their free colored lovers. Frequently, their families objected to their relationships, even when both partners were unmarried. This was the case of don Francisco de Saldías and María Nicolasa, who shocked his family by living together in a free union in Lima in 1668. Despite several jailings and fines (María spent six months in prison), Francisco refused to capitulate to his family's demands, declaring that it was simply not possible for him to "be a man" with any other woman. He and María eventually fled Lima and their prosecutors for Callao. Given these attitudes, it is no accident that public pressure led to sumptuary laws against colored women, from earliest times prohibiting them from wearing silks in public and displaying rich jewelry such as pearls. This was issued against both slave and free colored women in Panama in 1574, in Mexico in 1612, and in Lima in 1631. Due to noncompliance, much of this legislation had to be repeated over the centuries to little avail.

Free colored men also presented a problem for the white elite. In Mexico, for instance, the early 18th century was a time of economic recovery after years of sluggish growth and an ailing silver economy. As wealth increased, it seeped into the free colored class, as men and women found market opportunities and niches for advancing their careers. Some free coloreds became rather well-off in the process. During the 1720s and 1730s in the Mexican town of Puebla, Captain Joseph de Santander, a free colored militia officer, ran a successful enterprise as a master dyer. The business earned him enough money to dress in stylish imported British capes, to dine with place settings of fine china, and to relax in the comfort of his study reading Marcus Aurelieus while gazing upon paintings of historic European battle scenes. His brother, Captain Juan Santander, was even wealthier, possessing enterprises totaling more than 70,000 pesos, putting him among the ranks of the city's wealthiest individuals. Men like these had their pick of wives, and so did their subordinates. The city's free colored militia was stocked with soldiers who were taking advantage of job opportunities in textile production, leatherworking, and smithing. Of the hundreds of men who served, an inordinate proportion married white brides. In 1720, just 2 percent of the city's free colored males wedded white women. By the 1790s, that number had risen to 13 percent. But among free colored militiamen, a more successful economic class overall, these men married whites at exceptionally high rates—representing over 27 percent of their total marriages. Such marital behavior drew the ire of the colonial elite, particularly when these women were drawn from the upper social classes.

On the whole, studies of free colored marriage patterns suggest that racial endogamy was high. In Mexico City's central Sagrario parish in the 17th century, the 922 marriages recorded by color showed that free colored women married out of their ethnicity in only 27 percent of their unions, while just 18 percent of free colored males found partners who were not free coloreds. Among white women, however, only 3 percent married outside their race, compared with just 7 percent of white men. In the Mexican countryside, marital endogamy rates were equally telling. In rural Jalapa, 90 percent of white marriages were endogamous in 1645, as opposed to 82 percent of free colored and mestizo marriages, and 97 percent of Indian marriages. By the eve of independence, marital endogamy had relaxed considerably among rural whites. Nearly 79 percent of white marriages were endogamous, which exactly matched the rate of endogamy among free coloreds and mestizos. Meanwhile, native endogamy had increased, as 98 percent of their marriages were with each other. These small samples provide some insights to the larger picture of the colony. Quite simply, although marital endogamy was the norm for everyone, some groups were more endogamous than others, especially at particular moments in time and in different locations. By and large, natives were the most endogamous ethnic group, followed by whites, then mestizos and free coloreds. Marital exogamy also tended to increase over time, particularly in urban areas. Since free coloreds were among the most exogamous of the social classes, some have suggested that they may have played a critical role in bringing about *mestizaje*, the proverbial racial mixture that has been a trademark of the Mexican heritage. But at the same time, enough endogamy persisted in the colony throughout the colonial period that the *mestizaje* process was slow and staggered, especially in certain rural regions, like Igualapa (in the Mexican "Costa Chica"), where marital endogamy among free colored remained high, over 90 percent, into the late 18th century.

Some of the trends found in Mexico held elsewhere in Latin America. In Brazil, in the interior Minas town of Catas Altas do Mato Dentro, of the 260 free colored marriages between 1816 and 1850, the intermarriage rates ran higher than in Mexico, yet endogamy still prevailed. Here, 47 percent of the free colored women married outside of their racial group and just 11 percent of men. In the same town, white endogamy rates were quite high, and with far fewer white women marrying outside the race than men. Apparently, in this part of the world, it was free colored women and white men who were most responsible for racial mixture (*mestizaje*) within the framework of marriage. Some regional studies have also shown strong inclinations among free coloreds to marry slaves. In two parishes of Lima, Peru, between 1800 and 1820, a third, or 110 of 343 slave marriages, were contracted between slaves and free partners—and in this case all of the free spouses were blacks, mulattoes, or *castas* (members of the racially mixed castes). There are a few recorded instances of whites marrying slaves. An illustrative case comes from Quito in 1809, when the aunt and sister of the free white carpenter José Andrade denounced his decision to marry María de la Concepción Pastrama, a *parda* (dark, brown-skinned) slave. They argued that the marriage was denigrating to his social station. However, the president of the Audiencia (high court) ruled that since both had no legal impediments to marry, and Andrade, though legitimate and white, was not of noble status, nothing could prevent the wedding from taking place.

José Andrade and María de la Concepción's marriage reveals the blurring of status markers that took place over time, as free coloreds engaged in sustained interaction with the rest of society. The court's behavior in this instance underscores the permeability of certain legal barriers that gradually began to facilitate racial interaction. While the legal system continued to police certain boundaries of color, in time, it enabled others to be traversed. Symptomatic of these processes was the fact that in many documents showing plebian interactions there was great confusion about color status. People appearing in court cases and in various commercial transactions could be assigned different color definitions each time they were referred to by witnesses or officials. Over a lifetime, a person might even fluctuate from being *negro*, to mulatto, to mestizo. In some cases, individuals made calculated efforts to move and "pass" into a lighter, more socially acceptable caste status. In doing so, they typically found it easier to move between groups that were not greatly different from their own. For example, a *negro* (black) might find it easier to pass as a mulatto, or a mulatto might be able to slip into the status of a mestizo. However, engineering any major move across caste categories could involve significant alterations in one's social networks and considerable psychological strain. But these moves did not always have to be permanent. Free coloreds routinely moved fluidly, back and forth, between caste statuses, oftentimes as they traveled between cities, towns, rural estates, and colonies. For many, the effort was worth it. Itinerant free coloreds living in rural townships in parts of colonial Mexico sometimes found homes in indigenous communities (*pueblos de indios*). Here they occasionally became enveloped in native life and were eventually embraced as *indios* themselves. When census takers took note of the populations in these settlements, they often failed to record the free colored presence accurately, preferring to lump them into the general category of *indios*.

Such refashioning of caste status was largely unintentional on the part of free coloreds. But in colonial Quito, between 1678 and 1815, a total of 253 individuals aggressively petitioned the court (*declaratorias*), claiming that they were mestizos. They were actively attempting to escape one of the burdens of being a free person of color in colonial Spanish America—the obligation of paying a head tax (*tributo*), an amount that varied from colony to colony. For people from the lower and middling ranks of society, the fee represented a real and detectable loss of income—for wealthier free coloreds, the tax smacked of discrimination and reminded them of their racial origins. Mestizos, however, were excluded from payment. By and large, the petitioners in Quito were humble folk, peasants and lower-class laborers; yet many were indeed free coloreds who were legally liable to taxation. Through their measured efforts, several successfully claimed a mestizo identity, and they did so by appealing to their poverty. One of the unremarkable benefits of being a plebeian in the Hispanic world was that poverty tended to equalize everyone's lifestyle and dress. Hence, it became doubly difficult for administrators to distinguish between the plethora of races, given that the complexities of phenotype alone did not often provide a reliable guide. Ironically, therefore, the very poverty that the government intended to use to suppress the status of free coloreds, keeping them beneath whites and mestizos, actually became their route to advancing in caste status in Quito's *declaratoria* cases.

Unsurprisingly, given the multiracial composition of the plebeian sector, studies of housing in Mexico City and San Juan, Puerto Rico, show that free coloreds and whites lived together, rented rooms to each other, and shared the same buildings. In the few studies we have of racial distribution by housing, there is little evidence of sustained racial segregation, despite the best efforts of the early colonizers to impose a *traza* system in urban areas that relegated certain parts of towns to whites, and others to natives. In 19th-century Cuba, city officials in Havana did intentionally undervalue property just outside of the city's walls in 1846, so as to inspire free coloreds to abandon the downtown area. The attempt was successful, but not completely. While 72 percent of free blacks left the city proper, 34 percent of whites also moved into the areas beyond the walls, creating a racially mixed environment. Even the downtown neighborhoods continued to be home to some blacks, mainly slaves, but also some free colored families of wealth and means.

In contrast to the efforts of the Cuban officials, a number of explicitly free colored townships were created in the rest of the New World. One of the most integrated of these was the township of San Vicente de Austria (Lorenzana), founded in El Salvador in 1639. Residents here included both free coloreds and mestizos. But in Guatemala, a more exclusive town, known as Gomera, was founded between 1610 and 1611 by the president of the Audiencia of Guatemala. Located in a lowland coastal region near the Pacific, the town was intended to solve the colony's growing problem with blacks who illegally resided in native villages. At Gomera, blacks were enticed to settle by being granted control over local salt pans at Sicapate, as well as having access to their own governing apparatus, including a *cabildo* (town council) and *regidores* (councilmen). The community became a success as free coloreds settled and jealously guarded their rights from encroaching Spaniards. Other black municipalities developed more organically. In Costa Rica, the Puebla de Pardos was founded in 1655 in a section of Cartago. Over the 16th and 17th centuries, increasing free black migration into the hills of the region caused the government to seek ways to group them into a single settlement.

An opportunity began to present itself in the 1630s. Sometime between 1635 and 1638, a female mulatto firewood collector witnessed a miracle. While searching for wood in the forests around Cartago, she encountered a statue of the Virgin. Elated, she brought the image home and placed it carefully in her room. On her next outing she stumbled upon another image. Returning home again, she noticed that the first statue had mysteriously vanished! The events repeated themselves a third time, but during this instance the statue she recovered in woods was of a black Virgin. Interpreted as miracles, these religious happenings led to the creation of a Marian folk-cult devotion, the establishment of a shrine, and, ultimately, a religious confraternity.

By the 1650s, this spiritual anchor gradually supported a settlement, which became the Puebla de Pardos. A series of nonreligious institutions then quickly emerged in the municipality. One of the most important of these was a militia company for free colored soldiers. Adeptly, in exchange for their military services and fealty to the king, the militia's early officers made some demands from the Crown. They requested that the new community not be exploited by whites, and that they be granted specific land rights. They also pressed for the municipality to be allowed to possess its own free colored *cabildo* and police force, and that blacks living in Puebla de Pardos be granted the privilege of tribute exclusion. It took time for their requests to materialize. In the interim, a number of grave abuses were committed against the township's free colored residents. Since the settlement was located within the confines of Cartago, whites lived nearby and randomly entered the area, robbing free colored children, absconding with their wives, and impressing community members into exploitative labor. But as a solid base of privileges and protections finally coalesced, the Puebla de Pardos began attracting black settlers who voluntarily moved down from the hills to join the burgeoning community. Between 1700 and 1798, the settlement grew from 55 to 231 homes.

In such settlements, free coloreds reflected their broader composition in society. Most were working class, while a few managed to acquire positions of stature and influence. As a predominantly working-class people, free coloreds had high illegitimacy rates. Indeed, on the whole, free coloreds living virtually everywhere and in all types of communities possessed some of the highest rates of illegitimate births among all free persons in Latin American society. They also had among the largest number of consensual unions, though it is worth noting that in many cases, poor whites in the Ibero-American colonies were only moderately better off. The high free colored consensual union rates did not necessarily mean that these mulattoes and blacks had a greater degree of instability in family life, but they indicated a level of poverty in which church weddings were too costly an item to be worthwhile. On the other hand, all free coloreds baptized their children, and unlike slaves, they usually had both a godfather and a godmother present at the christening. But given that many free coloreds were striving for upward mobility in their new world of freedom, they tended to use the fictive kinship system in a more calculating way than either the master or slave classes. Like the upwardly mobile mestizos in Latin America, many freedmen listed successful whites as *copadres* and *comadres* in an effort to gain support in classes and caste groups above their own station. For these free colored parents, *compadrazgo* ties were used to forge patron and client relations and to boost their children's chances at upward mobility.

Despite fictive kinship ties to powerful white neighbors, ultimately, as seen in the Puebla de Pardos, free coloreds did build a powerful set of institutions that also strengthened their internal cohesion as Afro-Americans. This development of a community identity was of course aided by a continuing prejudice against blacks and mulattoes on the part of whites, of legal impediments that constantly reminded them of their partial rights, and by a government and Church that often insisted that they organize themselves strictly into color-based voluntary associations.

Undoubtedly, one of the most important of such political associations was the militia. Neither Spain nor Portugal maintained a large standing royal army in America. All defense was essentially in the hands of a small group of professional officers and soldiers, and a mass of civilian militiamen. Beginning in the 1540s, military service was required of all able-bodied freedmen, and it was not long before free coloreds began serving in the militias. In 1555, Cuba allowed blacks to serve in its companies as auxiliaries, followed by Puerto Rico (1557), Cartagena (1560, 1572), Mexico (1556–62), and Santo Domingo (1583). Tentative initial experiments in using blacks as auxiliaries quickly led to their incorporation as full-time militiamen, especially in strategically important coastal regions where exceedingly hot climates and the ravaging effects of yellow fever proved inhospitable to whites. Port cities such as Havana, Vera-cruz, and Cartagena soon became havens for free colored duty, and especially during the 16th and 17th centuries, when pirate activity was at its height, the services of the free colored militias provided an anchor to Crown military policy. Valiant services, such as the 1624 defense of Lima against Dutch corsairs, and the 1683 repulsion of the notorious Lorenzo de Graff (Lorencillo) from the shores of Mexico, brought free colored forces into the spotlight, providing them with important political capital they could use to improve their status as black civilians. Perhaps the most obvious benefit derived from duty was the right for free coloreds to carry weapons, an issue that was hotly debated in bureaucratic circles into the mid-1660s. Loyal militia service also did much to combat the stereotype that free coloreds, if given the opportunity, would ally themselves with maroons and bands of unconquered native groups to contest the governing regime. If anything, when emergency situations presented themselves, the Crown was able to find its greatest immediate support among free colored soldiers, since whites, particularly members of the merchant elite, usually shied away, claiming that serving active duty would place their businesses in jeopardy. Another concrete benefit of duty involved eliminating the dreaded tribute burden. Militia services garnered in the 1624 assault on Lima resulted in successful petitions by the militiamen to be released from the detested tax. This was followed by appeals from soldiers in the Yucatán (1630s), Nicaragua (1665–70), Costa Rica (1672), and Mexico (1678), among others. Relieving the tax burden was an important step toward increasing the attractiveness of military service for free coloreds and was also the beginning of wider appeals by free colored militia families (essentially noncombatants) to request exemption. As free coloreds lobbied for rights, they developed the legal arm of the militia institution and shared case infor-mation with soldiers in various regions and colonies. Consequently, they carefully created a network of contacts that widened their understanding of events happening among free coloreds in other parts of the colonial New World. In this sense, the militia served as a vehicle for a broad cohesion in which free coloreds understood their fate and fortunes to be linked with others of their kind.

These processes only increased in importance in the first half of the 18th century, especially in the Spanish colonies. During this time courtroom im-munities, known as the *fuero militar*, were conceded to free colored soldiers, and in some places militiamen began acquiring greater access to high-ranking officership posts. Among the more impressive of these were accomplishments in Mexico, where by the 1720s free coloreds had managed to acquire the post of colonel. In the 1740s and 1750s, Mexico's free colored soldiers even possessed their own black military inspector, responsible for supervising the militia forces of the colony at large. As this was occurring, militiamen at the local level began to imbricate themselves into local politics. In parts of rural Mexico it was not unheard of for local free colored captains to use their posts and their soldiers to intimidate local magistrates, mayors, and governors into submission. These tactics proved most effective in townships where free coloreds already comprised the majority of the nonnative population. Hence, in the Mexican coastal town of Acayucan in 1762, Lieutenant Juan Domingo Ramos mobilized troops to protest the punishment of Francisco Salomon, a *pardo* soldier who was slated to be whipped for resisting arrest. Spurred into action for reasons beyond martial camaraderie, Domingo Ramos was incensed that his subordinate was to be flogged like a slave, since "never before in Acayucan has a *pardo* been whipped," he exclaimed. Meanwhile, in Tamiagua, another Mexican coastal town, militia forces mobilized in 1710 and shot the local justice official. The murder had been called in retribution for his acts against the free colored soldier Joseph Alexandre, who had been accosted for owing a white merchant ten pesos. When not engaged in such blatantly defiant activities, militiamen also exercised their politics from within the system, serving as bailiffs or as the military arm of the provincial authorities. In this way, they amassed more political capital that enabled them to appeal for certain economic privileges, such as preferred fishing rights, land titles, and commercial contracts.

Clearly, the free colored militias offered concrete opportunities for its soldiers to operate successfully in colonial society, but it also developed certain identities for its members. In the Spanish kingdom, militiamen served in a variety of companies—some segregated by color called units of *pardos* (mulattoes), others for *morenos* ("pure" blacks), and still other units that were racially integrated (*de todos colores*), even to the point of including mestizos and whites. The classification of these units depended greatly on local and regional factors rather than on any consistent Crown policy. But given that these units were often racially constructed, opportunities arose for the development of racial consciousness based on color. In other words, the militia could help trigger racial affinities that moved beyond ethnicity and that were entwined with bonds generated by both martial service and color. But because the institution also provided soldiers with raw political power, militiamen could use this to refashion themselves, thereby transforming the very meaning of racial identity. Each time the militia scored a political victory or acquired a new privilege, it chiseled away at society's understandings of who free coloreds were and, in the process, gave free coloreds more confidence in expressing themselves as *negros*, *pardos*, mulattoes, or the like.

The degree to which race came to shape the identity of the militiamen can again be traced in Mexico. In the 1760s, the Crown directed a wholesale assault on free colored militia duty throughout the Spanish empire. In Mexico, as elsewhere, free colored militiamen were asked to relinquish autonomy over their units in favor of white officers, who were to promptly begin supervising their affairs. These shocks produced some unpredictable responses. As royal officials deliberated removing tribute exemptions in the province of Xicayan in the 1770s, free coloreds responded with a fascinating letter revealing tenets of their self-identity: "And this Sir? Why must the [mulatto] militias of Xicayan be perceived as useless and looked upon with disdain . . . and why must the blacks and mulattoes in the companies of Spaniards be looked down upon as well? Are we not coastal guardians?" In the rural Mexican town of Guajolotitlan, the response of some soldiers to the sweeping changes was potentially more sanguine, as Lieutenant Policarpio de los Santos attempted to rally free black soldiers to arms for "not allowing Spaniards to become officers in the [militia] companies under any circumstances." In Puebla, less conflict came about, since the militiamen were aware that they were operating in a city where they were outnumbered by other *castas*. Still, in their letters drafted to the viceroy and king, they expressed an identity as free coloreds. But they did so carefully, in ways that revealed a strategy of self-deprecation in order to try to uphold privileges: "we . . . serve Your Majesty, who must consider that *although we are pardo in color*, we are of noble heart to sacrifice our being and lives for the king as we have done on numerous occasions [emphasis added]."

Free colored militias also developed a class identity that could become enveloped with racial identity. In the French colony of Saint Domingue on the eve of the Haitian revolution, the island's free colored population was a divided one. In one of the several camps stood well-to-do mulattoes who associated with white planters and constituted an economic elite that was distant in its racial affinities with blacks. In another camp was the military group, essentially militiamen and some professional soldiers. Unlike mulatto planters, their wealth was created and sustained with great entrepreneurial vigor—typical of the risky business ventures one might associate with individuals who were only recently removed from slavery and who were willing to do whatever was necessary to advance into the upper tiers of economic success. But many free coloreds of the island's military group consciously retained African surnames and aggressively cultivated relationships with fellow free coloreds through fictive kinship and patronage. These individuals also became deeply involved in manumitting slaves—an additional source of patronage. By and large, their close proximity with free coloreds of varying social strata made the military group more of a leadership class for the free colored population as a whole.

While more research needs to be done on the topic, it appears that the basic patterns of this leadership class may have existed in other colonies, including those in the Spanish and Portuguese realm.

Of course, there were militiamen in all colonies who were little invested in the affairs of other blacks or free coloreds, and who utilized the institution solely for personal gain. Lower ranking soldiers frequently had minimal influence in the militia and could easily float in and out of the corps. The degree to which racial identity shaped their lives varied according to the individual, their commitment to their roles as *pardo* and *moreno* militiamen, and even their civilian roles in their communities. In Brazil as well as Saint Domingue, there were also specific units of soldiers dedicated primarily to the recapture of runaway slaves. Called *caçadores do mato* (bush hunters) in Brazil and the *maréchaussée* in Saint Domingue, these units were frequently composed of ex-slaves who were deemed knowledgeable in the habits of maroons. Thanks to their profession, these *caçadores do mato*, and especially their captains, could hold ambivalent relationships with the free colored community at large. On the one hand some free coloreds praised their activities, since they helped increase the feeling of safety and security in colonial life by reducing the real threat that maroons often posed on towns and settlements. Maroons were not necessarily discriminating in their raids, and free coloreds, as well as whites, could equally be the targets of attacks. But on the other hand, the *caçadores do mato* were individuals who were frequently rather close to slavery themselves, and their duties placed them at the margins, rather than at the center of free colored society.

In hindsight, it is probably no exaggeration to say that in Spanish and Portuguese America the vast majority of able-bodied freedmen did service at some time in their lives in the colonial military establishment, particularly during the 17th and early 18th centuries when the militia institution expanded to encompass regions beyond coastal zones. As might be suspected, in most cases the free coloreds were confined to serve in infantry units. Less often they could form into more prestigious cavalry units, and in the case of the major Caribbean fortress and port city of Cartagena, they controlled the two artillery companies in the city. Although the Spanish Crown disbanded many of these units by the end of the 18th century, their services continued in key strategic ports. In the vital center of Cuba in 1770, free coloreds made up a third of the armed forces in this heavily guarded island. In 1779 there were 3,413 black (*pardo*) and mulatto (*moreno*) soldiers organized into three battalions and several smaller companies, another 4,645 were white militiamen, and 3,609 were paid royal troops in this large armed force. Moreover, the Spanish government kept these militias in active service until the Esclaera conspiracy, and after a ten-year pause reestablished them in 1854 when six battalions of 1,000 men were created on the island.

Aside from the military, the Church for its part also encouraged free coloreds to form their own separate *cofradías* and *hermandades*, especially because many of the white ones refused to admit them into coequal membership. These fraternal and religious societies then became a major source for maintaining Afro-American religious cults, acted as mutual-aid societies, and cemented class and color friendships through ritual ceremonial activity. Though created for racist reasons and supported by a white society bent on maintaining a social order that was more separate than equal, these religious voluntary organizations became pillars of the community and gave free coloreds a sense of worth and identity, which, like their militia units, provided them with crucial supports in highly racist societies. These black brotherhoods existed in nearly every city and town that had a substantial population of free and slave blacks and mulattoes. In most larger towns, there were several such societies, and many of the brotherhoods admitted slaves as well. These organizations thus tended to maintain important ties between the two classes and counterbalanced the antagonisms that inevitably developed between those who had a firm stake in the status quo and those who inherently opposed it.

When examined over time, it is possible to detect an evolution in the social function of these organizations that paralleled the development of changes, both demographic and cultural, among the black population. In Mexico, for instance, colored confraternities on the whole seem to have functioned very differently in the 16th and 17th centuries than they did in the 18th century. While they always served as vehicles of black integration into local Hispanic culture, offering blacks a sanctioned space to practice Catholicism and public opportunities to participate collectively in religious festivals, such as during the processions of Holy Week, confraternities also fluctuated over time in the degree to which their religious devotion possessed African content. In the 16th and early 17th centuries, because a larger African slave population resided in the colony, and because many first-generation freedmen were either African-born or had relatives who were from the continent, there were notable African practices in a number of confraternal activities and devotions. As elsewhere in the New World, several confraternities were even organized by ethnicity, as "Angolans," for example, claimed membership in some organizations over others. Even the leadership structure of the colony's confraternities was impacted, in that the power and influence of African matriarchal patterns saw large numbers of women playing prominent roles in positions of authority. A few 17th-century confraternities were even founded by women. Interestingly, despite African cultural imprints, these confraternities also remained forces of Hispanicization. Some confraternities even boldly exhibited their Christian piety, to the extent that their membership even outperformed white Catholics in their devotion. Most vividly in this respect were the participants of flagellant confraternities, such as those of the brotherhood of Saint John in Zacatecas (1635), whose members walked the streets during religious processions, whipping themselves and drawing blood in penitence for Christ. These forms of Baroque piety, somewhat unique to Mexico's poor black community, began to give way in the 18th century. While such extreme forms of external devotion were deemed appropriate for a population of slaves and newly manumitted freedmen, as the composition of the black population gradually changed, transitioning into a population of more established free coloreds, the desire to follow these practices waned. Throughout Mexico in the 18th century, confraternities came to more closely resemble the practices of whites and mestizos, their leadership became more predominantly male (reflecting European patterns of patriarchy), and the institutions served to integrate blacks more deeply into the dominant culture. Nevertheless, greater Hispanicization never completely eliminated the possibility that these organizations retained some African roots.

Despite their function as institutions that ultimately supported the framework of Iberian hierarchy, the road to founding black confraternities was not an easy one. In the 16th century, as the colony of New Spain consolidated, colonial authorities questioned the role and trajectory of Mexico's black population and remained unsure if allowing its members to organize into confraternities was a good idea. Realizing that black confraternities had existed in Spain itself from the 1400s, slaves and small numbers of free coloreds petitioned the government to grant them permission to create confraternities and hospitals in Mexico, since they were being excluded from predominantly white, mestizo, and Indian organizations, and since they were poor and in need of charity. A black tailor named Juan Bautista lobbied on these grounds in 1568, but to no avail. Bureaucrats feared that confraternities might serve to foment rebellion, such as the foiled black conspiracy of 1536–37 in Mexico City. To some degree, they were right. When news of black rebellion circulated again in 1611–12, it was precisely within the confines of confraternities that insurrectionary plans were made. In 1611, a group of 1,500 black and mulatto confraternity members marched through the streets of Mexico City, protesting the killing of a slave woman who had been cruelly beaten to death by her master. They shouted at onlookers and hurled stones at public buildings before angrily approaching the offices of the archbishop and the Inquisition. When the confraternity's leader was publicly punished for these acts, the organization's members retaliated with plans for a more serious uprising to occur during Holy Week of 1612. The rebels were to be armed with weapons purchased by the confraternity.

Such dramatic political activities did not emerge as the norm in Mexico but did become stronger features of free colored Cuban *cabildos* (confraternities) of the 19th century. Cuba actually possessed a variety of related religious organizations—*cofradías*, which resembled the confraternities commonly found in other parts of the Spanish kingdom and had tight Church affiliations; *cabildos*, typically housed in the private homes of coloreds and that were more distanced from Church policy; and *sociedades de soccoros mutuos*, or mutual-aid, "Pan-African societies" that were less ethnically exclusive than either the *cabildos* or the *cofradías*, which gained prominence after 1850. In Cuba, it should be noted, African ethnicity and linguistic ties played a guiding role in who comprised the membership of certain *cofradías* and *cabildos* in the 19th century. In 1812, José Antonio Aponte, a former militia corporal and a priest in the Lucumí *cabildo* of Shango Tedeum, used his spiritual connections and ministry to foment a large-scale uprising. Among his goals was seeking independence from Spain and an end to slavery. To gather followers he conspired to entice slaves into believing that abolition had already occurred, but that others were preventing them from knowing it. Aponte also used the network of *cabildos* on the island, and the fact that they primarily spoke in African languages, to plan the revolt and to keep it secret. Despite the successful torching of a few sugar plantations, Aponte's plans were leaked and the revolt ultimately folded. *Cabildos* again, however, played a role in various moments of unrest throughout the 1830s, and in the planning of the widely feared Escalera conspiracy of 1844. But in the repressive aftermath of this plot, the prominence of Cuba's *cabildos* waned, and they started facing competition for membership from the emerging *sociedades de soccoros mutuos*. It was these Pan-African organizations that began playing a more formal role in politics, and that mainstreamed their members into Hispanic society. On their agenda were appeals for black suffrage, better access to education, the desegregation of public spaces, repeals of discriminatory legislation, the abolition of slavery, and the elimination of the caste system. This sweeping reform platform actually came about in stages between the 1850s and the 1890s. With help and pressure from black military leaders, especially those who had participated in the Ten Years' War, substantive changes in the lifestyle of free coloreds and slaves gradually emerged.

It has been claimed that most free colored persons in Brazil also belonged to brotherhoods and that a large number of slaves were members. As throughout Spanish America, these associations were dues-paying institutions that saw to the spiritual, physical, and burial needs of its members. While most confraternities in both the Spanish and Portuguese world were relatively poor (usually sharing an altar in a church), in a minority of cases they accumulated large amounts of real estate and had their own separate chapels and cemeteries. Some of these wealthier organizations were found in Brazil. Also, as seen in the Spanish territories, while many confraternities were open to people of all colors, others were divided by race and ethnicity. In 18th-century Salvador, one brotherhood was based on African birth in Dahomey, and another was maintained exclusively for Nago-Yoruba peoples of the Keu nation. The great period of development for these ethnically and racially divided Brazilian brotherhoods was the 18th and early 19th centuries. The city of Salvador at this time had some sixteen primarily black or mulatto brotherhoods. At the same time, there were twenty-one of these to be found in the towns of the mining districts of Minas Gerais.

Although they were allowed to elect their own officers in nearly all confraternities in the Spanish and Portuguese New World, there were usually provisos stating that slaves or illiterates could not become secretaries, presidents, or treasurers. Many of these rules were routinely broken. At least in the case of the Spanish colonial *cofradías* and in the Brazilian *hermandades*, the Church also went out of its way to control these associations. All were given white clergymen as guardians, and sometimes the government even forced these associations to accept whites to control their finances, despite vociferous protests, as occurred in the late 18th-century confraternity of Saint John the Baptist in Caracas, Venezuela. In most cases they played a subordinate role in much local religious activity, but in some regions they became major economic and social powers. Outstanding in this respect were the *hermandades* in the city of Bahia in the 18th and early 19th centuries, and those scattered throughout the major mining communities of Minas Gerais in the same period.

It was these black brotherhoods, as well as many white ones, that funded major artistic activity of mulattoes and blacks. In Minas Gerais the most famous sculptors and architects were free coloreds. António Francisco Lisboa, known as Aleijadinho, was the son of a slave woman and a white architect father. His sculptures and decorations of 18th-century churches in Minas earned him the reputation as Brazil's leading artist of the Rococo period. Another was the slave-born Manuel da Cunha, who was the leading portraitist of the age and also painted many walls and altars of Brazil's leading churches. He was trained in both Brazil and Portugal and had already achieved an outstanding career before his manumission. In music, the composers of Minas were all mulattoes. The most outstanding was Emerico Lobo de Mesquita, who was an organist to a major white brotherhood, a member of the mulatto brotherhood of Nossa Senhora das Merces dos Homens Pardos, and a composer totally current with the latest in European Baroque composition.

A more prominent, if less skilled, composer was the Jesuit Padre José Mauricio, whose mother was African-born and who himself was appointed court composer when the imperial family moved to Brazil in 1808. The Brazilian free-colored class even produced one of the giants of Latin American and world literature. In a class by himself was the 19th-century mulatto novelist Machado de Assis, who, though little conscious of his class or background in his own writings, was closely associated with the free colored intellectuals of his Northeast region. These exceptional artists of regional and even international stature were just the peak of a mass of free colored musicians, writers, and artists who produced for both the popular masses and the elite of their respective societies.

Free coloreds were also to be found in all the other professions of Brazilian and Spanish American societies. Sometimes they were forced to form their own separate craft corporations, but often they were members of the regular guilds. More common as apprentices and journeymen than as master craftsmen, they nevertheless could be found in every skilled occupation in these societies. Sometimes, however, they even became officially licensed masters of occupations legally denied to them. Thus in the officer class of the colored militias could be found goldsmiths, silversmiths, and jewelers, all occupations specifically banned to them in Iberian law. There were also entire occupations traditionally dominated by both free coloreds and slave artisans. The most important of such occupations was that of the barber surgeon, who often performed most of the major medical functions in the community. That the free coloreds served an important role in all skilled crafts, and even dominated a few crucial ones, does not mean that their color did not affect their economic lives. Colonial and 19th-century records are filled with complaints by white artisans against their free colored compatriots. For every free colored who made it to the top of his profession, color barriers always kept others from practicing that profession. Constant attempts were made by whites to force blacks and mulattoes to form their own craft corporations, or make them take more extensive examinations for a master's certification, or even deny them the right to carry out their craft on any level. But the Crown and royal officials usually accepted their right to existence, both on their credentials as workers but also on the pragmatic grounds that skilled artisans of any race were needed in the colonies to help rectify manpower shortages in key industries. Thus, while prejudice was current everywhere, so too was some social mobility and economic integration.

In less skilled occupations there was little opposition because whites were less numerous and less interested in competing. In domestic service, vending, stevedoring, and seafaring, free coloreds and slaves were dominant. These were the types of work, however, that offered less income and less mobility for ex-slaves and their offspring. But such labor did give them the economic independence that enabled them to survive in the competitive market economy that dominated the free world. Free coloreds could also be found among the servant class (known as *agregados* in Brazil) that labored in the households of many middle and upper-class persons. Thus, for example, in the sugar district of Itu in the province of São Paulo, in 1829 there were some 343 *agregados* (representing 9 percent of total free population), of whom half were free persons of color, mostly women. This ratio of free coloreds was actually probably lower than normal in Brazil, given the high concentration of slaves in this region. Finally, on the frontiers, in the mountains, on the lands surrounding the towns and cities, and in the lands abandoned by the plantations, the majority of ex-slaves built their lives as free peasants. In most cases they remained squatters, few possessing full title to their lands. But they were nevertheless a major element of the truck-farming industry and formed the bulk of the subsistence farming population in most areas where slavery was the dominant institution.

Given their entrance into the lowest classes of society, their lack of education and even of capital, the climb up the social ladder was slow and painful for manumitted slaves and freedmen, but they did progress. Cuba offers an excellent example of the odds against them. Here, freedmen experienced difficulty in entering primary and secondary schools, and in 1860 only 5 percent of the school population consisted of free coloreds. This was at a time when the free coloreds formed 16 percent of the national population. Also, the areas where free coloreds were most densely concentrated, the eastern half of the island, had the fewest schools and fewest social resources. Of the 14,000 property holders on the island in 1861, only 1,000 of them were freedmen of color, though in the poorer districts of Oriente province they were often the dominant landowners.

Fundamental to all free coloreds in Latin America, however, was the right to physical mobility. In only a few regions and during only limited periods did the colonial, republican, and imperial governments restrict the movement of the free colored population. This was in contrast to North America, where passports and other restrictions existed to tie the freedmen to their original communities. The right of internal migration was crucial for the ability of free colored persons to respond to market incentives and to negotiate better work conditions. Physical mobility was not an automatic guarantee of economic mobility, as the experience of Brazilian frontier squatters who were forced off their lands and became urban poor suggests, but it was a fundamental right that allowed freedmen to escape more oppressive exploitation by the elite.

In only one instance did a significant group of landowners emerge among the free colored class prior to abolition, and this was in the already mentioned case of late 18th-century Saint Domingue. From the second half of the 18th century there had developed in the western part of the colony a group of mulatto landowners who possessed large plantations with numerous slaves. This was apparently one of the only significant groups of free colored planters known to have existed in any slave society in America. Many of these freedmen had gotten their starts with small inheritances from their white fathers, and then through hard work they or their sons built small landholdings into large plantations. Several of these same families also succeeded in sending their sons to France for higher education, while many of them entered the liberal professions.

In the course of events this group should have blended into the white upper classes. Their orientation and disposition in the decades prior to the Haitian revolution indicated that they were poised for absorption into these economic and social sectors. But the French and creole whites in the West Indies became ever more frightened of this new brown elite as it gained more economic and educational power. Though the Code Noir of 1685 unqualifiedly granted full citizenship to these freedmen, all local legislation and many imperial laws in the 18th century tried to ghettoize them, close off the avenues of manumission, and deprive them of all rights that whites possessed. The bitter elite mulatto planters were thus eventually forced by whites to identify with their poorer free colored neighbors, despite their class position. The majority of the free coloreds in Saint Domingue, as in the other French American possessions, were apprentice and journeymen artisans and small-scale farmers who were primarily to be found in the lower ranks of society. In Saint Domingue they were distinguished by their higher level of education but otherwise looked like all such groups in American slave society. But they had a powerful leadership that fought for their rights throughout the slave era. Though mostly losing to the white racists, leaders such as Rigaud, Oge, and Labastille nevertheless had an impact on radical insular and French opinion. The outbreak of the French Revolution gave them a chance to fight back and reverse the tide of racist legislation that had restricted their lives. First winning over the French Assembly in 1789, which regranted them full citizenship, they would eventually organize large armies to defend their rights from the enraged local whites. Though triumphing over their white rivals, the armies of free mulattoes would eventually go down to defeat at the hands of the slave armies of the revolutionary era.

But the battle lost in Saint Domingue did not end the struggle among the free coloreds on Martinique or Guadeloupe. These more humble, but still educated, free colored farmers and tradesmen had to fight the racist struggle all over again from the Napoleonic period through the restoration monarchy. They campaigned actively at home and abroad and by 1830 convinced French metropolitan opinion once again of the justice of their cause. The July Monarchy thus both opened up the manumission process on a major scale for these islands and then finally abolished slavery altogether in its American possessions in 1848. So powerful a political force had the free coloreds become that they dominated the first delegation of islanders sent to the French Assembly in the next decade. Of the half dozen men sent as representatives to the French legislature, only one was a white, and he was the island's leading abolitionist.

Few other free colored classes under slavery ever demonstrated as much political power as the embattled French American community. But in the Iberian world individual leaders among the free coloreds did play major political roles in their respective societies, both identifying with their fellow freedmen and slaves and, as often as not, playing independent or even hostile roles. This more complex relationship, especially in 19th-century Ibero-American society, had more to do with their greater acceptance and the less effective racist oppositions in their own societies. Their political activities involved everything from being part of elected officialdom and holding appointive administrative and military posts, to the leadership of illegal revolutionary armies. Thus the Rebouças family in Brazil, whose black founding father was a lawyer and elected representative in the Bahian provincial legislature, and whose sons were engineers and administrators at the imperial court, represents one type of behavior, just as Antonio Maceo, the mulatto revolutionary hero of the 1868 war in Cuba, was another. In the Brazilian abolitionist movement were Luis Gama and José de Patrocinio of the free colored class, while the mulatto viscount Francisco de Soles Torres, a former minister and head of the Bank of Brazil, was a supporter of slavery. In the armies of both the Spanish royalists and the creole republicans in the American Wars of Independence (1808–25) appeared many famous free colored military leaders, several of whom would eventually establish major political careers in their respective republican governments. Moreover, in every region where independence was fought and slavery existed, the well-trained black and mulatto militias formed important elements in the armies of both sides, and during the worst of the fighting in such regions as Peru and Venezuela both sides freed numbers of slaves for military service.

Though attacked, despised, rejected, and feared as a class of nouveaux riches and potential competitors, the free colored class in Latin America grew rapidly under the slave regimes that created them. They proved able to forge a community of freedmen capable of integrating themselves into the free market economy. They fought bitterly and sometimes successfully for the right to social and economic mobility and for the legal rights of full citizenship. This was the most difficult struggle of all, and one that would go on long after the death of slavery. But it was this never-ending struggle of the freedmen for acceptance before abolition that ultimately prepared the way for all slaves to enter more successfully into free society after freedom was granted to all Africans and Afro-Americans.

II

Transition from Slavery
to Freedom

The Haitian revolution was but one manifestation of a growing attack on African slavery that had begun earlier in the 18th century. For the first time in western European history, there developed in many of the imperial and colonial societies associated with African slavery a popular abolitionist movement that challenged the very legitimacy of slavery. Though individuals had attacked slavery from its earliest development in the Americas, these were isolated voices, which never took on a mass following or significantly changed accepted opinion. But at the beginning of the 18th century, an increasing number of influential philosophers and religious leaders began to challenge the legitimacy and morality of the institution. French thinkers of the Enlightenment were to lead a fundamental attack on the underpinnings of the institution by their appeals to reason, the stress on a rationalist vision of the world, and a new sense of cultural relativism and a corresponding decline of Eurocentric views of the world. To this general shift in values was added a direct attack on the legitimacy of slavery by one of the century's most influential political theorists, Montesquieu, in his study *The Spirit of the Laws* in the late 1740s.

A more direct assault on the institution grew out of the radical and millenarian elements of 17th- and 18th-century Protestantism. Almost all these sects rejected slavery, but the most conservative of them, the Quakers, had been deeply involved in slaving and slavery in America. In the 1770s the inherent contradiction between their beliefs and their practices led the Quakers to begin attacking slavery both among their members and in the societies in which they lived. This same rejection of slavery was also to appear in the preachings of the newer evangelical Protestant movements, and in 1774

John Wesley attacked slavery as a sin against man. Finally, even the economic justifications of the institution began to be challenged. In 1776, in *The Wealth of Nations*, Adam Smith declared that slavery was an anachronism in modern society and could not compete with free labor.

Though abolitionism was still a minority position, it now was receiving fundamental intellectual and moral backing among a small group of influential theorists and clergymen. Instead of isolated voices of marginal critics, a growing consensus emerged among European elites that slavery, despite its extraordinary historical roots, no longer was a legitimate institution or one compatible with modern enlightened society. It was this consensus that explains the attacks on slavery in the metropolitan territories of the major European states, many of them possessors of slave colonies. It was now held that slavery was incompatible with traditional English, Portuguese, or French rights. In the 1770s, Portugal, England, and France all enacted decrees or supported judicial decisions that essentially abolished slavery within their territories on the continent and the nearby Atlantic islands.

This was followed by a growing abolitionist consensus of radical republicans and millenarian and evangelical Protestants in the northern colonies of North America at the time of the American Revolution of 1776. In these newly independent states, gradualist abolitionist schemes were developed in the 1770s and 1780s, which declared all newborn slaves to be free and which required their apprenticeship under their parent's masters well into early adulthood. The first regions in America to legislate abolition were the northern states of the new republic of North America: Vermont in 1777, and Pennsylvania and Massachusetts in 1780. Rhode Island and Connecticut followed with gradual abolition laws in 1784. All of these were areas that had relatively small populations of slaves, most of whom were in domestic service.

The first massive liberation of slaves as a result of the abolitionist movement dates from the French Revolution. Far more than the American Revolution of 1776, the French movement of 1789 directly confronted the contradiction of the enslavement of humans in an egalitarian society. In 1788 an antislavery society known as the Amis des Noirs was founded in France with support from British Quakers. But this upper-class organization had little impact until the French Revolution. Even then, it was only the growing debate over colonial representation and the civil rights of free mulattoes and blacks that finally permitted the Amis to extend the discussion of abolitionism to a mass audience. In the several French Assemblies, the abolitionists under Abbé Gregoire, Lafayette, and Mirabeau, among others, became ever more radical and a mainstay of the Girondist faction. But were it not for constant political and military pressure by the West Indian free colored, the issue would not have continued to agitate the metropolitan assemblies. From 1789 to 1793, the constant interaction between planter and free coloreds and finally slave rebels, along with increasingly radicalized French opinion, led in late 1793 and early 1794 to the abolition of slavery in the French colonies. The Assembly in February 1794 emancipated and apprenticed only the 491,000 slaves of Guadeloupe and Saint Domingue, since Martinique was temporarily seized by the British, and Cayenne by the Portuguese. Napoleon's overthrow of the abolition decree in 1802 pushed the black rebels into total independence and led to an immediate emancipation of all slaves remaining on Saint Domingue.

But the events of the French Revolution only moderately affected abolitionist sentiments in other American societies. There were some small protests or conspiracies in most Spanish American colonies and Brazil but little general movement. Given the effective resistance of entrenched planter elites and their influence upon metropolitan and local republican governments, it would take more than a consensus of radicals and evangelicals to destroy the institution. Thus began a campaign of mass mobilization within Europe against slavery. This campaign first concentrated on the most vulnerable part of the American slavery system, its reliance on the African slave trade. This proved a more inviting target for reformers because there was a widespread belief that trading in slaves was morally reprehensible.

In 1787 the Society for the Abolition of the Slave Trade was formed in England, which mounted a successful public opinion campaign against the trade. As early as 1788 it forced through amelioration legislation establishing a limit on the number of slaves carried by tonnage of ship. This simple tonnage-to-slaves measure proved inadequate for increasing the space given Africans aboard the ships, and in 1799 a measured space requirement was enacted. The long-sought demand of total abolition was enacted in 1807 and achieved in 1808, also included a prohibition of interisland slave trading. The anti–slave trade campaign quickly spread to all the nations of Europe and America. In 1787 the U.S. Congress abolished the slave trade as of 1808. In 1792 the Danes also decreed the abolition of the trade but closed it off as of 1802, thus becoming the first nation to stop its slave trade. Then in the 1810s and 1820s all the major new Latin American republics abolished the slave trade.

The English anti–slave trade movement now mounted a major effort to abolish the slave trading of all nations. The movement pressured the British government to force all governments to end the trade, demanding its total abolition. By the time of the Congress of Vienna in 1815, several nations renounced the trade under British pressure. The most important trader affected was France, a major carrier of African slaves in the period before the French Revolution, which had hoped to reenter the trade in the postwar era.

But Britain was adamant and forced the defeated French to accept its conditions. In separate treaties in 1815 and 1817 the British also extracted promises from the Spaniards and the Portuguese to begin a gradual abolition of the trade. In 1820 the British navy began its policy of patrolling the African coast, and the government extracted from various European powers the right to search their vessels on the high seas. By the 1840s most of the major European naval powers had granted Britain this vital right; the Brazilians followed in the 1850s, with the United States finally coming into line in the following decade.

In the period from 1808 to 1850 it was only the Spaniards and the Portuguese who refused to conform to these demands. It was thus a tenet of British foreign policy in the next half century to pressure both nations to end their slave trade. The British demanded that Spain, Portugal, and the then new nation of Brazil declare slave trading to be piracy. By the 1830s they had forced all these nations to accept mixed judicial commissions to condemn vessels caught in the trade. Through constant prevarication, both the Spaniards and the Portuguese were able to keep their trades alive until the second half of the 19th century. But British naval blockades and patrols made life increasingly difficult for the slave traders. By 1850 British military and diplomatic pressure on the more sensitive Brazilian empire finally forced an effective end of the slave trade. But the Spaniards, whose Cuban possession remained their most important colony, refused all demands for abolition or carried out meaningless abolition decrees that did not stop the trade. Although the minor trade to Puerto Rico was effectively terminated in the 1840s, it would take the combined U.S. and British blockade of the island in the 1860s to finally force the termination of the slave trade to Cuba. With this ending of the Cuban trade, the entire Atlantic slave trade was finally and successfully terminated.

Although many abolitionists were convinced that the end of the slave trade would automatically bring about the end of American slavery, this was not the case. The natural decline of the slave population gradually slowed with the end of the slave trade, and relatively quickly the American-born slave population began to achieve positive rates of growth in those societies where emancipation was kept to a low rate. Thus in Europe and America, from the 1810s to the 1840s abolitionist groups began gathering their forces for a frontal attack on the institution within America. But emancipation of the slaves was a far more difficult and costly affair than the abolition of the trade. Slave owners in every major American slave society fought the emancipationists, and in every case the abolition of slavery was achieved only through political and/or military intervention. Masters bitterly fought or delayed every move toward abolition and by all their actions indicated that they hoped to maintain their slave regimes intact to the very last moment. In the French and British West Indies and in the United States, Brazil, and the Spanish islands, the price of slaves remained high until the last years before abolition. This expression of faith by the slave owners in their system of control and domination made each abolitionist movement a hard-fought struggle. Even when they were forced to accept defeat, owners demanded cash compensation for their slaves and the right to freely use the emancipated slaves as "apprentices" for many years into the future. They thus sought to maintain control of the workforce long after official emancipation was enacted.

The growth of abolitionism within the various slave regimes proceeded at different rates. In Britain and France the abolitionists gathered strength in the 1820s and 1830s, especially as they grew frustrated after the anti–slave trade campaign bogged down in a costly confrontation with all the naval powers of the world. After numerous petitions to parliaments and great debates, along with major slave unrest and strikes in the West Indies and British Guyana, ending in the Jamaica rebellion of 1831–32, the British government finally abolished slavery in 1834. But the planters fought so hard that the metropolitan government acceded to their demands before freeing the 668,000 slaves British subjects owned in America. These included both a generous cash settlement and a six-year apprenticeship beginning in 1834 for all slaves. It was only bitter apprenticeship strikes and unrest by the ex-slaves themselves that finally put an end to this system of labor, which was abandoned in most of the colonies by 1838.

The British experience served as a model for French and Danish emancipationists a decade later. Again, bitter planter and owner opposition forced each government to provide financial settlements when both nations abolished slavery in 1848. But the opposition of the 174,000 French and 22,000 Danish ex-slaves and their constant agitation led both nations to abandon any attempt to introduce apprenticeship, and the emancipated slaves were given direct freedom. When it came time for the Dutch finally to free their remaining 45,000 slaves in Surinam and the Caribbean islands in 1863, they also made no attempt to deny the ex-slaves freedom of residence, occupation, and employment.

In the American slave societies that were republics and thus controlled by the master class, the movement toward emancipation went at a much slower pace. Protestant groups, which were so effective in the English abolitionist movement, were also important in the United States. But the initial thrust of those movements dissipated itself in the abolition of the trade and in the liberation of slaves in the northern colonies. A frontal assault on the plantation slave regime of the Southern states did not come until well into the 19th century.

Most of the Spanish American republics initiated gradual emancipation at the time of their independence by passing so-called free-womb laws, which liberated the children of all slaves. But long-term apprenticeship periods under the old slave masters were required for these newly manumitted *libertos* or *manumisos*, and at the same time no slave born prior to the 1820s decrees was freed. This meant that slavery would continue, with ever-declining numbers, well into the 1840s and 1850s in most of these states. Typical of this pattern was the emancipation process in the three republics of Venezuela, Colombia, and Ecuador, which at the time of independence in the 1820s together had a slave population on the order of 125,000 to 130,000 persons. The three governments initially obtained their independence under the leadership of Simón Bolívar as a unified confederation known as Gran Colombia. In 1821 this state freed all slaves born after July 1821 and then set up local *juntas de manumisión* to collect special taxes to be used to purchase the freedom of those born before that date.

With the breakup of the confederation government into three independent republics, the abolitionist movement lost its drive, and the slaveholders were usually able to manipulate the laws to their own advantage in the next two decades. Ages in apprenticeship contracts were changed from eighteen years to twenty-one and in one case even twenty-six years, thus guaranteeing that the *libertos* would serve as slaves well into the 1840s. Some of these states even returned to slave trade activities, with Colombia selling some 800 slaves to Peru in the 1840s. But by midcentury pressure for total emancipation again built up, with the result that in the 1850s each of these states carried through immediate abolition for the remaining slaves, though always promising financial compensation for their masters. In most cases, the slave population by the 1850s was one-third or less than at the time of independence. In Colombia the 54,000 slaves at the end of the colonial period numbered just over 16,000 by 1851. In Venezuela, the 64,000 slaves in 1810 by 1854 had decreased to just 33,000 slaves and *manumiso*, while Ecuador, with its 8,000 or so slaves at independence, had only some 2,000 left by the time of abolition in 1852.

The Peruvian experience followed closely that of its northern neighbors. The liberating army of San Martín decreed gradual emancipation with a free birth act in July 1821. But apprenticeship laws kept the *libertos* working for the masters of their parents well into the next two decades. Again slavery declined slowly, though not without a great deal of violence, including a major slave rebellion of sugar workers who temporarily captured the city of Trujillo in 1848. When slavery was definitively abolished in late 1854, the 89,000 slaves to be found in 1821 were down to an estimated 25,000 slaves, for whom masters received compensation. The other South American republics followed a similar path. Bolivia in 1831 declared all slaves born since independence in 1825 to be free, but it did not finally abolish slavery until 1851, at which time there were only

1,000 left. Uruguay decreed a free-womb law in 1825 but was still importing slaves from Brazil in the 1830s. The only variation here was that in 1842, when slavery was definitively abolished, no compensation was paid to the masters.

Chile and Mexico stand out somewhat in their almost immediate turn toward total abolition as their first acts. Chile in 1823 unconditionally freed its 4,000 slaves and was thus the first Spanish American republic to do so. Argentina was the first to begin emancipation, with a free birth law in 1813, but total abolition did not come until the Constitution of 1853. Mexico, which still retained 3,000 slaves just before its independence, had freed all of them by the early 1830s, while the few slaves in Central America were freed with compensation in 1824. Thus after a period of thirty years, all the continental republican governments had eliminated slavery, the majority through apprenticeship and partial compensation arrangements. This relatively slow and pacific withering away of the institution of slavery was not the experience of the remaining large-scale slave societies in the post-1850s period.

For Brazil, the Spanish islands, and the United States—the only major slave powers in the second half of the 19th century—abolition was a long and slow process. In the case of the United States a close tie between the English and North American antislavery movements meant a long and intense campaign that finally culminated in the 1840s and 1850s in a massive popular attack on the institution. The isolation of the movement in the Northern states guaranteed that the overthrow of slavery would only finally occur through civil war. It was the destructiveness and violence of this civil war in the 1860s that finally convinced Cuban and Brazilian intellectuals that slavery was ultimately a doomed institution. As a result, in the 1860s, a serious abolitionist movement finally began to develop in these two societies. In the case of Cuba and Puerto Rico, the problem presented itself within a complex imperial colonial relationship, which essentially involved a struggle over control of a relatively indifferent and often changing central government. From the beginning, abolitionism was associated with the liberal movement in Spain, but it was only a minor part of that reformist position. In fact, the most influential and important of the abolitionist leaders in Spain were always Cuban or Puerto Rican creoles. In the Cortes of 1811–13 it was colonial delegates who demanded gradualist emancipation in all the American possessions. This movement failed, and most of the effective action against the slave trade came from external British pressure. In 1815 and 1817 stringent but ineffective treaties against the trade were signed by the two countries, one provision of which was to set up mixed condemnation commissions in Havana to seize slave ships. British consuls in Havana thereafter became major advocates for abolition and were extremely active in local politics in the 1820s and 1830s.

Within Spain itself only the occasional coming to power of the Liberals even led to a discussion of slavery. This occurred in the Cortes of 1822 and 1823, when Cuban radicals raised the issue. But another such liberal government did not appear until the late 1860s. Despite all the stringent treaties signed with the British, which did end the minor trade to Puerto Rico by the 1840s, it was only the intervention of the Union navy in the period of the U.S. Civil War that brought an end to the trade to Cuba. It was also the North American civil war that stimulated the creation of the first Spanish abolitionist society, which was established by a Puerto Rican in Madrid in 1864. The creation of the first Spanish republic in 1868 finally led Madrid to accept a gradualist emancipation, which it decreed in September of that year. But the weakness of the government and the simultaneous beginning of an independence rebellion in Cuba prevented its enactment. Nevertheless, the Madrid government and all the major parties now believed that slavery was doomed, so even the conservatives supported the government decision in July 1870 to abolish slavery. The so-called Moret law provided for the freeing of all slaves born after its enactment and the assignment of these *patrocinados* to an overly generous apprenticeship lasting until twenty-two years of age, though with half wages to be paid them from the time they reached eighteen. All persons sixty-five years of age and older were also freed.

The first Cuban rebellion begun in 1868 guaranteed that the Moret decree would be applied only on the government side of the lines, but emancipation was effectively carried out in a series of enabling decrees in Puerto Rico in 1872 and 1873. Meanwhile, government action brought down the number of slaves rather quickly in Cuba. In 1869 there were 363,000 slaves, then 228,000 in 1878, half of this loss being accounted for by the Moret reforms. Although there was some delay after the defeat of the rebels, the Moret law was finally applied to Cuba in 1880, and by late 1883 there were only 100,000 slaves left on the island. As could be expected from the earlier English and French experiences, opposition to apprenticeship was strong among the ex-slaves, and many of the older slaves demanded immediate emancipation. In October 1886 all this agitation finally led the Madrid government to terminate the apprenticeship system altogether and free the last remaining slaves.

In contrast to the complex struggle between metropolis and colonies, the abolitionist movement in Brazil was a struggle between classes and regions within one nation. Because slavery was so embedded within Brazilian society, the attack on slavery developed much later than elsewhere in Latin America. This was especially the case given the unwillingness of the master class to argue for the positive benefits of slavery for blacks. Unlike in the United States, the Brazilian elite never made a positive defense of slavery and only defended its economic necessity until alternative labor could be found. They thus seemed to accept the idea of emancipation in some distant future. This made opposition difficult to mount for those who wanted an immediate end to slavery. But the delay did not prevent it from being one of the more bitterly fought of abolitionist struggles. Until 1850 an elite group of liberal urban intellectuals had fought for the abolition of the Atlantic slave trade. The signing of a treaty with the British outlawing the trade in 1831 had little effect, and so pressure built up until final abolition was forced on the empire in 1850, as much by internal popular pressure as by British military intervention in Brazilian ports. There then followed a ten-year period of tranquillity in which slavery remained unchallenged. But the U.S. Civil War and mounting international campaigns against Brazil finally forced a reopening of the question in the 1860s. All this led the government elite to move toward a gradualist abolitionary approach as the only answer to an inevitable confrontation.

In September 1871 Brazil therefore adopted a law of free birth. But these emancipated slaves (or *ingenuos*) had to serve an apprenticeship until twenty-one years of age before effective freedom was to be granted. A state-supported emancipation fund was also established to purchase freedom for those born before 1872. Government leaders thought they had resolved the issue, and, in fact, serious abolition agitation did disappear temporarily, so that until 1880 the planter class enjoyed relative peace and control over their slave force.

It was only after 1880 that Brazil finally began to experience a popular movement of abolitionism. This new mass movement quickly challenged the very foundations of slavery. Although the leadership typically came from elite families, Brazilian abolitionism was unusual in having a significant minority of mulatto and black leaders. They ranged from the engineer André Reboucas and the pharmacist José de Patrocinio to the politician Luiz Gama and the fugitive-slave leader Quintano Lacerda and his 10,000 runaway slave community in the port city of Santos. The abolitionist movement also included large numbers of free black workers on the docks and in the railroads, who refused to transport slaves and who assisted runaways. In the early 1880s the internal slave trade was finally abolished, and taxes were established on local sales of slaves. But these ameliorating decrees did not stem the rising tide of abolitionist activity. In 1884 abolitionists succeeded in proclaiming the northeastern state of Ceará as a free state. An active underground railroad immediately developed, with free persons helping individual slaves to escape their owners and reach Ceará. The slave owners bitterly fought this growing disobedience, and in another set of ameliorating decrees passed in September 1885 they obtained a harsh fugitive slave law. This severely punished anyone assisting a runaway slave and had the effect of provoking the abolitionist movement into taking a stand of civil disobedience.

Thus from 1885 onward the pressures increased. In each year more and more cities abolished slavery within their limits. The state of Amazonas joined the ranks of free Ceará, and, most importantly, São Paulo itself became a center of mass mobilization. In November 1886, strikes by free workers, many of them colored, finally forced the city of Santos to declare itself free, and by the end of the year 10,000 fugitives were living in the town. Though slave owners proclaimed their emancipationist sentiments and claimed that the 1871 and 1885 decrees were ending slavery, the radical abolitionists challenged these assertions. The Emancipation Fund in its entire period of operation from 1871 to 1888 freed only some 32,000 slaves. Three times that number of slaves purchased their own freedom or were granted manumission by their masters. Thus the immediate abolitionist leaders held that all the gradual decrees had little effect on the institution, which as late as 1885 still counted 1.1 million slaves.

It was this move toward confrontational politics on the part of the abolitionists in the post-1885 period that finally saw the dismantling of slavery. By 1887 the number of slaves had declined to 723,000 and was falling rapidly. The army and the local police now refused to return fugitives, so mass exodus from plantations was becoming common in the most advanced plantation counties of São Paulo. Almost all the major *paulista* cities were declaring slavery abolished and their territory a free zone, so that fugitive slaves had little difficulty in finding safe havens. The level of violence also escalated as arms were distributed to the fugitive slaves by the more radical abolitionists. Conflicts between police and armed slaves became common, and the agitation was even spreading to the most backward areas. When even members of the imperial family were converted to a radical abolitionist position, there was little hope left for the slave owners. In May 1888 the government finally decreed immediate and totally uncompensated emancipation for all slaves. Thus was the largest remaining slave regime in America destroyed, and with its destruction African slavery was finally brought to an end in all the Americas.

But the legal ending of slavery did not end its influence on American life. For a full generation or more after abolition, and in some areas at least until the second or third decade of the 20th century, ex-slaves and ex-masters fought to control the resources that had been created under slavery. The outcome of this struggle varied from region to region, but the process of transition was almost as long and as bloody as abolition and emancipation had been. The impact of this struggle in the Americas brought about one of the most fundamental changes in the world economy in the 19th century. It was a process that reallocated and destroyed large amounts of capital, and it brought about an immediate, if sometimes temporary, reduction of formerly slave-produced commercial agricultural exports to Europe and North America. The adjustment to free labor also brought about some major shifts in the centers of production, as the shock of transition often led to the collapse of older production centers. Abolition also profoundly transformed the nature of the labor force, as slaves abandoned plantations everywhere and were often replaced by new immigrant workers. Slave emancipation became the major impulse for the migration of Asian laborers to the Americas and was one of the key factors promoting the transatlantic migration of southern Europeans to Brazil. The flight of ex-slaves from the plantations promoted new centers of peasant agriculture in many parts of the continent, just as it changed the nature of plantation agricultural labor itself. From being a supervised labor force organized in groups and employing women in all aspects of basic agricultural production, plantation labor shifted to family units of production in which control over actual working conditions was given over to the individual workers themselves. The transition also meant an increasing sexual division of labor, as women shifted out of plantation field work. It even affected the rhythm of agricultural production, with the marked seasonal occupation of labor during harvesting and planting becoming a more pronounced aspect of plantation agriculture in the New World as the need to keep a servile labor force occupied full-time was eliminated.

This transition from slave to free labor also opened a new chapter in the struggle between ex-masters and ex-slaves for control of land and labor. In every former society these two groups fought bitterly to either maintain or destroy the traditional plantation system. The planters sought to continue as many of the old institutions and arrangements as possible. They wanted to retain the ex-slaves first as apprentices and then as cheap wage laborers who had no access to lands and few political, economic, or social rights. The freed slaves of the rural areas wanted to own their own lands, and they wanted freedom from any type of coerced labor. Their ideal everywhere was to own land and independently produce their own crops. They would work on the old plantations for their ex-masters only if they could not get access to their own lands or if they could find no alternative employment, urban or otherwise. If given no migration opportunities or access to land, they still refused to return to the old plantation working conditions. If they worked on the old estates, they demanded immediate withdrawal of their wives and daughters from field labor, an end to gang-labor arrangements, payment in money wages for all labor, and access to usufruct land for their own cultivation.

This struggle between planters and emancipated slaves would dominate the rural areas of the old slave regimes from the time of abolition until the first decades of the 20th century. The fight over land and labor was long and bitter and was accompanied by a high degree of local violence. Overseeing this conflict were the various local or metropolitan governments that often supported one or the other of the contenders. Though most of the governments were committed to maintaining the plantation economies, and often envisioned the role of the ex-slaves to be that of a landless rural proletariat, they never allowed a return to slavery or permitted formal peonage or the indenturing of black and mulatto workers.

This political, economic, and social conflict was in the end much influenced by the economic viability of the surviving plantation regimes. For those planters who had access to new or fertile soils and produced crops whose prices were stable or rising on the international market, there was an ability to control the outcome of the conflict. This might mean the use of the ex-slaves on the old estates, or it might mean the employment of immigrant indentured laborers. For those planters whose land contained older soils, or who worked crops whose prices were falling, there was a gradual surrender to the demands of the ex-slaves and often the withdrawal from plantation production. Sometimes the limitations on alternative lands or occupations for the slaves saved the marginal producers from going out of production, just as in some cases even best of local conditions could not prevent world economic conditions from throwing victory to the ex-slaves.

These various processes can be illustrated in the history of many of the slave plantation regimes. In such new sugar regions as Cuba, British Guyana, Surinam, and Trinidad, the planters could afford to maintain production despite the dramatic increase in labor costs under freedom. In the Cuban case, the previously isolated Oriente region now came into major commercial sugar production. Here and in the western half of the island profits were so high and the demand for labor was expanding so rapidly that indentured Chinese were imported even before the end of the slave trade. Thus free black wage laborers, Chinese indentured workers, and slaves were all laboring on the large estates at the time of transition, so it was a relatively simple process to shift into free labor. So wealthy were these new estates that they could even attract seasonal migrant harvest workers from among the black and mulatto subsistence peasant farmers. Without the need for maintaining the slave labor force on a yearly basis, these postemancipation sugar plantations became even more pronounced seasonal operations with a clearly defined "dead season" in which no work was performed.

Abolition also encouraged the total reorganization of sugar production itself in the most advanced regions. Following the earlier experiments in new mills (called *usines*) for sugar production in Guadeloupe in the 1860s, the Cubans in the last quarter of 19th century began to adopt the new *centrales* system of production on a major scale. This involved the creation of large, new steam-driven and railroad-fed central factories for milling and the renting out of the lands to entrepreneurs known as *colonos* who did the actual planting and harvesting of sugar. This, in many ways, was a return to the earlier Brazilian *lavradores de cana* system, in which the plantation owner became a refiner of sugar, and smaller planters, who were often landless, took on the costs of planting and harvesting. Throughout Cuba this process of central mill formation and intermediate rental or small-farm planters replaced the old sugar-mill estates.

In the Northeast of Brazil a similar process of adjustment occurred. First there was the early use of free wage labor from the abundant free colored, white, and *caboclo* (mestizo) subsistence peasant classes living near the sugar estates in Pernambuco and Bahia. There was a crisis in production as slaves left the estates en masse to take up squatting claims on frontier lands. But the retention of a growing national market, as well as continued world exports, enabled the Northeast sugar producers to find the capital to begin constructing the central mills (which Brazilians called *usinas*) in the last two decades before the end of the century. Also, a series of severe droughts in the Northeast that began in the 1880s, and the subsequent crisis in subsistence agriculture, forced many ex-slave peasants into part-time wage-labor on their old estates. The Brazilian sugar industry also experienced the new stress on marked seasonal production, which created a symbiotic relationship between peasant agriculture—which supported the workers most of the year—and seasonal wage labor on the plantation lands of the *lavradores* in the harvest season.

In the coffee fields of São Paulo, the transition was somewhat different. Coffee, like cotton, was an American crop for which world prices remained high throughout the transition period, providing the capital to aid the planters in their shift to free labor. This was crucial, since the coffee planters found their labor crisis even more acute than those in sugar because of the wholesale abandonment of the coffee *fazendas* by the ex-slaves. With the city of São Paulo and other large urban centers expanding in the heart of the coffee zones, and with an open and fairly prosperous local frontier available to them in the west, and poor abandoned lands in the old coffee regions of the Paraíba valley to the north, the manumitted slaves had enough land or occupational opportunities open to them so that they had no need to compromise with the planters. They simply disappeared from plantations and overnight were replaced by a white labor force.

The coffee planters had resisted the transition to the end, but in the 1870s and early 1880s they finally began to experiment with the use of European immigrant indentured laborers. Most of these early *paulista* experiments were failures, since the Europeans refused to accept the extremely restrictive labor contracts that Asians were forced to work under in other American regimes.

Immigrant labor strikes, the slowing of immigration, and threats of closure of emigration from European governments all put pressure on the planters to produce both a freer labor system and one with much higher returns for the workers. Even then, the immigrants found that the repayment of the original passage money put too much of a limit on their earnings, so they refused to migrate to Brazil. This was a period when the Italians who might emigrate to Brazil could also consider Argentina and the United States as viable alternatives. The end result was that the planters were required to absorb all transportation costs, just as they had to accept families rather than single male workers as the base for their labor force. Given the wealth of the coffee planters, due to market conditions and their power in local politics, they were able to force the government to use public revenues to subsidize the migration of Italian families. First the provincial government of São Paulo, and then the central government after the creation of the Republic in 1899, provided state subsidization for some 900,000 immigrants who came to work the coffee plantations. In all, in the decade after abolition, some 1.3 million immigrants arrived from Europe, of whom 60 percent were Italians.

The resulting labor of Italian families on Brazilian coffee estates led to a technical reorganization of the whole coffee production process. Trees were assigned to families, who worked individually and were paid for their planting, caring, and harvesting on a combination of sharing and piece-wage arrangements. This shift in labor and production arrangements was occurring as the coffee frontier was moving south and east into Paraná from São Paulo. This new frontier would be distinguished by small-farm production and the end of the old plantation organization. By 1910 the old planter class had given way to a new, largely Italian owned, small-farm frontier, and the small freehold estates of Paraná became the center of the Brazilian coffee industry from then onward.

In the Guyana territories of the Netherlands and Great Britain the transition had much in common with the Brazilian experience. Ex-slaves largely escaped the sugar plantations and were progressively replaced by immigrant indentured laborers. In these mainland colonies as well as in the French islands and the newer British sugar regions like Trinidad, there was experimentation with all types of immigrants. The French and British from the 1830s to the 1860s actually tried to bring in free African workers, but this was too reminiscent of the slave trade and was eventually stopped by the respective metropolitan governments. These areas, along with Surinam, brought in some 544,000 East Indians from the late 1830s until the 1910s to work in the sugar fields abandoned by the slaves. The Chinese indentured primarily went to Cuba, with some 125,000 arriving between the late 1840s and the 1880s, but another 18,000 were absorbed in the newer sugar zones of the West Indies.

Some 41,000 Portuguese Azorian workers went to Surinam and the British West Indies between the 1830s and 1880s to work in sugar, and the Dutch after 1900 even brought in 33,000 Javanese for the same purpose.

Although the newer sugar regions did well for most of the 19th century, they progressively lost ground in the 1880s and 1890s. The continued fall of world sugar prices due to the rise of beet sugar production and the increasing efficiency of first the Cuban and then the Santo Domingo sugar industry reduced the importance of these older sugar colonies. The result was that the Asian immigrants soon followed the path of the ex-slave into peasant commercial farming and urban activities. Trinidad and the Guyana territories thus became multiracial societies, with Asians and blacks forming complex social and political systems unusual in America.

In the mainland region of South America, abolition usually occurred in the middle decades of the 19th century to Afro-American communities that were already mostly free. Here the pattern was for the free colored to maintain their relative power in the artisanal, domestic, and unskilled urban marketplace, so long as there was no massive European immigration. Given that the remaining slaves were usually urban domestics, there was no rush of newly emancipated blacks and mulattoes to the frontier or into peasant agricultural activity when final abolition did occur. In selected urban areas of Mexico, Peru, and northeastern Brazil, the black and mulatto populations remained the basic force in the urban labor market and were well represented in most occupations and most skill categories. But in the southern cities of Brazil and in the major urban centers of Argentina and Uruguay, the relative economic position of the Afro-American community was threatened. This was due to the arrival of European immigrants, mostly Italians, who were willing to compete with the ex-slaves for even the most unskilled occupations. In these cases, black and mulatto workers lost ground to the immigrants and were usually found in a less competitive position than in societies where European immigration did not occur. In the cases of Argentina and Uruguay, where the emancipated group was small and European immigration overwhelming, the ex-slaves were eventually absorbed into a generalized, mixed racial, lower urban class, and by the early decades of the 20th century they were soon indistinguishable from the rest of the urban native-born proletarian population.

The experience of integration or decline and absorption in the urban areas was not the pattern in most rural zones. The majority experience was that found in the Caribbean islands and in most of central and northern Brazil, where the ex-slaves became the peasantry. Even where Asian and European migration had occurred, it was the blacks and mulattoes who made up the majority of the peasants. In the continental republics of Spanish America, where Afro-Americans had always formed a minority of even the rural population, ex-slaves tended to be found in relatively isolated and self-contained peasant communities that differed little from their neighboring mestizo or Indian communities except in their color. Along the Pacific coast of northern South America were isolated communities of black peasants or fisherman who maintained their distinctive culture intact into the modern period. In the Guayaquil area of Ecuador and the Pacific and Atlantic coastal regions of Colombia there were many such communities. The same occurred in Venezuela, and of course the Guyana area was filled with isolated Bush Negro communities, as well as ex-slaves in the major agricultural zones. In the Vera Cruz region of Mexico these black peasant communities distinguished by their isolation and self-awareness also existed. There were even such communities in the interior of Peru and Bolivia in the heartland of mainland South America. These were former plantation workers who now lived in closed communities within the larger peasant world in which they found themselves. Typical of such communities were the bilingual black towns in the traditional coca plantation areas of highland Bolivia known as the Yungas. Dressed in traditional Amerindian costumes, black ex-slaves spoke both Spanish and Aymara and carried on the same economic activities as their Aymara Indian peasant neighbors. But they did not intermarry, and they continued to maintain their cultural and social isolation well into the 20th century.

Thus the dual process of emancipation and transition to free labor had resulted in profound changes in the social, economic, and even geographic organization of most of the old slave societies. It had also led to varying patterns of integration and marginalization among the liberated slaves. In most cases, whether or not land was secured, ex-slaves found themselves still living in the areas of the old plantation regimes and mostly at the lowest level of their respective socioeconomic systems. Entering free society with little or no capital—often with skills only adaptive to a now declining plantation economy—and faced by continuing discrimination based on their color, most found it difficult to rise from the working class. In some societies the general economic stagnation that followed abolition guaranteed that mobility was a limited commodity available to only a very few. In other cases ex-slaves often found themselves in the most backward regions of even the most dynamic of nations. The former pattern was typical of many of the Caribbean islands, while the latter situation was one confronting ex-slaves in countries as diverse as Brazil and the United States.

For the sons and daughters of ex-slaves, therefore, only the escape out of the old plantation regions and islands provided any hope of advancement. In most cases, such migration would not occur until major changes developed in the world economy. The impact of World War I, with its new demands for labor in the industrial areas of the Western world, and the even more profound impact of World War II finally broke the isolation of the liberated slaves and their descendants. Although intraregional migration within the Caribbean and in South America from rural to urban areas had begun before 1914, these migrations were still only of a moderate size. The creation of the Republic of Panama in the new century and the building of the trans-isthmian canal created a demand for laborers that was met by English West Indian blacks. In Honduras, Belize, Guatemala and Costa Rica, the coastal communities of the Caribbean shore were also much influenced by migration of British West Indian blacks as well as Amerindian communities, such as the Caribs, heavily influenced by runaway slaves and their descendants.

The decline of local sugar industries in most of the British West Indies and the failure of export production in Haiti all encouraged local but intense migration patterns. In the 1840s and 1850s, for example, Barbadians migrated in significant numbers to Trinidad. Interisland seasonal migration was also important in supplying Haitian and British West Indian workers to the booming sugar fields of Cuba and Santo Domingo. The latter nation was the only one in America to get into sugar plantation agriculture after the end of slavery. Santo Domingo's low population densities and the expansion of its highly efficient sugar industry in the post-1880 period guaranteed a major demand for foreign labor that was satisfied by these quite local intra-Caribbean migrations.

But it was only in the middle decades of the 20th century that really massive migration of Afro-Americans got under way. These migrations were substantially different from these earlier intraregional movements. Although they were motivated by the search for new economic opportunities as before, they often involved either long-distance migrations or permanent residence outside the traditional centers. West Indians began major migrations to North America and Europe, just as Brazilians moved south into the booming urban centers and major industrial areas. Cubans and Peruvians moved to the cities, and even Ecuadorian villagers began to migrate to Guayaquil in search of education for their children and better lives for themselves.

The out-migration from the poor lands and marginal regions did not, however, end the legacy of slavery. Even for those who obtained the skills, education, and capital needed to rise above the working class, they found that mobility was not as open to them as to the poor whites. That black color was considered a negative identity, and that "whitening" of skin color was held a prerequisite for successful mobility, was part of the cognitive view of all American societies until well into the 20th century. What distinguished the

Latin American and Caribbean world was not so much the lack of prejudice as it was the subtle differentiations which that prejudice would create. Class was such a powerful determinant of position that the attributes of class would often influence the definition of color, whatever the phenotypic characteristics shown by the individual. Black lawyers were often defined as mulattoes, just as mulatto ones were defined as whites. In turn, successful Afro-Americans, accepting the views of their racist societies, often "married up" in color, thus "whitening" their offspring and having them move into the mulatto or white category. Since class had an important influence on color definitions, the role of prejudice was far more subtle and discrimination far less precise than in those societies such as the United States where color was defined solely by phenotype and origin.

While upwardly mobile mulattoes and blacks conformed to these racist views, the black masses did not totally accept these values. Many rejected this acculturation to "white" norms and the rejection of their color and culture this usually implied. The isolated village of ex-slaves preserving traditional ways was one response to this prejudice, but another was the elaboration of an even more vibrant alternative cultural expression. The new religion of Umbanda, along with the preabolition groups of Candomblé, Voodoo, Santería, and other cults, expanded under freedom. Though bitterly attacked by the white police in Cuba and Brazil and by the mulatto elite in Haiti as manifestations of idolatry and social disorder, the Afro-American cults publicly revealed themselves in the late 19th century and early 20th century and forced the dominant society to grant them recognition. First, isolated intellectuals and, then, important sections of the elite realized that these beliefs were too powerful to destroy, especially after the black masses obtained the vote and could influence the political process itself. More and more private churches and even street festivals were permitted, and by the mid-20th century they began to absorb mulatto and white adherents. What started as signs of protest and self-identity became, for better or worse, symbols of a diverse but integrated national culture, at least in the case of Brazil, if not that of Cuba and of Haiti.

Much of this slow erosion of the harsher manifestations of racial prejudice came from two different directions. The first was the growing political power of the black masses with the arrival of democratic or representative governments to all these former slave societies. By the late 19th century most of the British and French Caribbean islands permitted the Afro-Americans to vote, and by the early decades of the 20th century this occurred in Cuba and Brazil as well. The traditional elites were thus forced to compromise with the black masses. In the Caribbean colonial islands, where the whites were few and governance came from the central metropolis, this occurred much quicker. It came so fast in Jamaica that by the 1860s the whites gave up their political power to the Crown to prevent the aroused Afro-Americans from seizing control of the government. In the French islands, the blacks and mulattoes had dominated the islands' representation to the French National Assembly from the first elections in 1848 and 1849. Paris disenfranchised the islands from 1854 to 1870, but riots in Martinique finally led to permanent restoration of electoral rights in 1871. The result was the immediate return of black and mulatto representatives to Paris. In Brazil, blacks and mulattoes were early elected to the local provincial assemblies, but it was only in the 20th century that they made any headway against prejudice in the central administration, which was largely controlled by southern and central Brazilian whites. In Cuba, the republican governments were responsive to the black masses, though whites dominated the national government for most of the earlier decades.

Along with their growing political power, there was also an increasing acceptance of the black contribution to national culture and identity. Late 19th-century Latin American whites were influenced by the European ideas of racial ranking and were hostile to Afro-Americans and their culture. But the disaster of World War I challenged the legitimacy of white imperialism, while at the same time the growth of relativism in cultural analysis in European and North American social sciences provided radical Latin Americans with models to reevaluate their own national cultures. This led in the 1930s and 1940s to the rise of nativist schools that glorified the African contributions to national culture. Rather paternalistic in their initial manifestations, the new pro-Afro-American ideologies nevertheless gave a legitimacy to mass opposition to the "whitening" process and helped to reduce the high cultural costs of integration into the dominant society. In the Caribbean, similar forces gave rise to the movement of negritude, which proclaimed the legitimacy of popular mass culture. This time, however, the movement was led by black and mulatto intellectuals.

In all these societies, the degree of economic expansion, urbanization, European immigration, and Afro-American emigration would influence the relative rates of mobility of the descendants of the slaves. But in most of these Latin American and Caribbean nations enough mobility had occurred, and enough self-awareness existed on the part of the Afro-Americans of the legitimacy of their own cultural needs and demands, that relatively high rates of mobility and accommodation were achieved by the second or third generation after abolition. In the more competitive societies, the struggle was often more bitter and more costly for Afro-Americans, whereas in the more traditional societies there was greater security, especially where Afro-American cultures became frozen in isolation, but mobility was slower. Whatever the variations, however, in most of Latin America by the last quarter of the 20th century the Afro-American presence had become an accustomed and accepted part of the culture and national self-identity of most of the ex-slave societies. A century after the last slave was freed, the legacy of slavery is still seen in continuing poverty of many descendants of slaves, in ongoing prejudice against Afro-Americans, and in lower rates of mobility than among whites. But these class rigidities and color impediments notwithstanding, the descendants of the African slaves have achieved significant levels of socioeconomic mobility, political power, and cultural integration in the societies to which their forebears had been so brutally transported many years before.

Bibliographical Notes

GENERAL

The following bibliography is not intended to be a detailed listing of all works on the subject of slavery in Latin America and the Caribbean. We have cited only those studies used to support given discussions in the text, or modern works that are themselves summaries of a large previous literature and to which those wishing more detailed information may turn. Aside from these latter works, there are several useful bibliographical surveys, which include John David Smith, *Black Slavery in the Americas: An Interdisciplinary Bibliography, 1860–1980*, 2 vols. (Westport, Conn., 1982); the series of bibliographies of Joseph C. Miller, beginning with *Slavery: A Teaching Bibliography* (Waltham, Mass., 1977), continuing with Miller et al., *Slavery and Slaving in World History* (New York, 1998), and constantly updated in a series of articles usually entitled "Slavery: Annual Bibliographic Supplement" in the journal *Slavery and Abolition*, the latest of which is dated 2004 and appeared in vol. 26, no. 3 (December 2005). For the Atlantic slave trade, see Peter C. Hogg, *The African Slave Trade and Its Suppression: A Classified and Annotated Bibliography* (London, 1973), which can be supplemented with the bibliographies in the more recent surveys listed below.

CHAPTER 1.   ORIGINS OF THE AMERICAN SLAVE SYSTEM

In defining the institution of slavery, several recent works are fundamental. Orlando Patterson, *Slavery and Social Death: A Comparative Study* (Cambridge, Mass., 1982), provides a crucial guide through the maze of issues in delineating slavery from all other forms of servile and forced labor. The studies of Keith Hopkins, *Conquerors and Slaves* (Cambridge, 1978), and Moses Finley, *Ancient Slavery and Modern Ideology* (New York, 1980), are essential readings for the study of slavery in the classical world and the definition of a slave system.

Slavery in Europe in the postclassical period has been well analyzed in the numerous works of Charles Verlinden. For English readers his *The Beginnings of Modern Colonization* (Ithaca, 1970) is a good summary of his earlier findings. This should be supplemented with *Les origines de la civilisation atlantique* (Paris, 1966). His basic monographic research is contained in *L'esclavage dans l'Europe medievale*, 2 vols. (Bruges, 1955, Gent, 1977). The transformation from slave to serf labor in western Europe is discussed in Marc Bloch, *Slavery and Serfdom in the Middle Ages* (Berkeley, 1975), and the controversial study by Pierre Dockes, *Medieval Slavery and Liberation* (Chicago, 1979). William D. Phillips Jr.'s survey, *Slavery from Roman Times to the Early Atlantic Slave Trade* (Minneapolis, 1985), contains an updated bibliography of this field, and the recent volume by T. F. Earle and K. J. Lowe, *Black Africans in Renaissance Europe* (Cambridge, 2005), provides a comprehensive look at black life in Europe both within and outside the context of slavery.

Slavery in Africa has been the subject of wide interest and controversy in recent years. A good introduction to this debate can be found in Walter Rodney, *How Europe Undeveloped Africa* (London, 1972). A fine attempt at classification and historical analysis is Paul E. Lovejoy, *Transformations in Slavery: A History of Slavery in Africa* (Cambridge, 1983). For detailed case studies, see the selections in Jean Claude Meillassoux, ed., *L'esclavage en Afrique précoloniale* (Paris, 1975); Suzanne Miers and Igor Kopytoff, eds., *Slavery in Africa: Historical and Anthropological Perspectives* (Madison, 1977); James Watson, ed., *Asian and African Systems of Slavery* (Berkeley, 1980); J. E. Inikori, ed., *Forced Migration: The Impact of the Export Slave Trade on African Societies* (London, 1982); and Claire C. Robinson and Martin A. Klein, eds., *Women and Slavery in Africa* (Madison, 1983). For recent analysis of the African impact on America, see John Thornton, *Africa and Africans in the Making of the Atlantic World*, 2nd ed. (Cambridge, 1998); Linda M. Heywood, ed., *Central Africans and Cultural Transformations in the American Diaspora* (Cambridge, 2002); Selma Pantoja and José Flávio Sombra Saraiva, eds., *Angola e Brasil nas rotas do Atlântico do Sul* (Rio de Janeiro, 1999); José C. Curto and Paul E. Lovejoy, eds., *Enslaving Connections: Changing Cultures of Africa and Brazil during the Era of Slavery* (Amherst, N.Y., 2004); Manolo Florentino, ed., *Tráfico, cativeiro e liberdade, Rio de Janeiro, séculos XVII–XIX* (Rio de Janeiro, 2005); and José C. Curto and Renée Soulodre-LaFrance, eds., *Africa and the Americas: Interconnections during the Slave Trade* (Trenton, N.J., 2005). Another useful introductory text that outlines issues of slavery in Africa and the broader African Diaspora is Michael A. Gomez, *Reversing Sail: A History of the African Diaspora* (Cambridge, 2005).

For the Iberian experience with African slavery, there exists a model study by A. C. de C. M. Saunders, *A Social History of Black Slaves and Freedmen in Portugal, 1441–1555* (Cambridge, 1982). More local studies for Spain are those by Vicenta Cortés Alonso, *La esclavitud en Valencia durante el reinado de los reyes católicos* (Valencia, 1964), and Alfonso Franco Silva, *La esclavitud en Sevilla y su tierra a fines de la edad media* (Sevilla, 1979). Though dated, the older survey by Antonio Domínguez Ortiz, "La esclavitud en Castilla durante la edad moderna," *Estudios de Historia Social de España* vol. 2 (Madrid, 1952), is still useful. From a literary perspective, the work of Baltasar Fra-Molinero, especially his *La imagen de los negros en el teatro del siglo de oro* (Mexico, DF, 1995), is quite useful.

Slavery in the Atlantic islands is detailed in the work of Manuel Lobo Cabrera, *La esclavitud en las Canarias Orientales en el siglo xvi* (Tenenfe, 1982). The Portuguese Atlantic experience is analyzed in John L. Vogt, *Portuguese Rule on the Gold Coast, 1469–1682* (Athens, Ga., 1979); the background chapters in Stuart B. Schwartz, *Sugar Plantations in the Formation of a Brazilian Society (Bahia, 1550–1835)* (Cambridge, 1985), provide the best available survey of the Madeira and Azorian experience.

CHAPTER 2. THE ESTABLISHMENT OF AFRICAN SLAVERY IN LATIN AMERICA IN THE 16TH CENTURY

For determining the population movements of Indians, Africans, and Europeans in America in this first century, the best overall assessment will be found in Nicolás Sánchez-Albornoz, *La población de America latina desde los tiempos precolombianos al año 2000*, 2nd ed. (Madrid, 1977); and his more recent "The Population of Colonial Spanish America," in Leslie Bethell, ed., *Cambridge History of Latin America*, vol. 2 (Cambridge, 1984). Reliable numbers on the Indian population of Mexico are found in William T. Saunders, "The Population of the Central Mexican Symbiotic Region, the Basin of Mexico and the Teotihuacan Valley in the Sixteenth Century," in William M. Denevan, ed., *The Native Population of the Americas in 1492* (Madison, 1976); and for Peru in David Nobel Cook, *Demographic Collapse: Indian Peru 1520–1620* (Cambridge, 1981). For the Portuguese American territories in the same period, see Maria Luiza Marcílio, "The Population of Colonial Brazil," in vol. 2 of the *Cambridge History of Latin America*. The latest estimates for African forced migrants to America are found in David Eltis, "The Volume and Structure of the Transatlantic Slave Trade: A Reassessment," *William and Mary Quarterly*, 3rd ser., 58:1 (January 2001), which supplements the original estimates given by Philip Curtin in *The Atlantic Slave Trade: A Census* (Madison, 1969).

The first century of African slavery is dealt with in the Schwartz volume for Brazil, and for Mexico in Colin A. Palmer, *Slaves of the White God, Blacks in Mexico 1570–1650* (Cambridge, Mass., 1976). Also useful are David M. Davidson, "Negro Slave Control and Resistance in Colonial Mexico, 1519–1650," *Hispanic American Historical Review* 46 (1966) ; and Gonzalo Aguirre Beltrán, *La población negra de Mexico, 1492–1810*, 2nd ed. (Mexico, DF, 1972). A model study of urban slavery in this period is Frederick P. Bowser, *The African Slave in Colonial Peru, 1524–1650* (Stanford, 1974). For the growth of the internal Spanish American slave market, see Rolando Mellafe, *La introducción de la esclavitud negra en Chile: Tráfico y rutas* (Santiago de Chile, 1959); for a general overview of this earlier period, his study *Breve historia de la esclavitud en America Latina* (Mexico, DF, 1973) is still of utility.

Slaves in the early Mexican and Peruvian mining industry are discussed in the two fundamental studies of Peter J. Backwell, *Silver Mining and Society in Colonial Mexico, Zacatecas, 1546–1700* (Cambridge, 1971); and *Miners of the Red Mountain: Indian Labor in Potosí 1545–1650* (Albuquerque, 1984). The importance of mining in Quito has been explored in the classic work of Robert C. West, *Colonial Placer Mining in Colombia* (Baton Rouge, 1952). The themes in this book have been picked up by others who have examined

Quito, including Sherwin K. Bryant, "Slavery and the Context of Ethnogenesis: Africans, Afro-Creoles, and the Realities of Bondage in the Kingdom of Quito" (Ph.D. diss., Ohio State University, 2005); Germán Colmenares, *Historia económica y social de Colombia*, 2 vols. (Santafé de Bogotá, 1973, 1979); and see also chapter 2 in Kris Lane, *Quito 1599: City and Colony in Transition* (Albuquerque, 2002). An interesting assessment of black and native experiences in mining can be found in Lane, "Africans and Natives in the Mines of Spanish America," in Matthew Restall, ed., *Beyond Black and Red: African-Native Relations in Colonial Latin America* (Albuquerque, 2005).

The Mexican and Peruvian sugar plantation regimes have been examined in Ward Barrett, *The Sugar Hacienda of the Marqueses del Valle* (Minneapolis, 1970); and Nicholas P. Cushner, *Lords of the Land: Sugar, Wine and Jesuit Estates of Coastal Peru, 1600–1767* (Albany, NY, 1980); for slavery on the the Jesuit estates in Colombia, Ecuador, Venezuela and Mexico, see Germán Colmenares, *Las haciendas de los Jesuitas en el Nueva Reyno de Granada, siglo XVIII* (Bogotá, 1969); Jean Pierre Tardieu, *Noirs et nouveaux maîtres dans les "vallées sanglantes" de l'Equateur, 1778–1820* (Paris, 1997); Jaime Torres Sánchez, *Haciendas y posesiones de la Compañia de Jesús en Venezuela* (Seville, 2001); and Hermes Tovar Pinzón, "Elementos constitutivos de la empresa agraria jesuita . . . en México," in Enrique Florescano, ed., *Haciendas, latifundias y plantaciones en América Latina* (Mexico, DF, 1975). The idea of auxiliary slavery, as opposed to mass slavery (in classic plantation societies), is a concept articulated in chapter 7 of Matthew Restall and Kris Lane's *Latin America in Colonial Times* (Boston, 2007), as well as chapter 1 of Restall's *The Black Middle: Slavery Society and African-Maya Relations in Colonial Yucatan* (Stanford, forthcoming). This distinction is key for understanding features of Spanish American mainland slavery.

In this respect, good regional studies of aspects of slavery in mainland Spanish America include Jean Pierre Tardieu, *El negro en Cusco, los caminos de la alienación en la segunda mitad del siglo XVII* (Lima, 1998); Rafael Antonio Díaz Díaz, *Esclavitud, region y ciudad: el system esclavista urbano-regional en Santafé de Bogotá, 1700–1750* (Bogotá, 2001); and Maria Cristina Navarrete, *Génesis y desarrollo de la esclavitud en Colombia, siglos XVI y XVII* (Cali, 2005). Also see Germán Colmenares, *Cali, terratenientes, mineros, y comerciantes, siglo XVIII*, 4th ed. (Bogotá, 1997); and Hermes Tovar Pinzon, *Grandes empresas agricolas y ganaderas: Su desarrollo en el siglo XVIII* (Bogotá, 1980); and Sherwin K Bryant, "Finding Gold, Forming Slavery: The Creation of a Classic Slave Society, Popayán, 1600–1700," *The Americas* vol. 62, no. 3 (2006). For aspects of slavery specifically referring to Guatemala, see Robinson A. Herrera, *Natives, Europeans and Africans in Sixteenth-Century Santiago de Guatemala* (Austin, Tex., 2003); Christopher H. Lutz, *Santiago de Guatemala, 1541–1773: City, Caste, and the Colonial Experience* (Norman, Okla., 1994); Herrera, "Por que no sabemos firmar: Black Slaves in Early Guatemala," *The Americas* 57, no. 2 (2000): 247–67; Paul Lokken, "Marriage as Slave Emancipation in Seventeenth Century Guatemala," *The Americas* 58, no. 2 (2001): 175–200; and Lokken, "A Maroon Moment: Rebel Slaves in Early Seventeenth-Century Guatemala," *Slavery and Abolition* 25, no. 3 (2004): 44–58. For aspects of early slavery in Costa Rica, see Rina Cáceres, *Negros, mulatos, esclavos y libertos en la Costa Rica del siglo XVII* (Mexico, DF, 2000); and Kent Russell Lohse, "Africans and Their Descendants in

Colonial Costa Rica, 1600–1750" (Ph.D. diss., University of Texas at Austin, 2005). For Panama, see Arturo Guzmán Navarro, *La trata esclavista en el istmo de Panama durante el siglo XVIII* (Panama City, 1982); Luis A. Diez Castillo, *Los Cimarrones y los negros antillanos en Panama* (Panama City, 1981); Maria del Carmen Mena Garcia, *La sociedad de Panama en el siglo XVI* (Seville, 1984). For Honduras, see Rafael Leiva Vivas, *Tráfico de esclavos negros a Honduras* (Tegucigalpa, 1982); Melida Velásquez, "El comercio de esclavos en la alcaldía mayor de Tegucigalpa," *Mesoamerica* 22, no. 42 (2001): 199–222. For discussions of the Miskitu in Nicaragua, see Karl H. Offen, "The Sambo and Tawira Miskitu: The Colonial Origins and Geography of Intra-Miskitu Differentiation in Eastern Nicaragua and Honduras," *Ethnohistory* 49, no. 2 (2002); and Offen, "The Territorial Turn: Making Black Territories in Pacific Colombia," *Journal of Latin American Geography* 2, no. 1 (2003). A number of articles appear on topics of slavery and blackness in Panama, Nicaragua, Honduras, and Costa Rica in Luz María Martínez Montiel, ed., *Presencia Africana en Centroamérica* (Mexico, DF, 1993). Information on slavery in Bolivia can be found in Lolita Gutierrez Brockington, "The African Diaspora in the Eastern Andes: Adaptation, Agency, and Fugitive Action, 1573–1677," *The Americas* 57, no. 2 (2000); Gutierrez Brockington, *Blacks, Indians, and Spaniards in the Eastern Andes: Reclaiming the Forgotten in Colonial Mizque, 1550–1782* (Lincoln, 2007); and a broader temporal analysis is Max Portugal Ortiz, *La esclavitud negra en las epocas colonial y nacional de Bolivia* (La Paz, 1977). A dramatic increase in the literature on slavery in Mexico has taken place, represented by the following titles: Herman L. Bennett, *Africans in Colonial Mexico: Absolutism, Christianity and Afro-Creole Consciousness, 1570–1640* (Bloomington, Ind., 2003); Patrick J. Carroll, *Blacks in Colonial Veracruz: Race, Ethnicity, and Regional Development*, 2nd ed. (Austin, Tex., 2001); Frank T. Proctor III, "Afro-Mexican Slave Labor in the Obrajes de Paños of New Spain, Seventeenth and Eighteenth Centuries," *The Americas* 60, no. 1 (2003); Proctor, "Slavery, Identity and Culture: An Afro-Mexican Counterpoint, 1640–1763" (Ph.D. diss., Emory University, 2003); Adriana Naveda Chávez-Hita, *Esclavos negros en las haciendas azucareras de Córdoba 1690–1830* (Jalapa, 1987); Francisco Fernández Repetto and Genny Negroe Sierra, *Una población perdida en la memoria, los negros de Yucatan* (Merida, 1995); Lourdes Mondragón Barrios, *Esclavos africanos en la ciudad de México, el servicio doméstico durante el siglo XVI* (Mexico City, 1999); María Guadalupe Chávez Carvajal, *Propietarios y esclavos negros en Valladolid, Michoacán (1600–1650)* (Morelia, 1994); Lolita Gutierrez-Brockington, *The Leverage of Labor: Managing the Cortés Haciendas in Tehuantepec, 1588–1688* (Durham, N.C., 1989); and Dennis Nodin Valdés, "The Decline of Slavery in Mexico," *The Americas* 44, no. 2 (1987). While much of the newer work on Mexico written in Spanish is not cited here, an extensive bibliographical and historiographical survey can be found in Ben Vinson III and Bobby Vaughn, *Afroméxico* (Mexico, DF, 2004). For more on slavery in the city of Quito, see Manuel Lucema Salmoral, *Sangre sobre piel negra* (Quito, 1994). For an original survey of urban life of the period, see R. Douglas Cope, *The Limits of Racial Domination: Plebian Society in Colonial Mexico City, 1660–1720* (Madison, 1994). Note that several of the regional studies listed above are not limited to the 16th and 17th centuries but also address mainland Spanish American slavery in the 18th century. For 16th-century Brazil, the Schwartz work should be complemented with the two basic studies of F. Mauro, *Le Portugal et l'Atlantique au*

XVIIe siècle (Paris, 1960); and *Le Brésil du XVe a la fin du XVIIIe siècle* (Paris, 1977); as well as Charles R. Boxer, *The Dutch in Brazil, 1624–1654* (Oxford, 1957).

CHAPTER 3.   SUGAR AND SLAVERY IN THE CARIBBEAN IN THE 17TH AND 18TH
             CENTURIES

The growth of the sugar plantation system has been the subject of several fine studies, the most outstanding of which remains Noel Deerr, *The History of Sugar*, 2 vols. (London, 1949–50). A useful general survey is found in Alice Piffer Canabrava, *O açucar nas antilhas (1697–1755)* (São Paulo, 1981); also the Ward Barrett study "Caribbean Sugar-Production Standards in the Seventeenth and Eighteenth Centuries," in John Parker, ed., *Merchants and Scholars: Essays in the History of Exploration and Trade* (Minneapolis, 1965). Good surveys of slavery and colonization in the Caribbean include Michael Craton, *Sinews of Empire: A Short History of British Slavery* (New York, 1974); M. Devèze, *Antilles, Guyanes, la Mer des Caríbes de 1492 a 1789* (Paris, 1977); Eric Williams, *From Columbus to Castro: The History of the Caribbean 1492–1969* (New York, 1970); J. H. Parry and P. M. Sherlock, *A Short History of the West Indies*, 2nd ed. (New York, 1966); and Richard B. Sheridan, *Sugar and Slavery, an Economic History of the British West Indies 1623–1775* (Baltimore, 1973).

Specific local studies include Richard S. Dunn, *Sugar and Slaves: The Rise of the Planter Class in the English West Indies, 1624–1713* (Chapel Hill, 1972), on the Barbados experience, and Christian Schnakenbourg, "Notes sur l'orgine de l'industrie sucrière en Guadeloupe au XVIIe siècle, 1640–1670," *Revue Française d'Historie d'Outre-Mer* 55, no. 200 (1968), which challenges the earlier arguments in Mathew Edel, "The Brazilian Sugar Cycle of the Seventeenth Century and the Rise of West Indian Competition," *Caribbean Studies* 9, no.1 (April 1969). Still worth consulting are the older studies of L. Peytraud, *L'Esclavage aux Antilles francaises avant 1789* (Paris, 1897); and Gaston-Martin, *Histoire de l'esclavage dans les colonies francaises* (Paris, 1948). Michael Craton, *Searching for the Invisible Man: Slaves and Plantation Life in Jamaica* (Cambridge, Mass., 1978), summarizes a great deal of information on local Jamaican plantations in this earlier period, as does an innovative study by Arlette Gautier, *Les soeurs de solitude: la condition féminine dans l'esclavage aux Antilles du xviie au xix siècle* (Paris, 1985), for the special problems of female slaves.

For the 18th century there has been much new research on both the French and British West Indies. French dissertations have made some major contributions, one of which has been partly published: N. Vanony-Frisch, "Les esclaves de la Guadeloupe a fin de l'ancien régime d'après les sources notariales (1770–1789)," *Bulletin de la Société d'Histoire de la Guadeloupe* 63–64 (1985). Most of these follow the model set in the basic study by Gabriel Debien, *Les esclaves aux Antilles francaises (xviie–xviiie siècles)* (Basse-Terre, 1974). The best of the older theses remains that of Christian Schnakenbourg, "Les sucreries de la Guadeloupe dans la seconde moitie du xviii eme siècle (1760–1790)" (Ph.D. diss., Université de Paris II, 1973). Also useful is David Geggus, "Les esclaves de la plaine du Nord a la veille de la Revolution Française: Les equipes de travail sur une vengtaine de sucreries," *Revue de la Société Haitienne d'Histoire* 135–36 (1982); as well as the classic works by Moreau de Saint-Mery, *Description ... de la parte francaise de la'isle de Saint-Domingue*, 3 vols., new ed. (Paris, 1958); Bryan Edwards, *An Historical Survey of the French Colony in the Island of St. Domingue* (London, 1797); and Barre Saint Venant, *Du colonies modernes sous la zone torride, et particulierement de celle de Saint Domingue* (Paris, 1802), which are still important sources. For the basic statistics on production and trade, see J. R. McCulloch, *A Dictionary ... of Commerce and Colonial Navigation*, rev. ed. (London, 1838); along with Christian Schnakenbourg, "Statistique pour l'histoire de l'économie de plantation en Guadeloupe et en Martinique (1635–1835)," *Bulletin de la Société d'Histoire de la Guadeloupe*, 31 (1977). One of the best single studies of the slave population of the Caribbean remains Alex. Moreau de Jonnes, *Recherches statistiques sur l'esclavage colonial ...* (Paris, 1842).

CHAPTER 4.   SLAVERY IN PORTUGUESE AND SPANISH AMERICA IN THE 18TH
              CENTURY

Useful as starting points for a general view of Brazilian slavery are Mauricio Goulart, *A escravidão africano no Brasil* (São Paulo, 1949); Gilberto Freyre, *The Masters and the Slaves* (New York, 1946); Jacob Gorender, *O escravismo colonial* (São Paulo, 1978); Ciro Flamarion S. Cardoso, *Agricultura, escravidão e capitalismo* (Petrópolis, 1979); the recent survey by Katia M. de Queiros Mattoso, *To Be a Slave in Brazil, 1550–1888* (New Brunswick, N.J., 1986); and the older work of Agostinho Pedrigao Maiheiro, *A escravidão no Brasil*, 2 vols. (Rio de Janeiro, 1866), which remains fundamental for the legal aspects of the Brazilian slave regime.

The Brazilian economy of the 18th century and its slave labor force have been well studied. A general overall assessment is found in Charles R. Boxer, *The Golden Age of Brazil, 1695–1750* (Berkeley, 1966). This should be complemented by the earlier cited work of Mauro (1960, 1977) and Schwartz (1985), and the recent surveys of A. J. R. Russell-Wood, "Colonial Brazil: The Gold Cycle, c. 1690–1750," Dauril Alden, "Late Colonial Brazil, 1750–1808," and Stuart B. Schwartz, "Colonial Brazil, c. 1580–c. 1750: Plantations and Peripheries," all found in vol. 2 of the *Cambridge History of Latin America*. An excellent local study of slavery on the frontier is Alida C. Metcalf 's *Family and Frontier in Colonial Brazil: Santana de Parnaíba, 1580–1822* (Berkeley, 1992). For the important role of Indian slavery in this region, see John Manuel Monteiro, *Negros da terra; índios e bandeirantes nas origens de são paulo* (São Paulo, 1994). The most intensely studied regions in the pre-1800 period are those of Bahia and Minas Gerais; see A. J. R. Russell-Wood, *The Black Man in Slavery and Freedom in Colonial Brazil* (London, 1982); Francisco Vidal Luna, *Minus Gerais: Escravos e senhores (1718–1804)* (São Paulo, 1981); Francisco Vidal Luna and Iraci del Nero da Costa, *Minas colonial: Economia e sociedade* (São Paulo, 1982); and Iraci del Nero da Costa, *Populações mineiras: Sobre a estrutura populacional de alguns núcleos mineiros no alvorecer do século XIX* (São Paulo, 1981); Kathleen J. Higgins, *"Licentious Liberty" in a Brazilian Gold-Mining Region ... Eighteenth Century Sabará, Minas Gerais* (University Park, Pa., 1999); and Myriam Ellis, *A Baleira no Brasil colonial* (São Paulo, 1969). Two traditional studies that are still essential reading for regional developments are André João Antonil,

Cultura e opulencia do Brasil (1711; new ed., São Paulo, 1967); and W. L. von Eschwege, *Pluto Brasiliensis* (1833; 2 vols., São Paulo, 1944).

Slavery in the mainland Spanish American colonies in the 18th century has been less studied. Some of the better analyses are those for northwestern South America and especially the local Chocó mining industry, which include William F. Sharp, *Slavery in the Spanish Frontier: The Colombian Chocó, 1680–1810* (Norman, Okla., 1976); David L. Chandler, *Health and Slavery in Colonial Colombia* (New York, 1981); and Colin A. Palmer, *Human Cargoes: The British Slave Trade to Spanish America, 1700–1739* (Urbana, Ill., 1981); Jaime Jamarillo Uribe, *Ensayos sobre historia social colombiana* (Bogotá, 1968); and Adolfo Meisel R., "Esclavitud, mestizaje y haciendas en la Provincia de Cartagena, 1533–1851," *Desarrollo y Sociedad* 4 (1980). See also Robert C. West, *Colonial Placer Mining in Colombia* (Baton Rouge, 1952); Sherwin K. Bryant, "Slavery and the Context of Ethnogenesis: Africans, Afro-Creoles, and the Realities of Bondage in the Kingdom of Quito" (Ph.D. diss., Ohio State University, 2005); Germán Colmenares, *Historia económica y social de Colombia*, 2 vols. (Santafé de Bogotá, 1973, 1979); Kris Lane, *Quito 1599: City and Colony in Transition* (Albuquerque, 2002); and Kris Lane, "Africans and Natives in the Mines of Spanish America," in Matthew Restall, ed., *Beyond Black and Red: African-Native Relations in Colonial Latin America* (Albuquerque, 2005). Some interesting information on mining practices in Africa that have a New World impact can be found in Paul Lovejoy, *Transformations in Slavery: A History of Slavery in Africa*, 2nd ed. (Cambridge 2000); and Ivor Wilks, "Wangara, Akan, and Portuguese in the Fifteenth and Sixteenth Centuries," in Peter Bakewell, ed., *Mines of Silver and Gold in the Americas* (New York, 1997). For the cacao plantations of Venezuela, see Robert J. Ferry, "Encomienda, African Slavery and Agriculture in 17th-Century Caracas," *Hispanic American Historical Review* 61, no. 4 (1981); Miguel Izard, "La agricultura venezolana en una epoca de transición," *Boletín Histórico* 28 (1972); and Robert J. Ferry, *The Colonial Elite of Early Caracas: Formation and Crisis, 1567–1767* (Berkeley, 1989). For cacao plantations in Costa Rica, see Kent Russell Lohse, "Africans and Their Descendants in Colonial Costa Rica, 1600–1750" (Ph.D. diss., University of Texas at Austin, 2005). Slavery in the Veracruz sugar estates and local urban centers has been the primary region studied in 18th-century Mexico. The sugar estates have been analyzed in detail by Adriana Navela Chavez-Hita, "Esclavitud negra en la jurisdicción de la valle de Cordoba en el siglo xviii" (M.A. thesis, Universidad Veracruzana, 1977), and *Esclavos negros en las haciendas azucareras de Córdoba 1690–1830* (Jalapa, 1987). For the urban occupations and nonplantation lives of local slaves, see Patrick J. Carroll, "Black Laborers and Their Experience in Colonial Jalapa," in Elsa Cecilia Frost et al., eds., *El trabajo y los trabajadores en la historia de Mexico* (Mexico, DF, 1977). However, in Mexico, the region of Morelos has also been examined. See Cheryl English Martin, *Rural Society in Colonial Morelos* (Albuquerque, 1985). For the Andes, there is an important book by Alberto Crespo, *Esclavos negros en Bolivia* (La Paz, 1977); on Uruguay is the book by Emo Isola, *La esclavitud en el Uruguay... (1743–1852)* (Montevideo, 1975). For pre-19th-century Santo Domingo, see Ruben Silie, *Economia, esclavitud y población... en el siglo XVIII* (Santo Domingo, 1976); and Carlos Esteban Deive, *La esclavitud del negro en Santo Domingo*, 2 vols. (Santo Domingo, 1980). On urban slavery in the early 19th century, see Christine Hünefeldt, *Paying the Price of Freedom: Family and Labor among Lima's Slaves 1800–1854* (Berkeley, 1994).

CHAPTER 5. SLAVERY AND THE PLANTATION ECONOMY IN THE CARIBBEAN IN THE 19TH CENTURY

For 19th-century developments in the French and British colonies, there are many new studies of importance. B. W. Higman, in *Slave Population and Economy in Jamaica, 1807–1834* (Cambridge, 1976) and *Slave Populations of the British Caribbean, 1807–1834* (Baltimore, 1984), provides the best survey of slave demography both in Jamaica and throughout the British mainland and insular colonies. This should be supplemented with the study of Craton (1978) cited above and with the reinterpretation of the 19th-century slave sugar economy in Seymour Drescher, *Econocide: British Slavery in the Era of Abolition* (Pittsburgh, 1977). A survey of the process of appenticeship and emancipation is provided in William A. Green, *British Slave Emancipation: The Sugar Colonies and the Great Experiment, 1838–1865* (Oxford, 1976).

The post-1791 period in the French West Indies is treated in David Patrick Geggus, *Slavery, War and Revolution: The British Occupation of Saint Domingue 1793–1798* (Oxford, 1982); and "The Slaves of British Occupied Saint Domingue: An Analysis of the Workforce of 197 Absentee Plantations, 1796–1797," *Caribbean Studies* 18, nos. 1–2 (1978). For the other islands and colonies, see Christian Schankenbourg, *Histoire de l'industrie sucrière en Guadeloupe... la crise du systeme esclavagiste 1835–1847* (Paris, 1980); and Augustin Cochin, *L'Abolition de l'esclavage* (Paris, 1861).

Slavery and the plantation economy have received a great deal of attention for the Spanish islands. The classic work is by Fernando Ortiz, *Hampa Afro-Cubana: Los negros esclavos* (Havana, 1916), which can be supplemented by the older Hubert H. S. Aimes, *The History of Slavery in Cuba, 1522–1868* (New York, 1907). More modern studies include Herbert S. Klein, *Slavery in the Americas: A Comparative Study of Cuba and Virginia* (Chicago, 1967); Franklin W. Knight, *Slave Society in Cuba during the Nineteenth Century* (Madison, 1970) on the slave system; Manuel Moreno Fraginals, *El ingenio*, 3 vols. (Havana, 1978); and most recently the work of Laird W. Bergad, *Cuban Rural Society in the Nineteenth Century: The Social and Economic History of Monoculture in Matanzas* (Princeton, 1990), and his fundamental joint study of Cuban slave prices, in Laird W. Bergad, Fe Iglesias García, and María del Carmen Barcia, *The Cuban Slave Market, 1790–1880* (Cambridge, 1995). Important for all aspects of the 19th-century economy is Levi Marrero, *Cuba: Economía y sociedad. Azucar, ilustración y conciencia (1763–1868)*, 3 vols. (Madrid, 1983–84). One of the more complete demographic assessments of the slave population is found in Kenneth F. Kiple, *Blacks in Colonial Cuba, 1774–1899* (Gainesville, Fla., 1976); the best study on the coolie population is that of Juan Perez de la Riva, *Para la historia de las gentes sin historia* (Barcelona, 1976). Still fundamental are the contemporary studies of Alexander von Humboldt, *The Island of Cuba*, translated and with notes by I. S. Thrasher (New York, 1856); and Jacobo de la Pezuela, *Diccionario geográfico, estadístico, histórico de la isla de Cuba*, 4 vols. (Madrid, 1868–78).

The older study of Luis M. Díaz Soler, *Historia de la esclavitud negra en Puerto Rico* (Rio Piedras, 1969), has been supplemented by several innovative monographs on the unusual evolution of slavery and the plantation economy in Puerto Rico. The most important of these is Francisco A. Scarano, *Sugar and Slavery in Puerto Rico: The Plantation Economy of Ponce, 1800–1850* (Madison, 1984). Also useful are the studies of José Curet and Ramos Mattei contained in Andrés A. Ramos Mattei, ed., *Azúcar y esclavitud* (Rio Piedras, 1982).

CHAPTER 6.   SLAVERY AND THE PLANTATION ECONOMY IN BRAZIL
AND THE GUYANAS IN THE 19TH CENTURY

The literature on 19th-century Brazil is extensive. In addition to the works of Freyre, Schwartz, Mattoso, Perdigão Malheiro, and Goulart cited above for chapter 4, there is also a fine overall survey of the 19th-century experience with slavery in Minas Gerais to be found in Laird W. Bergad, *Slavery and the Demographic and Economic History of Minas Gerais, Brazil, 1720–1888* (Cambridge, 1999); and in São Paulo in Francisco Vidal Luna and Herbert S. Klein, *Slavery and the Economy of São Paulo, 1750–1850* (Stanford, 2003). Other regional studies include the work of Schwartz on Bahia (1985) and B. J. Barickman, A *Bahian Counterpoint: Sugar, Tobacco, Cassava, and Slavery in the Recôncavo, 1780–1860* (Stanford, 1998), which deals with slavery in nonplantation small farming; the best estimate of the size and importance of slave provisioning grounds in Bahia is his study " 'A Bit of Land, Which They Call Roça': Slave Provision Grounds in the Bahian Reconcavo, 1780–1860," *Hispanic American Historical Review* 74, no. 4 (1994). Older studies on local regions include Octavio Ianni, *As metamorfoses do escravo* (São Paulo, 1962); Fernando Henrique Cardoso, *Capitalismo e escravidão no Brasil meridional* (São Paulo, 1962); and Mario José Maestri Filho, *O escravo no Rio Grande do Sul: A charquedada e a gênese do escravismo gaucho* (Porto Alegre, 1984). The best studies on slave demography in Latin America remain Robert Slenes, "The Demography and Economics of Brazilian Slavery: 1850–1880" (Ph.D. diss., Stanford University, 1976); and Pedro Carvalho de Mello, "Estimativa da longevidade dos escravos no Brasil na segunda mitade do século xix," *Estudos Econômicos* 13, no. 1 (1983). These should be supplemented with Thomas W. Merrick and Douglas H. Graham, *Population and Economic Development in Brazil, 1800 to the Present* (Baltimore, 1979). The best work on the economics of slavery in Brazil has been done by Pedro Carvalho de Mello, "The Economics of Labor in Brazilian Coffee Plantations, 1871–1888" (Ph.D. diss., University of Chicago, 1977); and "Aspectos economicos da organizacão do trabalho da economia cafeeira do Rio de Janeiro 1850–1888," *Revista Brasileira de Economia*, 32, no.1 (1978).

General studies of regional industries or slave economies are found in Stanley J. Stein, *Vassouras:, A Brazilian Coffee County, 1850–1900* (Cambridge, Mass., 1957); Peter L. Eisenberg, *The Sugar Industry in Pernambuco, 1840–1910* (Berkeley, 1974); Warren Dean, *Rio Claro: A Brazilian Plantation System, 1820–1920* (Stanford, 1976); and Maria Thereza Schorer Petrone, *A lavoura canavieira em São Paulo* (São Paulo, 1968). While an overview of the coffee plantation regime is provided in C. F. van Deldein Laerne, *Brasil and Java: Report on Coffee Culture in America, Asia and Africa* (London, 1885); and Affonso de E. Taunay, *Historia do cafe no Brasil,* 15 vols. (Rio de Janeiro, 1939–43).

The unusual rural economy of Minas Gerais in the 19th century has been the subject of recent debate, which began with Amilcar Martins Filho and Roberto B. Martins, "Slavery in a Nonexport Economy: Minas Gerais Revisited," *Hispanic American Historical Review* 63, no. 3 (1983), with comments by Robert Slenes, Warren Dean, Eugene Genovese, and Stanley Engerman, and their reply in *Hispanic American Historical Review* 64, no. 1 (1984), has found a new synthesis in the major study of Bergad (1999). The special role of slavery in a local marginal economy has been provided in several fine articles by Luiz R. B. Mott; see especially his "Pardos e pretos em Sergipe, 1774–1851," *Revista do Instituto de Estudos Brasileiros* 18 (1976). Finally, the classic work of Sebastião Ferreira Soares, *Notas estadisticas sobre a produçãao agricola … no imperio do Brasil* (Rio de Janeiro, 1860), remains fundamental reading for agricultural production in general at midcentury.

There are numerous plantations or plantation family studies, among which are Herbert H. Smith, *Uma fazenda de cafe no tempo do imperio* (Rio de Janeiro, 1941); Carlota Pereira de Queiroz, *Um fazendeiro paulista no seculo xix* (São Paulo, 1965); Eduardo Silva, *Barões e escravidão: Tres generacoes de fazendeiros e a crise da estructura escravista* (Rio de Janeiro, 1984); and José Wanderley de Araujo Pinho, *Historia de um engenho do Reconcovo … 1522–1944* (Rio de Janeiro, 1946); along with the classic work of Gilberto Freyre.

Urban slavery is studied in Mary C. Karash, *Slave Life and Culture in Rio de Janeiro, 1808–1850* (Princeton, 1986). Also see Zephyr L. Frank, *Dutra's World: Wealth and Family in Nineteenth-Century Rio de Janeiro* (Albuquerque, 2004); João José Reis, " 'The Revolution of the Ganhadores': Urban Labour, Ethnicity and the African Strike of 1857 in Bahia, Brazil," *Journal of Latin American Studies* 29, no. 2 (May 1997); and Paulo Roberto Staudt Moreira, *Os cativos e os homens de bem, experiéncias negras no espaço urbano* (Porto Alegre, 2003). The only major studies of industrial slavery are by Douglas Cole Libby, *Trabalho escravo e capital estrangeiro no Brasil* (Belo Horizonte, 1984) ; *Transformação e trabalho: Em uma economia escravista: Minas Gerais no século XIX* (São Paulo, 1988); and "Proto-industrialization in a Slave Society: The Case of Minas Gerais," *Journal of Latin American Studies* 23, no. 1 (1991). Also see Luis Carlos Soares, "A escravidão industrial no Rio de Janeiro do século XIX," *Associação Brasileira de Pesquisadores em História Econômica (ABPHE) V Congresso Brasileiro de História Econômica,* 2003. It is mostly urban conditions that are examined in Gilberto Freyre, *O escravo nos anuncios dos jornais brasileiros do século xix* (Recife, 1963); the movement of largely urban slaves from the north to the south is studied in Evaldo Cabral de Melo, *O norte agrário e o império* (Rio de Janeiro, 1984).

For the French Guyanese experience with slavery in this period, useful studies include Ciro Flamarion Cardoso, *Economia e sociedade em áreas coloniais periféricas: Guiana francesa e Pará (1750–1817)* (Rio de Janeiro, 1984); Marie Louise Marchand Thebault et al., "L'esclavage en Guyane française sous l'ancien régime," *Revue Française d'Histoire d'Outre-Mer* 48 (1960); and, finally, Jean-Marcel Hurault, *Francaise et Indiens en Guyane* (Paris, 1972). Helpful as well are the general sources already discussed for the

French West Indies, which also include the mainland French experience. British Guyana is also evaluated in the works on the British West Indies cited above, which should be supplemented with Alan H. Adamson, *Sugar without Slaves. The Political Economy of British Guiana, 1838–1904* (New Haven, 1972); and Jay R. Mandle, *The Plantation Economy: Population and Economic Change in Guyana, 1838–1960* (Philadelphia, 1973).

The Dutch experience has been treated extensively. A good introduction is to be found in Cornelis Ch. Gosling, *A Short History of the Netherlands Antilles and Surinam* (The Hague, 1979). The best social history of the colony is given by R. A. J. Van Lier, *Frontier Society: A Social Analysis of the History of Surinam* (The Hague, 1971). More detailed studies of specific topics are R. M. N. Pandy, *Agriculture in Surinam, 1650–1950* (Amsterdam, 1959); and the studies of Silvia W. de Groot, *From Isolation towards Integration: The Surinam Maroons and Their Colonial Rulers 1845–1863* (The Hague, 1977), and "The Maroon of Surinam: Agents of Their Own Emancipation" (paper presented at the University of Hull, July 1983). For an analysis of a plantation workforce, see Humphrey E. Lamur, "Demography of Surinam Plantation Slaves in the Last Decade before Emancipation: The Case of Catharina Sophia," in Vera Rubin and Arthur Tuden, eds., *Comparative Perspective in New World Plantation Societies* (New York, 1977).

CHAPTER 7.   LIFE, DEATH, AND THE FAMILY IN AFRO-AMERICAN
SLAVE SOCIETIES

The modern study of the Atlantic slave trade begins with the work of Gaston-Martin, *Nantes au xviiie siècle: L'ère des négriers (1714–1774)* (Paris, 1931); and the excellent documentary collection of Elizabeth Donnan, *Documents Illustrative of the History of the Slave Trade to America*, 4 vols. (Washington, D.C., 1930). It was not until the last three decades, however, that this early work was built upon. The appearance of Philip Curtin's fundamental study *The Atlantic Slave Trade: A Census in 1969* coincided with a number of publications by scholars who were working on the trade from several different aspects. Thus Jean Meyer, *L'Armement nantais dans la deuxième moitié du XVIIIe siècle* (Paris, 1969), and Roger Anstey, *The Atlantic Slave Trade and British Abolition* (London, 1975), began the detailed reconstruction of the commercial organization and profitability of the slave trade; Herbert S. Klein, *The Middle Passage: Comparative Studies in the Atlantic Slave Trade* (Princeton, 1978), dealt with transatlantic mortality and the manner of carrying slaves among the major slave-trading nations; while António Carreira, *As companhias pombalinas de navegação comercio e trafico de escravos entre a costa africana e nordeste brasileiro* (Porto, 1969); Pierre Verger, *Flux et reflux de la traite des nègres entre le golfe de Bénin et Bahia de Todos os Santos, du dix-septième au dix-neuvième siècle* (Paris, 1968); and Manual dos Anjos da Silva Rebeho, *Relações entre Angola e Brasil, 1808–1830* (Lisbon, 1970), opened up the systematic study of the Portuguese trade to Brazil. On the broader international aspects of the early Brazilian slave trade, see Luiz Felipe de Alencastro, *O trato dos viventes: Formação do Brasil no Atlântico Sul, séculos XVI e XVII* (São Paulo, 2000); and on the trade to the port of Rio de Janeiro, see Manolo Florentino, *Em costas negras, uma história do tráfico de escravos entre a África e o Rio de Janeiro (séculos XVIII e XIX)* (São Paulo, 1997).

For the Spanish American trade, the best of the local studies include Elena F. S. Studer, *La trata de negros en el Rio de la Plata durante el siglo xviii* (Buenos Aires, 1958); Jorge Palacios Preciado, *La trata de negros por Cartagena de Indias* (Tunja, Colombia, 1973); and the previously mentioned work of Chandler (1981) and Palmer (1981) on the trade to the northern and northwestern coast of South America. Bibiano Torres Ramirez, *La compañía gaditana de negros* (Seville, 1973), deals with this special 18th-century monopoly company; for the earlier trade, Enriqueta Vila Vilar, *Hispano-America y el comercio de esclavos: Los asientos portugueses* (Seville, 1977), and Maria Vega Franco, *El trafico de esclavos con America...1663–1674* (Seville, 1984), have substantially revised and added numbers to the earlier work of George Scelle, *La Traite négrière aux Indes de Castille*, 2 vols. (Paris, 1906). Finally, the study of Robert Louis Stein, *The French Slave Trade in the Eighteenth Century: An Old Regime Business* (Madison, 1979), complements the earlier work of Meyer (1969) and Gaston-Martin (1931). The single best work on the important Dutch slave trade is found in the classic study of Johannes Postma, *The Dutch in the Atlantic Slave Trade, 1600–1815* (Cambridge, 1990).

There have also been several important collections of articles on the trade, which include Roger Anstey and P. E. H. Hair, eds., *Liverpool, the African Slave Trade and Abolition* (Liverpool, 1976); Henry A. Gemery and Jan S. Hogendorn, eds., *The Uncommon Market: Essays on the Economic History of the Trans-Atlantic Slave Trade* (New York, 1976); and the previously cited work of Inikori (1982). The trade of the 19th century is now being studied intensively; a good deal of this material is to be found in David Eltis, *The Nineteenth Century Atlantic Slave Trade* (New York, 1986). An overview of the entire trade is provided in Herbert S. Klein, *The Atlantic Slave Trade* (Cambridge, 1999).

There has been a lively debate on the profitability question in articles by J. E. Inikori, R. P. Thomas, and R. N. Bean, among others, which is summarized in two articles by B. L. Anderson and David Richardson, entitled "Market Structure and Profits of the British African Trade in the Late Eighteenth Century," *Journal of Economic History* 43 (1983) and 45 (1985). The ongoing debate about the numbers transported is reviewed and updated in the Paul E. Lovejoy, "The Volume of the Atlantic Slave Trade: A Synthesis," *The Journal of African History*, 23, no. 4 (1982) and the Eltis (2001) article cited above. A work comparable to the Donnan collection is Jean Mettas, *Repertoire des expeditions negrières francaises au xviiie siècle*, 2 vols. (Paris, 1978–84). A major collection of the extant slave voyages has been made available on CD; see David Eltis, Stephen D. Behrendt, David Richardson, and Herbert S. Klein, *The Transatlantic Slave Trade: 1562–1867: A Database* (Cambridge, 2000).

Of the recent surveys of all the slave trades from Africa, the most useful overview is found in François Renault and Serge Daget, *Les Traites negrieres en Afrique* (Paris, 1985). Also the health conditions of the slaves in the crossing have been analyzed in the books by Palmer (1981) and Chandler (1981) and in a recent study by Franz Tardo-Dino, *Le Collier de servitude: La condition sanitaire des esclaves aux Antilles francaises du xviie au xixe siècle* (Paris, 1985). A general survey of slave health is also found in Kenneth P. Kiple, *The Caribbean Slave: A Biological History* (Cambridge, 1985).

Finally, the impact of the migrating slaves on the native population was first analyzed in detail in Jack E. Eblen, "On the Natural Increase of Slave Populations:

The Example of the Cuban Black Population, 1775–1900," in Stanley Engerman and Euguene Genovese, eds., *Race and Slavery in the Western Hemisphere* (Princeton, 1975). It is also discussed in the previously cited work of Slenes (1976) and Carvalho de Melo (1984) for Brazil; in Higman (1984) and Craton (1978) for the English West Indies; and in two recent articles by Herbert S. Klein and Stanley L. Engerman, "Fertility Differentials between Slaves in the United States and the British West Indies: A Note on Lactation Practices and Their Implications," *William and Mary Quarterly* 35, no. 2 (1978); and "A demografia dos escravos americanos," in Maria Luiza Marcllio, ed., *Poblação e sociedade. Evolução das sociedades pre-industriais* (Petropolis, 1984).

CHAPTER 8.   CREATION OF A SLAVE COMMUNITY AND AFRO-AMERICAN CULTURE

A vast literature exists on the topic of African ethnicities in the New World, and this bibliography only points to a sample of works on the issue. Two important broad discussions of the clustering of African ethnicities in the Americas can be found in John Thornton, *Africa and Africans in the Making of the Atlantic World*, 2nd ed. (Cambridge, 1998), and Gwendolyn Midlo Hall, *Slavery and African Ethnicities in the Americas: Restoring the Links* (Chapel Hill, 2005). An important collection of essays addressing the theme is Michael L Conniff and Thomas J. Davis, eds., *Africans in the Americas: A History of the Black Diaspora* (New York, 1994). There are numerous discussions of the complexities of African ethnic survivals and slave identities in regional contexts. For Brazil, see James Sweet, *Recreating Africa: Culture, Kinship and Religion in the African-Portuguese World, 1441–1770* (Chapel Hill, 2003); Mary Karasch, *Slave Life in Rio de Janeiro, 1808–1850* (Princeton, 1987); Mieko Nishida, *Slavery and Idenity: Ethnicity, Gender, and Race in Salvador, Brazil, 1808–1888* (Bloomington, 2003). The work of Nicolás del Castillo Mathieu, *Esclavos negros en Cartagena y sus aportes Léxicos* (Bogotá, 1982), provides excellent ethnic information about slaves arriving to Cartagena who were subsequently shipped elsewhere in the Americas. Related information on slaves arriving to the ports of both Mexico and Panama can be found in Enriqueta Vilar Vilar's cited, *Hispanoamérica y el comercio de esclavos*. For information on the Bantu in Mexico, see Nicolás Ngou-Mve, *El Africa Bantú en la colonización de México (1595–1640)* (Madrid, 1994); "Huellas Bantúes en el noreste de Oaxaca," in María Elisa Velázques and Ethel Correa, eds., *Poblaciónes y culturas de origen africano en México* (Mexico, DF, 2005); and, for broader discussions of African ethnicity in early Mexico, see Herman L. Bennett, *Africans in Colonial Mexico: Absolutism, Christianity and Afro-Creole Consciousness, 1570–1640* (Bloomington, 2003). For ethnicities in Peru, see Jean-Pierre Tardieu, "Origins of the Slaves in the Lima Region in Peru (Sixteenth and Seventeenth Centuries)," in Dondon Diéne, ed., *From Chains to Bonds: The Slave Trade Revisited* (New York, 2001); and Frederick P. Bowser, *The African Slave in Colonial Peru, 1524–1650* (Stanford, 1974). For ethnicity in Cuba, see Manuel Moreno Fraginals, "Africa in Cuba: A Quantitative Analysis of the African Population in the Island of Cuba," in Vera Rubin and Arthur Truden, eds., *Comparative Perspectives on Slavery in New World Plantation Societies* (New York, 1977); María Elena Díaz, *The Virgin, the King,* and the Royal Slaves of El Cobre: Negotiating Freedom in Colonial Cuba, 1670–1780 (Stanford, 2000); Laird W. Bergad, Fe Iglesias García, and María del Carmen Barcia, The Cuban Slave Market, 1790–1880 (Cambridge, 1995). African ethnicities in Guatemala and Venezuela can be found in Robinson A. Herrera, Natives, Europeans and Africans in Sixteenth-Century Santiago de Guatemala (Austin, 2003); and Miguel Acosta Saignes, Vida de los esclavos negros en Venezuela (Caracas, 1967). The ethnicity of slaves in Chuao, Venezuela, is briefly mentioned in Robert J. Ferry, The Colonial Elite of Early Caracas: Formation and Crisis, 1567–1767 (Berkeley, 1989). Understanding the impact of African ethnicity in the French Caribbean can be appreciated in Hein Vanhee, "Central African Popular Christianity and the Making of Haitian Vodou Religion," in Linda M. Heywood, ed., Central Africans and Cultural Transformations in the American Diaspora (Cambridge, 2002); and David Geggus, "The French Slave Trade: An Overview," William and Mary Quarterly, 3rd ser., 58, no. 1 (2001); Geggus, "Sex Ratio, Age, and Ethnicity in the Atlantic Slave Trade: Data from French Shipping and Plantation Records," Journal of African History 30 (1989): 23–44. Broader patterns of Yoruba and Central African influences on the Americas can be found in two excellent edited collections, Toyin Falola and Matt D. Childs, eds., The Yoruba Diaspora in the Atlantic World (Bloomington, 2004); and Heywood, Central Africans and Cultural Transformations in the American Diaspora.

As the work of recovering African ethnicities transpires, Philip D. Morgan speaks of the inadvertent "orthodoxy" that can emerge as historians discuss slaves as "forming identifiable communities based on their ethnic or national pasts." His argument favoring heterogeneity over homogeneous ethnic African representations in the Americas can be found in "The Cultural Implications of the Atlantic Slave Trade: African Regional Origins, American Destinations and New World Developments," in David Eltis and David Richardson, eds., Routes to Slavery: Direction, Ethnicity and Mortality in the Transatlantic Slave Trade (London, 1997).

Of Afro-American culture, one of the more studied elements has been its religious organization and expression. The main work in this respect has been done by anthropologists, psychologists, and sociologists. Among the most prominent names have been those of Meville Herskovits, Alfred Metraux, and Roger Bastide. Bastide has summarized much of this literature in his book African Civilization in the New World (New York, 1971). The bibliography in this work can be supplemented with surveys by Angelina Pollak-Eltz, Cultos afroarnericanos (Caracas, 1977), and George E. Simpson, Black Religions in the New World (New York, 1978). The classic work on Voodoo is Alfred Metraux, Voodoo in Haiti (London, 1949); Roger Bastide, Les religions africaines aux Brésil (Paris, 1960), has written the definitive work on Condomblé and other Afro-Brazilian cults. Melville Herskovits; The Myth of the Negro Past, rev. ed. (New York, 1958), provides a good introduction to many of the religious activities in the English-speaking colonies. For Cuba the standard work remains Fernando Ortiz, Los negros brujos (Havana, 1906). On the interaction of African and Afro-Cuban religious and cultural experiences, the best source is the autobiography of Esteben Montejo in Miguel Barnet, The Autobiography of a Runaway Slave (New York, 1968).

On the African and Afro-American experience within the Catholic Church, one of the better-studied areas is that of Brazil. Important in this regard are the works of A. J. R. Russell-Wood, *Fidalgos and Philanthropists* (Berkeley, 1968); his article "Black and Mulatto Brotherhoods in Colonial Brazil," *Hispanic American Historical Review* 54, no. 4 (1974); and his book (1982) cited above. A fine study of an individual *cofradia* is that of Juanita Scarano, *Devoção e escravidão: A Irmadade de N.S. do Rosdrio dos Pretos no Distrito Diamantina no século xviii* (São Paulo, 1976); the African element in these *cofradias* is found in the recent study of Mariza de Carvalho Soares, *Devotos da cor: Identidade étnic, religiosidade e escravidão no Rio de Janeiro, século XVIII* (Rio de Janeiro, 2000). Emerging studies are appearing for other regions. Laura A. Lewis, *Hall of Mirrors: Power, Witchcraft, and Caste in Colonial Mexico* (Durham, N.C., 2003), offers an important survey of deviant religious behavior in the form of magic and witchcraft. In Mexico, witchcraft and religious nonconformity are also explored by Joan Cameron Bristol, "Negotiating Authority in New Spain: Blacks, Mulattos, and Religious Practice in Seventeenth Century Mexico" (Ph.D. diss., University of Pennsylvania, 2001); Bristol, "From Curing to Witchcraft: Afro-Mexicans and the Mediation of Authority," *Journal of Colonialism and Colonial History* 7, no. 1 (2006); and Nora Jaffary, *False Mystics: Deviant Orthodoxy in Colonial Mexico* (Lincoln, 2004). Work on Mexico can be complemented by studies in the Andes, such as Leo Garofalo's "Conjuring with Coca and the Inca: The Andeanization of Lima's Afro-Peruvian Ritual Specialists, 1580–1690," *The Americas* 62, no. 3 (2006); Rachel O'Toole's "Danger in the Convent: Colonial Demons, Idolatrous Indians, and Bewitching Negras in Santa Clara (Trujillo del Peru)," *Journal of Colonialism and Colonial History* 7, no. 1 (2006); and the fascinating account of a black Peruvian mystic by Nancy E. Van Deusen, *The Souls of Purgatory: The Spiritual Diary of a Seventeenth-Century Afro-Peruvian Mystic, Ursula de Jesús* (Albuquerque, 2004).

Two collections provide a wealth of information on the question of Afro-American languages. These are Dell Hymes, ed., *Pidginization and Creolization of Languages* (Cambridge, 1971); and A. Vaidman, ed., *Pidgin and Creole Linguistics* (Bloomington, 1977). A recent useful survey for Brazil is Yeda Pessoa de Castro, "Os falares africanos na interação social do Brasil colonial," *Centro de Estudos Baianos* 89 (1980).

For the occupational distribution on the plantations, the best data will be found in the Schwartz (1985) study of Bahia, the Stein (1957) analysis of the coffee estates of Vassouras, and the Debien (1974) and Vanony-Frisch (1985) studies of the coffee and sugar habitations of the French West Indies. Housing is discussed in Debien and in the major studies on 19th-century slavery in Cuba, those of Levi Marrero (1983–84) and Manuel Moreno Fraginals (1978).

The question of slave families has received considerable attention in studies on the North American slave system but has only recently become a major topic of concern in studying slavery in Latin America and the Caribbean. Fundamental for background reading is Herbert G. Gutman, *The Black Family in Slavery and Freedom, 1750–1925* (New York, 1976); and the critiques of his position given by Jo Ann Manfra and Robert R. Dykstra, "Serial Marriage and the Origins of the Black StepFamily: The Rowanty Evidence," *Journal of American History* 72, no. 1 (1985). There has been an outpouring of studies on Brazilian slave marriages. For older studies, see Iraci de Nero da Costa and Horacio Gutierrez, "Nota sobre casamentos de escravos em São Paulo e no Paraná (1830)," *História: Questões e Debates* (Curitiba) 5, no. 9 (1984); and chapter 14 in Schwartz (1985). For recent work, see Robert Slenes, *Na Senzala, uma flor: Esperanças e recordações na formação da família escrava—Brasil Sudeste. Século XIX* (São Paulo, 1999); the book of Carvalho Soares (2000); José Flávio Motta, *Corpos escravos, vontades livres: Posse de cativos e família escrava em Bananal (1801–1829)* (São Paulo, 1999); João Luis Ribeiro Fragoso and Manolo Garcia Florentino, "Marcelino, filho de Inocência Crioula, neto de Joana Cabinda:um estudo sobre famílias escravas em Paraíba do Sul (1835–1872)," *Estudo Econômicos*, 2 no. 17 (1987); Manolo Garcia Florentino and José Roberto Góes, "Parentesco e família entre os escravos no século XIX: Um estudo de caso," *Revista Brasileira de Estudos de População* 12, nos. 1 and 2,(1995); and by the same authors, *A paz das senzalas: Famílias escravos e tráfico atlántico, Rio de Janeiro, c.1750–c.1850* (Rio de Janeiro, 1997); José Roberto Góes, *O Cativeiro Imperfeito: Um estudo sobre a escravidão no Rio de Janeiro da primeira metade do século XIX* (Vitória, ES, 1993); plus a series of important studies that were published in the *Anais* of the Encontro da Associação Brasileira de Estudos Populacionais, in various years (available at http://www.abep.org.br/usuario/GerenciaNavegacao.php). These include Marcia Cristina Roma de Vasconcellos, "Casamento e maternidade entre escravas de Angra dos Reis, século XIX," *Anais XIV ABEP*; Jonis Freire, "Compadrio em uma freguesia escravista: Senhor Bom Jesus do Rio Pardo (MG) (1838–1888)," *Anais XIV ABEP*, 2004; Renato Leite Marcondes and José Flávio Motta, "A família escrava em Lorena e Cruzeiro (1874)," *Anais XIII ABEP*, 2000; Juliana Garavazo, "Relações familiares e estabilidade da família escrava: Batatais (1850–88)," *Anais XIV ABEP*, 2004; and Carolina Perpétuo Corrêa, "Aspectos da demografia e vida familiar dos escravos de Santa Luzia, Minas Gerais, 1818–1833," *Anais XIV ABEP*, 2004. Also see Linda Wimmer, "Ethnicity and Family Formation among Slaves on Tobacco Farms in the Bahian Recôncao, 1698–1829," in José C. Curto and Paul E. Lovejoy, eds., *Enslaving Connections: Changing Cultures of Africa and Brazil during the Era of Slavery* (Amherst, N.Y., 2004); Rômulo Andrade, "Ampliando estudos sobre famílias escravas no seculo XIX," *Revista Universitaria Rural, Serie Ciencias Humanas* 24, nos. 1–2 (2002); and Hebe Maria Mattos de Castro and Eduardo Schnoor, eds., *Resgate: Una janela para o Oitocentos* (Rio de Janeiro, 1995). On the question of legitimate slave births, see Ana Luiza de Castro Pereira, "A ilegitimidade nomeada e ocultada na vila de Nossa Senhora da Conceição do Sabará," and Vanda Lúcia Praxedes, "A teia e a trama da 'Fragilidade Humana': Os Filhos Ilegítimos em Minas Gerais (1770–1840)," both presented at the XI Seminário sobre a Economia Mineira (Diamantina, MG, 2004) and available on EconPapers online.

For a general reassessment of the family on the large latifundia and a critique of the older Freyre model, see Eni de Mesquita Samana, *A família brasileira* (São Paulo, 1983). For the West Indies, the most research has been done on the English islands; see Barry W. Higman, "African and Creole Slave Family Patterns in Trinidad," *Journal of Family History* 3, no. 2 (1978); and Michael Craton, "Changing Patterns of Slave Family in the British West Indies," *Journal of Interdisciplinary History* 10, no. 1 (1979). A pioneering study on naming patterns is found in John Thornton, "Central African Names and African-American Naming Patterns," *William and Mary Quarterly* 50, no. 4 (1993).

CHAPTER 9.   SLAVE RESISTANCE AND REBELLION

Our discussion of the legal structure of slavery is taken from several sources. For the European background, the first volume of Charles Verlinden's *L'esclavage dans l'Europe* is helpful. See the previously cited work of Klein (1967) for a survey of the Spanish legal codes; and for the Portuguese and Brazilian legal system, the already mentioned work of Saunders (1982) and Malheiro (1866), respectively. The French codes are analyzed in Antoine Gisler, *L'esclavage aux Antilles francaises (xviie-xixe siècle)*, rev. ed. (Paris, 1981), which should be supplemented by the study of Yvan Debbasch on the free colored, discussed with works related to the next chapter. One of the few detailed analyses of judicial precedents used in court cases is Norman A. Meiklejohn, "The Implementation of Slave Legislation in Eighteenth-Century New Granada," in Robert Toplin, ed., *Slavery and Race Relations in Latin America* (Westport, Conn., 1974).

Work on how slaves negotiated their position as religious subjects in the dynamics of the colonial world can be found in some of the emerging work on Mexico. Herman Bennett's *Africans in Colonial Mexico* offers one prominent example. However, work on the use of blasphemy is also prominent, as can be found in Javier Villa-Flores, "To Lose One's Soul: Blasphemy and Slavery in New Spain, 1596–1669," *Hispanic American Historical Review* 82, no. 3 (2002): 435–69; Frank T. Proctor III, "Slavery, Identity and Culture: An Afro-Mexican Counterpoint, 1640–1763" (Ph.D. diss., Emory University, 2003); Joan Cameron Bristol, "Negotiating Authority in New Spain: Blacks Mulattos, and Religious Practice in Seventeenth Century Mexico" (Ph.D. diss., University of Pennsylvania, 2001); Bennett, " 'Sons of Adam': Text, Context, and the Early Modern African Subject," *Representations* (Fall 2005): 16–41; and Bennett, "Genealogies to a Past: Africa, Ethnicity, and Marriage in Seventeenth-Century Mexico," in Edward E. Baptist and Stephanie M. H. Camp, eds., *New Studies in American Slavery* (Athens, Ga., 2005).

The literature on *marronage* is extensive. Useful as background is the collection edited by Richard Price, *Maroon Societies: Rebel Slave Communities in the Americas* (New York, 1973). The classic work on the French West Indies is Yvan Debbasch, "Le marronage: Essai sur la desertion de l'esclavage antillais," *L'Année Sociologique*, published in two parts in 1961 and 1962.

There is an extensive body of materials on Palmares and the Brazilian *quilombos*. The best general work is that of João José Reis and Flávio dos Santos Gomes, *Liberdade por un fio: História dos quilombos no Brasil* (São Paulo, 1996). The standard survey of the Palmares experience is Décio Freitas, *Palmares, a guerra dos escravos*, 4th ed. (Rio de Janeiro, 1982), along with Ernesto Ennes, *As guerras nos Palmares* (Rio de Janeiro, 1958), and Edison Carneiro, *O quilombo dos Palmares* (Rio de Janeiro, 1966). The best study to date on the great Bahian revolts is João José Reis, *Slave Rebellion in Brazil:, The Muslim Uprising of 1835 in Bahia* (Baltimore, 1993). A useful study on the largest participation of runaway slaves in a general popular rebellion is Maria Januária Vilela Santos, *A Balaiada e a insurreiçao de escravos no Maranhão* (São Paulo, 1983). For the conspiracies and rebellions in early Spanish America, the best single work to date is that by Carlos Federico Guillot, *Negros rebeldés y negros cimarones . . . siglo xvi* (Buenos Aires, 1961). Detailed studies on individual movements include María del Carmen Borrego

Plá, *Palenques de negros en Cartagena de Indias a fines del siglo xviii* (Sevilla, 1973); María Cristina Navarrete, *Cimarrones y palenques en el siglo XVII* (Cali, 2003); the previously cited article of David Davidson (1966) on 16th- and 17th-century Mexico; Patrick J. Carroll, "Mandiga: The Evolution of a Mexican Runaway Slave Community: 1735–1827," *Comparative Studies in Society and History* 19, no. 4 (1977), and Adriana Naveda Chávez-Hita, "La lucha de los negros esclavos en las haciendas azucareras de Córdoba en el siglo xviii," *Anuario del Centro de Estudios Históricos* (Xalapa), 11 (1980). The Venezuela situation is studied in Fedenco Brito Figueroa, *Insurreciones de esclavos negros en Venezuela colonial* (Caracas, 1960). A study of the Escalera conspiracy is provided in Robert L. Paquette, *Sugar Is Made with Blood: The Conspiracy of La Escalera...in Cuba* (Middletown, Conn., 1988). The best introduction to the complex patterns of rebellion in the British colonies of the Caribbean and South America is Michael Craton, *Testing the Chains: Resistance to Slavery in the British West Indies* (Ithaca, 1982). For some of the work on Esmeraldas, see Charles Beatty Medina, "Caught between Rivals: The Spanish-African Maroon Competition for Captive Indian Labor in the Region of Esmeraldas during the Late 16th and Early 17th Century," *The Americas* 62, no. 3 (2006); Baltasar Fra Molinero, "Ser mulatto en España y América: Discursos legales y otros discursos literarios," in Berta Ares Queija and Alessandro Stella, eds., *Negros, Mulatos, Zambaigos: Derroteros africanos en los mundos ibéricos* (Sevilla, 2000), 123–47; José Rumazo González, *Documentos para la historia de la Audiencia de Quito* (Madrid, 1948); Frank Salomon, *Los Yumbos, Niguas y Tsatchila o "Colorados": Durante la Colonia Española* (Quito, 1997); Rocio Rueda Novoa, *Zambaje y autonomia: Historia de la gente negra de la provincia de Esmeraldas, siglos XVI–XVIII* (Quito, 2001); Adam Szazdi, "El transfondo de un cuadro: 'Los mulatos de Esmeraldas' de Andrés Sánchez Galque," *Cuadernos Prehispánicos* 12 (1986–87): 93–142; and Kris Lane, *Quito 1599: City and Colony in Transition* (Albuquerque, 2002). For more on issues of *marronage* in Colombia, see Anthony McFarlane, "Cimarrones and Palenques: Runaways and Resistance in Colonial Colombia," *Slavery and Abolition* 6, no. 3 (1985). Interesting work on Santo Domingo can be found in Carlos Esteban Drive, *Los guerrilleros negros, esclavos fugitivos y cimarrones en Santo Domingo* (Santo Domingo, 1989). A broad-reaching analysis of Spanish efforts to counter *marronage* in the 17th century has been written by Jane Landers, "Una cruzada Americana: Expediciones españolas contra los cimarrones en el siglo XVII," in Juan Manuel de la Serna Herrera, ed., *Pautas de convivencia étnica en la América Latina colonial (Indios, negros, mulatos, pardos y esclavos)* (Mexico,DF, 2005). On the Haitian rebellion, the survey by C. L. R. James, *The Black Jacobins*, 2nd ed. (New York, 1963), remains the classic source. This should be supplemented by Carolyn E. Fick, *The Making of Haiti: The Saint Domingue Revolution from Below* (Knoxville, 1990), and Geggus, *Slavery, War and Revolution* and the works cited therein. Torcuato Di Tella, *La rebelión de esclavos de Haiti* (Buenos Aires, 1984), attempts a sociological reinterpretation of the movement, while the developments in Guadeloupe have been treated in Germain Saint-Ruf, *L'Épopée Delgres, La Guadeloupe sous la revolution française (1789–1802)*, 2nd ed. (Paris, 1977). Two stimulating recent works by Laurent Dubois both recast the Haitian revolution and resistance efforts in the broader French Caribbean. See *A Colony of Citizens: Revolution and Slave Emancipation in the French*

Caribbean, 1787–1804 (Chapel Hill, 2004); and *Avengers of the New World: The Story of the Haitian Revolution* (Cambridge, Mass., 2004).

Assessments of slave resistance also encompass the employment of legal strategies designed to ameliorate slavery, as well as activities that manipulated certain inconsistencies in the colonial conceptualization of honor. Also important were unique opportunities for liberty that were afforded by the particular geographic condition of certain regions in Latin America. A few of the titles exploring such themes include Sherwin K. Bryant, "Enslaved Rebels, Fugitives, and Litigants: The Resistance Continuum in Colonial Quito," *Colonial Latin American Review* 13, no. 1 (2004); Lolita Gutiérrez Brockington, "The African Diaspora in the Eastern Andes: Adaptation, Agency and Fugitive Action, 1573–1677," *The Americas* 57, no. 2 (2000); Rachel O'Toole, "In a War against the Spanish: Andean Protection and African Resistance on the Northern Peruvian Coast," *The Americas* 62, no. 3 (2006); María Eugenia Chaves, *Honor y Libertad: Discursos y recursos en la estrategia de libertad de una mujer esclava (Guayaquil a fines del período colonial)* (Güttenberg, 2001); Chaves, "Literate Culture, Subalternity and Resistance: The Case of Slave Women in the Colonial Courts," *Journal of Colonialism and Colonial History* 7, no. 1 (2006); Camila Townsend, " 'Half My Body Free, the Other Half Enslaved': The Politics of the Slaves of Guayaquil at the End of the Colonial Era," *Colonial Latin American Review* 7, no. 1 (1998); and Christine Hünefeldt, *Paying the Price of Freedom: Family and Labor among Lima's Slaves, 1800–1854* (Berkeley, 2004).

On violence to slaves and among slaves, there are some interesting works. Urban slave crime is dealt with in Suley Robles de Queiroz, *Escravidão negra em São Paulo: Um estudo das tensões provocadas pelo escravismo no século xix* (Rio de Janeiro, 1977); and Leila Mezan Algranti, "Ofeitor austente, estudo sobre a escravidão urbana no Rio de Janeiro, 1808–1821" (M.A. thesis, Universidade de São Paulo, 1983). Crimes against slaves have been studied in the works of José Alipio Goulart, *Da fuga ao suicidio: Aspectos da rebeldia dos escravos no Brasil* (Rio de Janeiro, 1972); and *Da palmatoria ao patibulo (castigos de escravos no Brasil)* (Rio de Janeiro, 1972); as well as in Ariosvaldo Figueiredo, *O negro e a violencia do branco (o negro em Sergipe)* (Rio de Janeiro, 1977).

Scholarship on slave resistance during the era of independence in Spanish America can be found in George Reid Andrews, *Afro-Latin America, 1800–2000* (New York, 2004); Peter Blanchard, "The Language of Liberation: Slave Voices in the Wars of Independence," *Hispanic American Historical Review* 82, no. 3 (2002); and Aline Helg, *Liberty and Equality in Caribbean Colombia, 1770–1835* (Chapel Hill, 2004). Two important reassessments of black participation in Cuba's independence wars are Ada Ferrer, *Insurgent Cuba: Race, Nation, and Revolution, 1868–1878* (Chapel Hill, 1999); and Aline Helg, *Our Rightful Share: The Afro-Cuban Struggle for Equality 1886–1912* (Chapel Hill, 1995).

CHAPTER 10.   FREEDMEN IN A SLAVE SOCIETY

An excellent introduction to the free colored population under slavery is the collection edited by David W. Cohen and Jack P. Greene, eds., *Neither Slave Nor Free: The Freedmen of African Descent in the Slave Societies of the New World* (Baltimore, 1972). The model work on the unusual free colored class in the French West Indies is Yvan Debbasch, *Couleur et liberte: Le jeu du critère ethnique dans un ordre juridique esclavagiste* (Paris, 1967). Aside from the articles by H. S. Klein on Brazil in the 19th century and A. J. R. Russell-Wood on 17th- and 18th-century Brazil in the Cohen and Greene collection, the book of Russell-Wood (1982) is also suggestive.

On the origins of this class within American slave regimes, the best work to date has actually been done for Latin American slave societies. These began with the article by Katia M. de Queiros Mattoso, "A proposito de cartas de alforria-Bahia, 1779–1850," *Anais de História* (Assis, São Paulo), 4 (1972), who called attention to the formal certificates of freedom for liberated slaves as a vital source of information. Mattoso followed through herself with a full-scale study "A Carta de alforria como fonte complementaría para o estudo de rentabilidade de mão de obra escrava urbana, 1819–1888," in Carlos Manuel Pelaez and Mircea Buescu, eds., *A moderna história econômica* (Rio de Janeiro, 1976). The colonial period was analyzed in Stuart B. Schwartz, "The Manumission of Slaves in Colonial Brazil: Bahia, 1684–1745," *Hispanic American Historical Review* 54, no. 4 (1974). These Bahian studies were followed by a detailed analysis of the manumission process in the sugar-producing and distilling center of Paraty, a *municipio* in the province of Rio de Janeiro, by James P. Kiernan, "The Manumission of Slaves in Colonial Brazil: Paraty, 1789–1822" (Ph.D. diss., New York University, 1976). Using these Brazilian studies as a model, Lyman L. Johnson produced his study, "Manumission in Colonial Buenos Aires, 1776–1810," *Hispanic American Historical Review* 59, no. 2 (1979). Recent additions to this literature have included the two books by Eduardo França Paiva, *Escravos e libertos nas Minas Gerias do século XVIII* (São Paulo, 1995), and *Esravidão e universo cultural na colônia, Minas Gerais, 1716–1789* (Belo, 2001); Mieko Nishida, "Manumission and Ethnicity in Urban Slavery: Salvador, Brazil, 1808–1888," *Hispanic American Historical Review* 73, no. 3 (August 1993); Enidelce Bertin, *Alforrias na São Paulo século XIX: Liberdade e dominação* (São Paulo, 2001); Douglas Cole Libby and Clotilde Andrade Paiva, "Alforrias e forros em uma freguesia mineira: São José d'El Rey em 1795," *Revista Brasileira de Estudos de População* 17, nos. 1/2 (2000); Cristiano Lima da Silva, "Senhores e pais: Reconhecimento de paternidade dos alforriados na pia batismal na Freguesia de Nossa Senhora do Pilar de São João del-Rei (1770–1850)," *Anais do I Colóquio do LAHES* (2005); Antônio Henrique Duarte Lacerda, "Economia cafeeira, crescimento populacional e manumissões onerosas e gratuitas condicionais em Juiz de Fora na segunda metade do século xix," *X Seminário sobre a Economia Mineira, Anais* (2002); Manolo Floreno, "Sobre minas, crioulos e a liberdade costumeira no Rio de Janeiro, 1789–1871," in Manolo Florentino, ed., *Tráfico, cativeiro e liberdade Rio de Janeiro* (2005), and his essay with José Roberto Pinto de Góes, "Do que Nabuco já sabia: Mobilidade e miscigenação racial no Brasil escravista"; and in the previously cited work of Paulo Roberto Staudt Moreira (2003), Higgins (1999), and Mary Karasch (1987). An earlier study still of utility was Frederick P. Bowser, "The Free Person of Color in Lima and Mexico City: Manumission and Opportunity, 1580–1650," in Engerman and Genovese (1975).

On the demographic dimensions of the free colored class, we have relied on Jonnes (1842), Cochin (1861), and the various censuses available for the 19th century in the countries studied. Useful on the social condition of free coloreds, which also overlap with poor whites, women, and other dependent groups under slavery, are the studies by Maria Sylvia de Carvalno Franco, *Homens livres na ordem escravocrata* (São Paulo, 1969); and Laura de Mello e Souza, *Desclassificados do Ouro: A pobreza, mineira no século xviii* (Rio de Janeiro, 1982); and on women, Maria Odila Leite da Silva Dias, *Quotidiano e poder em São Paulo no século xix* (São Paulo, 1984). Poor whites are also considered along with blacks and mulattoes, free and slave, in Verena Martinez-Alier, *Class and Colour in Nineteenth Century Cuba* (Cambridge, 1974).

In examining slave women's interactions with elite women, we have used Kimberly Gauderman, *Women's Lives in Colonial Quito: Gender, Law and Economy in Spanish America* (Austin, 2003); Kent Russell Lohse, "Africans and Their Descendants in Colonial Costa Rica, 1600–1750" (cited above); Frank Proctor III, "Slavery, Identity and Culture: An Afro-Mexican Counterpoint, 1640–1763" (cited above); Sherwin Bryant, "Slavery and the Context of Ethnogenesis: Africans, Afro-Creoles, and the Realities of Bondage in the Kingdom of Quito" (cited above); and Bianca Premo, *Children of the Father King: Youth, Authority, and Legal Minority in Colonial Lima* (Chapel Hill, 2006). For a broad treatment of slave and free colored women in Mexico, see: María Elisa Velázquez, *Mujeres de origen africano en la capital novohispana, siglos XVII y XVIII* (Mexico. DF, 2006).

The extensive literature on the caste system illuminates aspects of free colored life, since contained within these studies are often important demographic, occupational, and marital information. More recently, studies of the caste system have examined cultural phenomena and institutional relations—such as the caste ramifications of free colored religious behavior as seen through Inquisition trials. For some key studies, particularly on Mexico and Peru, see John K. Chance and William B. Taylor, "Estate and Class in a Colonial City, Oaxaca in 1792," *Comparative Studies in Society and History* 19 (1977): 454–87; Chance and Taylor, "The Ecology of Race and Class in Late Colonial Oaxaca," in David J. Robinson, ed., *Studies in Spanish American Population History* (Boulder, Colo., 1981); Dennis Nodin Valdes, "Decline of the Sociedad de Castas in Mexico City" (Ph.D. diss., University of Michigan, 1978); Magnus Mörner, "Economic Factors and Stratification in Colonial Spanish America with Special Regard to Elites," *Hispanic American Historical Review* 63, no. 2 (1983); Lyle N. McAlister, "Social Structure and Social Change in New Spain," *Hispanic American Historical Review* 43, no. 3 (1963): 349–70; Woodrow Borah and Sherburne F. Cook, "Sobre las posibilidades de hacer el estudio histórico del mestizaje sobre una base demografica," *Revista de historia de América* 53/54 (1962); Patricia Seed, "The Social Dimensions of Race: Mexico City 1753," *Hispanic American Historical Review* 62, no. 4 (1982); Rodney D. Anderson, "Race and Social Stratification: A Comparison of Working-Class Spaniards, Indians and Castas in Guadalajara, Mexico in 1821," *Hispanic American Historical Review* 68, no. 2 (1988); R. Douglas Cope, *The Limits of Racial Domination: Plebeian Society in Colonial Mexico City, 1660–1720* (Madison, 1994); Richard Boyer, *Cast and Identity in Colonial Mexico: A Proposal and an Example* (Storrs, Conn.; Providence, R.I.; and Amherst, Mass., 1997); Robert McCaa, Stuart B. Schwartz, and Arturo Grubessich, "Race and Class in Colonial Latin America: A Critique," *Comparative Studies in Society* and *History* 25 (1979); with a reply to this article by Chance and Taylor, "Estate and Class: A Reply," *Comparative Studies in Society and History* 25 (1979); Herman L. Bennett, "Lovers, Family, and Friends: The Formation of Afro-Mexico, 1580–1810" (Ph.D. diss., Duke University, 1993); Brigida von Mentz, *Pueblos de Indios, Mulatos y Mestizos: Los Campesinos y las transformaciones proto industriales en el Poniente de Morelos* (Mexico, DF, 1988); Bruce Allen Castleman, "Social Climbers in a Colonial Mexican City: Individual Mobility within the Sistema de Castas in Orizaba," *Colonial Latin American Review* 10, no. 2 (2001); Aaron P. Althouse, "Contested Mestizos, Alleged Mulatos: Racial Identity and Caste Hierarchy in Eighteenth Century Pátzcuaro, Mexico," *The Americas* 62, no. 2 (2005); David Cahill, "Colour by Numbers: Racial and Ethnic Categories in the Viceroy-alty of Peru, 1532–1821," *Journal of Latin American Studies* 26, no. 2 (1994); Ben Vinson III, "Estudiando las razas desde la periferia: Las castas olvidadas del sistema colonial mexicano (lobos, moriscos, coyotes, moros y chinos)," in Juan Manuel de la Serna Herrera, ed., *Pautas de convivencia étnica en la América Latina colonial (Indios, negros, mulatos, pardos y esclavos)* (Mexico City, 2005); Irene Silverblatt, *Modern Inquisitions: Peru and the Colonial Origins of the Civilized World* (Durham, 2005); Laura Lewis (2003), cited above; and the articles contained within the special issue of the *Journal of Colonialism and Colonial History (JCCH)* edited by Leo Garofalo and Rachel O'Toole entitled "Construct-ing Difference in Colonial Latin America," *JCCH* 7, no. 1 (2006). Research on blood purity (*limpieza de sangre*) is tightly linked to analyses of the caste system. Apart from many of the scholars mentioned above, the forthcoming work of Maria Elena Martínez will be influential in reshaping our understanding of *limpieza de sangre*, as is signaled by her unpublished paper entitled "Religion, Purity, and 'Race': The Spanish Concept of Limpieza de Sangre in Seventeenth-Century Mexico and the Broader Atlantic World" (working paper for the International Seminar on the History of the Atlantic World 1500–1800, Harvard University, 2000). The works of Laura Lewis and Irene Silverblatt also address the topic of *limpieza de sangre*.

Generally speaking, a growing trend in recent scholarship has been greater inclu-sion of blacks in local and regional studies. This means that much of the newer literature on Latin America contains some mention of free coloreds, as well as slaves. Likewise, works on slavery also address free colored life. Notwithstanding, some im-portant monographs and articles exist on the topic. For example, the free colored population in late colonial Puerto Rico is ably discussed by Jay Kinsbruner in *Not of Pure Blood: The Free People of Color and Racial Prejudice in Nineteenth-Century Puerto Rico* (Durham, N.C., 1996). For Florida, free coloreds and slaves are examined in Jane Landers, *Black Society in Spanish Florida* (Urbana, 1999). For Argentina, see George Reid Andrews, *The Afro-Argentines of Buenos Aires, 1800–1900* (Madison, 1980). A useful although dated essay on Afro-Uruguayan free coloreds is Carlos M. Rama, "The Passing of the Afro-Uruguayans from Caste Society into Class Society," in Magnus Mörner, ed., *Race and Class in Latin America* (New York, 1970). For free coloreds in Colombia, two important articles by Aline Helg include "The Limits of Equality: Free People of Colour and Slaves during the First Independence of Cartagena, Colombia, 1810–15," *Slavery and Abolition* 2C, no. 2 (1999): 1–30; and "A Fragmented Majority: Free 'of All Colors,' Indians, and Slaves in Caribbean Colombia during the Haitian Revolution," in David

P. Geggus ed., *The Impact of the Haitian Revolution in the Atlantic World* (Colombia, S.C., 2001). Free coloreds in Guatemala are examined by Christopher H. Lutz, *Santiago de Guatemala, 1541–1773: City, Caste and the Colonial Experience* (Norman, 1994); material can also be found in Paul Lokken, "From Black to Ladino: People of African Descent, Mestizaje, and Racial Hierarchy in Rural Colonial Guatemala, 1600–1730" (Ph.D. diss., University of Florida, 2000). Discussion of free colored townships and black neighborhoods can be found in the aforementioned work of Rina Cáceres, *Negros, mulatos, esclavos y libertos en la Costa Rica del siglo XVII*, and Paul Lokken, "Marriage as Slave Emancipation in Seventeenth Century Guatemala," as well as in the fine monograph by Philip A. Howard, *Changing History: Afro-Cuban Cabildos and Societies of Color in the Nineteenth Century* (Baton Rouge, 1998). Howard's book represents one of the best treatments of confraternity life in Cuba. In Mexico, a parallel study is that of Nicole von Germeten, *Black Blood Brothers: Confraternities and Social Mobility for Afro-Mexicans* (Gainesville, Fla., 2006). General discussion of free coloreds in Latin America can be found in the recently reprinted monograph of Leslie B. Rout Jr., *The African Experience in Spanish America: 1502 to the Present Day* (New York, 2003). Several edited collections address the lives of free coloreds in multiple regional contexts, as well as their interrelationships with natives, mainstream society, and slaves. Some of these include Luz Maria Montiel, ed., *Presencia Africana en Centroamérica* (cited above); Matthew Restall, *Beyond Black and Red* (cited above); María Elisa Velázquez and Ethel Correa, eds., *Poblaciones y cultura de origen africano en México* (cited above); Juan Manuel de la Serna Herrera, ed., *Pautas de convivencia étnica en la América Latina colonial* (cited above); and Adriana Naveda Chávez-Hita, ed., *Pardos, mulatos y libertos: Sexto encuentro de afromexicanistas* (Mexico, DF, 2001). Several edited volumes have appeared in Mexico on the black presence based on an annual series of conferences held by the "Third Root" movement. Only one of these influential volumes has been cited here. Four interesting articles on black interrelationships with natives are Laura Matthew, "Mexicanos and the Meanings of Ladino in Colonial Guatemala," *Journal of Colonialism and Colonial History* 7, no. 1 (2006); Andrew B. Fisher "Creating and Contesting Community: Indians and Afromestizos in the Late-Colonial Tierra Caliente of Guerrero, Mexico," *Journal of Colonialism and Colonial History* 7, no. 1 (2006); Fisher, "Free Blacks in an Indigenous World: Three Centuries in the Tierra Caliente," in Ben Vinson III and Matthew Restall, eds., *Black Mexico* (Albuquerque, forthcoming); and Patrick J. Carroll, "Black Aliens and Black Natives in New Spain's Indigenous Communities" in Vinson and Restall, *Black Mexico*. Finally, a treatment of free colored tribute policy in Spanish America is featured in Cynthia Milton and Ben Vinson III, "Counting Heads: Race and Non-native Tribute Policy in Colonial Spanish America," *Journal of Colonialism and Colonial History* 3, no. 3 (2002).

On the military role of the free coloreds in the colonial and national periods, see Ben Vinson III, *Bearing Arms of His Majesty: The Free Colored Militia in Colonial Mexico* (Stanford, 2001); Herbert S. Klein, "The Colored Militia of Cuba, 1568–1868," *Caribbean Studies* 6, no. 2 (1966); Michele Reid, "Protesting Service: Free Black Response to Cuba's Re-established Militia of Color, 1854–1865," *Journal of Colonialism and Colonial History* 5, no. 2 (2004); Alan Keuthe, "The Status of the Free Pardo in the Disciplined

Militia of New Granada," *Journal of Negro History* 56, no. 2 (1971); David Sartorius, "My Vassals: Free-Colored Militias in Cuba and the Ends of Empire," *Journal of Colonialism and Colonial History* 5, no. 2 (2004); Stewart R. King, *Blue Coat or Powdered Wig: Free-People of Color in Pre-revolutionary Saint Domingue* (Athens, Ga., 2001); and Hendrik Kraay, *Race, State and Armed Forces in Independence Era Brazil: Bahia, 1790s–1840s* (Stanford, 2002). Useful for the special context of Cartagena is Aline Helg, *Liberty and Equality in Caribbean Colombia, 1770–1835* (Chapel Hill, 2004). A recent compilation of articles addressing the black presence in the colonial military forces of Haiti, Brazil, Guatemala, and Cuba is Ben Vinson III and Stewart R. King's special issue of the *Journal of Colonialism and Colonial History*, entitled "The New African Diasporic Military History," *JCCH* 5, no. 2 (2004).

CHAPTER II .   TRANSITION FROM SLAVERY TO FREEDOM

Placing the whole abolitionist movement in the context of the times is the work of David Brion Davis, *The Problem of Slavery in the Age of Revolution, 1770–1823* (Ithaca, 1976). His more recent reflections on this theme are found in *Slavery and Human Progress* (New York, 1984). On the campaign to abolish the slave trade, and then slavery in the British Empire and then throughout America, the place to begin is with Eric Williams, *Capitalism and Slavery* (Chapel Hill, 1944), which is then challenged in the work of Roger Anstey (1975) discussed above. Drescher's (1977) book is also part of this ongoing debate, as is the Anstey and Hair (1976) volume. The process of emancipation is dealt with in the book by William Green (1976). The ending of slavery in metropolitan Portugal is studied in Francisco C. Falcon and Fernando A. Novais, "A extinção da escravatura africana em Portugal no quadro da politica econômica pombalina," *Anais de VI Simpósio Nacional dos Professores Universitários de História* (São Paulo, 1973).

The British-led campaign to abolish the Atlantic slave trade has come under considerable scrutiny in the past few years in both a quantitative and a qualitative fashion in such works as E. Philip LeVeen, *British Slave Trade Suppression Policies, 1821–1865* (New York, 1977); Leslie Bethell, *The Abolition of the Brazilian Slave Trade* (Cambridge, 1970); José Capela, *As burgesias portuguesas e a abolição do tráfico da escravatura, 1810–1842* (Porto, 1979); Arturo Morales Carrión, *Auge y decadencia de la trata negrera en Puerto Rico (1820–1860)* (Rio Piedras, 1978); David Murray, *Odious Commerce: Britain, Spain and the Abolition of the Cuban Slave Trade* (Cambridge, 1980); and David Eltis and James Walvin, eds., *The Abolition of the Atlantic Slave Trade* (Madison, 1981).

A quick survey of emancipation in 19th-century Spanish America is found in Leslie B. Rout Jr., *The African Experience in Spanish America* (Cambridge, 1976). A detailed study of the Venezuelan experience is given by John Lombardi, *The Decline and Abolition of Negro Slavery in Venezuela, 1820–1854* (Westport, Conn., 1971). On the development of abolitionism in Cuba, Puerto Rico, and Spain, see Arthur F. Corwin, *Spain and the Abolition of Slavery in Cuba, 1817–1886* (Austin, 1967). The Argentine experience with abolition and afterward is dealt with in George Reid Andrews (1980). An analysis of the last years of slavery in Cuba is Rebecca J. Scott, *Slave Emancipation in Cuba: The*

Transition to Free Labor (Princeton, 1985). For an assessment of the planter expectations about slavery as seen in the prices they were paying for slaves, see Manuel Moreno Fraginals, Herbert S. Klein, and Stanley L. Engerman, "Nineteenth Century Cuban Slave Prices in Comparative Perspective," *American Historical Review* 88, no. 4 (1983).

The materials available for studying the emancipation process in Brazil are extensive. A useful survey is that of Suely R. Reis de Queiroz, *A abolicão da escravidão* (São Paulo, 1982), which cites many of the local regional studies. Two major works on the final years are Robert Toplin, *The Abolition of Slavery in Brazil* (New York, 1972), and Robert Conrad, *The Destruction of Brazilian Slavery, 1850–1888* (Berkeley, 1972). The most detailed of the regional studies include Ronald Marcos dos Santos, *Resistencia e superacão do escravismo na provincia de São Paulo, 1885/1888* (São Paulo, 1980); Vilma Paraiso Ferreira de Almada, *Escravismo e transição: O Espirito Santo (1850–1888)* (Rio de Janeiro, 1984); and Diana Soares de Galliza, *O declino da escravidão na Paraíba, 1850–1888* (João Pessoa, 1979). Lively debates about the causes of abolition are found in Paula Beiguelman, "The Destruction of Modern Slavery: The Brazilian Case," *Review* (the Fernand Braudel Center) 6, no. 3 (1983); J. H. Galloway, "The Last Years of Slavery in the Sugar Plantations of Northeastern Brazil," *Hispanic American Historical Review* 51, no. 4 (1971); and Jaime Reis, "The Impact of Abolitionism in Northeastern Brazil," in Rubin and Tuden (1977).

For a general discussion of the transition from slave to free labor in the Spanish Caribbean, see Manuel Moreno Fraginals Frank Moya Pons, and Stanley L. Engerman, eds., *Between Slavery and Free Labor: The Spanish Speaking Caribbean in the Nineteenth Century* (Baltimore, 1985). The model of the transition from slave to free labor that we present here was first elaborated in Herbert S. Klein and Stanley L. Engennan, "Del trabajo esciavo al trabajo libre: Notas en torno a un model económico comparativo," *HISLA, Revista Latinoamericana de Historica Económica y Social* (Lima) 1, no. 1 (1983). The transition in Brazil is discussed in Emilia Viotti da Costa, *Da senzala a colonia* (São Paulo, 1966); Warren Dean, *Rio Claro; a Brazilian plantation system, 1820-19201820–1920* (Stanford, 1976); Thomas H. Holloway, *Immigrants on the Land: Coffee and Society in São Paulo, 1886–1934* (Chapel Hill, 1980); Eisenberg (1974); and Jaime Reis, "From bangue to usina: Social Aspects of Growth and Modernization in the Sugar Industry of Pernambuco, Brazil, 1850–1920," in Kenneth Duncan and Ian Rutledge, eds., *Land and Labor in Latin America* (Cambridge, 1977). A general survey of the entire field of postemancipation contract labor is dealt with in Stanley L. Engerman, "Contract Labor, Sugar and Technology in the Nineteenth Century," *Journal of Economic History* 43, no. 3 (1983).

Tables

TABLE 1. Estimated Slave Population in America in the Late 18th Century

Region/Colonies	Numbers
Caribbean	**1,122,000**
French West Indies	575,000
British West Indies	467,000
Spanish West Indies	80,000
Brazil	**1,000,000**
U.S.A.	**575,420**
Mainland Spanish America	**271,000**
Mexico and Central America	19,000
Panama	4,000
Nueva Granada	54,000
Venezuela	64,000
Ecuador	8,000
Peru	89,000
Chile	12,000
Rio de la Plata	21,000
TOTAL	2,968,420

Sources: For the West Indies, Alex. Moreau de Jonnes, *Recherches statistiques sur l'esclavage colonial...* (Paris, 1842), 14 ff.; Maria Luiza Marcilio, "The Population of Colonial Brazil," and Nicolás Sánchez Albornoz, "The Population of Colonial Spanish America," both in Leslie Bethell, ed., *The Cambridge History of Latin America* (Cambridge, Eng 1984), vol. 2; Leslie B. Rout Jr., *The African Experience in Spanish America* (Cambridge, 1976), 95. For the United States data, Bureau of the Census, *Historical Statistics of the United States* (Washington, D.C., 1975), 2:1168.

TABLE 2. Estimated Free Colored Population in Late 18th-Century America

Region/Colony	Numbers
Caribbean	**212,000**
French West Indies	30,000
British West Indies	13,000
Spanish West Indies*	169,000
Brazil	**399,000**
U.S.A.	**32,000**
Mainland Spanish America	**650,000**
TOTALS	**1,293,000**

Sources: Same as table 1, and David W. Cohen and Jack P. Greene, eds., Neither Slave Nor Free: The Freedmen of African Descent in the Slave Societies of the New World (Baltimore, 1972), 335 ff.

Notes: *This total figure breaks down into 54,000 for Cuba (1792), 35,000 for Puerto Rico (1775), and an estimated 80,000 for the Spanish colony of Santo Domingo, which had a majority of its population in this category and included runaway slaves from the French colony of Saint Domingue.

TABLE 3. Estimated Slave and Free Colored Population in America in the 1860s/1872

Region/Colony	Slave	Free Colored	Total Colored
Spanish West Indies	412,291	473,530	885,821
Cuba (1861)	370,553	232,493	603,046
Puerto Rico (1860)	41,738	241,037	282,775
U.S.A. (1860)	3,953,696	488,134	4,441,830
Brazil (1872)	1,510,806	4,245,428	5,756,234
TOTAL	5,876,793	5,207,092	11,083,885

Source: Same as table 1, plus K. B. Kiple, Blacks in Colonial Cuba, 1774–1899 (Gainesville, Fla., 1976), 63; for Brazil, H. S. Klein in Cohen and Greene, Neither Slave Nor Free, 320; for the United States, ibid., 339, and Bureau of the Census, Historical Statistics, 1:14; and for Puerto Rico, Luis M. Diaz Soler, Historia de la esclavitud negra en Puerto Rico (Rio Piedras, 1953), 259.

Notes: *Of this total of freedmen in the United States, 261,918 were living in the Southern slave states, and the rest resided in the free Northern states.

Index

Abolition: effect on labor relations, 236–37; effect on world economy, 237
Abolitionism, 224, 227–28; growth of, 231. *See also specific countries*
Africa: Portuguese, in Dutch wars of independence, 50; slavery in, 9–11
African slaves: in Europe, 13–14; Europeanized, 14; importation to America (*see also* African slave trade; Atlantic slave trade; Slave trade); used to develop American export industries, 22
African slave trade, 58; internal, 10–11; international, 10–11; intra-continental, 9–11; northern and eastern, 9–11; as target for reformers, 229
Africans, suppliers of slaves, 123
Afro-American culture, 135–64; belief system in, 156–57; common features, 143–44; development of, in slave villages, 146; influenced by European beliefs, 143; kinship arrangements in, 146, 150–51; purposes served by, 163–64; religious organization and expression in, 143–44, 147, 157–63; and self- identity, 161
Afro-American language, 135. *See also* Pidgin speech; Creoles: language of

Afro-Americans: contributions to national culture and identity, 244–46; migration patterns, 242–43; mobility of, 244, 245–46; political power, growth of, 244–45; prejudice against, 244; socio-economic status of, 244–45; whitening of, 244
Agricultural production, slaves as factor in, 12
Agriculture: Brazilian, slaves in, 111–13; of Brazilian Indians, 45; mechanization of, in Cuba, 92–96; in Puerto Rico, 96–98; peasant, after emancipation, 237
Aleijadinho (António Francisco Lisboa), 220
Algarve, sugar production in, 8
American Revolution, 228
Amis des Noirs, 85, 228
Angola, 136, 137, 141–42; slaving in, 24, 127–29
Annotto, 114
Apprenticeship, of emancipated slaves, 231–32, 234, 235
Argentina, African ethnic identity in, 138–39; free coloreds in, 197; slave armies of, 190
Armação, 70–71; slave workers in, 71

CPSIA information can be obtained at www.ICGtesting.com
Printed in the USA
BVOW070741100212

282640BV00001B/6/P